The New Deal
The Depression Years, 1933–40

T0119247

The New Deal
The Depression Years, 1933–40

Anthony J. Badger

IVAN R. DEE
Chicago

Library of Congress Cataloging-in-Publication Data:
Badger, Anthony J.
   The New Deal : the Depression years, 1933–1940 / by Anthony J. Badger.—
1st Ivan R. Dee pbk. ed.
      p. cm.
   Originally published: New York : Hill and Wang, 1989.
   Includes bibliographical references and index.
   ISBN 1-56663-453-9 (acid-free paper) ISBN: 978-1-56663-453-3
   1. New Deal, 1933–1939. 2. United States—Politics and government—
1933–1945. 3. United States—Economic conditions—1918–1945. I. Title.

E806.B24 2002
973.917—dc21
                                                        2002067690

For Ruth

Contents

Acknowledgements

My purpose is to interpret a substantial secondary literature on the New Deal. The many debts I have incurred in writing this book are entirely disproportionate to its modest aim. It is nevertheless a pleasant duty to acknowledge them.

My first obligation is to all those scholars whose work I have ransacked. To those who may feel that I have inadequately acknowledged their contribution or that I have distorted what they wrote, I can only plead inadvertence. My accomplices have been the unfailingly efficient Inter-Library Loan staff of Newcastle University Library, without whose assistance I could never have contemplated writing this book.

The book originated in a special subject course on the New Deal which I taught in Newcastle from 1974 to 1984. I am indebted to all the students who worked together with me to teach ourselves about the 1930s. I owe a special debt to the graduates of 1982 and 1984.

At an early stage I participated in an intensive symposium on the New Deal at the David Bruce Centre at the University of Keele. The other participants will recognise their contributions all too clearly in the pages that follow. David Adams organised and hosted the symposium with characteristic efficiency and generosity. Soon afterwards, a fellowship from the American Council of Learned Societies enabled me to start putting my ideas down on paper. The friendship and hospitality of Dan and Jane Carter at Emory University gave me the perfect environment to do so.

Invitations, first from Bruce Collins and Rhodri Jeffreys-Jones, then from Stephen Baskerville and Ralph Willett, to contribute to collections of essays gave me a much-needed opportunity to find out what I really thought about local studies of the New Deal and about Huey Long. Maldwyn Jones invited me to respond to the

1986 Commonwealth Lecture. John L. Thomas's brilliant lecture 'The Road Not Taken: Perspectives on Post-Frontier America, 1920–1940' made me explore aspects of the 1930s that I had hitherto resolutely ignored.

I have been fortunate in having friends who have not entirely allowed affection to cloud their critical faculties. Howell Harris has taught me all I know about organised labour and has acted as an instant bibliographical guide on everything. Bill Speck strove to excise the worst solecisms. Stephen Baskerville attempted in vain to make me understand economic thought. Bob Reinders put me right on social workers and on much else besides by meticulously scrutinising the whole manuscript. Jim Patterson, who more than anyone has influenced my work over the past twenty years, unerringly exposed great expanses of sloppy thinking and expression. The errors that remain despite their best endeavours are testimony to my own obstinacy.

Many others have helped this project, sometimes unwittingly, notably Malcolm Call, Stephen Constantine, Charlotte Erickson, Peter Fearon, John Harper, Michael Heale, Paul Metcalfe, Iwan Morgan, Jack Pole, Jim Potter, John Rowett, David Saunders, Patricia Sullivan, and Philip Taylor.

I have sorely tried the patience of Sarah Mahaffy, Vanessa Couchman, and Vanessa Graham as editors. The delivery dates I promised them usually proved as chimerical as Roosevelt's balanced budgets. Nevertheless, they did not allow me to give up. At a late stage, Arthur Wang made many consistently helpful suggestions.

Janice Cummin and Julie Savage typed assorted drafts with a speed, accuracy, and good humour that belied the pressure imposed on them by my illegibility and tardiness.

Finally, I want to acknowledge two personal debts. I only hope that this book in a small way repays the many kindnesses Alger Hiss and Isabel Johnson have shown me. It is customary for academics to acknowledge long-suffering partners. Those who know Ruth will know that she has not suffered in silence. Suffice it to say that without her love, tolerance, and constant encouragement this book would never have been completed. I dedicate it to her.

The New Deal
The Depression Years, 1933–40

Introduction

In May 1985 Jessica Lange, Sissy Spacek, and Jane Fonda brought
unprecedented glamour and publicity to a meeting on Capitol Hill
of a committee that did not normally attract crowded audiences
and flashing cameras: the House Democratic Caucus Task Force
on Agriculture. The film stars had come to dramatise the plight of
thousands of farm families being driven off the land. To do so,
they each evoked memories of the 1930s. Jessica Lange's father
had lost his land in the Depression; Sissy Spacek's had been a
county agent administering New Deal farm programmes in Texas;
Jane Fonda's had particularly loved playing Tom Joad, the mi-
grant Okie, in the film of John Steinbeck's *The Grapes of Wrath*.

It was not only the plight of dispossessed farmers that reminded
Americans in the 1980s of the Great Depression of more than half
a century earlier. Large banks failed in the Midwest; oil prices
plummeted in Texas; drought devastated southern farmers; criminal charges followed financial malpractice on Wall Street.
Congress and president struggled unavailingly with budget deficits.
The volatility of the stock market and Republican tax cuts for the
affluent prompted economist John Kenneth Galbraith to explore
the parallels between the unstable economy of 1986 and the
circumstances leading to the Great Crash of 1929. In 1987 Galbraith's academic concerns became stunning reality as the Dow
Jones stock-market index fell by over 508 points on 19 October,
twice the loss of the worst one-day collapse in 1929.

It is not surprising that Americans today cannot easily escape
the memories of the 1930s: they work out their lives in a political
economy that still bears the imprint of Franklin D. Roosevelt's
New Deal. Bankers and financiers are regulated by institutions
created by the reform legislation of 1933–35. Management and
workers confront each other under the watchful eye of the

National Labor Relations Board established by the Wagner Act of 1935. The poor receive their welfare payments from the complex framework of a social security system set up in the same year. Farmers are sustained by price-support loans first provided by the New Deal. Even President Reagan spent his way out of the deep recession of 1981 utilising the fiscal tools with which the New Deal had ultimately attempted to direct the economy. Nor could the economic, demographic, and ideological upheavals of the 1970s and 1980s entirely obliterate the political legacy of Franklin Roosevelt: a liberal national Democratic Party backed by organised labour, blacks, and other lower-income voters still confronts a conservative coalition of the South and West.

Historians have found it difficult to escape the effect of the persistent resonance of the 1930s for contemporary Americans. They have often appeared to be trapped in a cycle of lamentation or celebration of the New Deal: they have spent more time denigrating or championing it than explaining it.

In the post-war years conservatives condemned Roosevelt for introducing socialism: liberals applauded him for extending the responsibility of the federal government to cover the economic security of individual citizens. Most historians identified with the Democratic Party and liberalism and in the 1950s and early 1960s many aspects of the New Deal appealed to them. Unprecedented prosperity suggested that expert management of the economy, utilising the fiscal legacy of the New Deal, was successful. It appeared that Roosevelt had struck the right balance between government and private enterprise. The war-time threat of Fascisim and the Cold War threat of Communism highlighted the dangers of ideology and dogma: the allegedly pragmatic, non-ideological bent of the New Deal seemed all the more attractive. At a time when irrational mass movements seemed to produce a Hitler, a Stalin, or even a Joseph McCarthy, the 'broker state' of the New Deal whereby interest groups mediated between the government and the people seemed admirable.

If there were faults in American society – racial discrimination, private affluence but public squalor, sluggish growth and persistent poverty – they could be eradicated by activist presidents such as Harry S. Truman, John F. Kennedy, or Lyndon B. Johnson, seeking to extend New Deal reforms. Arthur M. Schlesinger Jr, the chronicler of both the New Deal and the New Frontier, likened

Kennedy's publicly cool and rational pragmatism to that of the New Dealers. Lyndon Johnson, who had first been elected to Congress in 1937 as an enthusiastic supporter of Roosevelt's court-packing plan, was anxious to turn the Mekong Delta into a giant Tennessee Valley Authority. He envisaged his Great Society as completing the unfinished business of the New Deal in civil rights, health care, education and rural and urban poverty.

Both conservative critics and liberal defenders of Roosevelt believed that he had instituted a massive break with the past. Radical historians in the 1960s saw the New Deal differently. Acutely conscious of continuing racism and poverty in the 1960s, they believed that the New Deal had merely served to sustain the hegemony of corporate capitalism. They argued that the New Deal, like Progressivism earlier and reforms of the 1960s, was not a popular movement designed to reform and curb business but a tool of the more sophisticated leaders of America's largest corporations and financial institutions. To the radicals the New Deal years were particularly tragic. The 1930s, they said, offered the great opportunity for substantial reform – a sad story, wrote Paul Conkin, 'of might have beens'. The New Deal did not nationalise the banks or discipline American businessmen; rather the corporate leaders themselves drafted the financial and industrial stabilisation legislation. Reform defused the threat of radical protest by incorporating potentially threatening groups into the system. Measures designed to help large commercial farmers at the expense of the rural poor alleviated farm discontent. Recognition of trades unions channelled the militant protest of rank-and-file industrial workers into the safe and responsible unionism of the post-war world. Shrewdly calculated relief and welfare measures for the hungry and unemployed, which could be cut back once the crisis was over, averted the danger of civil disorder. Limited concessions, the radicals argued, undercut radicalism's appeal.

Historians who came to the defence of the New Deal in the face of the New Left assault conceded the essentially limited nature of the changes wrought in the 1930s. But while the radicals stressed the conservative purposes of corporate liberalism defenders emphasised the constraints within which New Dealers operated, notably the persistence of conservative strength and the inhibiting effect of localism.

In the 1970s ideologues of the right challenged the notion that

New Deal change had been minimal: they argued, instead, that the
New Deal had set the American political economy decisively and
inexorably on the wrong course. Government exacerbated rather
than solved social problems. Government spending fuelled inflation. Union demands threatened to bankrupt major cities. Government undermined entrepreneurial spirit. Scholars had earlier
praised the New Deal's creation of a 'broker state' to act as a
neutral arbiter between competing interest groups. In the 1970s,
however, they often feared that interest groups simply bid up the
level of government spending to benefit themselves. Until the
1970s economists had usually favoured Keynesian policies: policies
which stressed the positive role of government spending and
taxation in creating sufficient demand in the economy. After 1970,
they were likely to argue that taxation, regulation, and spending
distorted the operation of the free market. The aims of liberal
reformers from the 1930s onwards, they complained, might have
been worthy, but their methods were counter-productive. Everywhere individual freedom was curtailed at both a moral and an
economic cost. Right-wing intellectuals saw the Reagan victory of
1980 as the turning-point when the American people reversed a
half century's drive towards collectivism and chose freedom instead.

Reassessments of the New Deal from both left and right have
accompanied a change in the topics historians have emphasised. In
the 1950s liberal historians focused largely on Roosevelt himself,
the drama of events in Washington, and the clash of ideas and
personalities among New Deal policy-makers. In the 1960s historians began to study New Deal programmes in action and to look
at the impact of the New Deal at the local level. Too many of the
changes that had looked impressive in Washington looked less
successful at the local level. The frantic bursts of legislation and
the explosion of the federal bureaucracy did not, they thought,
necessarily produce changes of equivalent proportions in the
localities.

These state and local case studies of the New Deal tended to be
interested in state government, local administrators, and political
leaders. They tended to look at actual members of the unemployed, individual workers, and farmers as passive objects acted
upon by New Deal programmes. Historians have recently become
very interested in the history of 'the inarticulate many as well as

the articulate few'. Taking advantage of oral history and the vast amount of social investigation carried out in the 1930s, they have started to focus on the experience during the Depression of the unemployed, of particular ethnic groups, of blacks, of Indians, of women, of the rural poor. Some of this work naturally highlights grass-roots radical protest in the 1930s – by rank-and-file labour militants, by tenant farmers' unions, or by Unemployed Councils. Some by contrast emphasises the persistence of conservative traditions of deference and individualism amid extraordinary economic distress.

The pendulum therefore has swung from diatribe to encomium and back. The perspective on the New Deal has shifted from Washington to the localities and from policy-makers to ordinary Americans. I have attempted to take stock of a vast and rapidly increasing literature and to make sense of the conflicting impressions.

My aim has not been to write another chronological account of the New Deal or another account of Franklin Roosevelt in the presidency.

No historian of the New Deal can ignore the dominating figure of Roosevelt himself. For seven years he grappled with the worst depression in American history. Then he led the United States in its first and only global war. After the Japanese attack at Pearl Harbor in December 1941, he directed a war effort primarily aimed at the defeat of Nazi Germany in Europe. He authorised the development of the first atomic bomb. He devised plans for the post-war world in which the hitherto isolationist United States would be one of the Four Great Policemen responsible for the maintenance of world peace. For twelve years Roosevelt faced awesome responsibilities: few presidents have seemed so personally untroubled in the exercise of such vast powers.

Few images are as familiar as that of Roosevelt with half-glasses, the broad smile, and the cigarette holder at a jaunty angle. Roosevelt also quickly established first-name familiarity with everyone he met. Yet not many people could claim to know Roosevelt well enough to penetrate the public mask of easy affability and light banter. Throughout his presidency many depended on him for reassurance, approval, and support. Yet cabinet members, administrators, and congressional leaders needed Roosevelt far more than he needed them. FDR allowed no one – not even faithful cabinet members like Frances Perkins, Harold Ickes, and Henry Morgenthau Jr who were still with him in 1945 – to come too close to the private Roosevelt. Only Louis Howe, the gnome-like newspaperman who masterminded his political career from his earliest days as a state legislator in New York, and Harry Hopkins, who served as his trusted emissary to Churchill and Stalin, had any claim to be indispensable to the president.

If the private Roosevelt was an enigma, the public figure was paradoxical. Born in 1882 the son of a wealthy upstate New York landowner, overly protected by a doting and domineering mother, educated at Groton and Harvard, Roosevelt had the background of an upper-class gentleman farmer who might dabble in the law, as he did half-heartedly, or in politics, which he entered with the same gusto as his distant cousin Theodore. The young Roosevelt elected to the state legislature in 1910 was an aloof, self-righteous figure concerned about rural affairs, conservation, and the elimination of corrupt politics. But the dilettante aristocrat was to become the national standard-bearer of urban liberalism: social justice measures designed to benefit the mass of ordinary lower-income Americans. This patrician figure aroused the fierce loyalty of millions of small farmers, industrial workers, and blacks.

Roosevelt was not an intellectual. Nothing in his record suggested that he had the expertise or the rigorous analytical mind of his predecessor, Herbert Hoover. His knowledge of economics was sketchy. John Maynard Keynes, the British economist, who met Roosevelt in 1934, was surprised that the president was not more 'literate, economically speaking'. But Roosevelt surrounded himself with intellectuals. Running for the presidency he assembled a Brains Trust of academics who put before him wide-ranging policy options. His New Deal gave 'service intellectuals', as Richard S. Kirkendall has described them, their chance to shape and implement policy. A remarkable host of young, bright, idealistic lawyers, social workers, and engineers descended on Washington to staff the proliferating New Deal agencies.

There was little ideological coherence in the New Deal. Roosevelt had a flypaper mind that could assimilate contradictory ideas in a way that was logically inconsistent but politically feasible. He championed the idea of experimentation in the face of economic crisis that overwhelmed orthodox remedies. Yet New

Deal policy-making was scarcely conducive to controlled experimentation and Roosevelt rarely acknowledged that any New Deal experiment had failed, even when he was unceremoniously abandoning it. There was an underlying commitment to certain basic simple goals of immediate relief to the distressed, the creation of more responsible and accountable economic institutions, and the long-term economic security of ordinary Americans.

Before 1928 Roosevelt's electoral success had been confined to election as editor of the Harvard student newspaper and twice as a state legislator from his home county in New York. Appointed Assistant Secretary of the Navy in the Wilson administration, he had been defeated in his 1914 bid for the US Senate seat from New York and was overwhelmingly defeated in 1920 as the vice-presidential candidate on the Democratic national ticket. Yet, after narrowly winning the governorship of New York in 1928, he won by a record margin in 1930, and went on to win the presidency four times and secure startling bursts of reform legislation from Congress in the First Hundred Days (1933) and the Second Hundred Days (1935).

In contrast to the dour suspicious Hoover, Roosevelt delighted in the open exercise of his personal political skills. Crippled by polio in 1921, able to walk with braces only with great difficulty, Roosevelt was nevertheless a highly visible president both on the campaign trail and on presidential tours of inspection. He early mastered the medium of radio. As president, the patrician tones of his fireside chats were unmistakable. Yet the simple exposition of the problems facing the government and the measures he was taking to solve them evoked a unique response from ordinary citizens. In 1933 they undoubtedly lifted the paralysing fear that had settled on the country. Afterwards thousands of the unemployed and dispossessed scrawled letters in pencil on scraps of paper in the faith that there was in the White House a personal friend who could help with their problems. In addition, Roosevelt's relaxed and informal press conferences and his easy banter with working journalists gave him a mastery of the press that no amount of editorial criticism could gainsay. He was therefore the first modern American president who could carry his message directly to the people, circumventing the traditional political organisations. Here were the weapons of a strong charismatic national leader.

In Washington, Roosevelt was a master of the art of personal political persuasion. He could win over an influential Catholic cardinal who was an inveterate autograph collector by a brief personal note on the cardinal's birthday. He could 'stroke the hand' and massage the ego of the most disgruntled cabinet member. He could flatter and assuage the most surly and self-important congressional leader. But critics complained that he failed to use the full power of his charismatic authority. He compromised too much. He allowed himself to be the prisoner first of southern conservatives, then of isolationist public opinion. He sorely tried the patience of congressional leaders by sudden and pre-emptory demands for legislation on which he had not con-sulted them. He tried the loyalty of congressional rank-and-file liberals by failing to consult them. He could be immensely considerate of and loyal to close political associates. Yet he could be petty, vindictive, and cruel. Politicians as diverse as Burton K. Wheeler, James A. Farley, Jesse H. Jones, James F. Byrnes, and Tommy Corcoran had reason to feel personally betrayed by a president who abandoned them in the interests of whim or his own personal political advantage.

Roosevelt could also be careless of civil liberties. He authorised the rounding up of Japanese-Americans in World War II into concentration camps. He allowed FBI and Internal Revenue investigations of political opponents. He taped White House conversations and tolerated segregation and discrimination against blacks. Yet his administration conducted a world war without the wholesale infringement of civil liberties that had occurred between 1917 and 1920. He refused to sacrifice members of his government who were pilloried for Communist affiliations by outraged con-gressmen, and he and his wife became folk-heroes to blacks.

A president of unprecedented popularity, Roosevelt also aroused a hatred unequalled in its intensity. The rich scored him as a traitor to his class; businessmen railed against his devious imposition of government controls; isolationists believed he had cynically led the nation into war by the back door; Republicans alleged that he had secretly sold out Eastern Europe to the Russians at Yalta.

Liberals loved him for the enemies he made. Although the New Deal had been largely stalemated after 1938 and Roosevelt had explicitly abandoned divisive reform measures during the war, young New Dealers maintained an almost mystical faith that Roosevelt would once more be able to lead the country to fresh reform efforts after the war. Many looked on Roosevelt as a 'father figure' and were bereft when he died in 1945. No leader since has satisfied their desire for another strong, activist, charismatic leader to champion the liberal cause.

I have not attempted to explore these themes in detail in this book. The figure of FDR does not loom as large in this account as in some others. There are more than enough good biographies of Roosevelt. I have also deliberately eschewed discussion of the dramatic foreign policy developments of the 1930s – the recognition of the Soviet Union, the Good Neighbor Policy in Latin America, the diplomatic and economic efforts to halt Japanese expansion in the Far East, the conflicting goals of neutrality and aid to the victims of Fascist aggression in Abyssinia, Spain, and ultimately the whole of Europe. To understand the evolution of New Deal foreign policy it is essential to penetrate Roosevelt's mind, to understand his personal preoccupations and perceptions. But the president's thinking is not so important in attempting to understand the domestic New Deal.

I do not argue that there could have been a New Deal without Roosevelt. It is difficult to imagine the frantic excitement in Washington between 1933 and 1936 if John Nance Garner, Albert Ritchie, or Newton D. Baker had been elected in 1932, as they easily might have been. FDR's personal political skills, which neither his predecessor, Herbert Hoover, nor his post-war successors possessed in like measure, made the New Deal possible.

Nor do I argue that Roosevelt's own ideas were unimportant. His personal interest in programmes like the Civilian Conservation Corps, which sent the young urban unemployed to work in forestry camps, and the Shelterbelt project, which planted millions of trees to act as a windbreak for the Great Plains, was decisive in their formulation and implementation. Equally, his lack of interest in low-cost urban housing was important in launching a belated and wholly inadequate programme. His personal indecision on industrial strategy and on deficit-spending was crucial.

Nevertheless, to understand the New Deal the historian has to look not only at FDR but at the programmes he authorised, the administrators he gave free rein to, the long-term ideological and social developments the New Deal interacted with. I have therefore not attempted another chronological narrative of the New Deal but have taken in turn important aspects of New Deal activity – in relation to industry, organised labour, agriculture, welfare, and politics – and tried to focus on some of the major problems of interpretations on each topic. I have tried to show how individual programmes operated and to give some indication of the local dimensions of such activities. My preconceptions and conclusions will soon become clear: that the New Deal did represent a sharp break with the past; that the New Deal's impact was nevertheless precisely circumscribed, often constrained by forces over which the New Dealers had little control; that in the end the New Deal functioned very much as a 'holding operation' for American society; and that for many Americans the decisive change in their experiences came not with the New Deal but with World War II.

1
Depression America

'This depression has got me licked', wrote a Houston mechanic in the fall of 1930 before he committed suicide. 'There is no work to be had. I can't accept charity and I am too proud to appeal to my kin or friends, and I am too honest to steal. So I see no other course. A land flowing with milk and honey and a first-class mechanic can't make an honest living. I would rather take my chances with a just God than with unjust humanity.' The national suicide rate rose from 14 per 100,000 in 1929 to 17.4 in 1932. In 1931 Detroit suicides were 30 per cent above the previous 5 year average. In Minneapolis the suicide rate peaked at 26.1 per 100,000 in 1932. So many people in Memphis jumped off the Hanrahan Bridge into the Mississippi that the telephone numbers of local clergymen willing to counsel would-be suicides were listed in the press. The efficacy of this assistance was substantially lessened by the newspaper headline 'Memphis Preacher Jumps Off'.

On the Navajo reservation in Arizona and New Mexico huge snowfalls in the winter of 1931–32 prevented Indians from feeding their livestock. As the Navajos confronted temperatures as low as −20°F, they trekked on foot into the trading posts. There they found food and shelter for the night but little or no rations to take back with them. In the spring, hundreds of thousands of dead cattle and sheep littered the range. The Navajos stripped wool from the sheep carcasses in desperation but could get almost nothing for it from the traders. By summer the stench of dead sheep hung over every trading post.

In 1932 in Temple, Texas, a cotton-picker explained why he was not working in the fields: 'I picked all week and made 85¢. I can starve sitting down a lot easier than I can picking cotton.'

A year later an Oklahoma editor reported:

> Not a blade of wheat in Cimmaron County, Oklahoma; cattle
> dying there on the range; a few bushels of wheat in the Perryton
> area against an average yield of from four to six million bushels
> ... ninety per cent of the poultry dead because of the sand
> storms; sixty cattle dying Friday afternoon between Guymon
> and Liberal from some disease induced by dust – humans
> suffering from dust fever – milk cows going dry, turned into
> pasture to starve, hogs in such pitiable shape that buyers will not
> have them.

In the coal-mining communities of West Virginia an agent of the
State Board of Children's Guardians found one farmer cremating
his dead infant because he could not afford a funeral. A mother,
insane from hunger and worry, drowned her two children. A
ten-year-old girl, whose father had been arrested, had been alone
for five days, except for the companionship of a small brown dog
and a black hen. She had a cataract in one eye and was almost
blind in the other. She had gone barefoot in the winter; one of her
toes had frozen but had healed.

In Detroit the Department of Public Welfare surveyed 1,286
families in 1931. Only 34 per cent of the heads of families were
actually on a payroll. Their median average weekly earnings had
fallen by 67 per cent since 1929. 145 of them were paying
mortgages. Of these, 14 had lost their homes, 63 were in arrears
with their repayments, 98 were delinquent in their tax payments.
Of the 828 tenants, 269 were in arrears, 28 had been evicted. One
quarter of the families had not provided milk for their children in
the previous two days. Their plight showed 'the dismal signs of
pauperizing, that is rapidly reducing the proud American citizen to
a level of insecurity and want, and destroying what had once been
known as the American standard of living'. That summer a mother
removed from the welfare rolls killed her four-year-old son for
fear that he would starve to death. The Recorder's Court found
her not guilty of murder.

In Gary, Indiana, employees of the United States Steel Company earned $1.75 a week in the summer of 1932. They worked
one day every fortnight. The Company forbade them from applying to public agencies or private charities for relief.

In Chicago a correspondent for the *New Frontier*, a fortnightly paper published by the Workers' Committee on Unemployment, reported on conditions at the Roseland Garbage Dump:

> About twenty-five men and boys and one woman stood in two rows all day, all the way down to the garbage hill waiting for that load to come down. And then, like a flock of chickens, they started to scratch in that smelly pile, and pick out certain things, which they deposited in baskets they had with them. Apples seemed most popular even when half rotted away. Carrots, potatoes, and bread also found their way into the baskets. . . . Some claimed they were taking the stuff for rabbits and chickens, but I noticed that a pile of lettuce and spinach leaves, which would have been ideal feed, were left untouched. Most of them admitted that it was for their supper.

In Philadelphia a settlement house worker described a landlord's plight. Mr Lazar had worked all his life as an unskilled worker but had managed to buy two family houses which he had converted into four apartments. He lost his job; his tenants could only pay rent sporadically; he exhausted the $1,000 he had saved; he borrowed all he could on his property. His two older girls dropped out of school to save on bus fares and shoes. His youngest child was refused free milk at school because his father owned property.

Robert Ozment's father was a railroad engineer in Texas. In 1929 the family had a new Overland Whippet car, were buying a home, had money in the bank and plenty of food and clothing. By 1933 all this had gone except the Whippet. They lived in a rent-free house on the edge of the black section of town. They had little to eat except oatmeal. They had no electricity and few clothes. Ozment remembers the house well 'because it had no coverings on the splintery old floors. My one pair of shoes had to be saved for winter use, and during the summer my feet were constantly bandaged from the thrust of splinters.' As for the car, it sat in a shed because they had no money for either petrol or tyres.

Diana Morgan's father was a prosperous cotton merchant and owner of a small general store in North Carolina. Her father went bankrupt. The first thing she noticed about the Depression 'was that my grandfather's house was lost, about to be sold for taxes'.

In her junior year at college, the phone was disconnected, the cook and the cleaning women were gone. There was dust under the beds and the curtains were not as clean as they used to be. Then came the final blow. 'Our own house was sold. It was considered the most attractive house in town, about a hundred and fifty years old. We even had a music library. Imagine my shock when it was sold for $5,000 in back taxes.'

These random cameos illustrate the shame, anger, destitution, and tragedy that Americans experienced during the Depression. But they also highlight the national and pervasive scope of the Depression in the United States. In Britain the traditional industries of coal-mining, ship-building, and textiles bore the brunt of the inter-war Depression. Regions like the Midlands and the south-east of England avoided the worst of the recession. Indeed for skilled workers in new industries and for the middle class in a time of deflation the slump brought prosperity. But in the United States, the Depression blighted countryside and city, inner-city and suburb, old industries and new, blue-collar and white-collar workers. No region escaped. And this economic catastrophe blanketed the nation with the most inadequate and antiquated welfare system of any Western industrialised country.

1 On the land

'Everybody talks of the Crash of '29. In small towns out West, we didn't know there was a Crash. What did the stock market mean to us? Not a dang thing. If you were in Cut Bank, Montana, who owned stock? The farmer was a ping-pong ball in a very tough game.' Farmers who made up more than 30 per cent of the workforce already had more than enough problems to contend with before the Great Crash wiped $26 billion off the value of shares on the New York Stock Exchange in October and November 1929.

Farmers had not participated in the prosperity of the 1920s: per capita farm income was one third the national average. Encouraged to expand production during World War I, farmers had continued to increase their output in the 1920s. Better seeds raised yields per acre, new tractors brought more and more acreage into production, particularly in the Great Plains. Farmers borrowed enthusiastically to purchase the new machinery and the new land: by 1929 total farm debts stood at $9.8 billion. Revived world agricultural production meant that at the end of the decade American farmers were already producing too much.

Then came twin hammer blows: foreign markets disappeared in the world depression; domestic markets sagged when urban demand collapsed in the United States after 1929. It was a tragedy to be producing food that starving city-dwellers could not afford to buy. But there was an even more cruel irony. Drought affected almost every farm state at some time between 1930 and 1936. Whichever way the farmer turned, he lost. Mounting surpluses meant that a good harvest yielded rock-bottom prices. Drought, on the other hand, eliminated farm income altogether. The fall in annual net farm income from $6.1 billion in 1929 to $2 billion in 1932 revealed the stark dimensions of the catastrophe.

The western farmers of the mountain and plains states suffered the most dramatic fall in income. Relative prosperity in the 1920s was wiped out by drought. Demand for beef had remained high through 1929 but from 1930 the ranchers of Wyoming and Colorado saw their cattle emaciated for lack of feed. Farmers in Idaho, angry at being excluded from a private, irrigated reclamation project, dynamited the controls of the project's reservoir. Relentlessly optimistic wheat farmers in the plains states had recklessly pushed forward into new acreage, previously considered uneconomic. Drought was soon followed by dust storms which blew the top soil away. In Cimarron County, Oklahoma, farmers had doubled their acreage between 1925 and 1930. Local boosters in 1930 fantasised that 'Soon you will have your own Empire State Building right across from Kirby's Kash Grocery'. Instead, the wheat harvest which yielded $700,000 that year and $1.2 million in 1931 produced only $7,000 in 1933. It cost North Dakota farmers 77¢ to produce a bushel of wheat in 1932: the price they received was 30¢. Kansas farmers were spared the worst of these calamities because they were more diversified and benefited from slightly greater rainfall but their plight was bad enough. Their income from cattle fell by half between 1930 and 1932 while local wheat prices slumped from 99¢ a bushel in 1929 to 33¢ in 1932.

The midwestern corn belt saw the most violent demonstrations of farmer anger. It was the precipitate drop in prices for previously prosperous farmers that sparked the unrest. The year 1931 saw the sharpest yearly decline ever in hog prices. In the spring of 1932 Milo Reno, the former president of the Iowa Farmers' Union, launched the Farmers' Holiday Association: the ultimate sanction of farmers would be to withhold their produce from market. FHA leaders were uncertain when and how such strikes would actually materialise. Local dairy farmers took the matter out of the leaders' hands by striking in Iowa and Minnesota in August and September 1932, and in Wisconsin in February 1933. Although the fall in dairy prices had been relatively modest, dairy farmers were the easiest to organise for strike action since theirs was a perishable commodity and they farmed in a small area near their market. But local farm strikes were futile: the strike had no impact on prices, so that farmers were not compensated for the income they lost in the strike.

What worried corn-belt farmers even more than low prices was their indebtedness and the threat to the land they owned. As prices fell, so they found it increasingly difficult to meet mortgage repayments and tax obligations. The length to which angry farmers were prepared to go to defend their farms took even FHA leaders by surprise. In January and February 1933 there were 76 penny-auctions in 15 states where violent neighbouring farmers scared off prospective bidders and restored land to its original owner. The impact of these auctions and farmer demonstrations in state capitals in the winter of 1932–33 was considerable: insurance companies voluntarily suspended foreclosure suits and the states, either by law or by governor's proclamation, declared moratoria on mortgage repayments.

In the South the collapse of export markets for cotton and tobacco exacerbated existing problems of overproduction. In the 1920s cotton farmers had had to cope with the ravages of the boll weevil and the 1927 Mississippi flood. Mounting stocks were boosted by the expansion of production in the south-western states: Texas and Oklahoma had almost doubled their cotton acreage in the 1920s. The 1929 crop yielded $1.5 billion; the 1930 crop a mere $826 million.

Drought in 1930 presaged worse to come. Local planters in Arkansas denied that anyone was suffering because they did not want outside assistance until their tenants and labourers had harvested the crop. But an Extension Service official noted that 'practically one half of the farm population of the state will be destitute if measures are not taken for relief'. A local minister summed up the effect of falling prices and drought:

> We have no well-to-do people. Our merchants are practically insolvent. All of us have been helping the destitute about us to the extent of our ability and it is useless to attempt to raise money among people who do not have it.

In England, Arkansas, in January 1931, 300 farmers threatened to loot stores if they did not receive food. Frightened merchants hastily arranged to disburse $1,500 worth of staples. By the end of the winter the Red Cross had aided 2.7 million drought sufferers.

What was happening to cotton farmers was not just a natural disaster: overproduction was still the problem. In August 1931 the federal crop Reporting Division predicted that the coming crop would be 15.5 million bales – the third largest cotton crop in history – which would bring a likely $100 million loss to cotton and its related businesses in the South. Large planters in Louisiana persuaded their governor, Huey Long, to call for a cotton holiday – a complete ban on cotton planting in 1932. Long used the largest privately-owned radio station in the United States – KWKH – to drum up mass meetings of farmers throughout the South to press other states to follow Louisiana's example. The Texas governor and legislature resisted Long's blandishments and threats and the movement for a cotton holiday collapsed.

The next summer the cotton crop yielded only $465 million dollars. By then in Mississippi times were reported to be 'as tough as jailhouse stew'. Per capita income fell from $239 in 1928 to a mere $117 in 1933. Over one third of the banks in the state failed. On one day in April 1932 one quarter of the land in the state was sold at sheriff's sales. This paralysis of credit was paralleled in the tobacco belt. Total receipts for the cigarette tobacco crop in 1932 were one third those of 1929. In one tobacco county there were 3,500 foreclosures in one year on the county's 5,280 farms. As banks collapsed, those that remained open did not want to lend to farmers; it became clear that landlords simply did not have the money to finance their usual crop. There was, reported two time-merchants from eastern North Carolina, 'no money or credit available. Worthless farmers and tenants cannot be carried and the more worthy must go without financial aid.' Extension Service officials estimated that between fifteen and twenty thousand tenants would not be retained for the 1932 crop.

No area of rural America escaped the Depression. Small diversified farms in Virginia and in New England might suffer less than the producers of great staples. As one Virginian recalled almost lyrically:

> We were largely self-sufficient. Our life style was simple but we were happy as we had a large family and a happy one. We were concerned about our neighbors. We cooperated and helped each other. We traded items or lent items to each other if the need was there.

But others recalled that money for necessities was scarce, for luxuries non-existent. 'People were in a daze-shock actually.' Relatively few farmers in Vermont lost their farms but its small dairy farmers went on strike in 1932, squeezed between high feed costs and falling milk prices. They needed every possible advantage to make money from their tiny dairy herds. In 1932 those advantages simply did not exist.

2 In the towns

Depression came as inexorably to industry. In 1930 unemployment had risen to 8.7 per cent of the non-agricultural workforce from 3.2 per cent in 1929. At that point it was possible to argue that the unemployment rate was no worse than during the 1920–21 recession. But the 1931 figure of 15.9 per cent swept away any notion that the economic downturn was temporary. By 1933 one in four of the workforce was unemployed. The unemployment statistics were notoriously unreliable. It is quite likely that one third of those available for work were jobless. No other industrial country experienced as much long-term unemployment as the United States. Only Germany for a brief period saw as many of its workforce thrown out of work. The jobless figures do not capture the full plight of industrial workers. Those who worked suffered wage cuts. A survey of 1,500 firms by the National Industrial Conference Board suggested that workers lost 32 per cent in real income between 1929 and 1932. Many were working short-time.

One economist in January 1932 estimated that half of those with jobs were only working part-time.

The first industries to suffer were the 'sick' industries of the 1920s, coal and textiles, which had failed to prosper then because of overproduction and falling demand.

Despite political fulminations against the 'Coal Trust', coal was a chaotically organised industry made up of relatively small operators who had, after World War I, rejected plans to continue war-time policies of price-fixing and market-sharing. Mechanisation, the restoration of European production, the competition of oil and natural gas, and the decline of the railroads created excess capacity in coal. The operators responded by seeking desperately to lower labour costs. In Illinois and the Central Competitive Field of Ohio, Indiana, and Pennsylvania cost-cutting meant breaking the back of the United Mine Workers' Union; elsewhere, it meant moving production to the non-union areas of Alabama, West Virginia, and Kentucky. Demand fell further during the Depression: 1932 production was the lowest since 1904, 300,000 miners lost their jobs and those who were employed worked on average only 146 days that year, at wage rates for a third of them of less than $2.50 a day. Destitution and malnutrition scarred the mining communities. Governor Gifford Pinchot of Pennsylvania reported that 'in the whole range of the depression there is nothing worse than the condition of the soft-coal miners'. In Harlan County, Kentucky, 231 children died of malnutrition-induced disease between 1929 and 1931.

Conditions were so bad that miners responded to wage cuts with desperation militancy: in 1931, 2.2 million man-days were lost in strikes, 32 per cent of all those lost in the nation; in 1932, 6 million man-days; 58 per cent of the national total. The strikes were hopeless. The strikers could look for little assistance to the United Mine Workers' Union: its strike fund had been exhausted even before the Depression. Most commonly, as in Pennsylvania, Ohio, and Harlan County, they were backed by the Communist National Miners' Union. But although the Communists were capable of mobilising and organising strikes, they were no more capable than the United Mine Workers of winning them. National publicity, which the Communists secured in abundance, was of little avail to striking miners evicted from their homes, terrorised by company guards whom local sheriffs deputised, and denied local relief or

Red Cross assistance. Communists might be able to organise blacklisted unemployed miners in Harlan County: they could do little to protect miners against scab 'barefootmen', hungry men desperate for any job no matter how low the wage.

An atomised industry, overproduction, company towns, and desperation militancy also characterised the textile industry. As production in England and the Far East was restored in the 1920s and the competition from fibres like silk and rayon increased, so cotton textile executives sought to expand production and lower costs in the South. By 1930 three-quarters of the firms were losing money. Workers faced especially drastic wage cuts and the 'stretch-out' – the stepping-up of individual work loads. Given the plantation-like dependence of the workers in many mill villages, it was a measure of their desperation that they struck in great waves of unrest in the southern Piedmont in 1929 and 1931. Once again, Communists led the most notable of these conflicts in Gastonia, North Carolina. As in coal, so in textiles, the strikes were doomed to failure. Red-baiting, vigilante mob violence, the presence of trigger-happy deputies and the National Guard, eviction from company houses, and the pervasive presence of the employers' influence in churches and welfare agencies, assured defeat.

The Depression, however, was not confined to the 'sick' atomised industries of the 1920s. It was also marked by the collapse of the technologically advanced, consumer durable industries which had led the way to prosperity in that decade. Both the automobile and electrical manufacturing industries, dominated by a few large corporations, saw their sales shrink by over two-thirds between 1929 and 1932.

In 1921 Americans bought almost 1.5 million motor vehicles: in 1929 they bought almost 4.5 million. Affluence, new-found leisure time, suburban development, and the availability of instalment buying dramatically widened car ownership: probably two-thirds of the nation's families owned a car by the end of the decade. Yet communities dependent on automobile manufacturing were already feeling the first tremors of economic collapse before the end of 1929. In the last four months of the year unemployment in Michigan quadrupled. The average number of people employed in factories in the Detroit area fell by 21.5 per cent from the same period the previous year. By April 1930 Michigan's unemployment rate had risen to 10.2 per cent compared to the national rate of

6.6 per cent. In Detroit and Flint the figure was over 13 per cent.

Car sales plummeted: just over 1,000,000 new cars were sold in 1932. Ford in Detroit employed 120,000 workers in March 1929; by August 1931 the workforce had shrunk to 37,000. Edmund Wilson reported that 'The enormous organism of Detroit is now seen, for all its Middle Western vigor, to have become atrophied. It is clogged with dead tissue now and its life is bleeding away.' A year later over 50 per cent of the city's workforce was estimated to be jobless. In Toledo, Ohio, Willis-Overland employed 28,000 workers in March 1929; by the spring of 1932 only 3,000 remained. Between 30 and 40 per cent of the male population were out of work.

The value added by manufacture in the electrical industry had more than doubled between 1919 and 1929. The industry, dominated by General Electric and Westinghouse, had previously concentrated on heavy electrical equipment but in the 1920s it sought successfully to educate consumers to new standards of domestic living. Over seventeen million households were wired for electricity and the manufacturers sought to install electric appliances from irons to washing machines in all of them. In 1922 they sold 100,000 radios: in 1929 they sold 4.9 million. The scope for future expansion seemed limitless yet the Depression ravaged the industry. The value added by manufacture fell by over 70 per cent between 1929 and 1933. Worst hit of all were capital goods as utilities and steel companies cancelled orders for motors and generators. Expensive consumer items like electric cookers fared as badly. Only refrigerators and light bulbs held their own. General Electric's net income fell from $60.5 million in 1930 to $14.17 million in 1932. Its payroll fell from 87,933 in 1929 to 41,560 in 1933. Westinghouse slashed its workforce by 54 per cent between 1929 and 1932 but still lost money in 1931, 1932, and 1933.

In many communities construction workers were among the first to feel the pinch. An 82 per cent decline in residential construction between 1929 and 1932 and a 75 per cent fall in other construction devastated the building trades. Construction contracts amounted to $6.6 billion in 1929, but only $1.3 billion in 1932. Houston vividly illustrated this collapse. Building permits worth $29 million were issued in 1929, but only $2.5 million worth were granted in 1932. Industries that depended on construction were inevitably hit. In Oregon employment in lumber and timber manufacturing fell by 60 per cent in three years. Professionals did not escape either: more than one third of the nation's civil engineers and architects were out of work.

Iron and steel production fell by 59 per cent between 1929 and 1932. The United States Steel Corporation's full-time payroll stood at 225,000 in 1929: half its workforce even then was working part-time. By the end of 1931 three-quarters of its payroll worked part-time. By April 1933 all of its workers were part-time. The collapse crippled steel communities. In Pittsburgh, shanty towns sprang up and Father James Cox's church reputedly provided two million free meals from its soup kitchens. By 1933, 31 per cent of the city's white workforce and 48 per cent of its black workers were jobless. Birmingham, Alabama, was labelled the hardest hit city in the nation. US Steel paid its workers there between 10¢ and 15¢ an hour, often in scrip redeemable only at the company store. By early 1932, 25,000 of the city's workforce of 108,000 were out of work and most of the remainder were employed part-time. The city's community chest usually helped 800 families a year. In 1932 it had to care for 9,000.

Particular circumstances could cushion the Depression's impact. Cities dependent on commerce and finance fared better than those dependent on manufacturing. Diversified light industry offered more protection than a single heavy industry. Thus, cities as diverse as New York, Boston, Dallas, Houston, and Memphis did not feel the full weight of the Depression till 1932. The presence of a military base, a major state university, or the seat of state government could also help sustain employment levels. Similarly, the recent arrival of new industry (Fort Wayne, Indiana), a local oil boom (Kilgore in north-east Texas), or the presence of a depression-proof industry like cigarette manufacturing (Louisville and Richmond) could delay the inevitable. In general, southern towns experienced the worst later than midwestern and north-eastern communities. Cities on the West Coast like Oakland experienced the economic downturn six months later than the rest of the country. But by 1933 not even the most optimistic local boosters could claim that their community had escaped the trauma of mass unemployment.

3 Poverty and subsistence

The 1920s may have seen the unprecedented availability of consumer goods. But the decade was also characterised for many Americans by low wages and irregular employment. Even without a Depression many of them could ill-afford to join the consumer society. In 1930 an estimated 16 million families, 60 per cent of the total, representing 70 million people, received less than $2,000 a year, the figure which the Brookings Institution calculated was 'sufficient to supply only basic necessities'.

Most working-class males and many in the middle class were not paid enough to support their families above a subsistence level on their own. They needed supplementary wage-earners. In the past, children, particularly from immigrant families, had often served that role. Increasingly, women had to work. In 1930 women constituted 24.3 per cent of the workforce. A quarter of women over the age of 16 worked, 28 per cent of them were married.

The Depression put intense pressure on these working women. It sent them, in Alice Kessler-Harris's words, a 'curious double message'. Their earnings became particularly crucial for working-class families where husbands were thrown out of work. For many middle-class families, a wife's income was the only means of sustaining the levels of consumption enjoyed in the 1920s. The percentage of married women working rose 50 per cent in the 1930s to 35 per cent of the female labourforce.

At the same time, there was substantial opposition, voiced in the press, women's magazines, and later in the opinion polls, to the idea of married women working. They were, it was argued, selfishly responsible for male unemployment. In 1930–31 over three-quarters of American school systems refused to hire women employees if they were married. Half dismissed women teachers if they married. Section 213 of the Economy Act passed by Congress in 1932 in a vain effort to curb federal government spending required that married employees, with a spouse also working for the government, were the first to be dismissed in the event of job reductions. 1,500 women were dismissed under this provision in the first year. In addition, some ethnic groups, notably Italians and Mexican-Americans, maintained their traditional cultural hostility to married women working outside the home. These formidable ideological constraints helped explain why, despite economic need, only 15.2 per cent of married women were working in 1940.

In general, female unemployment rose faster than male jobless-ness in the first years of the Depression. Low-wage, unskilled women in manufacturing were likely to be laid off first: by January 1931 female unemployment in that sector was already 30.3 per cent. Women in domestic service were also vulnerable: their jobs were often the first casualties of household economies. 24.2 per cent were out of work by January 1931.

The impact of the Depression on the 14 per cent of female workers who were in professional jobs was perhaps less dramatic. Nevertheless, a quarter of them saw their earnings fall in the decade after 1929, 30 per cent reported in 1934 that they had been unemployed at some point in the past year, and their share of the female labourforce declined slightly during the decade to 12.3 per cent. Women had failed to make significant advances in the professions in the 1920s and they found it difficult to reverse that trend in the Depression.

Women teachers epitomised some of the problems facing pro-fessional women during the Depression. Four out of five teachers were women in 1930. Job losses were relatively small: only 8 per cent of teaching jobs had gone by 1933. But those teachers in jobs had to endure savage pay cuts and lengthy periods without pay as hard-pressed local school boards struggled to meet payrolls. Chicago was the most notorious example of local penury. First, the city paid its teachers in tax warrants, then in the winter of 1932–33 it paid them nothing at all. In some areas teachers distributed clothing and food to needy children to enable them to come to school; in others, parents organised bake sales to raise the bus fares for needy teachers to travel to work. In the 1930s the absolute number of women teachers fell, as did their share of jobs in the profession.

Despite the difficulties facing working- and middle-class women, the Depression did not completely devastate female employment as it might have done if women's jobs had merely been marginal to the economy. Ruth Milkman, Julia Blackwelder, and Alice Kes-sler-Harris have demonstrated some of the forces that enabled the female share of the workforce to creep up to 25 per cent by 1940. Women were protected by their concentration in clerical and service sectors which recovered more quickly than manufacturing. They also benefited from the decision of some manufacturers, notably in textiles, cigar-making, and the garment industry, to rationalise and modernise their equipment. These employers were happy to bring more low-paid women in to do the routine, unskilled jobs they were creating. Finally, women were also protected by the sexual stereotyping of many of their jobs. Despite the economic pressure on male workers, men were either not brought in, or did not want, to replace women in these jobs.

The need for women to work highlighted the generally low level of incomes for many ordinary Americans even during the prosperous 1920s. But there was a substantial segment of the population – an estimated 40 million people – whose plight was even worse: an estimated third of the population with income below $1,200 a year. This core of the permanently poor were also largely invisible – either because they were unorganised and unrecognised – the old – or the subjects of moral disapproval – single parent families – or geographically removed – the rural poor – or black.

Blacks had flocked from southern farms to the cities during World War I and had continued to migrate in the 1920s. One in five of the nation's blacks was an urban dweller by 1930. Restricted to domestic service and unskilled and casual jobs, crowded into ghetto slums, most eked out a bare subsistence living. The Depression made their grim plight worse. In southern cities whites moved into jobs hitherto earmarked for blacks: street cleaning, garbage collection, domestic service, even as bellhops in hotels. Desperate whites organised vigilante groups like the Black Shirts in Atlanta to deprive Negroes of jobs. By 1931 one third of blacks in southern cities were unemployed. A year later the proportion rose to over a half. For the two million blacks in the North the prospect was little better. An Urban League survey of 106 American cities suggested that the proportion of blacks unemployed was anywhere between 30 and 60 per cent greater than for whites. St. Louis blacks who constituted only 9 per cent of the population made up 60 per cent of relief cases. Blacks were disproportionately concentrated in industries that suffered early, notably soft-coal and construction. Black, marginal, and unskilled workers were usually the last to be hired and the first to be fired. The Depression also threatened the precarious toehold in the middle-class economy that black businessmen had gained in the ghetto. In Harlem the percentage of property owned or managed by blacks fell from 35 per cent in 1929 to 5 per cent in 1935. The median income there for skilled workers fell by a half between 1929 and 1932.

Urban blacks could do little in the political arena to alleviate their plight. Republican politicians in the North tended to take support from the black ghetto for granted. Democratic politicians in cities like Kansas City and Detroit were only just beginning to be alerted to the possibility of competing for that black vote. Most blacks in the urban South could not vote: only in San Antonio and Memphis did white machine politicians trade a modest provision of public services to local leaders in return for bloc black support.

The American population was ageing. Those over 65 were 4.9 per cent of the population in 1929, 6.9 per cent in 1940. The bulk of the 6.6 million aged in 1930 lived on or below the poverty line. Their dependence was increasing. In 1920 an estimated one third relied on someone else's resources; in 1930 two-fifths; in 1940 two-thirds. They could not turn to the government for assistance. An earlier generation had received Civil War pensions which by the turn of the century were probably assisting two-thirds of native whites in the North over 65. As those pensions lapsed, the Fraternal Order of Eagles pushed the states for state pension laws. But in 1929 only eleven states provided pensions for the needy aged and aided a mere one thousand people. The pensions were often discretionary and required humiliating means tests. In California, which passed the first mandatory state pension law in 1929, only those over 70 were eligible and the monthly pension averaged only $22 a month between 1930 and 1932.

Private pension plans helped only a few. Established by some large firms in an effort to ease out inefficient workers, lessen labour turnover, and undercut the spread of trades unions, they offered only grudging and discretionary benefits to a few long-service workers. In 1925 only 36,000 former employees received assistance from some 500 pension plans. Old people were therefore thrown back on their own resources. They had either to keep working, use their own savings, or rely on their families for support. The humiliating alternative was the county poorhouse.

The spectre of the poorhouse loomed larger during the Depression. Older workers were the first to be let go and found it difficult to get another job. 'What chance,' asked the superintendent of the San Francisco Relief home, 'has the man not of seventy, but of fifty to reestablish himself today with thousands of boys who have left school in the past three years who were not fitted into any sort of job and will do anything at any price to get a job?' The number of people over 65 increased by 24 per cent in the 1930s, but the number employed declined by 22 per cent. Savings were rapidly exhausted or lost in banks which collapsed; the value of stock investments was wiped out. Family resources were stretched to the limit.

Another major group of the permanently poor were families where there was no father present. There were 3.8 million families with no adult male breadwinner in 1930. Twenty-six states offered pensions for these families with dependent children. Yet the eligibility requirements were so tightly drawn that only 93,260 families received a pension in 1931. The aim was to help only those deemed morally worthy, mainly widows. In Mississippi for example only 34 families received pensions in June 1931. All the beneficiaries were white, 30 of the 34 grants went to widows. Only one went to a mother with an illegitimate child.

The rural poor constituted the other great sector of the pre-Depression poor in America. There were three main groups on the land who were permanently poor. Subsistence farmers on submarginal land in the Appalachians or the cut-over regions of the Great Lakes lived isolated lives remote from modern communications and commercial markets. Their farms were too small, the soil was exhausted, their population growth was the highest in the nation. The Depression made matters worse by cutting off alternative sources of income from coal mining and lumber. But the poverty of their existence and the resilience of their culture was on the whole little affected by either the Depression or the New Deal.

Migratory farm labourers, particularly, on the factory farms of California, were economically dependent and politically powerless. They were usually Mexican, often illegal immigrants, who lived in squalid labour camps and had little leverage against employers and local sheriffs who constantly held over their heads the threat of deportation. Communist efforts to organise them into unions in 1931 foundered on racial tension and vigilante violence.

The largest group of the rural poor was comprised of the 8.5 million people living in tenant and sharecropper families in the South, 3 million of whom were black. The dimensions of their poverty had remained largely unchanged since the end of Reconstruction. Cotton did not generate enough income at the best of times to support so many people. Dependent on their landlords for housing, and the supplies and credit with which to farm, the tenants had almost no guarantee that landlords would fairly divide the proceeds of the crop at the end of the year. They had little bargaining power since in any case there were too many people on the land. Nor could many leave the land. The urban economy did not grow fast enough in the 1920s to absorb them and in the 1930s there were no jobs to be had in the depressed cities. Almost the only form of protest available to them was to leave one landlord and work for another. As many as 40 per cent of Mississippi tenants did this in 1930. More substantial protest invited violent retribution, at its most extreme the lynching of 'troublesome' blacks. When Communists organised a sharecroppers' union in Tallapoosa County, Alabama, in 1931 an indiscriminate shoot-out by local deputies at Camp Hill led to the death of one black farmer and was the prelude to white posses rampaging through the countryside in search of non-existent carloads of black Communist invaders. Dirt, dilapidation, and disease characterised living conditions. Cash income for families rarely topped $100 a year, and black incomes lagged behind white. The hopelessness was summed up by one Alabama tenant: 'Ain't make nothing, don't speck nothing more till I die. Eleven bales of cotton and the man takes all. We just work for de oder man. He git everything.' Or as one rural Georgia black wryly commented, 'Most blacks did not even know the Great Depression had come. They had always been poor and only thought the whites were catching up.'

Only one group perhaps endured a worse fate: American Indians. Under the Dawes Act of 1887 a policy of rapidly enforced assimilation followed a century of conquest. But the Act achieved the worst of both worlds. The land policy, the Bureau of Indian Affairs, boarding schools, and Christian missionaries attempted to destroy traditional Indian community organisation, but failed in turn to assimilate the Indians. Individual allotments of land were too small to turn Indians with little agricultural experience into self-sufficient farmers. In debt, the Indians consequently sold their lands to whites who coveted the rich mineral resources. Indian land diminished from 139 million acres in 1887 to 48 million acres in 1932.

In 1928, 55 per cent of Indians had a per capita income of less than $200 a year. Only 2 per cent had incomes greater than $500 a year. Almost half the Indians on the reservations were landless and over-grazing was denuding what land they had. Their infant mortality rate was three times that of whites and alcoholism and crime were widespread.

4 What had gone wrong?

In 1928 Herbert Hoover accepted the Republican nomination for the presidency by proclaiming that 'We in America today are nearer to the final triumph over poverty than ever before in the history of any land'. When he took office in 1929 the prospects continued to look bright: profits were high, wages and prices stable, and industrial capacity plentiful. What caused the dramatic collapse which gave Hoover's words such a hollow ring?

Economists for a long time highlighted the structural weaknesses of the American economy in the 1920s. Because of the maldistribution of income and the flaws of the banking system and the operation of the stock market, there was insufficient demand in the American economy to sustain the great gains made in productivity by American industry and agriculture. This lack of demand was not offset in the early years of the Depression by any compensatory government spending. More recently, analysis of this lack of demand was refined to focus first on the downturn in construction and automobiles, then on the decline in agricultural income and the loss of wealth caused by the stock market crash.

The implications of such an analysis was that a Keynesian economic policy was an appropriate remedy for depression. To monetarists such an analysis was anathema. As Milton Friedman complained, an expanded role for government was no solution for a crisis caused by government itself in the first place. To Friedman and his followers, the Depression was caused by the fall in the money supply by a third. The body responsible first for not checking this fall, then for making it worse, was the Federal Reserve Board. The Board made two crucial mistakes. First, it failed to stop the collapse of rural midwestern and southern banks in 1930 and failed to protect the essentially sound Bank of the United States in New York when it too came under pressure. Second, when Britain went off the gold standard in 1931 the FRB raised interest rates. Both errors caused the money supply to contract unnecessarily. What the FRB should have done was to purchase on the open market large supplies of government bonds in order to make more credit available to the banks. Only briefly and reluctantly did the Board pursue this policy in 1932.

Elaborate econometric calculations have not resolved the conflict between monetary and spending hypotheses of the cause of the Depression. But there is surely a *prima facie* case for arguing that there was insufficient purchasing power in the economy to sustain the growth of the 1920s, particularly in consumer durables. Too many Americans received incomes that could only sustain subsistence purchases. When in 1929 Americans ceased to consume at previous rates, inventories grew, manufacturers reassessed their futures, and declining confidence started the economy on a downward spiral. As businessmen started to cut back, they created the very conditions they feared. The downward spiral was speeded up by particular structural weaknesses in both the US and the international economy. Forces that in themselves were not responsible for the Depression combined to send the economy from a cyclical recession into a depression of unprecedented severity.

The lack of consumer purchasing power to sustain the growth of the 1920s seems clear enough. The agricultural sector was, as we have seen, doing relatively badly. While all per capita income rose 28 per cent during 1920–29, farm per capita income rose only 10 per cent. The industrial and urban economy simply did not grow fast enough to absorb the surplus rural population. Nor did lower-income workers proportionately share in the fruits of prosperity. Profits gained from rising productivity were not translated into higher wages. While the per capita income of the top 1 per cent of the non-farm population almost doubled, that of the lower 93 per cent rose only by 6 per cent. Structural poverty, irregular employment, and low wages meant that America was a consumer society without the capacity to consume.

Any slowdown as manufacturers found it hard to sell their goods was exacerbated by other structural weaknesses in the economy. America may have been a self-sufficient nation but it was not isolated from the international economy. The US emerged from World War I as a creditor nation. It would be difficult for European nations to sell enough goods on the American market to repay their war loans. The record levels of the Smoot-Hawley tariff in 1930 made it even harder. Large corporate profits, tax changes in favour of capital gains which made available money previously invested in tax-free municipal bonds, and low US interest rates combined to boost American investment overseas. American holdings of foreign securities trebled between 1925 and 1929 as American bankers made unsound loans to Latin America and invested to sustain German recovery to enable Germany to pay its reparations to the Allies, who could in turn pay back their war loans to the United States. The consequences were specific: Federal Reserve policies designed to protect the international gold standard so that American investors would not be hurt by European devaluation; the freezing of American assets in the European financial collapse that followed the collapse of the Austrian bank, Credit-Anstalt, in the spring of 1931; and severe pressure on the dollar and American banks once Great Britain went off the gold standard in 1931. The international events of 1931 certainly hurt the US at a time when economic recovery in the US demanded that credit be available to businessmen to renew investment.

The fragile US banking structure also hastened the deflationary spiral downwards. Almost 5,000 banks collapsed between 1923 and 1930 even before the Depression. In the absence of branch banking, too many banks in rural areas were small and lacked sufficient reserves to weather inevitable economic fluctuations. In 1930 as agriculture collapsed these banks were particularly vulnerable. 1,345 failed that year and their failure in turn made the plight of farmers worse. As banks ran into trouble, so investors withdrew their funds to safeguard their assets and to meet Depression expenses. Their withdrawals put yet more pressure on the banks. The banks then tried to improve their cash position. They put more pressure on debtors, froze more assets, and slowed the economy further. As the economy worsened, the banks suffered once more. 2,294 banks failed in 1931, 1,453 in 1932. The crisis spread from the rural banks to the large metropolitan institutions and in the autumn of 1932 moved from a crisis of individual banks to the complete collapse of credit in whole states. Governors closed banks in their states to halt the withdrawal of cash. These bank holidays started in Nevada, but the final collapse started with the closing of banks in industrial Michigan. By March 1933 governors in 34 states had closed their banks.

Questionable loans from banks for speculative purposes had

been one of the contributing factors in the boom on the stock market. This was fine as long as the stock market continued to rise. Similarly, the practice of buying on the margin, where the investor pays only a small part of the purchase price, was satisfactory as long as share prices continued to rise and the investor could sell profitably. The rise in share prices was spectacular from 1927 to October 1929. However, once confidence snapped, and investors sold rather than bought, investors who had borrowed or who had bought on margin were anxious to sell as quickly as possible to minimise their losses. This, in turn, quickened the fall in share prices which they had been anxious to avoid. The Great Crash in October 1929 was followed by a much longer and larger fall in values that both reflected and contributed to the economic downturn. $85 billion in share values were wiped out.

It is not clear what the FRB could have done to avert the collapse. In the 1920s it encouraged overseas investment by low interest rates in the US which were designed to protect the gold standard and overseas investors. In 1929 the Board faced an insoluble dilemma. If it raised interest rates to curb speculation it would take much needed credit from industry and agriculture. Keeping rates low meant a speculative boom and a disastrous bust. In 1930 the Board was reluctant to lower rediscount rates and purchase bonds on the open market which would have increased the credit available to the hard-pressed banks. In 1931 it raised interest rates to protect the dollar against European speculation. When rediscount rates were finally lowered in 1932 and open-market purchases stepped up, banks were so anxious to make their own position liquid and businessmen had so little confidence that the increased availability of credit made little difference. The FRB can scarcely be said to have made much contribution to recovery.

5 Coping

Job insecurity and irregular employment was a common experience for most Americans before the Depression. Traditionally, families survived periods of joblessness by turning to informal kin and ethnic networks. As the Depression took hold after 1929, they turned to these well-tried remedies.

Middle-class women looked for jobs, let their domestic servants go, made 'endless little economies' at home, canned their home-grown food, and made their own clothes. Families used up their savings, opted not to buy a new car (although few Americans gave up a car altogether in the Depression – car registrations and petrol sales held up), attempted to reschedule mortgage repayments or moved to cheaper accommodations. These efforts were often not enough to save their homes. In 1930 about 150,000 non-farm households lost their property through foreclosure; in 1931 this increased to almost 200,000; in 1932 to 250,000. By the spring of 1933 half of all home mortgages were technically in default; foreclosures had reached 1,000 a day.

Working-class families sent wives out to work, doubled up households to mind the children and save on rent, and took in lodgers. A survey of workers laid off by the United States Rubber Corporation in New Haven and Hartford, Connecticut, noted, 'Whole families combine in a sort of super family, so that one rent will do instead of two. Relatives of all degrees gather round an income like flies round a honey-pot – anyone who has an income will find himself swamped either with appeals for help or with non-paying guests.' The birth-rate slowed, engaged couples delayed getting married, children decided not to get married, handed over pay cheques to support bankrupt fathers or left home and became hoboes, travelling around the country in a vain search for work.

Such family strategies to combat the effect of unemployment could put great strains on families. Fathers lost the status and respect that came from being the chief provider; mother had to fulfil dual roles of breadwinner and homemaker; overcrowding produced domestic tension; children resented forced sacrifice, increased domestic responsibilities, and the loss of affluence. The evidence suggests, however, that the Depression tended to break up and disorganise only the families that were already unstable. If anything the fight for survival drew families together and strengthened the commitment of both adults and children to the institution of the family and to the conventional roles of men and women within the family.

Neighbourhood and ethnic networks helped as well. Neighbours served community dinners for all the families on the street or contributed a dollar a week to help the unemployed on the block. In Detroit the Hungarian Free Kitchen and the Jewish Emergency

Relief Fund provided free meals. In Steelton, Pennsylvania, the unemployed turned to the Croatian Fraternal Union. Inner-city churches ran soup kitchens. A small number of the unemployed received assistance from their former employers. For example, the unemployment fund operated by General Electric in Schenectady, New York, ensured that no GE employee had approached the city for relief by June 1931.

Nevertheless, where family and neighbourhood resources might earlier have seen families through hard times, the extent and duration of the Depression after 1929 exhausted these traditional remedies. Only a handful of firms operated 'welfare capitalist' unemployment schemes and falling profits forced most of them to abandon these by 1932.

A persistent theme, both in contemporary accounts by relief workers and in oral history interviews, is the reluctance of most Americans to abandon familiar strategies and seek charity or government assistance. The lengths that individuals went to avoid seeking help testified both to the strength of their own beliefs in individual responsibility and to the extent to which conservative assumptions underpinned existing welfare provision in the US.

Great Britain and Germany had had social insurance schemes for many years: in the United States prevailing welfare practice was more akin to the operation of the Old Poor Law. Assistance was first and foremost a local responsibility: for example in Pennsylvania it was the responsibility of 425 Poor Boards. Counties aimed to help the 'deserving poor' who were poor through no fault of their own – the aged, the infirm, and the mentally incapacitated. Assistance to these categories tended to be 'indoor relief': placement in a county poorhouse that would deter all but the most genuine cases. For those in distress for any other reason, the 'undeserving' poor, outdoor relief was designed to be as minimal and degrading as possible to deter idleness. Welfare recipients were in some cases required to sign paupers' oaths, denied the right to vote and even to marry. Counties usually had to bear the financial burden of welfare without any state government help.

Those who were temporarily unemployed in an economic downturn were expected to receive assistance from private charities: the embodiment of the conscience of the community. In the 1920s professionally-trained social workers employed by these charities relied on an individual case-work approach to poverty. Poverty, they seemed to believe, was the result neither of the general environment, nor of economic conditions, but of personal inadequacy. As late as 1932 social work students at Western Reserve University produced only one thesis on social conditions: more typical of their concerns was a dissertation on 'The Development of Basketball as a Leisure-Time Sport in Greater Cleveland'. Some private welfare agencies refused aid to clients unless psychiatric help was needed.

These private charities were not equipped to cope with a mass of able-bodied unemployed facing long-term joblessness. Individual case work was impossible as case loads multiplied. As *Survey* said, in the America of 1930, 'The niceties of modern social work, the careful process of building and rehabilitation are going overboard. The struggle is reduced to the simple elements of food and shelter for the hungry and the homeless.' Mass unemployment rendered personal inadequacy as an explanation of misfortune obsolete.

In any case, private charities could not raise enough money to meet their burgeoning commitments. Community Chests, first established in Cleveland in 1913 to fund and coordinate local charities, successfully boosted their fund-raising from $73 million in 1929 to $101 million in 1932. But these funds were still insufficient to meet the demands being made on the charities. Often fund-raising fell far short of its targets. In Detroit the Emergency Relief Fund aimed to raise $3.5 million in 1931 but collected a mere $645,000; San Antonio raised only $6,000 of its $20,000 target. In Boston the Salvation Army had to reduce its fund-raising goals in 1931 and 1932. Associated Jewish Philanthropies raised $900,000 in 1930 but only $615,000 to meet much greater need in 1931. In Pittsburgh 75 business leaders organised by H. J. Heinz and Robert Mellon financed over $1,000,000 of city improvements but their funds ran out in March 1932.

The unemployed had therefore to turn to local government for help. But cities were often totally ill-equipped to give assistance. Birmingham, Alabama, for example had abolished its Welfare Department in the 1920s. Most cities did not have the personnel to operate a wide-ranging relief effort. As late as August 1933 Cleveland relied on the private charities to distribute its relief funds. All cities found that they had to help ever-increasing numbers of unemployed when their own revenues, chiefly from property taxes, were declining. In Detroit a third of the taxes levied for 1932–33 could not be collected. Many cities were still servicing debts they had incurred in the construction boom of the 1920s. It was difficult to borrow more money: state constitutions often restricted urban borrowing and by 1932 it was almost impossible to find a market for municipal bonds.

Cities were increasingly the prisoners of unsympathetic bankers, who demanded the right to examine proposed budgets in detail and insisted on drastic economies before making any loans. Their demands were often unrealistic. As the mayor of Houston lamented, 'Of course we could fire all the policemen and let the people carry arms and try to protect themselves. We could discharge all the firemen and let the insurance rates swallow the city. We could nail up the front door of the city hall.' As it was, cities cut back essential services, dismissed staff, and turned the street lights off. They defaulted on debt repayments, were late in meeting monthly payrolls, and often had no alternative but to pay their employees in scrip.

The urban financial crisis had a devastating effect on assistance to the unemployed. Detroit and Boston were two of the most generous cities in the nation in public help for the jobless. The Detroit Department of Public Welfare, rather than private charity, had previously cared for the unemployed: between 1929 and 1933 public funds provided over 90 per cent of spending on unemployment relief. But in the summer of 1931 Mayor Frank Murphy explained that the dilemma was to 'feed half the people or half-feed the people' as relief rolls were slashed by almost half. The following year relief funds ran out in May, rents could not be paid, 150 tenants a day were being evicted, and food was temporarily provided on credit by the grocery chains, a practice they stopped on 1 August. In Boston, the number of families aided by the Overseers of Public Welfare increased sixfold between 1929 and 1932 but the city was still only aiding one in four of jobless families. In Philadelphia, which prided itself on its private philanthropy, a Committee of One Hundred raised $4 million and the city borrowed $3 million but public and private funds were exhausted by the end of 1931. A further charity drive by the United Campaign raised another $5 million but as the relief load increased by 2,000 families a week this money ran out in 3 months. In mid-June 1932 Philadelphia was forced to leave its 57,000 relief families to fend for themselves.

The unemployed often did not escape the traditional moralistic hostility to the 'undeserving' poor. Soup kitchens and feeding stations reminded one relief client of 'refugee feeding during World War I'. Relief was granted in many cases as food orders rather than cash on the assumption that the unemployed could not be trusted to spend money wisely. In Pennsylvania these food orders were redeemable at stores in which members of the Poor Board sometimes had an economic interest. The weekly relief grant in Pennsylvania was only one tenth of what it was ten years earlier. A family of three was expected to survive on three dollars or less a week for food. In Chicago the unemployed were first given cash but as funds ran out they received grocery orders instead: there had been complaints that the cash had been spent on cigarettes and sweets. Finally, the city found it even cheaper to buy food wholesale and hand out food boxes. In New York City a monthly food order was arbitrarily refused to one family in ten to save money and discourage the undeserving. In many cases, relief agencies refused to pay rent, even when the unemployed were on the verge of eviction. Often, clients were required to work for whatever pittance they received in order to test their real need and to protect their moral fibre.

Even when it became clear that cities faced financial catastrophe, state governments were reluctant to help. Legislatures in which rural areas were over-represented were unsympathetic to the plight of the cities. Constitutional restrictions often hamstrung their efforts to help. Where states were prepared to spend money it was often on highway projects which provided employment in rural areas and small towns rather than in the big cities. In September 1931, however, New York State pioneered with the direct granting of relief money to the local governments and six states followed suit in the winter.

Private charities and local governments had taken unprecedented steps to accept responsibility and aid the unemployed. But many local élites still did not accept that the Depression was more than a small temporary economic downturn. As a city councilman stated in Detroit in June 1931, 'This is a glorious time for a lot of people who have never worked in their lives and never will work.' It took a long time for the beggars and the breadlines to disturb the massive complacency of civic leaders in places like

Boston, Muncie, Indiana, and San Antonio. Businessmen, philan-
thropists, and civic leaders for the most part failed utterly to
respond to the plight of the millions of unemployed Americans.

6 Apathy or rebellion

How did the unemployed themselves respond? One view, summed
up by Arthur M. Schlesinger Jr, is that the Depression numbed the
jobless: 'People were sullen rather than bitter, despairing rather
than violent'. They 'sat at home, rocked dispiritedly in their chairs
and blamed conditions'. Some argue that the unemployed blamed
themselves for their plight. Imbued with the success ethic and the
American Dream, the unemployed felt that they, not the system,
had somehow failed. Sherwood Anderson in 1936 argued that
'There is in the average American a profound humbleness. People
seem to blame themselves.'

A diametrically opposed interpretation argues that the unemployed rebelled. Far from being imbued with middle-class ideas of
the success ethic, the unemployed became radical and approached
class-consciousness. According to Frances Fox Piven and Richard
Cloward, it was 'the specter of cataclysmic disorder' created by the
violence of the unemployed rebellion that eventually coerced
welfare concessions from the New Deal.

It is not easy to assess the mood of the unemployed in the 1930s.
They were often invisible. Newspapers sometimes chose not to
report demonstrations by the jobless. Until the late 1930s there
was no scientific polling of public opinion. Unlike politicians, the
unemployed did not leave manuscript collections to libraries. But
we do have oral history interviews, including a vast number carried
out by the New Deal's Federal Writers' Project, and a large
number of investigations conducted by zealous sociologists and
later by New Deal field workers.

These indicate that some of the unemployed took action. One
estimate suggests that as many as two million people took part in
some form of collective protest in the 1930s ranging from self-help
barter groups to the organised looting of food to mass demonstrations and hunger marches. Militants, notably the Communists,
organised the unemployed in Unemployed Councils and Leagues.
These organisations functioned as local welfare rights groups.

They demonstrated at local relief offices to force welfare officials to put their members on the relief rolls or to reinstate relief payments that had been stopped. There were an estimated 566 such incidents in Chicago in 1932 alone. They also organised mass resistance against evictions; local groups tried to put families back into their houses after bailiffs had put them on the streets. In New York Unemployed Councils allegedly restored 77,000 families to their homes. In Detroit and Chicago they claimed success in virtually halting evictions. The Unemployed Councils also took to the streets in local demonstrations behind the slogans of 'Work and Wages' and 'Fight, Don't Starve' to pressure local authorities to aid the unemployed. In New York a demonstration on 16 October 1930 was followed by the first one-million-dollar appropriation for relief by the city. In 1931 demonstrations in Chicago and St. Louis won immediate relief payments or the rescinding of relief cuts. Finally, there were well-publicised demonstrations aimed at dramatising the plight of the unemployed. Thousands took to the streets in cities across the nation on 6 March 1930, including an estimated 35,000 in New York, and clashed with police. In March 1932 the Hunger March on the Ford plant at Dearborn led to four people being killed. 20,000 people marched in the funeral procession.

There were, however, limits to the radical impact of these activities. Probably less than 5 per cent of the unemployed were engaged at any one time in the Councils and Leagues. As radical politicians admitted, the more successful the local group, the busier the local officials were in dealing with practical welfare matters. They had little time to educate politically their clients. The Communists, for example, added few party members as a result of their work with the jobless. The radicals found it difficult to sustain the organisations. Less than six months after the notable March 1930 demonstrations, Communist officials were reporting that 'organized councils are almost non-existent' and that 'the Unemployed Councils are dying out'. Just over a year after the Dearborn Hunger March, Unemployed Councils in Detroit were reported to be 'completely out of existence'. Often organisations were little more than the paper creations of party functionaries. Earl Browder, Communist Party secretary, reported at the end of 1931 that the Councils 'remain narrow cadre organizations that do not have day to day contact with the masses'. Intense Communist suspicion of other radicals fuelled this tendency. The party's organiser of the unemployed, Herbert Benjamin, noted, 'Where non-Party members are attracted to our movement, they find themselves excluded from all participation in the actual work of planning and leading actions'.

If there were precise limits to radical action by the unemployed, what was the psychological impact of unemployment on the jobless? Surveys reported a common pattern of response in both America and other industrialised countries: an initial optimistic but feverish search for jobs, followed by disillusion, then by apathy. As Lorena Hickok reported from New York in 1933 the unemployed were 'so apathetic that they accept without questioning us whatever we give them, no matter how pitifully inadequate it is or how badly administered'.

There may have been some difference between those who had been out of work before the Depression and those who were facing economic insecurity for the first time. Those who had previously been able to support themselves went to great lengths to avoid going on welfare. As an unemployed white-collar worker in Detroit explained, he was avoiding relief because 'It seems to me that I have lost all my ability as a responsible man. It seems to me that I have some shortcomings somewhere.' When they finally had no alternative, they tended to be apologetic and deferential to welfare officials. People who had received welfare before 1930 by contrast were likely to be among the earliest applicants for relief and were more likely to be aggressive towards relief officials.

As the Depression wore on there is also evidence to suggest that the unemployed became less acquiescent, less willing to accept middle-class values and blame themselves for their plight. Mass unemployment made personal inadequacy a less plausible explanation for failure. Lorena Hickok herself, as she investigated relief conditions in 1933–34, found signs of the unemployed expecting assistance as a matter of course and bitterly criticising the quality of aid they were receiving. Under the New Deal rising expectations seemed to have fuelled dissatisfaction with welfare assistance, particularly when economy drives led to cuts in relief.

The unemployed seem to have been neither rebellious nor the deferential victims of bourgeois hegemony. If E. Wight Bakke, who carefully surveyed the unemployed in New Haven, is right, employment gave workers many of the values they cherished:

status vis-à-vis their fellows, economic security, and a reputation as a good provider. The goal of the unemployed was to restore those values. A job would give them control of their own fate and restore their reputation for providing economic security for their families. Their goals were defined neither by dreams of upward mobility nor by political beliefs in the rights of their class. They were defined instead 'in terms of possibilities revealed by experience'. What characterised the American workers' response to unemployment was tough-minded realism. Such stoicism and resilience might militate against political radicalism but it did not signify self-blame, indifference, or hopeless despair.

7 Herbert Hoover and voluntarism

The man who had to cope with the first consequences of the Depression was vilified by Democratic publicists as a callous, dogmatic, and incompetent president. Few Democratic presidential candidates ever since have allowed the electorate to forget Herbert Hoover as the symbol of Republican responsibility for hard times and of Republican indifference to the poor. The picture of Hoover as a conservative ideologue devoted to nineteenth-century ideals of *laissez-faire* individualism has largely been rejected by historians. They now portray the president as a humane technocrat who attempted to rationalise and maximise the efficiency of American economic resources. Hoover's reluctance to expand state and bureaucratic power has won the admiration of New Left historians. They see his fear of state power as a perceptive warning of the development of corporatism under the New Deal. They applaud his defence of the values of the community against bureaucratic infringement.

Hoover was a rich man. As a geologist and engineer he had been at the forefront of mining developments on the frontiers of three continents. He believed that if a man 'has not made a million by the time he is forty he is not worth much'. By 1918 this poor Quaker boy from Iowa was worth $4 million. But he was also a humanitarian public servant. As administrator of relief to the starving Belgians in 1915, then as Food Administrator during the war, and finally as overseer of relief to the ravaged Europe of the post-war years, Hoover developed an immense reputation as a compassionate but remarkably efficient organiser. Several strands stand out in his career as a heroic expert in good works. He was not shy of publicity. He had a keen sense of public relations and the promotion of his public image. He shared acclaim grudgingly. He wielded vast personal powers and had little need to compromise or tolerate disagreement. But he used this vast power to stimulate voluntary endeavour. Wherever possible, he attempted to encourage cooperative activity and to mobilise local resources and initiative. He had enough experience of price-fixing during the war to convince him of the undesirability of coercive state action.

Hoover championed American individualism and celebrated the freedom of opportunity the nation provided. Yet distinctively American individualism was not the wasteful and cut-throat competition of *laissez-faire*, but an individualism that accompanied a capacity for cooperative activity. This bent for voluntary association, the combination of altruism and self-interest, was the key to American economic growth. It was the job of government not to sit idly by, but positively to encourage voluntary cooperation so that America's vast resources could be managed in the most efficient way. Hoover's views, as admirably summed up by Ellis Hawley, 'combined the outlook and optimism of modern management with deep-seated reservations about the competency of statist institutions'. Hoover was, in short, 'an anti-statist planner'.

Hoover's role as Secretary of Commerce from 1921 to 1929 amply confirmed his restless progressivism. There was scarcely an aspect of American economic life that he did not try to improve. He opposed Secretary of the Treasury Andrew Mellon's tax cuts for the wealthy and advocated instead a stiff graduated tax on legacies and gifts. He repeatedly urged the Federal Reserve Board to curb speculation by restricting credit. He stressed that traditional employers' attitudes to their workers were incompatible with efficiency: higher wages and labour standards were needed to ensure that a market existed to sustain the tremendous economic growth caused by the productivity gains of the decade. To that end, he worked to eliminate the twelve-hour day in steel; he also embraced schemes of worker representation. After the Mississippi flood of 1927, he advocated the thorough-going restructuring of southern agriculture to enable tenants and sharecroppers to own their land. Above all his department encouraged the activities of trade associations. Trade associations, especially in industries where there was excessive competition and wild fluctuations in demand, would enable businessmen to exchange information about their pricing policies and their inventories, standardise products, and eliminate wasteful competition. With more informed decisions, businessmen could plan sensibly without direct state intervention.

It was an impressive record. Combined with a talent for securing maximum public exposure, it made Hoover the unchallenged candidate for the Republican presidential nomination in 1928. In the election his rural, Quaker background and his intimate connection with Republican prosperity made him an unbeatable opponent for the hapless Al Smith. The Democratic candidate struggled in vain to overcome the handicaps of his Roman Catholicism, his opposition to Prohibition, and an urban power base in a party which still relied heavily on its rural, Protestant, dry southern and western base.

But there were flaws in Hoover's record. Despite his advocacy of genuine worker representation, in the end he acquiesced readily in the employee representation schemes of his business friends, schemes which were designed to inhibit the growth of genuine trades unions and give virtually unrestricted power to the employers. His grandiose plans for tenants and sharecroppers were never funded: any possible funding from the private foundations vanished in the Depression. His advocacy of trade associations did not go as far as some businessmen wanted and left many confused. Hoover refused to advocate suspending or revising the anti-trust acts. He favoured trade association activity that eliminated waste and promoted stability; he opposed activity that protected inefficiency and fostered monopoly. The dividing line was elusive. What was the difference between an open-price system – in which members of the association shared the information on which each other's pricing policies were made – and price-fixing? But elusive or not, the distinction to Hoover was crucial. Acceptable trade association activity was the epitome of the American system at its best; unacceptable activity was not simply misguided, but immoral, illegal, and un-American. His righteous conviction that such a narrow distinction was self-evidently correct, his willingness to acquiesce finally in conservative policies, his determination to rely on private initiative when it had clearly failed and the alternative was inaction, all would make his life difficult in the White House.

Even before the Great Crash, Hoover took bold steps to put his ideas on rationalisation and efficiency into effect in agriculture. Throughout the 1920s, farm belt politicians had advocated McNary-Haugen legislation to alleviate the farmers' plight, particularly that of the grain farmers. The scheme involved a two-price system. Surplus production would be dumped overseas at the world price, but at home crops would be sold at a tariff-protected price. Losses would be met by an equalisation fee levied on the farmers. Hoover as Secretary of Commerce was the legislation's most cogent and formidable critic and influenced President Calvin Coolidge to veto it. His objections were persuasive: dumping overseas would guarantee retaliation and an international trade war; higher food prices would lead to increased wage demands and inflation; the bill would not discourage overproduction; it would benefit larger producers and tend to promote oligopoly; it would politicise the economy and lead other groups to demand special treatment from the government.

Hoover's alternative policy was enacted in the Agricultural Marketing Act of 1929. It established the Federal Farm Board with a capital of $500 million to foster the formation and development of agricultural cooperatives and to establish stabilisation corporations to purchase surplus commodities. Aid to cooperatives was at the heart of the bill and exemplified Hoover's ideals. Cooperatives would lower farm costs by eliminating waste in purchasing and marketing. Existing small farm units would be maintained. Better-informed farmers would diversify their production and thus eliminate surpluses. Above all, the state would not have to intervene directly in the market. The 1929 Act was not a second-rate substitute to fob off farmers pushing for McNary-Haugenism; it was a massive effort by the government, funded on an unprecedented scale, to promote the rationalisation and prosperity of agriculture within the existing political economy.

When the general economic downturn came after the Great Crash, Hoover naturally turned to an earlier example of his own successful efforts to combat an economic downturn. In 1921 he had coordinated the Harding administration attempts to beat the recession. He had organised conferences of businessmen, local government officials, and private charity representatives to persuade them to maintain wages, to speed up public works and investment, and to coordinate local efforts at unemployment relief. Arthur Woods, who in 1930 was to oversee Hoover's relief drive, in 1921 had organised the Committee on Civic and Emergency Measures which acted as clearing house for 225 local committees. Hoover repeated this overall strategy in 1929 and 1930 in an effort to put a floor under the deflationary spiral, to stop that seemingly inexorable downward spin when businessmen cut wages and jobs in order to cut prices and remain competitive, which leads to a further fall in demand, which in turn leads to further price and wage cuts.

After conferences in Washington with leading businessmen, Hoover encouraged the formation of the National Business Survey Conference, under the auspices of the United States Chamber of Commerce. The conference monitored the efforts to maintain wage levels and to continue stock purchases. Meanwhile a conference of mayors promised to speed up public works projects already scheduled. Hoover saw the Depression as a correctable slowing down of credit and that the fundamental structure of the American economy was sound. Once business confidence was restored, once businessmen were convinced that his measures to check the deflationary spiral were working, then Hoover expected recovery would follow. This analysis prompted a succession of optimistic statements from the president, notably one in March 1930 that predicted recovery in 60 days. Not only was his a reasonable policy to try to instil confidence – Franklin Roosevelt as governor of New York was saying much the same thing in the winter of 1929–30 – but it also seemed for a long time that the economic downturn was no worse than the recession of 1920–21. In May 1930 stock market prices had only fallen to their May 1929 level. Unemployment, insofar as the figures were accurate, had not yet reached the peaks of 1921. In addition to persuading businessmen not to deflate, Hoover also sought to make credit more readily available by enlisting the assistance of bankers. He sought to ease the supply of credit and also to persuade bankers to use their own resources to safeguard threatened banks. In 1931 when Britain went off the gold standard, thus increasing the pressure on the dollar and US gold reserves, the president persuaded bankers to organise a National Credit Corporation to pool private credit resources in order to protect the nation's financial institutions.

Similarly in the provision of unemployment relief, Hoover sought to tap the spirit of voluntary cooperation in the country.

First through the President's Emergency Committee on Employment, then through the President's Organization for Unemployment Relief, the government attempted to stimulate the wealthy and private charities to contribute to relief and publicised the initiatives of local governments. Hoover himself made substantial private contributions to charity, persuaded Will Rogers, the humorist, to head a Red Cross fund-raising drive, arranged for the American Friends Service Committee to feed coal miners' children, and tried to find a small group of wealthy men to give five to ten million dollars to handle relief in Pennsylvania. This reliance on private and local community effort was the way the American people had handled crises in the past, and Hoover was confident that they would rise to the challenge again. He did not want the federal government to give direct financial aid to the unemployed. This reluctance sprang not from any callousness on his part, nor from any conservative fear that relief would sap the morale of the recipients and weaken the incentive to work. Rather, Hoover feared the effect on the morale of the wealthy and the local communities. If the federal government gave direct assistance, local communities would shirk their responsibility for the welfare of their neighbours. This presidential vision of community values has been saluted by the doyen of New Left historians, William Appleman Williams:

> Hoover told us that if we [the neighbours of the stricken] cannot be roused to provide such help, and if the way the government helps them in lieu of our direct assistance is not handled very carefully . . . there will be hell to pay . . . bureaucratic statism that would devalue the human beings it claimed to save . . . imperialism in the name of welfare . . . violence in the name of peace. We now know these were legitimate fears.

However noble Hoover's aspirations, the fact remained that his anti-Depression offensive failed. As this became apparent, the president was sometimes forced to abandon his voluntarist preferences. But at other times, Hoover clung doggedly to his anti-statist principles, often wilfully refusing to acknowledge the extent of the failure of his policies.

In agriculture, the formation of cooperatives might marginally lower farmers' costs but it did nothing in the short term to affect prices, debts, or the problem of overproduction. Mounting surpluses meant that stabilisation corporations for grain and cotton played a far larger role than Hoover had intended. For a time purchases by these corporations held farm prices up: wheat for example was held at 80¢ a bushel in the US until February 1931 while the world price fell to 50¢. But the Farm Board did not have unlimited funds. The hope was that keeping surpluses off the market would force prices up. When prices continued to fall, not only did the stabilisation corporations have to stop purchases, but they also had to unload some of their stocks, further glutting the market and depressing prices. The president's only response was to exhort farmers to reduce production. But farmers were not going to do that unless they had some guarantee that other farmers would do the same. Federal exhortation, together with the efforts of Huey Long to organise prohibition of cotton planting through the state governments for 1932, failed.

In industry, repeated assertions of confidence by the president, and the efforts of leading businessmen to maintain wage, price, and employment levels, may have worked through 1930. Large corporations like US Steel maintained wage levels, but only at the expense of laying people off. In September 1931 US Steel finally instituted a 10 per cent wage cut. Within 10 days as other industries followed suit over 1.7 million workers saw their wages slashed. Spending on public works speeded up: outlays on projects tripled in three years. But that increase in no way offset the drastic drop in private construction. Making more credit available was of limited use if businessmen refused to borrow. Efforts to stimulate voluntary agreements among financial institutions also collapsed. At the end of 1931 leading bankers failed to support the National Credit Corporation. Hoover was furious at their selfishness. His own Secretary of the Treasury, Andrew Mellon, refused the president's request to help save the Bank of Pittsburgh.

As exhortation failed, Hoover increasingly interpreted America's problems as international in origin. His voluntarist efforts to foster recovery, he believed, had been working until the economy was thrown off course by the European financial collapse of 1931. His efforts to secure recovery now focused on two tactics. Overseas, he tried to solve the problem of war debts and reparations. He negotiated a moratorium on the payment of war debts. At home, he attempted to shore up the financial institutions with the intention of making credit available and giving businessmen the confidence to use that credit. It was to be recovery from the top downwards. As his new Secretary of the Treasury, Ogden Mills, maintained, 'I want to break the ice by lending to industry so that somebody will begin to spend in a big way'. After the failure of the National Credit Corporation, and under pressure from Congress, Hoover established the Reconstruction Finance Corporation modelled on the War Finance Corporation of 1917. Capitalised at $500 million and authorised to borrow $1.5 billion, the RFC could bail out banks, railroads, insurance companies, and other large lending institutions. Shortly afterwards, the Glass-Steagall Act lowered the FRB's rediscount rates to make more reserves available to banks.

Giving business the confidence to borrow was another matter. Hoover believed that confidence depended on a sound currency, the maintenance of the gold standard, and a budget that, if not actually balanced, was not threatened by wild spending programmes. According to Hoover, nascent recovery following his remedial action of the winter of 1931–32 was thwarted by business fears of precisely such wild spending sprees launched by an irresponsible Democratic Congress and an equally irresponsible and radical presidential nominee, Franklin D. Roosevelt. Nonetheless, Hoover continued to try to get business to take advantage of the new credit opportunities. He returned to the idea of business conferences to do so. He turned to the Banking and Industry Committees of the twelve Federal Reserve districts. In August 1932 a conference of those committees set up twelve national committees to stimulate the offering of credit. The business press, by prearrangement with Hoover, gave the committees an enthusiastic response and tried to convey the impression that they were successful. The most conspicuous committee, under Walter C. Teagle of Jersey Standard, urged employers to spread work amongst the workforce to enable more men to be hired. Even if successful, share-the-work plans did not promise to increase total purchasing power. In some industries cutting hours to enable work-sharing would have driven already low wages below subsistence levels. In any case, businessmen who refused to take advantage of credit opportunities also failed to respond to the work-sharing proposal. Members of the Banking and Industry Committees themselves notably failed to set an example.

Hoover's faith in voluntarism was above all put fully to the test in the provision of unemployment relief. The local agencies in which he put his faith clearly could not cope. The demands of mass distress overwhelmed private charities. City governments were squeezed between the demands of their creditors and taxpayers and the needs of their unemployed. Hard-pressed state governments were unsympathetic to the cities' plight. Congress eventually forced Hoover to agree that the Reconstruction Finance Corporation should lend money to states in the summer of 1932 for relief, loans to be paid back out of later road-building grants. Such stringent conditions were placed on the states receiving such loans that Governor Gifford Pinchot of Pennsylvania complained that 'The result of these measures is to convince the people of Pennsylvania that the RFC intends to let us have as little relief as possible and that little after the longest possible delay'. Some $133 million of the $300 million appropriated was not used by March 1933 because of the so-called 'pauper's oath' demanded of the states. The public works spending authorised under the same act had yielded only $20 million disbursed by the end of the Hoover administration.

For all his activism, and concessions to political pressure, Hoover had firmly drawn the line against greater federal coercion: farmers would not be forced to curtail production, their prices would not be fixed; there would be no legislative setting of minimum wages and prices in industry; there would be no large-scale federal spending on public works; there would be no direct federal grants for relief. Such relief options were explicitly discussed. But Hoover equally explicitly rejected them.

Economist M. L. Wilson was busy convincing congressmen and policy-makers that agricultural overproduction could be curbed by paying farmers to curtail their acreage. Even the Federal Farm Board eventually endorsed this notion. But when the proposals surfaced in Congress Hoover firmly set his face against direct government involvement in controlling output.

The inability of business conferences and exhortation to maintain wages and employment led to suggestions that some form of legislative remedy was needed to check the deflationary spiral. The natural vehicle for such a remedy seemed to be the trade association. If, by suspending the Sherman Anti-Trust Act of 1890, businessmen could be allowed to agree on minimum prices, wages, and production, the economy could be stabilised. The main advocates of such proposals came from industries that had not done particularly well in the 1920s, like textiles and coal, or from natural resource industries like lumber and oil. All these industries suffered from a large number of small operators who produced more and cut wages and prices in an effort to maintain a competitive edge. To combat this destructive competition, the Cotton Textile Institute launched a sign-up campaign to persuade mills to limit their shifts to 55 and 50 hours a week. But the most dramatic proposal for suspension of the Sherman Anti-Trust Act came in September 1931 from Gerard Swope of General Electric. He proposed that, in return for suspension of the Sherman Act, trade associations should be able to cooperate on price and production plans on condition that they maintained labour standards by providing agreed workmen's compensation, employee pensions, and unemployment insurance. Trade associations would be able to compel members of the industry to participate.

Industries suffering from destructive competition had an obvious interest in confining their competitors to agreed labour and production standards. But a leading producer of consumer durables like General Electric also had a vested interest in price and cost stability; the level of investment required for electrical manufacturing made long-term planning essential. In addition General Electric's own programmes of welfare capitalism were collapsing under the weight of the Depression. They could be sustained only if all their competitors were forced to meet similar welfare costs. Finally, Swope may have been anxious to pre-empt radical proposals for government schemes of social insurance. Hoover's reaction to Swope's scheme was damning: the plan was 'an attempt to smuggle fascism into America through the backdoor'. Hoover's Department of Justice in fact stood firm against any efforts to spare trade associations from anti-trust prosecution. Hoover was prepared to approve voluntary efforts to curtail production like those of the Cotton Textile Institute; he was prepared to allow considerable leeway to attempts to eliminate wasteful competition in a natural resource industry like oil; but in general he appeared sensitive to charges that his earlier sponsorship of trade associations had been designed to foster and benefit trusts. Thus, businessmen seeking some help from Hoover in planning for their own industries were thwarted.

The most important alternative proposals for injecting purchasing power into the economy came from Senators Robert La Follette Jr of Wisconsin and Robert Wagner of New York, who championed the cause of large-scale spending on public works and direct federal grants for unemployment relief.

Wagner, from New York City, epitomised that strand of progressivism identified by his biographer Joseph Huthmacher as urban liberalism. Politicians in the northern cities representing lower-income, new-stock voters had been more ready than other progressives between 1900 and 1920 to advocate the use of government power to meet the welfare and economic needs of their constituents. Whereas older machine politicians relied on informal means to protect their voters, the newer breed of machine Democrat like Robert Wagner and Al Smith were prepared to use government to regulate wages, working conditions, and housing. While Al Smith became increasingly conservative on economic matters, Wagner took from Tammany Hall to Washington a conviction that only the federal government could protect workers from economic insecurity.

Before the Depression Wagner had been working on a package of measures designed to make the economy operate more smoothly. A federal public works board would have $150 million at its disposal to prime the pump of the economy whenever it threatened to slow down. To ensure that unemployed workers were most efficiently matched to available jobs, the government would fund an adequate system of state employment services. In order more accurately to assess the need to reflate the economy, the government would for the first time collect unemployment statistics. All these measures passed Congress, though Hoover vetoed the employment exchange bill as a coercive infringement of states' rights. The extent of the Depression soon convinced Wagner of the need for more substantial remedies. While Hoover sought recovery through the protection of the financial structure and the provision of credit, Wagner favoured a massive injection of purchasing power at the bottom of the economy through $2 billion of public works spending, federal spending on unemployment relief, and unemployment insurance.

Robert La Follette Jr also rapidly became convinced of the need for federal spending on relief and public works. His father's progressivism, as well as political exigencies in Wisconsin, gave the younger La Follette an awareness of both the need for farm relief and the urban dimensions of economic distress. Traditional progressive commitments to the public development of electric power, fairer taxation, the regulation of monopolies, and the defence of organised labour were joined during the Depression to a relentless determination to discover the real extent of unemployment and to canvass wide-ranging remedies. His committee hearings on unemployment highlighted his own scheme for planning by a National Economic Council and drew a vivid picture of the collapse of local relief efforts. La Follette fought the complacency of administration spokesmen. While officials of the President's Organization for Unemployment Relief boasted that private fundraising was exceeding its targets, La Follette was gathering facts from the nation's mayors to show just how inadequate those private and local relief resources were. As William Hodson, relief director in New York City, facing a monthly wage loss of $80–90 million, explained, he was able to supervise the distribution of only $4 million a month in relief. The Russell Sage Foundation showed that public money made up 70 per cent of relief money, and the city mayors mostly testified that they simply could not provide enough public money. The only solution according to La Follette was direct federal relief grants to the states. La Follette also favoured $5 billion in federal grants for public works. Advocacy of such proposals by two of the most hard-working and intelligent senators did not convince Hoover. He detested congressional progressives and stuck firmly to his belief that there should be no federal bureaucratic intervention in unemployment relief and that the only spending on public works should be on self-liquidating (self-financing) projects.

Hoover had convinced himself of the rightness of his stand against increased statist power in the economy. His was the only American way to recovery. This certainty convinced him that other politicians who disagreed were irresponsible and selfish opportunists. He had little but contempt even for his own party leaders. So awkwardly did he handle the Republican Congress of 1929–30 that even a sympathetic journalist described him as 'the most left-handed President politically the world ever saw'. Hoover was determined not to call a special session of Congress in 1931: he was determined to tackle the Depression without congressional advice. He viewed the return of Congress in November 1931 with alarm: action by Congress could only harm business confidence. When politicians did cooperate with him, as the Democratic leadership did from December 1931 to March 1932, Hoover could not resist seeking the monopoly of political credit. Equally, he engaged in a petty 'credit' war with Wagner over employment legislation.

The combination of high-mindedness and pettiness made the president an all too inviting target for political critics in both parties. It was also easy to portray Hoover not as a tireless progressive, but as an insensitive reactionary. He might despise Old Guard Republicans and deplore the selfishness of business-men and bankers, but the overwhelming imperative of keeping business confidence and his ready acquiescence in conservative public positions tended to confirm the public image of the die-hard conservative.

No issue more dramatically highlighted that image than the president's handling of the Bonus Army. World War I veterans had been rewarded in 1924 for their sacrifices with a bonus, in effect an insurance policy which could be cashed in in 1945. With the coming of the Depression unemployed veterans on the West Coast, especially transients who were hoboes, searching for work and ineligible to receive most local relief, agitated for immediate payment of the bonus. Their demand was echoed by politicians like Wright Patman of Texas who were anxious to secure almost any measure of currency inflation. In 1932 some 25,000 veterans marched to Washington. They quickly disowned Communist lead-ership and, apart from one incident of Communist-inspired break-away violence, they assembled and lobbied peacefully. The Washington Superintendent of Police, Pelham Glassford, arranged for them to set up an orderly and properly maintained camp on the Anacostia Flats across from Congress. Hoover in fact quietly worked behind the scenes to help Glassford and ordered the impatient and ambitious General Douglas MacArthur to take action only on orders from Glassford. MacArthur was specifically ordered to use force to evict veterans only from government buildings. Hoover twice ordered the general not to enter the camps on Anacostia Flats. Yet when MacArthur sent tanks and men with bayonets drawn to rout the veterans and burn their camp, Hoover did nothing to stop or disown him. Aware of the peaceful nature of the veterans' demonstrations, he nevertheless capitulated to a conservative and hysterical reaction to the alleged danger of violent revolution. The sight of troops so thoroughly routing helpless, unemployed veterans, women, and children froze Hoover's uncaring image in ice.

8 The political alternative

The president's stubborn performance nevertheless looks a little more impressive when compared with the record of his political opponents. Many of Hoover's critics, despite their vitriolic denunciations of him, advocated fundamentally conservative policies. Their support of alternative policies was often inconsistent and uncomprehending. There was also little evidence of a clear political mandate for a more radical approach.

The opposition Democrats who controlled Congress after 1930 were led by conservatives who vied with the president in their commitment to fiscal orthodoxy and a balanced budget. Party leaders – former presidential candidates James Cox, John W. Davis, and Al Smith, Senate Majority Leader Joseph Robinson, House Speaker John Nance Garner, and Jouett Shouse and John J. Raskob from the National Committee – publicly pledged their cooperation with the president in his efforts to fight the Depression. Until well into 1932 Congress followed their lead. They were profoundly influenced by the ideas of renowned financier Bernard Baruch, who had financially backed the Senate campaigns of 14 Democrats in 1930. Baruch believed that retrenchment and a balanced budget were the only ways to restore business confidence. 'No government agency', he proclaimed, 'can cure this situation!' 'The country is in a highly excited condition. What it needs is rest not any more changes.' Joseph Robinson loyally echoed these sentiments. 'I grow more and more impressed with the necessity of conservative action.' Influential northern Democrats with close ties to business and the financial community looked round for a suitable candidate to carry the party's banner in 1932 and to head off the appeal of the unreliable Franklin D. Roosevelt. These conservatives favoured a policy that stressed repeal of Prohibition and offered little to cure the Depression except retrenchment and the maintenance of the gold standard. Their candidate was Al Smith, who for all his progressive legisla-

tion as governor of New York earlier, in 1932 denounced demagogic appeals to class consciousness and championed repeal of
Prohibition. If Smith could block Franklin D. Roosevelt, conservatives believed they could actually nominate a leading industrial statesman like Owen D. Young, an old-style progressive like
Newton D. Baker, or a colourless governor like Albert Ritchie of
Maryland, who was only famous for balancing his state budget and
supporting repeal. Candidates like these offered no significant
remedy for the Depression, no alternative expansion of government responsibility for the economy.

The support of alternative taxation and spending policies in
Congress fell to an unstable coalition of western Republicans,
western and southern agrarian Democrats, and some northern
urban Democrats. What linked these disparate groups was a
suspicion of recovery policies that were geared to the needs of big
business and some perception that purchasing power needed to be
given to workers and farmers. As Tom Walsh of Montana said,
'The first reason for the business depression was the inability of the
consuming masses to buy'. This coalition could on occasion be
mobilised to surprise conservative congressional leaders. When
conservative Democrats sought to balance the budget by a sales
tax in 1932, maverick Republican Fiorello La Guardia from New
York City and staunch North Carolina Democrat Robert L.
Doughton organised a successful revolt. Instead Congress went on
to pass a Revenue Act which raised surtaxes, corporate income
taxes, and estate taxes to World War I levels.

But this coalition was difficult to mobilise in support of a
positive recovery programme. The western progressive Republicans were extraordinarily difficult to organise. As newspaper
columnists Drew Pearson and Robert S. Allen lamented, 'Indi-
vidually they are the most righteous and forward-looking men in
the capital. . . . Collectively they have been without plan or
purpose, unorganised and ineffectual.' They were united on the
need for farm relief, but even here were not agreed on specific
remedies, beyond a general feeling in favour of currency inflation
to raise farm prices and ease the burden of debt. Nor did suspicion
of monopolies and hostility to a high tariff constitute an industrial
recovery programme. Running through all their ideas was a
reluctance to see federal bureaucracy expand. Even George Norris
was uneasy about the Reconstruction Finance Corporation, which

put the government into business, far beyond 'the wildest flights of my imagination'. Suspicion of federal intervention and a commitment to a balanced budget were bound severely to limit their conception of what the government could do to inject purchasing power into the economy.

Similarly the small-town rural-oriented businessmen and lawyers who made up the southern and western Democrats offered little positively to the debate over recovery. Support for a low tariff, calls for farm relief, and populist denunciations of the malign influence of big business and eastern bankers accompanied a faith in the existing local political and social structure. In 1932 congressional progressives could not even unite on public works and relief legislation. Supporters of the La Follette–Costigan bill for direct federal relief grants helped defeat the Wagner–Walsh–Black–Bulkley bill for loans and work relief, whose supporters in turn voted to defeat the La Follette proposal. Only in the summer of 1932, under the pressure of the impending election, was there any consensus that some form of relief and public works spending was essential. By that time, supporters of government spending had to compromise with the president to secure the Emergency Relief and Construction Act, which provided for the RFC loans to the states.

Lack of imagination in Washington was matched by mediocrity at the state level. State governments, as James T. Patterson has shown, responded to the Depression first with complacency, then bewilderment, but above all with conventional policies of retrenchment, balanced budgets, and regressive taxation, notably sales taxes. Such policies gave little scope for providing relief for the unemployed and did little to sustain mass purchasing power.

Some of the most effective grass-roots political pressure during the Depression came from organisations of taxpayers anxious to cut government spending in order to relieve their own tax burdens. Farm organisations in Kansas, the Chamber of Commerce and the National Economy League in Boston, the Farmers and Taxpayers League in South Carolina, and farmwomen storming county courthouses in Colorado sought to ease the weight of property taxes. They put far greater pressure on politicians than did unemployed groups who demanded greater local spending for relief. The budget director in Oregon described the consequences of such pressure when he called the 1933 legislature 'the worst' in the state's history, consisting of 'a lot of wild jackasses who believed they heard the call of the people and were willing to destroy anything and everything so long as they could make a show of saving a nickel'.

When voters did express their dissatisfaction with the existing conservative political establishments, they often elected colourful and demagogic politicians who, for all their rhetorical denunciations of the corporations, Wall Street, and the 'fat cats', offered conservative remedies to economic ills. William 'Alfalfa Bill' Murray in Oklahoma was prepared to use the National Guard to curb the overproduction of oil, but was hostile to the very idea of unemployment relief. Mayor James Curley in Boston toyed with expensive public works programmes, but feared the dole and unemployment insurance. Robert R. Reynolds in North Carolina won election to the Senate preaching a doctrine allegedly 'so strange and radical that it had never been heard before by this generation in North Carolina', but his programme simply called for the repeal of Prohibition, the insurance of bank deposits, and the payment of the veterans' bonus. He did not want to increase government spending for unemployment relief or industrial and agricultural recovery. Eugene Talmadge in Georgia rejoiced in the title of 'The Wild Man from Sugar Creek' and vowed 'Sure I'm wild and I'm going to stay wild' but his red-gallused appeal to the small farmers was for rigid economy; he was against high taxes and high government spending. Often local elections did not focus on the major question of how to tackle the Depression. In Idaho for example the main issue in the gubernatorial election in 1930 was the use of a state car for campaign purposes. Prohibition in many areas remained the salient issue. As late as 1933 high-school students in the most devastated state in the nation, Mississippi, could list pressing national issues in order of importance as strong drink, illicit sex, idleness, gambling, narcotics, pornography, and, last of all, poverty.

9 The Roosevelt challenge

Hoover's political contemporaries in both Washington and around the country offered little in the way of a radical coherent alternative to the president's policies. But Hoover was convinced that his presidential opponent in 1932, Franklin D. Roosevelt, was a stalking horse for revolutionary and un-American change. Roosevelt threatened, so one of the president's political allies warned him, 'a radical form of socialism'. In fact, despite Roosevelt's promise of a New Deal and 'bold, persistent, experimentation', the election of a man dismissed by Walter Lippmann, the noted columnist, as an 'amiable boy scout' did not suggest a mandate for radical change.

Since 1910 recent immigrants and lower-income voters in the northern cities had increasingly supported the Democratic Party. This shift, given added impetus by the prominence of Al Smith in the 1920s, offered the party the chance of national electoral success if this new-found support could be wedded to the party's solid base in the South and its support in the West. The national successes of the Wilson years, however, had not been repeated in the 1920s. The ethnocultural issues which were so salient in that decade – the Klan, Prohibition, immigration, and Roman Catholicism – were precisely the issues which split the Democratic Party between the urban, Catholic, wet East and the rural, Protestant, dry West and South. The bitterness of the split was exemplified by the deadlocked nominating convention of 1924, divided between Al Smith and William Gibbs McAdoo, and the desertion of five southern states from the Democratic column in 1928 when Al Smith was finally nominated.

Few candidates appeared better equipped to unite the rural and urban wings of the party than Franklin D. Roosevelt. He had nominated Al Smith in the famous 'Happy Warrior' speech of 1924 and had bowed to Smith's pleas to run for governor of New York in 1928. He was elected and two years later he was re-elected by a record 700,000-vote margin. But if he was a formidable figure in the urban East, he was also an attractive figure to the rest of the country. He was no product of the city machines, but rather a patrician politician from upstate New York, first elected to the state legislature from his rural home county. His consistent interest in conservation, his awareness of farm issues, and his advocacy of the development of public power all won him admirers among western Democrats. As Assistant Secretary of the Navy in the Wilson administration under the tolerant tutelage of Josephus Daniels he had learnt to cultivate southern congressional leaders. These cordial ties were strengthened during his long spells of convalescence at Warm Springs, Georgia, after his crippling polio attack of 1921. These links with the South and West survived Roosevelt's identification with the divisive Smith candidacies of 1924 and 1928.

After both elections Roosevelt deliberately set out to establish or maintain contacts with party leaders across the country. His recurring theme was that the Democrats could only succeed if they were perceived as a 'progressive' rather than a business-oriented party. Roosevelt had no sympathy with the conservative campaign of John W. Davis in 1924. In 1928 he was appalled when, under John Raskob's influence, Smith virtually ignored the South and West and concentrated on winning over the business conservatives of the North-East. Roosevelt despaired of Smith's gratuitous emphasis on repeal of Prohibition and his casual attitude to southern and western loyalists. When Roosevelt cautiously endorsed repeal in 1930 southern and western politicians were prepared to tolerate his stand: they accepted that 'Bread, not booze' mattered. What they were not prepared to accept was the determination of Smith, Raskob, and others that repeal should be the most important and visible issue stressed by the party.

As the front-runner for the Democratic nomination, Roosevelt was soon picking up endorsements from state organisations in the South and West. But he was unable to translate these into the two-thirds vote needed to clinch the party nomination. The two great obstacles were Al Smith and California. Latent suspicions between Roosevelt and Smith had come into the open during Roosevelt's governorship when he snubbed some of Smith's protégés. Conservative Democrats believed that a resentful Smith could pick up enough delegates from urban, industrial states to deny Roosevelt the nomination and pave the way for an acceptable compromise candidate like Newton D. Baker. City machine politicians had little love for Roosevelt but immense loyalty to Smith. Their support for Smith could only be strengthened by the futile and inept attempt by the Roosevelt forces to defeat Smith in the Massachusetts primary. As New York governor, Roosevelt could not even count on the support of New York City Democrats who feared that he would hound Mayor Jimmy Walker and his corrupt Tammany associates. Ironically liberals were scathing about the governor's delay in prosecuting Walker.

In California, William Gibbs McAdoo had little confidence that

Roosevelt would be sufficiently anti-business. He favoured the candidacy of a more populist-sounding candidate like the narrow, shrewd John Nance Garner. Isolationist newspaper magnate William Randolph Hearst was deeply suspicious of Roosevelt's internationalism. Roosevelt, who had campaigned for the vice-presidency in 1920 on a ticket loyal to both the League of Nations and Woodrow Wilson, distanced himself from the League in early 1932 to the chagrin of old Wilson loyalists. But his concession failed to satisfy Hearst, who continued to support Garner. The Speaker thus controlled two powerful states in the convention: Texas and California.

These obstacles almost proved fatal to the Roosevelt candidacy. The first three ballots at the Chicago convention saw his campaign manager, Jim Farley, eke out a few more votes each time, but none of the delegations with favourite sons came forward to put Roosevelt over the two-thirds figure. It appeared when the convention adjourned that Roosevelt would be beaten. Instead, Garner released his delegates and McAdoo announced decisively that California's votes would go to Roosevelt. It is still not clear what swung the result Roosevelt's way: Hearst disliked the prospect of the staunch internationalist Newton Baker as an eventual candidate and hated Smith. McAdoo hated Smith as well and disliked the likely conservative outcome of a successful 'stop Roosevelt' drive. Garner had no wish to see a deadlocked convention throw the election to the Republicans again. All three had only gradually realised that Smith intended to stay in the race to the bitter end.

What is clear is that Roosevelt almost lost the nomination: and that if he had been beaten, the successful nominee would have come from the right, rather than the left, of the party. Candidates like Smith, Baker, Garner, Governor Ritchie, and Melvin Traylor of Illinois (a banker who could not even attend the convention because of a run on his bank) would have advocated none of the expansion of federal government power in the economy that characterised the New Deal. Historian Elliot A. Rosen is surely correct in concluding that 'the principal alternative . . . came not from the minuscule and impotent Left but from a potent and powerful Right'.

Neither Roosevelt's career nor his campaign in 1932 seemed to offer much promise of radical change. Before 1929 his progressivism seemed essentially an amalgam of charitable instincts, respect for efficiency, and distaste for corruption. His concerns for conservation and the public development of electric power, the touchstones of progressivism in the 1920s, put him more firmly in the liberal camp. So did his awareness of the need for farm relief. As early as 1929 he contended that 'if farmers starve today, we will all starve tomorrow'. Little in his speeches or in his speculative business ventures in the 1920s suggested any prescience about the structural flaws of the economy. As governor his response to the Depression was innovative only in comparison to the arch-caution of his fellow governors. He was reluctant to drain the Treasury to spend on public works and he seemed anxious to keep unemployment relief a state responsibility. His only distinctive commitments on welfare were to support his Commissioner of Labor, Frances Perkins, in her efforts to expose the flimsiness of the Hoover statistics on unemployment levels, to launch an investigation of the possibilities of unemployment insurance, and to squeeze $20 million from the state legislature to fund a Temporary Emergency Relief Administration headed by Harry Hopkins.

But when Roosevelt assembled a group of academics from Columbia University to advise him on national policy in March 1932 he was given both a coherent analysis of the Depression and a recovery programme that profoundly differed from Hoover's.

What Raymond Moley, Rexford Tugwell, and Adolf Berle Jr of the Brains Trust had in common was a dissatisfaction with existing academic orthodoxy. Moley was perhaps the most conventional. As a young student he had been a disciple of the municipal progressivism of Tom L. Johnson of Cleveland, who struggled against the privileges of monopoly to introduce a cheaper street railway fare. Later political scientist Moley became director of the Cleveland Foundation, a business-sponsored attempt to find local solutions to city problems by utilising the latest academic research. Moley's Cleveland Crime Survey led to his appointment at Columbia University to direct similar studies of the administration of justice in other cities. As research director of the New York Crime Commission he met Roosevelt's devoted assistant, Louis Howe.

Tugwell had grown up in upstate New York the son of an orchard farmer. His earliest work as an economist had been on milk distribution and the need to regulate prices in the public interest. He had been at Columbia since 1920. He regarded himself as an 'experimental economist' who sought to study the discipline 'not from dogmatic principles, but towards favorable results'. *Laissez-faire* was an outdated prescription for the problems caused by imbalances between technological change, productive capacity, and consumer income. Both the United States experience in World War I and the Soviet experiment in the 1920s showed the possibilities of intelligent government planning of the nation's economic resources which would eventually eliminate private profit-making as the dominant economic principle.

Berle was a prodigy who graduated from Harvard at the age of 18. Steeped in the Social Gospel as the son of a Congregationalist minister, he had been imbued at Harvard Law School with the principles of the new jurisprudence that the law could not be separated from economics and could be a vehicle for social engineering. In 1927 he had gone to Columbia Law School to bring their courses on corporate law up to date to reflect the problems caused by existing corporate practice. Using a grant from the Social Science Research Council he worked with economist Gardiner C. Means to publish in 1932 *The Modern Corporation and Private Property*. This study showed how much economic power was concentrated in the hands of a small number of corporations, controlled not by the mass of shareholders but by a few corporate managers. The problem government had to address was how to exercise effective control of this concentration of power, and to hold these managers accountable.

The Brains Trust had its moment of glory in 1932–33 as it laid out many of the ideas and debated the issues that would shape the New Deal. Once the New Deal was launched, its members played a rather peripheral role. Moley was a ubiquitous figure in the interregnum, the banking crisis, and the First Hundred Days. But he was in an anomalous position as Assistant Secretary of State in Cordell Hull's State Department and his prestige slumped after the failure of the London Economic Conference. He left government and went into magazine publishing but remained in close contact with Roosevelt, particularly as a speech writer, until 1936. But he believed that the New Deal had substituted radical class politics for the policies of business–government cooperation and he became increasingly identified with the conservative wing of the Republican Party. Tugwell remained a close friend of Roosevelt's but his prominence always attracted accusations of Soviet or

Utopian influence. As Undersecretary of Agriculture he was unhappy when Henry Wallace sacrificed young radicals in 1935 to satisfy the demands of southern politicians and large cotton planters. He had a more congenial time in 1935 and 1936 as head of the newly-formed Resettlement Administration, which supervised the resettlement of farm families and the creation of Greenbelt New Towns. He resigned in order to protect the resettlement programme from the criticism his controversial presence inevitably attracted. Later he was appointed governor of Puerto Rico. After Roosevelt's death, Tugwell wrote extensively on the New Deal, accounts which reveal deep sympathy and affection for Roosevelt and a lament for the missed opportunities for imposing greater planning and collectivist organisation on the economy. Berle viewed the domestic New Deal with rather Olympian detachment from the State Department. By the 1950s he had become an apologist for the large corporations he had dissected in the 1930s, arguing they had finally acquired the social responsibility which he had called for then to accompany their economic expertise and efficiency.

What Moley, Berle, and Tugwell argued in 1932 was that the Depression was national, not international, in origin. The basic structure of the domestic economy was not, as Hoover argued, sound. The essential balance of the economy had broken down. The economy was an organic interdependent whole. When parts of it malfunctioned, ultimately the whole economy suffered. What had gone wrong in the American economy, they argued, was not simply a correctable slowing down of credit that could be cured by rescuing financial institutions as Hoover believed. They identified a fundamental maldistribution of income that brought on a crucial loss of consumer purchasing power. The lack of income in the farm sector, the rigidity of industry's prices, and the failure of workers' wages to rise fast enough meant that Americans could not consume what the economy had the capacity to produce.

Conventional remedies would solve little according to the Brains Trust. An international settlement of the debts and reparations question would do nothing to correct the structural flaws at home. The restoration of business confidence was an illusory goal since there was, in the absence of real change, little reason for businessmen to have confidence. If businessmen did not have confidence in the Hoover government, then it was difficult to see that more conservative policies could possibly attract business trust. Nor would old-fashioned trust-busting or the denunciation of alleged banking and stock exchange wrongdoers bring recovery. The banking system and the securities system needed regulation to control them, not moral indignation. Large-scale concentrations of economic power were unavoidable in the modern economic state. What was needed was not to break up the modern corporation but to make it more accountable, to ensure that business made the right investment, pricing, and wage decisions to create the necessary purchasing power so that America's capacity to consume could match its capacity to produce.

The Brains Trust was not clear how this could be achieved. Moley and Berle wanted government to allow businessmen to cooperate to regulate themselves, Tugwell hankered after a greater degree of discipline imposed by government through some sort of planning council. Idle corporate surpluses could be put to use more productively through an undistributed profits tax. From the bottom the necessary purchasing power would be created through the restoration of farm purchasing power – the domestic allotment plan advocated by M. L. Wilson appealed to them as the means to achieve this – and through spending on unemployment relief and ultimately schemes of social insurance. Equally important, the burden of debt had to be lifted. Here their concern was not with banks and other institutions that provided the credit but rather with their debtors. The crippling burden of debt on the railroads, on the urban home mortgage market, and on farm mortgages had to be lifted in order to unfreeze these vast assets. The federal government would have to intervene to refinance these debts at lower, more realistic interest rates.

Roosevelt allowed only isolated snatches of the Brains Trust's vision to be shown to the electorate. He did emphasise that the problem was one of underconsumption and that domestic change in the economy had to occur; he hinted at some form of planning to achieve a concert of interests in the economy; his farm speech calling for a voluntary, decentralised, self-financing farm programme was probably a coded endorsement of the domestic allotment plan; his speech in San Francisco was seen as an endorsement of business plans to seek anti-trust revision. But for the most part Roosevelt's speeches were designed to satisfy, or at least not completely alienate, as many people as possible, in particular nervous conservatives in his own party. His farm speech at Topeka did not fully convince any farm leaders, but neither did it offend any of them, and following their own conversations with Roosevelt, they could interpret the speech as an endorsement of their own pet farm plan. His tariff speech at Sioux City was a famous attempt to 'weave together' two contradicting drafts. Attacked by Hoover for allegedly dangerous views that threatened a sound currency and fiscal responsibility, Roosevelt made some of his most definite campaign statements in favour of clearly conservative policies. He attacked Hoover's reckless extravagance and promised to cut government expenses by 25 per cent. This seemed completely at odds with the Brains Trust's ideas for spending on unemployment relief and sustaining demand, but Roosevelt's promise did not simply reflect an opportunist move to placate the fiscal conservatives in his own party. His promise did reflect the commitment even in the Brains Trust to the desirability of a balanced budget.

Roosevelt believed that he was keeping his options open; Tugwell believed that he was making commitments to assuage politicians who would foreclose his options to experiment later. But Roosevelt's campaign was designed to reassure an electorate whose resentment against Hoover was strong, but whose commitment to traditional values had by no means collapsed. Once elected Roosevelt still played his cards close to his chest. He refused to be trapped by Hoover into any cooperation over international economic negotiations or the banking crisis that might have committed him to an internationalist and sound money programme. He gave little hint during the interregnum of what his plans for the New Deal actually were.

2
Holidays, Eagles, and Deficits: Finance and Industry

The success of New Deal efforts to secure industrial recovery was strictly limited. Between 1933 and 1937 the American economy grew at an annual rate of 10 per cent, but output had fallen so low after 1929 that even this growth left 14 per cent of the workforce unemployed. A recession in 1937 quickly shot the unemployment rate back up to 19 per cent. Well into 1941 unemployment remained at over 10 per cent.

There was an underlying goal to New Deal efforts to restore the economy. Recovery measures were meant to restore mass purchasing power. To achieve this, structural changes would be needed in the economy. However, the details of implementing such a policy were anything but coherent. The National Recovery Administration gave businessmen and the government almost wartime powers over production, wages, and prices and exempted business from anti-trust prosecution. Once the Supreme Court ruled the Industrial Recovery Act unconstitutional in 1935, the administration tried to perpetuate the principles of the NRA in certain industries. Yet at the same time the anti-trust division of the Justice Department flexed its muscles and New Deal spokesmen increasingly dwelt on the evils of monopoly. In 1933 a massive public works programme had been launched through the Public Works Administration to prime the pump of recovery. $3.3 billion on the PWA was accompanied by unprecedented relief expenditures. Yet Roosevelt constantly tried to reduce the budget deficit and almost succeeded in eliminating it in fiscal 1938. The ensuing recession forced the president to resume large-scale spending. But neither he nor Congress was happy with deficits. By 1940 the New Deal seemed resigned to the idea that the economy had reached maturity and that unemployment could not be eliminated. New Dealers did not appear to have found a mechanism that could engineer a major expansion of the economy.

For radical critics the failure to solve the problems of industry was a sad story of what might have been. The New Deal had missed a glorious opportunity to take control of the nation's financial institutions. With the nation's banking system in complete disarray in March 1933, Roosevelt failed to nationalise the banks and instead patched up and underwrote the existing system. When the economic conditions cried out for central economic planning, corporate liberals made the NRA into an agency that sanctioned cartels. At a time when wealth and power were discredited as never before in America, the New Deal failed to break up the concentrations of wealth and power either by taxation or by anti-trust prosecution. Lastly the radical critics claimed that the Roosevelt administration did not spend enough money fast enough to produce full employment.

The explanation of New Deal limitations lies less in a failure of radical will, and more in the dictates of the economic emergency which demanded speed of action and its vital corollary: the consent of the participants. The constraints of the emergency were compounded by both ignorance of some policy alternatives, like fully-fledged deficit spending, and the incapacity of the existing state apparatus to implement others, like central planning of the economy. Political realities sharply limited the room of New Deal policy-makers to manoeuvre.

As a result, it was World War II, not the New Deal, that was to shape the political economy of industrial and financial America. On the one hand massive government spending during the war stimulated unprecedented economic growth; on the other, the war confirmed and strengthened the position of large corporations in the US economy.

1 Closing the banks and reopening them

At 2.30 a.m. on the morning of Roosevelt's inauguration, 4 March 1933, Governor Herbert Lehman closed down the banks in New York; an hour later Governor Horner closed the banks in Illinois. The financial and credit system of the United States had come to a halt. Even before the two great financial centres of the nation had closed, 5,504 banks with assets of $3.432 billion had been shut down.

In 1930 and 1931 the Depression had ravaged a banking system that already had serious internal weaknesses. The presence of too many rural, small, undercapitalised banks, the absence of branch banking, criminal practices by some bankers, and a willingness to make too many speculative loans combined to make banks vulnerable. But in the winter of 1932–33 the cumulative effects of the Depression which froze so many of the banks' assets put strains on the strongest banks. As Roosevelt said, 'my thought is that on present values very few financial institutions anywhere in the country are actually able to pay off their deposits in full, and the knowledge of this fact is widely held'. The economic downturn eroded the savings of millions of depositors. As particular banks in individual states ran into difficulties, so frightened depositors, anxious to protect whatever savings they had left, moved to withdraw their holdings from other banks as well. In the winter of 1932–33 successive state governors had to call a halt to banking operations in their own states to prevent the complete collapse of every bank.

The first state banking holiday occurred in Nevada, where 80 per cent of the banking resources were owned by one man. His banks had made loans to ranchers on sheep at $8 a head. When the banks foreclosed on the 150 ranches that grazed 70 per cent of the cattle and sheep in Nevada, they received back on the drought-ridden animals 25¢ a head. At the end of October 1932 the governor called a temporary bank holiday in order to reorganise the state's banks. They were still closed in March 1933. In December the Reconstruction Finance Corporation stepped in to save banks in Wisconsin, Pennsylvania, Minnesota, and Tennessee. In January the RFC averted panic in a number of cities, but bankers were increasingly cautious about mobilising and risking reserves quickly to help threatened banks. At the beginning of February Huey Long saved a leading bank in New Orleans by proclaiming a state holiday, a day after the anniversary of Wilson's declaration of war on Germany, so that Long could mount a rescue operation for the bank.

In Michigan the crisis could not be averted by gubernatorial legerdemain. While livestock were the problem in Nevada, in

Michigan it was cars. The Union Guardian Trust Company, the automobile bank, was still paying out dividends, lending money to its officers for speculation on inadequate collateral, and making loans on the strength of bank stocks which were falling in value. However, 84 per cent of its assets were in fact frozen, many of them in loans to car workers who had defaulted on their mortgages, but whose houses could not be sold. At the same time, the First National Bank of Detroit, which was also still paying out dividends, thoroughly re-examined its loans. RFC aid for Union Guardian was conditional on Henry Ford agreeing not to withdraw his deposits. Not only did Ford refuse to agree, he threatened to pull out deposits from the ailing First National if Union Guardian was allowed to collapse. Faced with imminent failure of the state's two leading banks, a reluctant governor had little option but to call a banking holiday to try to reconstitute a bank from the Detroit wreckage. 550 banks and $1.5 billion held for 900,000 depositors were tied up. By 4 March the Detroit banks had still not been reorganised.

Governors in Indiana, Arkansas, and Oklahoma closed their banks to forestall withdrawals in the aftermath of the Michigan collapse. Meanwhile an investigation headed by Ferdinand Pecora for the Senate Banking and Currency Committee produced nine days of hearings which ruthlessly exposed the malpractices of leading American bankers. The cross-examination of Charles Mitchell of National City Bank revealed a web of loans to bank officers which had been written off, huge bonuses to senior staff, loans to insiders, and high-pressure sales techniques to sell securities to unsuspecting investors. As confidence in the banks plummeted, so European governments also sought to remove funds in the final week before Roosevelt's inauguration. Three-quarters of a billion dollars was withdrawn from New York banks and the Federal Reserve itself began to run out of money.

Hoover tried to secure Roosevelt's cooperation in stemming the drain of confidence and funds. On the one hand, Hoover wanted his successor to support his use of the wartime Trading with the Enemy Act to move against currency hoarding and, if necessary, to call a national bank holiday. On the other, he wanted Roosevelt to promote confidence by proclaiming his determination to balance the budget, safeguard credit, and avoid currency inflation. Roosevelt refused. He believed Hoover had all the authority he needed to act. He did not wish to dissipate his prestige in a futile attempt to shore up the existing banking structure and he did not want to close off his policy options.

As soon as Roosevelt took office he moved decisively to use the Trading with the Enemy Act to proclaim a national bank holiday from Monday 6 March to Thursday 9 March and asked Congress to assemble in special session on 9 March to pass legislation to enable the banks to reopen. A rescue package for the banks had to be put together very quickly and Roosevelt had few options. For all his denunciations of money changers and his indignation at the reckless practices of bankers, he knew that the hopes of millions of depositors and the starting up again of the economy depended on the return of confidence and the speedy reopening of the banks. Otherwise business would come to a standstill. The basic structure of the banking system therefore had to remain the same. Nationalisation of the banks was simply not a viable alternative. Nor was it seriously advocated. Progressives and historians later lamented this missed opportunity for radical action. But at the time Senator Robert La Follette and Senator Edward Costigan, far from advocating nationalisation as Arthur Schlesinger Jr had suggested, simply called for greater government control of the banks under licence from the Secretary of the Treasury. Rex Tugwell argued that the president could have used the nation's post offices as the new banking system, but this was an option that could have been implemented in weeks and months not days.

It was natural that Roosevelt should turn to conservative advisers to supervise the reopening of the banks, since the president wanted the return of conservative sound banking that would inspire confidence. Treasury Secretary William Woodin turned to Hoover's advisers for detailed and technical assistance. They knew what to do while the bankers themselves were, in Woodin's words, 'much at sea as to what to do'. Under the proposed legislation, the Treasury Secretary would decide which banks could safely reopen, conservators would have the authority to reorganise the remaining banks and to decide when, if at all, they could reopen. To ensure that there was enough currency to meet demand, the government decided not to issue scrip but to allow the Federal Reserve Board to print money against the assets of sound banks. The Reconstruction Finance Corporation would be able to buy preferred stock of both state and Federal Reserve member banks to give them sufficient capital. Congress passed this legislation in under eight hours on 9 March and the bank holiday was extended to the weekend to allow Treasury officials time to decide which banks could reopen the following Monday. On the Sunday night, Roosevelt went on the radio to deliver the first of his fireside chats to explain the crisis and the government's response in simple terms, 'I can assure you', he told his listeners, 'that it is safer to keep your money in a reopened bank than under the mattress'.

The greater the number of banks that opened, the greater was the likely revival of confidence. But the reopening of one unsound bank could have disastrous consequences. Treasury Secretary Woodin insisted that the requirements of soundness be interpreted as liberally as possible. It was a gamble. Much of the information Treasury officials had was a year old. They often depended on the good judgement of the local bankers themselves. When the San Francisco Reserve Board demurred at the reopening of the giant Bank of America with its 410 branches in California, Woodin gave the Board little alternative but to sanction its reopening. The gamble paid off. Confidence in the banking system flowed back. On the first day after the holiday deposits exceeded withdrawals. Within a month 70 per cent of banks had reopened.

The reopening of other banks was a more cautious business. Conservators wanted to make some of their deposits available to hard-pressed customers and then to reorganise their operations on a sound footing. Once again, the government lacked the information to make an informed judgement. Again, conservators had to rely on the trust and integrity of the local bank officers. By the end of June 90 per cent of US banks were open. A key influence in successful reorganisation was the injection of capital by the RFC into ailing banks. The RFC invested some $1.171 billion in over 6,000 banks. The Corporation only lost $13.6 million in the 106 banks that closed despite its assistance.

Bailing out the banks in an emergency would be of little value if the faults in the system were not remedied at the same time. The passage of a Banking Act during the Hundred Days – the first days of the New Deal when Congress passed so much dramatic legislation – went some way towards eliminating the most glaring deficiencies. The stress was on a return to conservative banking practices which would foster investor confidence: tighter control of bank officials, greater capital requirements for national banks and the separation of commercial and investment banking. These were measures designed to curb irresponsible officials making speculative loans from undercapitalised banks. In addition, Congress forced the banks and the president to accept the federal guarantee of bank deposits through the Federal Deposit Insurance Corporation. Though the stress was on conservative banking practices, the act was not a reform dictated by the interest group that was to be regulated. On the contrary, the bankers, as one student concluded, 'made few positive contributions to the banking reform legislation'. They favoured self-regulation, rather than separation, of investment affiliates and bitterly opposed deposit insurance out of fear that strong banks would have to bail out small, inefficient rural banks.

The issues which the 1933 Banking Act sidestepped were unified national control of the banking system and the extension of branch banking. Since the overwhelming majority of banks that had failed since 1920 had been single unit banks under state control, there was a strong argument for making all banks members of a single national banking system. Since neighbouring Canada with extensive branch banking had avoided bank failures while suffering much the same economic problems as the United States, there was also some powerful backing for the extension of branch banking. Western and southern politicians, however, wanted neither to see their state banks put under the control of a New York-dominated Federal Reserve, nor their single unit banks to compete with the branches of giant national banks. As a result, the 1933 Act had left the system of competing state and federal jurisdictions intact. A limited extension of the power of national banks to form branches on a citywide or statewide basis within existing state laws did little to extend the scope of branch banking.

Marriner Eccles, the Utah banker appointed by Roosevelt as governor of the Federal Reserve Board, wanted to increase federal government control of the Federal Reserve system as a key element in his plans to control credit and manage the economy. He assuaged the fears of centralisation expressed by western and southern politicians because central control of the Federal Reserve under his proposals would rest not in Wall Street but in Washington. Under the 1935 Banking Act the existing Federal Reserve Board was replaced by a board of governors appointed by the president, subject to Senate confirmation. The appointed governors of the regional Federal Reserve Banks would now be subject to veto by the Washington FRB. Control of the crucial open-market committee (which had operated so inefficiently during the Depression) was taken away from the twelve regional governors and placed under the FRB and representatives of the regional banks. The bill scarcely made the FRB the 'instrument of despotic authority' that one banker predicted, but it did give the federal government the power more intelligently to fine-tune the economy.

As for the banks themselves, they prospered under the new regulations. Fewer banks failed during the first two terms of the Roosevelt presidency than during any previous administration. In 1936 for the first time for 59 years, no national bank closed its doors. From 1921 to 1933 depositors had lost on average $156 million a year or $0.45 per $100 in commercial banks. From the establishment of deposit insurance to 1960, losses averaged only $706,000 a year or less than $0.002 per $100, with more than half of those losses occurring during 1934.

2 The triumph of business self-regulation: I The National Industrial Recovery Act

In debates with Roosevelt during the 1932 campaign, Brains Truster Rex Tugwell argued that 'a punitive programme for bankers was an avoidance of the lesson to be learned from the depression'. When Roosevelt called for reforms in Wall Street, Tugwell labelled the proposals 'irrelevant, evasive and untimely'. Reforms were necessary, Tugwell argued, but they did nothing to achieve the central task: the recovery of the economy. In 1933 this problem outlined by Tugwell was forcibly brought home to Roosevelt. Solving the immediate banking crisis and reopening the banks was a precondition for economic recovery but the measures did not in themselves put a single American back to work. With Congress in session and a wide range of nostrums in the air, Roosevelt could not escape the responsibility of acting.

Roosevelt's advisers' first thoughts for securing recovery turned to agriculture. Proposals for farm relief had been clearly worked out and could be presented both to farm leaders and to Congress almost at once (see Chapter 4). No such consensus had been reached, however, on industrial recovery. Some voices called for protection of business from excessive competition and from anti-trust prosecution, others called for the restoration of vigorous competition. Some called for massive government spending, others called for rigid government economy. It was congressional pressure to pass a share-the-work measure which would have restricted workers to 30 hours a week that finally forced the administration to try to resolve these conflicting ideas. The result – the major industrial recovery measure of the early New Deal – was the National Industrial Recovery Act. The Act provided for codes of fair competition which would eliminate unfair competitive practices in particular industries, lay down wage and hours standards, and guarantee workers the right of collective bargaining. Industries under those codes would be exempt from anti-trust prosecution. In addition $3.3 billion was appropriated for public works, to be spent over two years.

To radical critics of the New Deal, the National Recovery Administration which implemented the Act epitomised the capture of a regulatory agency by the special interests who were supposed to be regulated. Contemporaries on the left saw the NRA as dangerously akin to fascism. To those who later interpreted the New Deal as a corporate liberal effort to protect big business, the NRA represented the key attempt by large corporations to extend their hegemony by securing government support for the cartelisation of the economy. Businessmen certainly played a key role in drafting the Recovery Act and an even greater role in administering it. But a corporate liberal interpretation of the NRA underestimates the conflicting impulses that led to the Recovery Act, overestimates the degree of business support for the NRA, especially among the large corporations, and ignores the practical and political constraints on alternative policies.

Codes of fair competition protected by exemption from the Sherman Anti-Trust Act had been advocated by trade associations during the 1920s and had been loudly championed in 1931 by Gerard Swope of General Electric (see Chapter 1). It was natural that these ideas should be embraced by the two men most influential in the drafting of the Recovery Act: Ray Moley and Hugh Johnson. Moley, one of the Brains Trusters, had learnt much of his progressivism from the New Nationalism of Theodore Roosevelt and, in particular, from *Concentration and Control* by

Charles Van Hise. Large concentrations of economic power were inevitable; they were the product of economic efficiency; to break them up through anti-trust prosecution would be futile and retrogressive. General Hugh Johnson drew on his war-time experience as the army representative on the War Industries Board under the financier Bernard Baruch, who would become Johnson's mentor. The WIB had given business its head to determine its own price and production policies free from the anti-trust threat and business had triumphantly succeeded in meeting the formidable needs of the wartime economy. To Moley and Johnson, the Depression had been caused not by monopoly power but by destructive competition. As businessmen desperately cut prices and increased production to keep their share of declining markets, so they relentlessly shaved costs by cutting wages and thus further reduced consumer purchasing power and further exacerbated the problem of overproduction. By exempting cooperating businessmen from anti-trust prosecution, the codes could stabilise prices, production, and wages and eliminate the 'chiseller'.

This sort of business self-regulation promised exactly to fit the needs of a trade association like the Cotton Textile Institute. Its vain efforts to curb overproduction by voluntary agreements to limit the hours the machines operated could now be given teeth by federal regulation. Similarly, these ideas seemed to serve the needs of the major oil companies and the American Petroleum Institute. Their efforts to curb the overproduction in oil that followed the opening up of the East Texas fields in 1931 had failed. State regulation, federal allocation of state production quotas, the imposition of martial law, and negotiations of an interstate compact had all been ineffective. Now a code could give federal sanction against the interstate shipment of so-called 'hot oil' in excess of state quotas.

But aside from the major oil companies and individual voices like Gerard Swope's, it was not the representatives of the 'center firms', the large corporations in industries like steel and automobiles, who were demanding federal sanction of business self-regulation. After all, major steel and automobile companies were oligopolies that already exercised quasi-monopolistic control over their markets. It was middling or smaller-size firms that saw their salvation in codes of fair competition. Textiles was an industry of relatively small units. In oil, small inefficient producers in the old

Kansas fields saw codes as a means of protection against the new efficient independents of East Texas. Small retailers saw codes as a safeguard against the chain stores like Woolworth's and A & P. It was predatory price-cutting by the large chains that could afford loss leaders that had driven half the small retailers in the country out of business between 1929 and 1933.

Nor was it simply businessmen who saw self-regulation as the answer. Labour leaders in sick industries like soft coal and the needle trades had long advocated the elimination of destructive competition as a solution to their industries' problems. The United Mine Workers had sponsored legislation, opposed by most coal operators, that would have allowed operators to fix minimum prices and set production quotas, in return for guarantees of collective bargaining. The Amalgamated Clothing Workers of America under Sidney Hillman made similar proposals. Their arguments influenced Senator Robert Wagner and his advisers who joined Moley and Johnson's drafting team. It was Wagner's group that initiated Section 7a which gave workers the right to bargain collectively in the codes, a provision that Congressman Clyde Kelly brought straight from his bill for coal stabilisation.

To put faith in 1933 in the same businessmen who had so signally failed to make wise decisions in the 1920s seemed perverse to many. To some the logic was instead to call for much greater federal planning of the economy. It was not necessary to be a Communist to be impressed by the apparent success of the Soviets in planning their economy at a time when the capitalist West was in disarray. Advocates of greater government planning accepted the argument that large concentrations of economic power were the inevitable product of economies of scale and technological innovation. But these corporations were unaccountable. They had set prices excessively high, oversaved, and failed to redistribute the gains of productivity with higher wages. As a result there was insufficient purchasing power in the economy to consume the products of technological advance. A strong federal presence was needed to plan the economy to control the businessmen, eliminate waste, and ensure the adequate provision of consumer demand. Planning was something of a fad in the early 1930s, espoused not only by institutional economists like Rex Tugwell but by liberal intellectuals like George Soule and Stuart Chase of the *New Republic* and by progressives like the La Follette brothers. There was little idea how such planning should work. Even Tugwell did not seem to envisage much coercion by the federal government; rather he called for a national industrial council which could exhort businessmen to more responsible behaviour. Such proposals highlighted a major defect of planning proposals: there was simply not the state capacity to plan the economy.

As we shall see, the federal government lacked both the information and the personnel effectively to control economic decision-making. In any case, as Robert Himmelberg and Elliot Rosen have shown, Rex Tugwell's vision of centralised overhead planning was simply not one of the options considered in the drafting of the Recovery Act. Roosevelt had long since rejected such an alternative as politically impractical. It was in the Department of Agriculture, where Tugwell was Undersecretary, that people with similar ideas to his could be found. Nevertheless, the Act did contain a provision for government licensing of corporations. The provision originated with Undersecretary of Commerce John Dickinson, who had been in contact with the planners in Agriculture, and it certainly gave greater scope for government control and planning in the operation of the codes than the advocates of business self-regulation envisaged. The latter expected government simply to sanction the privately arrived at decisions of the industry groups. The supporters of planning expected the government to dictate and impose decisions on industry.

The planners and the champions of business–government cooperation accepted large corporations as a natural part of economic life. In doing so, they ran counter to a profound tradition of anti-monopoly sentiment in the United States which held that concentrated economic power was inimical to American democracy. The tradition had its most obvious manifestation in the Sherman Anti-Trust Act, a clumsy and often ineffective instrument which nevertheless could be used against the more blatant trusts. A more sophisticated version of this tradition came in the measures of Woodrow Wilson's New Freedom under the intellectual influence of Boston lawyer Louis Brandeis. Large corporations were the product not of natural economic forces but of financial manipulation and abuse. They needed to be broken up but, once broken up, there needed to be permanent government regulation by bodies such as the Federal Trade Commission to ensure that they did not reappear. In the 1930s Brandeis, now a Supreme Court justice, eschewed direct political controversy. But his admirers, like Felix Frankfurter of the Harvard Law School, who placed so many young lawyers in the burgeoning New Deal agencies, argued like the planners that monopolistic concentrations of power in the economy contributed to the Depression with their rigid and excessive prices and their failure to redistribute income and restore purchasing power. Unlike the planners, however, men like Frankfurter argued for the restoration of free market conditions, coupled with reforms to eliminate financial and banking malpractice.

Just as Theodore Roosevelt had denounced the New Freedom as 'rural toryism', so Moley and Tugwell derided Brandeis and his followers as irredeemably nostalgic, yearning for an America of 'small proprietors, of corner grocers and smithies under spreading chestnut trees'. Such criticism was misleading. The financial abuses and chicanery denounced by the market restorers were real enough, particularly in the complex holding company empires that had been established to control public utilities. Further, Brandeis did not deny that large-scale enterprise could be the natural and efficient consequence of technological progress. He accepted that a steel company needed to be large. What he denied was that a soup-maker like Campbell's needed to be a large national corporation. Nor did Brandeis have a naive faith in anti-trust prosecution to break up trusts. He had little faith in a remedy that had been tried for 50 years and found wanting. Progressive taxation was the vehicle which he believed could change the structure of the American economy.

The market restorers had little influence in the drafting of the Recovery Act but they were a powerful political force, as the NRA was later to discover. The proposals in the Act for anti-trust exemption alarmed progressive western Republicans like William Borah and some southern and western Democrats, notably Huey Long. Suspicion of eastern corporations and concern for the 'little man' was a potent political concoction. Fears of corporate dominance of the NRA were not assuaged by the arguments that the codes were designed to protect small businessmen against the predatory practices of large corporations. But the critics had to be satisfied with a vague amendment which provided that codes should not 'promote monopolies or monopolistic practices'.

War Department and the War Industries Board. This role led him to a long association with financier Bernard Baruch, who employed him after the war and bequeathed him to the Brains Trust after Roosevelt won the nomination at Chicago in 1932. Johnson was impressed by the degree of national unity that the war-time emergency had engendered and the degree of economic cooperation that could be secured not by coercion but by appeals to the national interest. The businessmen he associated with convinced him that the enemy of that cooperation was the chiseller, the selfish individual who cut prices and destroyed labour standards. The energetic, colourful Johnson was ideally suited to mount a war-time-style propaganda campaign to enlist the nation in support of the NRA under the symbol of the Blue Eagle.

In 1935 Johnson similarly organised the Works Progress Administration in New York City in three months. He then resigned. For that sort of short-term mobilisation he was excellent. For long-term organisation he had little aptitude. He was inclined to trust business goodwill rather than establish detailed policy guidelines. He resorted to exhortation and appeals to patriotism rather than to carefully crafted institutions. Opponents and critics were extravagantly ridiculed as traitors. He was particularly savage in condemning strikers who threatened the recovery programme. He was an increasingly erratic administrator: heroic bursts of energy were followed by equally heroic drinking binges when he disappeared for days on end, protected to a large extent by his devoted secretary and mistress, Frances Robinson. As he floundered amidst increasing criticism, critics suspected his sentimental love of Italian opera masked an admiration for Mussolini's ideals of corporatism. Arbitrary whim and maudlin self-pity paralysed his leadership. He was incurably suspicious of his subordinates, who in turn made it clear that he was impossible to work with. By September 1934 Johnson had to go.

When Johnson had been appointed to administer the NRA in 1933 he had expected also to control the Public Works Administration, which was to handle public works spending. Johnson saw rapid public works spending as the mechanism that would put people back to work quickly: the codes of the NRA would ensure that this sharp boost would be sustained on a sound and stable footing. Instead, Roosevelt appointed Secretary of the Interior Harold L. Ickes to run the PWA.

Ickes had been appointed to recognise the contribution of western progressives to Roosevelt's election. Franklin D. Roosevelt turned to him for the Interior slot after independent Republicans Hiram Johnson of California and Bronson Cutting of New Mexico both opted to remain in the Senate. Ickes had a long and largely unsuccessful career in reform politics in Chicago, vainly working for a series of reform candidates who challenged machine politics and the control of the utilities in city politics. Nationally he had also been associated with lost causes: the Progressive Party of 1912 and the presidential aspirations of Hiram Johnson. Roosevelt plucked him at the age of 59 from relative obscurity and Ickes rewarded the president with fierce, but not uncritical, loyalty through twelve years at Interior.

Ickes was one of the most fiercely combative of the New Dealers: he delighted in extravagant rhetorical attacks on the Republicans and on 'the interests'; he was one of the most outspoken and undiplomatic critics of Hitler; he also jealously fought fellow New Dealers to protect both his own bureaucratic empire and his position with the president. He remorselessly struggled with Harry Hopkins for control over public works appropriations: Hopkins occupied 83 closely typed index cards in the index to Ickes's 6-million-word diary. Later Ickes fought a fruitless campaign to secure the transfer of the Forestry Service back from the Department of Agriculture to Interior. Sensitive to real and imagined slights, he often reacted by offering his resignation to the president. Roosevelt always knew how to reassure his often exasperating subordinate by small personal gestures that cemented Ickes's loyalty. Harry Truman was not so patient. When Ickes resigned in 1946 over Truman's appointment of oilman Edwin Pauley as Under secretary of the Navy, Truman was only too happy to accept the resignation.

Ickes worked very long hours to transform the Interior Department from a corruption-ridden agency tainted by the Teapot Dome scandal into a diligent trustee of the nation's natural resources. He succeeded partly because of his genuine devotion to conservation and his wholesome suspicion of predatory private interests, partly because of the grip he maintained on his own bureaucracy, a control his departmental solicitor credited to his 'generally wholesome talents for terror'. In running his department Ickes forcefully attempted to protect Indian rights and was also one of the few New Dealers actively to seek to eliminate discrimination against blacks.

Ickes brought these qualities of hard work, watchful vigilance against any hint of corruption, and bureaucratic empire-building to his administration of the Public Works Administration. The irascible Ickes was determined that no money under his jurisdiction should be wasted or corruptly spent. His meticulous and cautious approach meant that in the first six months only $110 million of the $3.3 billion allocation was spent. One of his assistants commented in exasperation, Ickes 'may be a great man, sound on oil, Indians and Interior . . . but he has still to learn . . . that the Administrator of a $3 billion fund hasn't time to check every typewritten requisition'. Ickes in time created a remarkably graft-free and efficient public works empire. But any hope Johnson may have had of a boom generated by the 'quick fix' of public works in 1933 were soon dashed.

As a result the burden of putting people back to work fell on the NRA. Codes had to be drawn up quickly. But even the hard-driving, restless Hugh Johnson could not sign up American industry at once. Consequently, Johnson launched what was essentially a gigantic propaganda drive to increase wages and limit hours. Employers were urged to sign the president's Reemployment Agreement, a blanket code which provided for a 35-hour week and a 40¢-an-hour minimum wage for industrial workers. Cooperating employers displayed the symbol of the Blue Eagle and proclaimed 'We do our Part'. Anyone who cheated on the agreement, Johnson warned, would be subject to the full wrath of an aroused citizenry. Johnson was trying to stimulate the same coercive community pressure for conformity that had been so successfully invoked in World War I. It was no coincidence that the NRA's publicity director, Charles F. Horner, had been involved in the drive to sell Liberty Bonds. In the heady days of August and September 1933 Johnson's flair for publicity and the massive parades and demonstrations in favour of the Blue Eagle gave some cause for hope. Singer Al Jolson even told newsreel cameras that the day of the mammoth NRA parade in New York City was the most exciting day of his life, more exciting than the day he got married. But all too soon the Reemployment Agreement drive faded. There was no evidence of sustained gains in either jobs or income, and public opinion was no sanction against the determined chiseller. Appeals to community sentiment and voluntarism were no more successful·for the flamboyant Johnson than for the austere Hoover.

Exhortation under the Reemployment Agreement failed, but the slowness of public works pump priming and the failure of the NRA codes in themselves to guarantee increases in total demand meant that Johnson had time and again to resort to appeals to goodwill and the public-spiritedness of businessmen. In early October 1933 he launched a 'Buy Now' campaign, in the spring of 1934 he called for a 10 per cent increase in wages and a 10 per cent cut in hours. Later, he despairingly cried, 'Keep prices down. For God's sake, keep prices down.' That he had to resort to these increasingly futile and discredited appeals was testimony to the lack of a recovery mechanism in the NRA that could stimulate mass purchasing power.

The need for speed in the summer of 1933 meant that the codes could not be imposed on American industry: codes would require the consent of the businessmen themselves if they were to be put into operation quickly. The decision to put faith in businessmen's desire for self-regulation in part reflected Johnson's personal preference born of his First World War experience. In part, the decision resulted from advice given Johnson by Alexander Sachs, the head of the NRA Research and Planning Division, that the NRA could not withstand a challenge in the courts to its constitutionality. Above all, the government had neither the staff nor the information to impose conditions on American industry. The Agricultural Adjustment Administration, for example, could turn to a disinterested bureaucracy of 'service intellectuals' in the Bureau of Agricultural Economics, or in the land-grant colleges, which had acquired detailed information about American agriculture over the previous decade. No such body of expertise was available to the NRA, certainly not in the Department of Commerce. Seeking to staff its operations, the NRA had to ask businessmen, just as the War Industries Board had done, sixteen years earlier, to come to serve in Washington. These men were naturally imbued with ideals of business self-regulation, not government planning.

As codes were negotiated therefore in 1933 it was no surprise that businessmen achieved most of the goals they had set for themselves. In industry after industry, the employers were organised, they knew what they wanted, and they had a monopoly on information about how their industry worked. The government could not hope to compete. Johnson's staff was disposed to be cooperative in the first place and they were in any case often inexperienced and uninformed. Milton Katz, a 26-year-old Harvard Law School graduate, recalled that within hours of arriving in Washington from his honeymoon, he had to sit down as a representative of the NRA Legal Division with lawyers from the major oil companies and draft the petroleum code, about which he knew nothing, so that it could be ready for the president's signature at 8 a.m. the following morning. Government negotiators were also hampered by the sheer number of codes they had to draft: they had no chance to establish clear policy guidelines. It was not until the end of October, for example, that the NRA produced a policy memorandum on minimum prices, by which time all the major codes had been signed. Johnson's own quixotic interventions in negotiations further weakened the NRA's bargaining position. In the coal industry, just as southern coal operators were ready to accept Section 7a and collective bargaining, Johnson suddenly turned up and offered to 'clarify' 7a to their satisfaction, thus conceding the government's advantage. What James P. Johnson has said of Hugh Johnson's interventions in the coal negotiations, applied to all the NRA chief's interventions: 'the general knew little about the industry, spent only 15 minutes at the open hearings, and lacked the steadiness for sustained negotiation'.

If the government could not counter business influence in the negotiations, consumer and labour representatives were even less equipped to do so. It was only in mid-September that an opinion was required from the Consumers Advisory Board before a code could be promulgated. The Labor Advisory Board only had leverage in code drafting in those cases where unions were already strong in the particular industry. In negotiating the textile code, the Labor Board could make only a limited protest about a minimum wage of $11 a week ($10 in the South) for a 40-hour week since those provisions had already been accepted by the president of the United Textile Workers.

The one lever available to the government to extract concessions from business was the promise of exemption from anti-trust prosecution. But that lever was only effective in industries where excessive competition was the problem. It was no coincidence that the first industry to sign a code was cotton textiles. So desperate were their representatives to curb overproduction that they were prepared, in return for restricting mills to two 40-hour weekly shifts, to go further than the draft code and concede in the public hearings the elimination of child labour and a $13 minimum weekly wage ($12 in the South). But in industries like steel and automobiles, dominated by a few major corporations, the offer of anti-trust exemption carried little weight. The major corporations already exercised sufficient control over production and prices within the existing law. What alarmed these industrialists was not overproduction but the prospect that they might lose control of their costs if they were unionised. The thought that Section 7a might bring unions into their plants made steel and auto executives obdurate. There was little the government could do to extract concessions from them, so that steel and automobiles were the last of the major industries to sign codes. They made almost no concessions on wages and hours and secured the most favourable interpretation of 7a. The automobile code did not outlaw any unfair trade practices, set wages below prevailing minimums, and contained a merit clause which seemed to undermine Section 7a. This clause affirming the employers' right to hire and fire on individual merit seemed to give them a licence to dismiss troublesome union members.

Even an atomised industry like soft coal, plagued as was textiles by excessive competition and overproduction, was difficult for the government to sign up. While northern operators wanted codes so that production quotas could be allocated, southern operators feared that code wage provisions would erode their regional competitive advantage: an advantage that would be further weakened if 7a brought unionisation to the southern mines. It took a series of violent strikes in Pennsylvania and the direct threat by Roosevelt that he was willing to dictate a code to the industry before the operators finally signed.

It was the tobacco industry that most graphically illustrated government impotence. The oligopolistic control of the market enjoyed by the Big Four cigarette manufacturers gave them no incentive to sign a code. In addition, the industry had been virtually depression-proof. Code negotiations dragged on till February 1935 and in the end the NRA, as union leader Sidney

Hillman complained, acquiesced in 'miserable' wages, at a time when the industry was making 'gigantic profits'. Such was the lack of enthusiasm in the White House by this time that Roosevelt actually lost the code temporarily. Yet despite the cigarette manufacturers' intransigence, the chairman of R. J. Reynolds, one of the Big Four tobacco companies, became chairman of the Recovery Board which ran the NRA after Hugh Johnson resigned in September 1934.

The consequence of business domination of the code-drafting process was that NRA codes did little to stimulate mass purchasing power or increase employment. Wage provisions made little difference to existing wage levels even in an industry like steel which had been singled out for condemnation by New Deal spokesmen for its appalling wages. Similarly, the hours provisions did little to share the work in the way congressional supporters had hoped. Here the precedent was set by the 40-hour week in textiles which the AFL had challenged in vain. Black and women workers suffered in particular. Exemptions from code coverage for some workers, e.g. cleaners in cotton mills, often therefore exempted black and female workers. Employers often reclassified blacks and women into exempted occupations. Regional wage differentials often hid racial differentials. Sexual differentials were often explicit. Almost a quarter of the codes established rates for women that were from 14 to 30 per cent lower than for men. Custom was the only defence of this discrimination. In addition codes only covered half the women in the workforce. Since domestic service was not covered by the NRA, blacks and women again suffered disproportionately.

What the codes did provide was a series of price-fixing and production control devices which businessmen had long wanted to implement but which the threat of anti-trust prosecution had inhibited. While few codes provided for direct price-fixing, over 400 codes, nearly 80 per cent of the total, had provisions against selling below cost, and some 60 required open-price filing. Over 60 codes had restrictions on the operations of machines and plant.

Business dominance of code-drafting naturally led to business dominance of code administration. The deputy administrators, the key figures in each code, were usually men in sympathy with the idea of business self-regulation. The code authorities were often the trade associations of the industries concerned: in autos, the

National Automobile Chamber of Commerce; in cotton, the Cotton Textile Institute; in steel, the American Iron and Steel Institute; in lighting, the National Electric Manufacturers Association; in the southern lumber industry, the Southern Pine Association. Fewer than 10 per cent of code authorities had consumer or labour representatives. Government representatives were often too busy, or were disinclined, to offer an independent voice. In addition, the code authorities often controlled the statistical information by which their performance might be assessed. For example, in order to judge whether the cotton code authority was fairly applied, the government had to rely on whatever information the Cotton Textile Institute saw fit to let it see. Labour complaints about code violations in textiles were referred back by the code authority to local employers. Not surprisingly, few code violations were ever acknowledged in textiles.

4 The fall of business self-regulation: the failure of the NRA

The effect of business control of the NRA was to dash the hopes of virtually all the groups whose ideas had influenced the Recovery Act.

Advocates of government planning were outraged that Johnson had apparently conceded whatever was necessary to business to get the codes into operation. Radicals outside the government saw the NRA less as a tool of the planned society, and more as an instrument of the corporate state reminiscent of Italian and German fascism. Rex Tugwell argued in vain on the short-lived Special Industrial Recovery Board that overall standards in the public interest needed to be established to which individual codes would have to conform. Otherwise, he argued, across-the-board price increases would offset any rise in purchasing power. Price rises under the NRA convinced Senators Wagner and La Follette that the codes could not be expected to produce the revival of purchasing power needed for recovery. Wagner therefore began to consider legislative proposals to protect trades unions as the best means of workers getting for themselves the necessary wage increases. La Follette turned in 1934 to progressive taxation as the means of redistributing income to those who could foster economic revival.

Price increases also upset a host of interest groups. Organised labour saw them racing ahead of wage increases; labour also saw employers easily evading Section 7a (see Chapter 3). Farmers saw the prices they paid for goods soar, while the benefits they received from the AAA were delayed. While unorganised consumers suffered, the Consumers' Advisory Board could nevertheless muster support from powerful groups that were the victims of price increases: government relief agencies, purchasing agents for government departments and the military, and large retail organisations. These complaints about prices merged with the complaints of small businessmen that they were being squeezed out by the monopolistic practices, particularly production restrictions, of the larger corporations who controlled the code authorities.

These protests were grist to the mill of those who had always favoured the restoration of market and the breaking of monopoly control. Midwestern progressives, notably Gerald P. Nye of North Dakota and William E. Borah of Idaho, launched a relentless attack on the NRA in the Senate in November 1933. They deplored the trend to monopoly and the deleterious effect on farmers and small businessmen. They called for revival of the anti-trust laws, and demanded a Federal Trade Commission investigation of price-fixing in steel. They documented price increases of between 60 and 120 per cent and called for the publication of the business connections of all NRA employees and code authority personnel. The NRA, Nye concluded, 'was going back to the practices that brought on the depression'.

Hugh Johnson believed that the small businessman championed by Gerald Nye was not the exemplar of moral liberty, but all too often the chiseller who ran a sweatshop. But Johnson knew that Nye and his colleagues who were celebrating the virtues and plight of 'the little man' were invoking a formidable and politically persuasive ideological heritage. Johnson therefore agreed to the establishment of a Recovery Review Board under noted lawyer Clarence Darrow to investigate the impact of the NRA on small business. Darrow's investigators easily found what they wanted to find. The Board's report, with its sad litany of small business grievances and its complaint that the NRA was cruelly oppressing them, was meat and drink to critics of the agency.

These criticisms from planning advocates, labour, consumers, and anti-trusters were scarcely surprising in view of the triumph of

ideas of business self-regulation and the dominance by industrialists of code administration. What was surprising was the extent of
business criticism of the NRA. The extent of its opposition
certainly undermines the idea that the NRA was a corporate
liberal ploy designed to extend corporate hegemony.

In part, businessmen objected to the paperwork and the
bureaucracy that government regulation generated. The NRA had
not been content with codes for the major industries. There were
instead over 546 codes. Henning Prentiss, head of Armstrong
Cork, had benefited from the Depression-inspired boom in the
sale of food preserving jars since his firm was the largest producer
of bottle corks in the country. But he was exasperated by the 34
NRA codes under which his vertically integrated firm had to
operate. Although small retailers generally favoured the NRA,
hardware stores opposed it because they operated under 19 codes,
including one for air-conditioning units and another for upward-
outward opening doors. An assessment for each code was collected from each store and owners ended up paying their employees different rates of pay at different times of the day.

In part, opposition to the NRA came from the resentment of
small businessmen who found themselves forced to violate codes
in order to compete with their larger competitors who dominated
the code authorities. The opposition of the National Association
of Manufacturers however cannot be simply explained in these
terms. The NAM, after being almost bankrupted in 1932, revived
by becoming the organisation not only of small firms, but also of
middling-size steel interests run by Ernest Weir and Tom Girdler
and of representatives of large-scale heavy industry like the Du
Ponts of General Motors.

In part, criticism of the NRA reflected sectional and regional
tensions amongst businessmen within particular industries. Thus,
in oil, East Texas independents clashed with the majors over
production quotas; in coal, southern operators clashed with their
northern competitors and fought amongst themselves over efforts
to divide regional markets.

Nevertheless, the most revealing opposition to the NRA came
from the very people who were considered to be archetypal
corporate liberals. The Business Advisory Council set up by
Secretary of Commerce Daniel Roper has been portrayed as a
body of welfare capitalists anxious to use the NRA to promote

corporate stability. Yet by the end of 1933, Gerard Swope, the man most identified with ideas of industrial self-government, was calling for less government interference in the NRA. The United States Chamber of Commerce soon argued that the government should do no more than veto or approve codes drawn up by business. In 1934 the BAC could do nothing to prevent mass resignations of businessmen from the NRA and was unable to persuade industrialists to go to Washington to take their place. The steel, automobile, rubber, and chemical industries effectively broke off relations with the government. Why did the business-dominated NRA arouse such corporate hostility? Business opposition highlighted how few businessmen had been positively in favour of the ideas of business–government cooperation in the first place. Most of them had never seen the NRA as a means of extending corporate hegemony. Rather, they saw it as an unavoidable reform which they would have to make the best of by trying to control code drafting and administration. What distinguished men like Gerard Swope and fellow members of the BAC from more unrestrained business opponents of the New Deal was their belief that it was important to keep channels of communication open to the New Deal in order to defuse or deflect the worst proposals for reform.

Most businessmen feared that the NRA could become what government planners and anti-trusters lamented that it had not become: an effective restraint on the untrammelled right of business to manage its own affairs. The political power which consumer, labour, and anti-monopoly critics had outside the NRA did show signs of winning some influence inside the agency. In 1934 Leon Henderson had come in to head the Research and Planning Division and throughout the organisation consumer and labour voices were increasingly heard. Occasionally they had some policy successes. In the spring of 1934 many small industries were exempted from the codes. Office Memorandum 228 outlawed price-fixing in any future codes. Anti-trust rhetoric from the president down increased. There was more talk of progressive taxation. Government officials were developing for the first time independent information which could be used to challenge the assumptions of the business representatives. One reason negotiations on the cigarette manufacturing code dragged on for so long was that, once the industry had failed to sign up in the rush of

1933, labour and consumer representatives developed the figures to show that a special 25 ¢-an-hour rate for hand-stemmers was not the humanitarian gesture to feeble workers pictured by the employers, but a calculated effort to pay exceptionally low wages to the bulk of the workforce.

These developments rarely directly threatened business control of the code authorities themselves. General policy victories made little difference to the day-to-day running of the codes. But liberals in the NRA were able to prevent businessmen serving on the code authorities from extending their power. Leon Henderson, for example, thwarted the efforts of the textile code authority to restrict production even further. Stalemate was reached. Planners and anti-trusters could prevent businessmen from extending ideas of business self-regulation any further, but the businessmen running the code authorities could prevent liberal policies actually being put into practice. Nevertheless, the partial success of the liberals raised an alarming spectre for most American businessmen. Rather no government regulation at all, they felt, than the unpredictable state intervention of the New Deal.

Businessmen might still have accepted the NRA for all its dangers if the NRA had delivered economic recovery. But it did not yield the economic benefits that might have offset business's alarms. The NRA only restored modest profitability to American business, if it restored any at all. Even in the sick industries like coal and textiles whose executives had been so enthusiastic about market stabilisation and minimum prices, the NRA failed to deliver economic recovery. There was a brief boom in textiles. Firms operated at a net profit for the first time in four years in 1933 but in 1934, 481 out of 918 companies ran at a net deficit. Despite production controls, the industry was still producing too much. In coal, the industry's net deficit did decline from $51.5 million in 1932 to $7.6 million in 1934 and $15.5 million in 1935. But not until 1940 did the industry get back into the black. In both textiles and coal, the NRA hindered inevitable rationalisation, kept marginal operators in business, and did nothing to halt the long-term switch either to rayon or to alternative energy supplies. What the NRA simply could not provide was an increase in total aggregate demand that might have put people back to work in significant numbers and dramatically increased business turnover and profitability. Businessmen were not prepared to trade off marginal improvement in economic stability for the potential hazards of bureaucratic control and intervention that the NRA represented.

The NRA therefore stumbled towards the end of its two-year authorisation from Congress with few friends. Businessmen were unhappy at their lack of power in the agency; their critics balked at the extent of their control. The differing perceptions of the NRA were reflected in the different proposals to extend its life. Almost nobody supported an extension of the agency in its original form. Proposals ranged from the provision for purely voluntary codes to the continuation of codes with wage and hours standards but stripped of all price and production controls.

The Supreme Court put the NRA out of its misery on 27 May 1935. The NRA's enforcement of compliance with the codes had always been ambiguous. At first, NRA officials were reluctant to risk a constitutional challenge. Officials in the Justice Department Anti-Trust Division who insisted on maintaining control of prosecutions sponsored by the NRA Legal Division were uneasy about enforcing codes whose practices, particularly regarding price-fixing, would normally have been the subject of anti-trust prosecution. By the end of 1933 the Compliance Division of the NRA had a backlog of 10,000 complaints of violations. The dilemma for the NRA lawyers was that a vigorous enforcement policy would mean prosecuting a large number of small businessmen who in a desperate effort to stay in business had been driven to evade code standards imposed by their larger competitors. On the other hand, the failure to enforce could and did lead to the total breakdown of some codes. In vain, the NRA looked for large-scale businesses to prosecute. Instead, the cases which slowly moved towards the Supreme Court all involved small firms. In the end, the constitutional fate of the NRA rested on what its Legal Division head regarded as 'the weakest possible case': the prosecution of a kosher poultry dealer in New York City for paying below-code wages, not killing poultry in the required 'straight' manner, and selling diseased birds. The Schechter brothers ran one of the 500 small stores in the graft-ridden poultry industry in New York, but their appeal to the Supreme Court was financed by the Iron and Steel Institute anxious to see the end of government interference. The Supreme Court had no difficulty in declaring the NRA unconstitutional on the grounds that the Recovery Act attempted to regulate commerce that was not interstate in charac-

ter, and that the codes represented a wholly unacceptable delegation of power to the executive from the legislature, without
adequate policy and procedural guidelines.

5 After the NRA: plan, regulate, tax, or prosecute?

The end of the NRA saw Roosevelt embark on a second Hundred
Days of reform legislation as he forced a weary Congress to remain
in session through the ugly Washington heat until the end of
August 1935. The Wagner Labor Relations Act, soak-the-rich
taxation, the Public Utilities Holding Company Act, and the
Social Security Act were the most prominent features of this
so-called Second New Deal. To Basil Rauch commenting in the
1940s these legislative achievements represented a dramatic shift
in 1935 to the left, as Roosevelt abandoned the NRA approach of
conciliation with business. In place of cooperation came an
anti-business, pro-labour policy aimed at redistributing wealth and
power to the less privileged. But to New Deal advocates of
cooperation with business like Ray Moley or champions of collectivism like Rex Tugwell, the change of direction in 1935 marked
not a radical departure but a conservative return to the atomistic
philosophy of the Frankfurter-Brandeis group. The retreat to
nostalgic trust-busting was accompanied by easy attacks on business that appeared to be stealing the radical thunder of critics like
Huey Long, but were in fact a substitute for realistic organisation
of the modern economy.

Arthur M. Schlesinger Jr followed and developed this analysis
of the Second New Deal. The abandonment of the continuous
intervention of the NRA for a policy of simply telling business
what not to do symbolised for Schlesinger a retreat from ambitious
designs to restructure American society in every field of policy.
The purge of the liberal defenders of tenant farmers in the
Agricultural Adjustment Administration consolidated the triumph
of the prosperous commercial farmers in farm policy (see Chapter
4). The victory in the Tennessee Valley Authority of David
Lilienthal's ideas of grass-roots democracy over Arthur E. Morgan's coordinated vision of central planning restricted the TVA
simply to serving the interests of the local farming power structure
(see Chapter 4). The failure to adopt a federal system of social

security (see Chapter 5) fatally compromised the emerging welfare state. The failure of the Reconstruction Finance Corporation to act as an instrument of planned government capital allocation ended any real opportunity of economic planning through government direction of investment. Everywhere, the grandiose goals of reordering and directing American society were abandoned for the more limited and prosaic vision of piecemeal and pragmatic reform that catered to the needs of particular interest groups. This conservative shift, argued Schlesinger, was masked only by the aggressive radicalism of the Second New Deal's rhetoric and politics.

The New Deal's rhetoric and politics were more aggressively radical from 1935. Attacks on big business linked to a more consciously class-based appeal to lower-income voters were at the core of Roosevelt's appeal. But it is difficult to argue that this radical rhetoric obscured a conservative shift in policy. The New Deal's increased radicalism was firmly grounded in the protection of organised labour by the Wagner Act, the provision of jobs for the unemployed through the Works Progress Administration, and the promise of long-term economic security under the Social Security Act.

It is also difficult to describe a Second New Deal in 1935 as a coherent ideological retreat from the central planning philosophy of the First New Deal to the Brandeis-Frankfurter decentralised, atomistic vision of the Second. Overhead planning had never been at the core of industrial policy even in 1933. From the start, New Dealers had also aimed to regulate business abuses. Ideological continuity characterises the banking and securities legislation of 1933–35 and the public utility regulation of 1935, just as continuity characterises agricultural policy.

Changing circumstances and pragmatic concerns, rather than ideological shifts, account for much of what happened in 1935. Long-term reforms like social security could not be introduced overnight in 1933: by 1935 the policy-making groundwork had been completed and the political climate was right. A major work relief programme like the WPA was necessary when it became clear that the need for unemployment relief was not going to disappear quickly. The Wagner Act placed on the statute book the industrial relations procedures that the National Labor Board had been trying to impose under the NRA.

There was also no clear triumph in 1935 of the ideology of Brandeis and Frankfurter. Frankfurter influenced many New Deal appointments – but while 'the happy hot dogs' usually shared a common Harvard Law School background they did not necessarily share a common neo-Brandeisian philosophy. Only the taxation proposals of 1935 aroused the enthusiasm of the old Justice. He had little interest in the Wagner Act or the WPA; he was uneasy because the Social Security Act did not require the states to adopt the Wisconsin unemployment insurance plan; and he continued to dislike the AAA.

What did happen in 1935 was that Roosevelt lost patience with corporation leaders and younger New Dealers came to the fore who shared his reluctance to make concessions to conservative business opinion. Administrators who had made their names running large-scale spending programmes, lawyers who had successfully drafted reform legislation and shepherded it through Congress, liberal congressmen, anxious about any loss of New Deal momentum and alert to the threat of dissident demagogues, all worked to ensure that Roosevelt moved left in 1935.

Advocates of national planning in the administration did not disappear. But after 1935, as before, they had little direct impact on industrial policy. Some of the most committed advocates of economic planning remained in the Department of Agriculture. Not only was Henry Wallace turning the Bureau of Agricultural Economics into an instrument of the long-term rationalisation of American agriculture, but Wallace's advisers like Louis Bean and Mordecai Ezekiel were increasingly concerned that the failure to secure industrial recovery and to sustain mass purchasing power in the non-farm sector was inhibiting attempts to produce agricultural recovery. Along with Gardiner Means at the National Resources Planning Board, these economists believed that administered prices by monopolies created an economics of scarcity that precluded the creation of mass purchasing power and prevented economic expansion. Breaking up monopolies would be futile; instead they wanted continuous government involvement in economic decision-making in the private sector. Conscious of the opposition to centralised direct planning, their planning proposals were variants on earlier schemes for advisory national economic councils. The one government agency that might have served their purpose by systematically directing investment failed to do so. The

Reconstruction Finance Corporation under Texas banker Jesse Jones tended to pump capital into institutions that were good enough risks to have secured capital on the open market in any case.

Nor did ideas of business self-regulation disappear completely. Congress passed legislation perpetuating some of the NRA price and production controls for particular industries. With the support of northern coal owners and the United Mine Workers, Congress approved first the Guffey-Snyder Act in 1935 and then the Guffey-Vinson Act in 1937 to enable a national coal commission to set minimum prices for coal and to check any erosion of labour standards. In oil, the Connally Act continued the prohibition on the shipment of oil in excess of state quotas. Small retailers, who had never lost their enthusiasm for the protection the NRA offered them against the price-cutting chain stores, secured resale price maintenance under the Miller-Tydings Act. But it took a particular conjunction of favourable circumstances to produce legislative support for business self-regulation: in coal, a united employer and union stance; in oil, the arguments for conservation and the backing of state governments; in retailing, the politically potent appeal of small store owners. Industries like textiles and lumber lacked these advantages and failed to secure legislation.

Above all no one any longer advocated a policy of business self-regulation, of government sanctioned cartels, as a means of securing overall economic recovery. Men with overriding faith in the virtues of business cooperation did become rare. By 1935 Hugh Johnson and Ray Moley had already gone. Donald Richberg failed to find an influential niche in the government after the Schechter decision and set up a law office in Washington. The men around Roosevelt were now highly sceptical of the ability of business to act in the national interest. The men who had reassured business and the party elders in 1933 were much less visible in 1935. The figures who were increasingly prominent were Harry Hopkins, masterminding a new works programme, Harold Ickes, the proven administrator of PWA, Frances Perkins, the overseer of the Social Security Act, and Henry Wallace, responsible for the demonstrably popular farm programmes. In the lower echelons of the New Deal younger iconoclastic administrators were coming to the fore. As Aubrey Williams noted, they regarded a person like Jesse Jones as little more than a crook. In

Congress, the initiative was taken less by the traditional southern leaders, more by progressive politicians like Wagner and La Follette who were responsive to the needs of lower-income voters.

Faith in the willingness of business to regulate itself had been on the wane at least since early 1934. The NRA had discredited any naive faith in the selflessness of business. Roosevelt, angered by what he considered the ungrateful and increasingly strident hostility of the business community, was only too willing to attack big business, the malefactors of great wealth, and in the 1936 campaign to welcome their hatred. Roosevelt's shift in rhetoric was not complete. He never disowned the principles of the NRA. He often, like Theodore Roosevelt, distinguished between 'good' and 'bad' businessmen. Good, responsible businessmen tended to be the ones he knew well. Late in 1935, again in 1937, then in 1939 he made conciliatory gestures to the business community. But these did not represent major policy initiatives. He was never ready to make the concessions on taxation, spending, and labour that a partnership with the business community would have required. The fate of the Business Advisory Council indicated the precise limits to the New Deal's accommodation to business. The BAC was never the instrument of corporate liberalism that historians have suggested. Rather than being a group of far-sighted business leaders sponsoring reform to extend their control over the economy, the BAC was essentially defensive and reactive. Their beleaguered position was even clearer after 1935. While most business organisations broke off relations with the New Deal, the BAC consisted of those few business leaders who believed that maintaining some tenuous links with the New Deal offered the best opportunity to limit the damage that would otherwise be done by radical New Deal legislation.

Telling business what not to do also did not come to the fore of New Deal policy suddenly in 1935. Regulation of financial abuses and malpractice had been a concern of New Dealers from the start. We have seen that the Banking Acts of 1933 and 1935 sought to eliminate unsound banking practices and to assert greater public control over the Federal Reserve Board. It was also essential to restore confidence that had been badly shaken in that other basic prop of the financial order – the marketing of investment securities. The aim of the Securities Act of 1933 and the Securities and Exchange Act of 1934 was fundamentally conservative, as had been the purpose of the banking legislation. As Felix Frankfurter noted, 'conservative banking, within its appropriate function, has nothing to fear and everything to gain from the Securities Act'. The administration of the Acts confirmed that conservative intent and by the end of the decade many sections of the financial community acknowledged the contribution reform had made to financial stability. But in 1933 and 1934 most businessmen and financiers were terrified of federal regulation and denounced it bitterly.

States had always found it difficult to protect investors from fraudulent and worthless securities. In the 1920s investment bankers themselves admitted that the great expansion of equity shares had outstripped their own capacity to provide adequate information on the issuers of securities. The 1933 Securities Act attempted to protect securities purchasers by forcing the disclosure of accurate information about securities issues. False statements regarding the sales of securities were outlawed. Prospective issuers of securities had to file detailed financial statements with the Federal Trade Commission and wait for twenty days before the securities could be issued. Directors and everyone responsible for the registration statements, underwriters and dealers were all liable for the accuracy of the statements. This regulation capitalised on the deep suspicion, particularly among southern and western congressmen, of financial institutions. But it also drew on the detailed knowledge of corporate law, organisation, and practice of two of Frankfurter's protégés, Ben Cohen and Tommy Corcoran. According to New Deal congressional leader Sam Rayburn, the legislation drafted by Cohen and Corcoran passed so easily either 'because it was so damned good or so damned incomprehensible'.

Control of the mechanisms of marketing securities was the next stage. The untrammelled operation of the stock exchanges and the uncontrolled credit available for exchange trading had led to financial malpractice, the creation of huge paper profits for favoured individuals, and had fed the speculative booms such as the one that contributed to the Great Crash. The 1934 Act created a Securities and Exchange Commission to regulate the markets; it required the detailed financial reports of listed corporations to be filed with the Commission, restricted the ability of floor traders and insiders to manipulate the market, and gave the Federal

Reserve Board power to control credit available for trading by regulating margin requirements.

The regulatory framework established for the nation's financial institutions was characteristic of a consistent New Deal attitude to business. Between 1934 and 1941 the SEC increased its staff from 696 to 1,678, established 10 regional offices, and operated an annual budget that rose from $1.5 million to $5.3 million. The SEC regulated 20 stock exchanges, 7,000 brokers and dealers, and trading in 3,000 listed securities and 90,000 over-the-counter securities. This expansion confirmed the worst fears of its business enemies. Yet the SEC was not anti-business. Rather it served carefully to eliminate the worst abuses of corporate power. Its function, in the words of one of its commissioners, Jerome Frank, was 'primarily to preserve the capitalist form'. In some ways it was the quintessential reform of Felix Frankfurter and his disciples. Complex economic affairs could not be regulated by the courts simply applying statute law; they could only be effectively handled by the administrative attention of highly expert, technically equipped mandarins who as disinterested lawyers, preferably trained by Frankfurter himself, could protect the economic sound-ness of the industry. The SEC under not only its first chairman, buccaneering businessman Joseph P. Kennedy, but also his succes-sors, lawyers James M. Landis and William O. Douglas, favoured negotiation rather than litigation, self-enforcement rather than coercion, and voluntary decrees rather than court orders. By the end of the 1930s the SEC had halted the issue of $155 million of fraudulent securities, but it had also permitted the New York Stock Exchange to reform itself from within, and had allowed over-the-counter dealers to regulate themselves through the National Securities Dealers Association. By the end of the decade, financiers reluctantly accepted that the SEC had brought order to the financial markets.

Given the way that the SEC operated, it is not surprising that Frankfurter did not see the same great ideological divide between himself and some of the advocates of the First New Deal that later historians have identified. As he wrote to Ray Moley, 'Neither you nor I are doctrinaires either about the curse of bigness or the blessings of littleness. Like most things that matter in this world, it's a question of more or less, of degree, of when big is too big, and little is too little.' Both Frankfurter and his followers were certain however that the size of large corporations was not always the result of the natural forces of economic efficiency, but could be the result of financial chicanery. Frankfurter had always pointed to the giant companies which supervised power companies throughout the nation as the most glaring example of economic wastefulness and corporate abuse. A small number of holding companies were able through a complex pyramid of intermediary organisations to control scattered electric power companies in many states. The top holding company secured lucrative management fees and dividends from its subsidiaries, hindered improved service, and effectively escaped state or federal regulation. The holding company structure was so complex that Associated Gas and Electric had 264 corporate entities, including 40 pure holding companies. 'It is like', one critic complained, 'the Hanging Gardens of Babylon, a pyramidal structure built in weird design, worthy of a Nebuchadnezzar.' By 1929, 16 holding company groups controlled 92 per cent of private electrical power output.

Roosevelt did not have to shift in 1935 to move against these giants. His concern in New York for public power and cheaper electricity rates had led him to develop more personal expertise in the field of power policy than in any other aspect of economic development. While many of his advisers favoured some form of regulation of the holding companies or an assault on them by taxation, Roosevelt simply wanted to abolish them since he felt it would be impossible to regulate them. The Wheeler-Rayburn bill in 1935, drafted once more by Cohen and Corcoran, proposed a death sentence whereby the SEC could compel the dissolution of holding companies unless they formed a 'geographically and economically integrated system in two or more contiguous states'.

This threat to their very existence prompted a formidable propaganda counterattack from the holding companies who emphasised the harm such a measure would do, not to big business but to small investors and charities whose fortunes depended on shares in power companies. But Democratic congressmen from the already industrialised sections of the North-East and the upper South also feared the bill. The economic development of their regions would almost certainly depend on private power. They saw the assault on the holding companies as part of a wider New Deal power policy that would finance hydro-electric schemes and rural electrification in the less developed regions of the country and thus create industrial competitors. Roosevelt was forced to compromise. What opponents won was a longer period before execution and the possibility of a reprieve for companies which operated two separate but integrated systems, but in the end the death sentence remained.

The utility magnates, advised by John Foster Dulles, in vain fought the Act in the courts and the SEC made slow progress in reorganising the holding groups. By 1946 the 13 largest systems had only reduced their own corporate entities from 670 to 446. But the SEC kept plugging away. The Commission refused to suspend reorganisation because of the war and in the end leaders of the utilities would see that geographical integration made sense. Companies that were divested tended to be scattered individual properties that were a burden on the entire system. Holding companies that were reorganised made impressive market gains. Once again, federal regulation served to the advantage of business; but it was despite the best efforts of the businessmen that it did so.

Taxation had been one of the suggested ways of breaking up holding companies. Use of the taxing power, rather than anti-trust prosecution, was the device favoured by Brandeis for breaking up large concentrations of wealth and capital. Many in the New Deal and in Congress shared the distaste felt by Brandeis and Frankfurter for bloated salaries and fortunes. Taxation was also a possible key to the wider distribution of purchasing power which could prompt economic recovery where NRA codes had failed. Roosevelt's decision in 1935 to side with the advocates of soak-the-rich taxation was one instance where his actions that summer did mark a sharp break with the past.

Before 1935 New Deal taxation had not been based on the ability to pay. The people who could least afford to pay shouldered the heaviest burden. Indirect taxes on consumers constituted 55 per cent of federal tax collections in 1934 while individual and corporate income taxes yielded only 27 per cent. In contrast, income taxes in 1926–30 had yielded 64 per cent of tax collections compared to the 16 per cent raised by excise taxes. In part, the New Deal was relying on the excise taxes levied under Hoover in 1932, particularly on cars and petrol. But it also contributed an excise tax of its own on liquor after the repeal of Prohibition, and added the processing tax on agricultural products. Later, social security was partly financed by another regressive tax, the payroll tax.

The regressive impact of early New Deal taxation sprang from a reluctance to increase direct taxation during a depression: taxpayers were already up in arms about state and local taxes. But in the early New Deal, when so much hope was placed on cooperation with business to produce recovery, Roosevelt was reluctant to jeopardise that cooperation by increasing the corporate tax burden.

By 1935 however Roosevelt was no longer trying to woo the business community. He was under pressure to push for more progressive taxation from Treasury officials anxious for greater revenue, from men like Frankfurter who saw the chance to tax inflated salaries and big corporations, and from Robert La Follette and others in Congress who sought a wider distribution of purchasing power to hasten recovery. La Follette had already succeeded in the 1934 Revenue Act in forcing those who earned over $9,000 to pay more. One reason why progressive supporters of the president like La Follette and Harold Ickes were anxious to push Roosevelt out of the apparently conservative drift of early 1935 was their perception of the threat posed by radical dissidents who were complaining that the New Deal was not going far enough. The most visible and potent of these dissidents was Huey Long, whose Share Our Wealth scheme promised a massive redistribution of income and wealth. The threat of his third-party candidacy sent shivers down the spines of both national Democratic Party officials and established conservative southern congressmen. Driven from the right, pulled to the left, Roosevelt was ready in June 1935 to urge on Congress the 'very sound policy of encouraging a wider distribution of wealth'. He targeted in particular incomes over $1 million, vast fortunes created by inheritance, and big corporations. Huey Long said 'Amen' when the message was read in the Senate chamber.

The 1935 Revenue Act eventually hoisted top personal income tax rates from 63 per cent to 79 per cent, sharply graduated the income tax to penalise big corporations, and boosted estate taxes. The next year Congress passed an undistributed profits tax, taxing corporations which retained their profits rather than distributing them as dividends. Roosevelt needed extra revenue because of Congress's decision to pay the veterans' bonus in 1936 rather than

1945 and the Supreme Court's decision to invalidate the agricultural processing tax. The undistributed profits tax aimed to force corporations back to the securities market to raise capital, to prevent 'oversavings' by corporations, and to give stockholders greater control of the corporations they owned.

This profits tax was a lightning rod for business attacks on the New Deal particularly after the recession of 1937. But as Mark Leff has shown, the impact of New Deal taxation was largely symbolic. The New Deal did not break up large fortunes or concentrations of corporate wealth. The distribution of personal income remained largely static in the 1930s: the top 1 per cent retained one eighth of all personal income, almost as much as the poorest 40 per cent. The top 5 per cent retained over one quarter. In personal wealth, the share of the top 1 per cent rose from 28.3 per cent in 1933 to 30.6 per cent in 1939.

It was unreasonable to expect taxation to make significant changes when the federal government receipts were never more than a tenth of national income. But the failure to redistribute lay deeper than either the relative unimportance of taxation or a lack of radical will on the part of the president or Congress. When fewer than 10 per cent of American families earned as much as $3,200 a year and only 1 per cent drew over $10,000, simply raising taxes on the highest incomes would have made little difference to the distribution of income, even if the New Deal had soaked the rich more effectively. Taxing the highest incomes was simply not an effective revenue raiser. In the three years after the 1935 Revenue Act only one man, John D. Rockefeller, was subject to the highest tax rate. Genuine redistribution of income and wealth could only come by lowering tax exemptions dramatically to widen the tax base and to tax the middle class. A few politicians like Robert La Follette realised this but his efforts in 1934 and 1935 to lower exemptions were in vain. Most radical politicians preferred simply to denounce the super-rich. Most congressmen were scared stiff of alienating middle-class voters.

The characteristics of the modern tax system came not from the New Deal but from World War II. Less than 5 per cent of the population paid federal income taxes in the 1930s. During the war the figure rose to 74 per cent. In the 1930s taxes were paid in quarterly instalments a year after earnings. As more people paid larger sums in taxes, estimated taxes after 1943 were deducted from pay cheques. But the fact that far more Americans paid taxes did not mean that the tax system was fairer. Middle-income Americans remained relatively lightly taxed.

In 1935 Frankfurter reported that Brandeis's 'eyes became glowing coals of fire and shone with warm satisfaction' at Roosevelt's tax plans. But neither taxation nor government regulation had changed the basic structure of American industry. By 1936 and 1937 both advocates of market restoration and advocates of greater government planning feared that monopolies were stifling New Deal recovery by administered prices and restricted employment which crippled mass purchasing power. The recession of 1937–38 confirmed their worst fears. Anti-trust prosecution, however unsatisfactory, was one of the few methods of attack open to them. After all, even a champion of the control, rather than the break-up, of economic concentrations like Theodore Roosevelt had recognised that anti-trust suits were sometimes needed to deal with flagrant and unethical monopolies.

The Anti-Trust Division of the Justice Department had been anxious to resume prosecutions throughout the NRA. In 1938 its new chief, Thurman Arnold, strove to develop a realistic and sophisticated anti-trust policy. Arnold had few illusions about anti-trust policy and little sympathy for moral outrage as a basis for policy. 'Men like Senator Borah', he had written, 'had founded political careers on the continuation of such crusades which are enormously picturesque.' Arnold had little interest in 'trust-busting for the sake of trust-busting'. But he did believe that 'the sole weakness of the Sherman Act in the past has been the lack of an enforcement organization'. He persuaded Congress to grant him the funds to increase his staff from 48 to 200. By 1940 he had initiated 93 suits and 215 investigations. He pioneered the use of consent decrees which demanded, in return for suspending criminal prosecution, not merely a promise of reform in the future, but a detailed plan for the reorganisation of the industry. In particular, he worked to eliminate the distribution roadblocks which he thought were checking recovery. 'In order to keep prices up, industry is choking off its own avenues of distribution, decreasing employment and widening the disparity of prices.'

Arnold did not always get his own way in the administration. In oil, for example, Harold Ickes intended that the government should adopt wide planning powers over the industry but was anxious to preserve the existing structure of the industry, dominated by the major oil companies. At the same time, the Anti-Trust Division was planning to prosecute Standard Oil and other major companies. But Arnold received powerful backing from traditional congressional hostility to big business. Senator Joseph O'Mahoney, from Wyoming like Arnold, headed the Temporary National Economic Committee which carried out unprecedented investigations of monopolistic conditions in many sections of the American economy. The TNEC accumulated an amazing amount of information for the first time to show how the economy actually worked. Meanwhile, Arnold's staff went after the oil and car companies, the dairy industry, Paramount Pictures, the building and construction industry, the fertiliser industry, and tyre manufacturers.

Even this activity did not lead to any significant change in the structure of American industry. The TNEC's 37 volumes of evidence and 43 volumes of reports largely gathered dust to be used not for legislation, or for prosecution, but for later academic study of the workings of the economy. The anti-trust approach had inherent limitations. There was little support from any pressure groups. Organised labour, hostile to Arnold's attacks on their own monopolistic practices, in particular offered little backing. Even if Arnold's men were successful in court, the Anti-Trust Division was not equipped to keep a further eye on industries once it had moved on to other firms to prosecute.

But it was primarily World War II that aborted the New Deal's anti-trust drive. Ideas of business self-regulation triumphed once again, as they had in World War I. As in 1933, the emergency dictated the consent of businessmen. Business was reluctant to convert to defence production in 1939 at the start of the European war. Even after the attack on Pearl Harbor in December 1941 business was reluctant to expand war production to the necessary levels. Automobile manufacturers enjoying a belated boom in sales were reluctant to switch to tank and plane production. Businessmen feared dependence on government contracts and thought they would be left with inflated capacity at the end of the war. Secretary of War Henry Stimson succinctly summed up the government's response to this problem: 'If you are going to try to go to war, or to prepare for war in a capitalist country, you have got to let business make money out of the process or business won't work.'

As a result, businessmen flocked to Washington as dollar-a-year men in the war-time production agencies. Mouth-watering incentives were offered to industry in the form of tax write-offs, guaranteed profits, and government-financed plant construction. Anti-trust suits were suspended where they might slow down essential war production. Oil was a striking case. In order to secure the cooperation of the major companies in the war effort, the Justice Department had to sacrifice its anti-trust programme, suspending its prosecution of the American Petroleum Institute, 22 major companies and 344 subsidiaries, and Harold Ickes had to give up his ideas of government planning of the industry. Instead the government financed construction of the East Texas–Atlantic Coast pipeline and sanctioned the major companies' dominance of the industry. Robert Patterson, speaking for the armed services, claimed that 'we had to take American industry as we found it'. But the business dominance of the war agencies meant, as Richard Polenberg has argued, that they by no means left it as they found it. Two-thirds of military contracts went to 100 firms; the services preferred to deal with the large firms they already knew. When proponents of small businesses argued that they should be allowed to reconvert to peace-time production before the larger corporations in order to have an advantage in the post-war economy, both the armed services and businessmen in government insisted that there should be no premature reconversion.

Arnold himself was under no illusion as to what had happened. He recalled:

> FDR recognizing that he could have only one war at a time was content to declare a truce in the fight against monopoly. He was to have his foreign war; monopoly was to give him patriotic support – on its own terms.
>
> And so more than 90 per cent of all war contracts went to a handful of giant companies, many of them formerly linked by strong ties with the corporations of the Reich. The Big Fellows got the contracts, the little fellows were dependent upon sub-contracts with the big boys.

But it was going to be difficult to dislodge the large corporations.

New Deal liberals were increasingly aware of the dangers of big business dominance and monopoly control. The National Resources Planning Board in its report calling for expanded welfare in 1943 also called for vigorous anti-trust prosecution. This report was the basis for Roosevelt's Economic Bill of Rights, outlined in his State of the Union address in 1944. During the 1944 campaign he reaffirmed his opposition to corporate monopoly. Liberals were convinced that cartels would revert after the war to an economics of scarcity, of high prices, restricted production, and unemployment which would worsen what liberals regarded as the inevitable post-war depression. After Roosevelt's death in 1945, the Truman administration ignored liberal fears and opted for a reconversion policy that allowed business to throw off war-time controls as quickly as possible. When the anticipated depression failed to materialise, beleaguered liberals had lost any leverage they might have had for the imposition of government planning or controls or the revival of anti-trust prosecutions. With the unprecedented success of the post-war American economy, it was not long before liberal economists once again abandoned their anti-trust prescriptions, accepted the inevitability and desirability of large corporations, and advocated instead the concept of countervailing power to sustain their goal of social justice.

6 To spend or not to spend

Those New Dealers who attacked large corporations had a powerful moral case. But it was not clear that social justice in itself could generate economic recovery. The restoration of competition under fair and regulated terms and the rejuvenation of small businesses did not in the 1930s appear likely to produce new jobs. The attack on monopoly did promise to remove certain obstacles to recovery: oversavings and the maldistribution of purchasing power. Liberal fear that monopoly capitalism fed on an economics of scarcity grew stronger during the war. But the removal of such obstacles and the restoration of competition did not in themselves positively produce economic growth and extra jobs.

In the end, anti-trusters and liberal planners of the late 1930s found the answer in deficit spending. But it was not until 1938 that Roosevelt in any way consciously committed himself to spend his way out of the Depression and it was only World War II that demonstrated the exciting potential of deficit spending as an engine of economic expansion. Yet deficit spending appeared to be a perfect New Deal prescription. It promised economic growth with neither the creation of a large bureaucracy nor any infringement of management prerogatives. Why did it take so long for the New Deal to embrace this solution?

The economic theory to justify unbalanced budgets was available. Keynes's *General Theory* was not published until 1936, but he was a relentless populariser of his own ideas and his student R. F. Kahn made the principles of the multiplier widely known amongst economists on a visit to the United States in 1933. In any case some economists in the US were strongly influenced by J. A. Hobson's explanations of the capacity of economies to produce more than they could consume. Two of the most prominent economists, Waddill Catchings and William Foster, had advocated large-scale public works expenditure to offset shortfalls in purchasing power repeatedly in the 1920s and analysed the Depression in underconsumptionist terms. The idea that lack of purchasing power was the root cause of the Depression was a central tenet of the Brains Trust and fitted the ideas of institutional economists like Rex Tugwell. In April 1932 economists from the University of Chicago told a Senate committee that public works spending without raising the taxes to pay for it was the way out of the Depression.

Marriner Eccles, the Utah banker and Roosevelt's chairman of the Federal Reserve Board after 1934, told the Senate Finance Committee early in 1933 that a balanced budget should be deferred in favour of increasing mass purchasing power. Unaware of Keynes or his works, Eccles argued from 'naked-eye observations and experience in the inter-mountain region' that a balanced budget would inhibit recovery. The time to balance the budget was when recovery was assured: what was needed instead was an increase in national income through deficit spending. Eccles believed that unfettered economic individualism brought collective chaos. The government needed to exercise 'public control' of the economy through the 'compensatory instruments' of government spending, taxation, and monetary control. Unlike the 'direct control' of government planning, these indirect controls would preserve the maximum degree of freedom for businessmen in a liberal democratic capitalism.

Eccles consistently reassured leading New Dealers like Harry Hopkins and Henry Wallace that their spending on behalf of the unemployed and farmers was justifiable not only on humanitarian grounds but also on economic grounds. He also maintained close contacts with younger economists in the lower echelons of the New Deal, like Mordecai Ezekiel, Leon Henderson, Lauchlin Currie, and Gardiner Means, who eagerly devoured the new Keynesian analyses because they fitted in so well with their own perceptions.

Keynes's ideas also found favour with Felix Frankfurter, who saw them as the solution to the problem of financing public works on the scale that Justice Louis Brandeis envisaged. During the academic year 1933–34, which Frankfurter spent in England, he did his best to publicise Keynes's theories back in America. His efforts included arranging a famous, if mutually uncomprehending, meeting between Roosevelt and the English economist.

At the same time, there were politicians willing to advocate large-scale spending on public works as a means of 'priming the pump'. Progressive senators like La Follette and Wagner called for far greater spending than the New Deal envisaged in both 1933 and 1935. In any case, essential New Deal spending on relief for the unemployed made it impossible to approach a balanced budget through fiscal 1936.

But there were limits to any consensus in favour of government spending. Most New Dealers believed that recovery would come from the revival of private investment. That was why it was so important to restore confidence by reforming the marketing of securities and by afterwards reassuring business in the administration of the SEC. Government spending would simply prime the pump to set off the revival of private spending. Similarly, business advocates of spending in 1933 saw public spending as a 'quick fix' designed to 'start up' the economy, not a permanent crutch. Most supporters of government spending did not want to unbalance the budget. Increased spending would have to be paid for by increased revenue in the near future. Even La Follette in 1934 was pushing forward his tax reforms as a means of increasing revenue in order to limit the budget deficit. Further, as a panacea for recovery, fiscal policy took second place to monetary policy. Price rises through inflation were familiar demands of southern and western farmers. Going off the gold standard in 1933 partly satisfied that demand. For a time late in 1933 Roosevelt believed that the 'commodity dollar' theories of George Warren and Frank Pearson would bring instant recovery. Manipulating the price of gold by government purchases, it was believed, would raise the price level. Such solutions promised quicker and more painless results (even if they did not deliver them) than pump-priming.

Roosevelt himself accepted unbalanced budgets only reluctantly. In his Pittsburgh campaign speech of 1932 he had castigated Hoover for extravagance and had rashly pledged to reduce government expenditure by 25 per cent. He was embarrassed by Republican criticism of the budget deficits under the New Deal. He justified them by arguing that it was only extraordinary spending for humanitarian reasons that unbalanced the budget; the ordinary budget of the government, he argued, was balanced. He looked for ways to show that deficits were being scaled down so that he could promise a balanced budget for fiscal 1938. He could cite the declining deficits as evidence that the economy was recovering. In 1936, an election year, he was even prepared to cut spending on the Civilian Conservation Corps, arguably the New Deal agency that had more congressional support than any other.

As a result, federal spending from 1933 to 1936 was never more than 5.9 per cent of Gross National Product (in contrast to state and local government spending which in fiscal 1936 was 9.6 per cent of GNP). Budget deficits of $3.63 billion in fiscal 1934 and $4.43 billion in fiscal 1936 did help to raise GNP to its 1929 level and reduce the jobless total to 14.3 million. But those deficits did not produce full recovery. After all, Hoover had run deficits of $2.74 billion and $2.6 billion in his last years in office. In addition, state governments rigorously attempted to balance their budgets during the early New Deal, thus offsetting much of the expansionary effect of federal spending. The calculations of economic historians E. Cary Brown and Larry Peppers show how far New Deal spending was from the level of deficits needed to create a full employment GNP.

In December 1936 Roosevelt was given a clear choice as far as fiscal policy was concerned. His chairman of the Federal Reserve, Marriner Eccles, argued that the federal government would have to continue spending to continue the move towards recovery, since private enterprise was not yet ready to take up the slack if the government cut back. The government should act as a 'compensatory agent' in the economy for the failings of the private sector. Roosevelt's Secretary of the Treasury, Henry Morgenthau Jr, argued that in order to revive the private investment necessary for full recovery, the federal budget must be balanced so that business would have the confidence to invest. If the budget could be balanced, that would be the final evidence that recovery had been achieved. 'This was the moment . . .', Morgenthau argued, 'to throw away the crutches and see if American private enterprise could stand on its own feet.'

The opportunity to confound his conservative critics was too tempting for Roosevelt to resist. Tax revenues were up; the costs of relief and recovery programmes seemed to be falling; even Eccles and Hopkins were worried about inflationary pressures, particularly the impact of the price of materials in the construction industry. Roosevelt then opted for the conservative course. Government spending fell from $10.3 billion in 1936 to $9.6 billion in 1937. The budget would certainly have been balanced in fiscal 1938 if government revenues had held firm. The combination of cuts in government spending, the collection of regressive social security taxes, and high interest rates imposed by the Federal Reserve Board was catastrophic. The country fell into deep recession. The steady rise in GNP was reversed. Production declined by 70 per cent in steel, 50 per cent in automobiles, 40 per cent in rubber, and 75 per cent in electrical manufacturing. Five million workers lost their jobs as unemployment reached almost 20 per cent in this 'Roosevelt recession'.

Once again, Roosevelt was given a choice. Morgenthau, backed by conservative cabinet members like James Farley, argued that the recession demonstrated that business did not yet have the confidence to invest. It was therefore all the more important to secure that confidence by balancing the budget and abandoning labour and tax reforms that so disturbed businessmen. 'What businessmen want to know', said Morgenthau, 'is are we headed toward State socialism or are we going to continue on a capitalistic basis.' To the Secretary of the Treasury, balancing the budget had now become a test of the New Deal's moral credibility. The balanced budget was no longer a welcome indicator of recovery; it was to be the instrument to secure recovery. The spenders, led by Eccles, Harry Hopkins, and Harold Ickes, argued the reverse. The recession demonstrated that business was not ready to take up the slack. The government had to resume spending. They joined their pleas for more spending to attacks on monopoly capitalism which was threatening recovery through high prices.

The recession caused a profound crisis of confidence for New Deal liberals. Their liberalism put great store by bold presidential leadership, yet the president was now floundering. The lack of ideological coherence of the wide variety of programmes that constituted the New Deal did not trouble them as long as economic recovery accompanied the social gains that they had achieved. As that recovery daily eroded, there were inevitable twinges of doubt: perhaps their conservative critics had been right after all. The stakes were high: the price of failure awful to contemplate. As they watched authoritarian and fascist regimes triumph overseas, they pondered the possibility of a fascist victor in the United States if big business triumphed over Roosevelt.

Roosevelt hesitated through the winter of 1937–38. In the spring it looked as if Morgenthau and the conservatives would prevail. Many of Roosevelt's instincts favoured a balanced budget. Moreover, Morgenthau, his Dutchess County neighbour and oldest political friend, seemed to be in a powerful position to win the day for the budget balancers. But the conservative option was not politically appealing. It invited an activist president to do nothing. It required concessions to a business community which had long exhausted Roosevelt's patience. Advocates of spending at least offered him the chance to act, and they could remind the president of Hoover's fate as a powerful antidote to inaction.

In April 1938 Harry Hopkins, recuperated at last from major surgery for cancer, ambushed Roosevelt at Warm Springs. Hopkins, fully in sympathy with Eccles's pleas for renewed spending, was accompanied by Leon Henderson, Aubrey Williams, and Beardsley Ruml, a Macy's executive appointed to the New York Reserve Board by Eccles and already influenced by Keynesian economics. Their data convinced the president to agree to a $3.75 billion spending package. By the time Morgenthau saw him on his return to Washington it was too late to change his mind. The Secretary of the Treasury was left to fume that Roosevelt had 'lost all sense of proportion'.

Roosevelt told the nation that the budget could only be balanced if national income increased. Congress, with its eyes on the 1938 elections, agreed. By January 1939 Roosevelt was talking frankly about his 'compensatory fiscal policy'. For fiscal 1939 the deficit climbed back to $3.8 billion. Recovery came quickly as modest deficits were outstripped by the needs of defence spending as Roosevelt first prepared for, then embarked on war.

Younger New Dealers now eagerly turned to Keynesian economics as an intellectual justification for what they were doing. Keynes's ideas triumphed as well among American academic economists. Yet Roosevelt was still uncomfortable with a Keynesian approach. Lauchlin Currie succinctly summed up the president's dilemma for him in March 1940: 'I have come to suspect that you are somewhat bothered by the apparent conflict between the humanitarian and social aims of the New Deal and the dictates of "sound economics" '. Currie assured Roosevelt that 'sound economics' were not in conflict with New Deal social goals: on the contrary the increase in national consumption needed to produce full employment demanded that New Deal social goals be fulfilled. By the time of his State of the Union address in 1944 Roosevelt seemed to have accepted his economists' advice.

Roosevelt's failure in the 1930s to contemplate large enough budget deficits had two consequences beyond the simple failure to bring full employment. First, limits on New Deal spending did seriously affect its ability to meet its social goals: unemployment relief, housing, rural poverty programmes, jobs schemes, all were handicapped, often disastrously, by inadequate appropriations. Second, the Roosevelt recession, due in part to the inadequate fiscal policy, gave a tremendous boost to the conservative critics of the president. Before 1937 conservative critics had to concede that for most Americans conditions were better than they had been before Roosevelt took office. During the Roosevelt recession these same critics could gleefully maintain that their traditional arguments had been right all along. The recession gave a sharp impetus to the growing bipartisan coalition of congressional conservatives. In the Conservative Manifesto, the ideological underpinning of that coalition made public in December 1937, Senator Josiah Bailey of North Carolina powerfully rehearsed the traditional arguments for limited government. A balanced budget by cutting government spending, reductions in the tax burden on business, the removal of government competition with business, the end of disincentives to work, and the breaking up of the government's partnership with organised labour were the preconditions for business confidence and economic growth.

The ability of the New Deal to counter this conservative vision was sharply limited by its failure to find the key to full employment. Many New Dealers indeed believed that the American economy had reached maturity: that there might be a permanent army of 6,000,000 unemployed which New Deal agencies would have to cater for. This vision of the future was much less appealing than the simple certainties of the conservatives to a people whose traditional notions of individualism and opportunity were so persistent.

The war dramatically shifted the focus of the debate and seemed to demonstrate the efficiency of Keynesian economics. Government spending rose to over a third of GNP; the budget deficits soared from a 1930s high of $4.43 billion to over $57 billion. GNP almost doubled between 1939 and 1942 and over 17,000,000 new jobs were created in 5 years. At long last, New Dealers did seem to have found the key to a full employment economy. In Henry Wallace's formulation, the government could aim to provide 60,000,000 jobs, provided monopoly capitalism did not block its efforts and provided purchasing power was equitably distributed along the lines laid down in the Economic Bill of Rights. To the surprise of the liberals, war-time growth was sustained after the war. Liberals had foreseen a demobilisation-inspired post-war depression. Instead, consumer purchasing power, pent up during the war by the shortage of consumer goods, was released to maintain demand and to fuel an unprecedented boom between 1948 and 1952. It seemed that full employment could be achieved without the redistribution of existing resources but rather through the simple expansion of the available resources. The economic cake could be increased, not merely sliced up differently.

At the same time, the war educated important segments of the business world to the benefits of government links and the advantages of government spending. In the late 1930s Keynesian ideas began to have some appeal to those businessmen like the members of the Business Advisory Council who still retained links with the New Deal. Men like Donald Nelson were immediately available to head war-time production agencies. By 1938 others, like Ralph Flanders, Lincoln Filene, Morris Leeds, and Harry Dennison, looked to deficit spending as a relatively safe and conservative way to bring about economic recovery, if it could be stripped of New Deal reformism. By 1942, Robert M. Collins has shown, these more positive business responses to the New Deal had coalesced to form the Committee for Economic Development, an organisation for research and publicity under Paul Hoffman of the Studebaker automobile company; the Committee saw its central concern as mapping out the joint role of business and government in creating full employment in the post-war world. Here was the evidence of corporate liberalism that New Left historians have searched for in vain in the 1930s. Yet even the Committee for Economic Development represented a minority of businessmen and its driving forces were not themselves representative of the centre firms of the American economy. At the end of the war, most businessmen reverted to knee-jerk hostility to government interference and government spending.

7 New Deal limitations

It is easy enough to list the limitations of New Deal policies for industrial recovery. Recovery did not come until the war; the NRA was dominated by the businessmen it was supposed to regulate; banking and securities reform simply stabilised the capitalist order; taxation and anti-trust policy neither redistributed wealth or income nor wrought any changes in the structure of American industry; for the most part the New Deal relied on private investment to stimulate recovery yet its rhetoric precluded the private confidence to invest; fiscal policy did not become a consciously expansionary tool until the war.

If the New Deal helped make the world safe for capitalism, that had always been Roosevelt's intention. If large corporations came out of World War II benefiting from a stable, ordered, and rapidly growing economy, that was not evidence that the New Deal was simply a 'corporate liberal' plot to extend corporate hegemony. The NRA, banking and securities reform, and deficit spending – all seen by radical critics as devices to perpetuate conservative and business strength – were all at the time bitterly opposed by their supposed corporate beneficiaries. The war, rather than the New Deal, was responsible for the restored popular legitimacy of corporate leaders and the close alliance of the industrial-military complex.

It is not easy to see how the New Deal could have pursued more radical or effective policies. The economic emergency of 1933 created constraints as well as opportunities. The chance to nationalise the banks was largely illusory when the nation's capital and cash resources had to be unfrozen as quickly as possible. Cooperation with businessmen in the NRA was inescapable if NRA codes were to be implemented quickly in the interests of recovery.

Alternative policies were neither necessarily available nor guaranteed to succeed. Neither in 1933 nor later did there exist the mandate or the state capacity to plan the economy in an overhead and central fashion. A more vigorous drive against monopoly would have met even more bitter business opposition than government planning. In itself, such a campaign offered no means of creating new jobs. A genuinely redistributive tax policy would have involved the politically impossible task of broadening the tax base and heavily increasing middle-class taxation. It is not even clear that an earlier commitment to a more expansionist fiscal policy would have worked. Could policy-makers in the 1930s have devised ways of spending enough money to secure full economic recovery? Did the expertise and mechanisms exist for a larger public works programme than that operated by the PWA? How big did the deficit need to be to secure full employment? Would such a deficit have been politically feasible and economically successful in the face of intransigent business opposition? Do Keynesian economic policies work only in time of war or cold war?

3
Strife and Satisfaction: Labour

More important to American workers than the faltering steps taken by the New Deal towards economic recovery was the startling growth of organised labour. The New Deal may have failed to disturb the basic structure of American business, but it did appear to have facilitated the formation of a countervailing force in the trades union movement. The 1930s saw the largest ever growth in union membership in a single decade in both absolute and relative terms: trades union membership trebled; by 1940 23 per cent of the non-agricultural labour force was organised. The gains were to be decisive and permanent: by 1945 the war had consolidated the growth in membership at 25 per cent of the workforce. Thereafter there would be no significant increases.

As important as the size of the growth was its distribution in the economy. In the 1920s organised labour had been hemmed into the railroads, coal mining and the needle trades (all sick industries), and craft unions of skilled workers, particularly in construction. The great majority of semi-skilled and unskilled, often immigrant, workers in the mass production, basic manufacturing industries were unorganised. By 1940 those great centre industries of autos, steel, rubber, and electrical goods, dominated by large national corporations and opposed to organised labour, had been unionised. Labour appeared to have climbed, if not captured, the commanding heights of the economy. At the same time labour's political position had been transformed. Traditionally, the labour movement had been non-partisan. So weak was the political leverage of the American Federation of Labor in 1933 that Roosevelt had been able blithely to ignore its opposition to his appointment of Frances Perkins as Secretary of Labor. By 1940, however, the unions were an integral part of the Democratic Party: their funds made the largest contribution to the party's campaign chest; their members were a crucial element in the New Deal electoral coalition; as war approached, their leaders could demand representation at the highest levels of government policy-making.

1 Government and the union leadership

Two of the most obvious weaknesses of the labour movement before 1933 had been the hostility of the government and the cautious conservatism of the union leaders. Under the New Deal, government and the law came down firmly on the side of union organisation and a dynamic and militant leadership came to the fore in the unions themselves.

Before the New Deal the coercive power of the state had been largely arrayed against labour. Neither the courts nor local, state, or federal governments acted to restrain determined employers from using a battery of anti-union devices: firing and blacklisting union organisers, espionage, violence against strikers, and the use of strikebreakers. Courts willingly issued wide-ranging injunctions that hamstrung union organisers, pickets, and strikers. Local government officials tended to act as an arm of the employer, not only in the mining, steel, and textile communities where a single company dominated the town, but also in more heterogeneous communities where local officials deferred, nevertheless, to the politically powerful middle-class support for employers. Thus, union organisers were harassed, beaten up, and driven out, strikers and their families were denied public and private relief, picket lines were broken up, and employer and vigilante violence tolerated. State governors reinforced this bias by a willingness to send in the National Guard, ostensibly to maintain law and order, in practice to protect scabs, keep plants open, and break strikes. The federal government had similarly used troops and sought crippling anti-union injunctions in a number of major disputes. What protection the federal government did offer organised labour was either temporary (under the National War Labor Board in World War I) or in railroads (where a clear constitutional mandate existed) or under the Norris–La Guardia Act of 1932 (which outlawed the injunctions that upheld 'yellow dog' contracts), which was not declared constitutional until 1938.

Section 7a of the National Industrial Recovery Act required that NRA codes guarantee workers the right of collective bargaining. As they attempted to assert this right in practice in an unprecedented series of strikes in 1933, so the administration established a tripartite National Labor Board which attempted to hammer out an acceptable body of procedures that would translate the general intent of 7a into practical application. The Board tried to settle strikes on the basis of the Reading Formula, which it had devised to settle a strike of hosiery workers at the Berkshire Knitting Mills: strikers were to be rehired without discrimination, the Board would hold elections among the workers to choose their representatives, and the organisation which won the majority of votes would exclusively represent all the workers. In the summer of 1934 Roosevelt sought to augment the Board's authority by creating a National Labor Relations Board, which proceeded to hammer out a body of labour common law, based on the Reading Formula, and tried to define and proscribe a whole series of unfair practices by the employers.

The difficulty of enforcing the Labor Board's decisions, coupled with the collapse of the NRA, led to the Wagner National Labor Relations Act of 1935, which effectively gave statutory authority to what the NLRB bureacrats had been attempting to do. Not only was a new independent three-man National Labor Relations Board empowered to hold employee elections based on majority rule and exclusive representation; but the Act also outlawed company unions and proscribed unfair labour practices by the employer (some defined in the Act, others interpreted in later NLRB rulings). The law, which had previously offered little or no protection against an anti-union employer, now gave unions a means to compel employers to recognise them as a result of NLRB elections, banned a major employer weapon, the company union, and provided unions with redress against a whole series of unfair employer tactics: discriminatory discharge, espionage, blacklisting, and unfair propaganda.

Nor could employers any longer rely as a matter of course on the use of troops by state and federal governments to break strikes. This became most obvious during the tumultuous automobile workers' sitdown strike at General Motors' Fisher Body plants in Flint, Michigan, in 1937. Similar occupation of plants by strikers eventually would be denounced by the Supreme Court, and in the

1937 dispute General Motors twice secured injunctions to remove the men. But Roosevelt made it clear that he wanted the strike settled without force and Governor Frank Murphy was determined not to cause bloodshed by sending in troops to evict the strikers. Murphy did send in troops after the Battle of the Running Bulls, when the men at Fisher Body Number 2 plant violently repulsed the attempt by the company and the police to blockade the plant and cut the food supplies. However, he used the National Guard not to remove the strikers and break the strike, but strictly to maintain the status quo and to act as a buffer between the strikers and the company. By denying the company the means of recapturing its plant, Murphy effectively guaranteed the eventual triumph of the strikers. Some other Democratic governors (although not in Ohio and Connecticut) in the northern industrial states made equally clear their reluctance to do the employers' dirty work for them.

Linked to this new protective government attitude was a second major change: the willingness of some union leaders to seek out and organise hitherto unorganised semi-skilled and unskilled workers into industrial unions. Before 1933 the strength of the American labour movement, with the notable exception of the United Mine Workers, lay in craft unions in which skilled workers, for example machinists or carpenters, would join others of the same craft, irrespective of the sector of industry they worked in. This was a historically appropriate mode of organisation for skilled workers employed in small units where their hard-won skill gave them considerable leverage over their employers. It had far less relevance in mass-production industries where technological change enabled employers to bring in rapidly trained semi- and unskilled workers. Leaders of the traditional craft unions showed little interest in organising these, often new immigrant, workers and were ill-prepared to take advantage of the opportunities offered by the New Deal.

Three union leaders, however, saw Section 7a as a golden opportunity to capitalise on government support, recapture members for their struggling unions, and compel recognition from the employers: John L. Lewis of the United Mine Workers, Sidney Hillman of the Amalgamated Clothing Workers Association, and David Dubinsky of the International Ladies' Garment Workers' Union. Both coal mining and the needle trades had been sick industries in the 1920s. They suffered from chronic overproduction and excessive competition. Each union had seen its membership dwindle, but the NRA seemed to offer just the sort of economic stabilisation that their leaders had called for. They organised feverishly and fought successful strikes to secure favourable codes and contracts. As a result, the UMW was recognised in mines that moved over 90 per cent of the nation's soft coal, Hillman more than doubled his union's membership by the end of 1933, and the ILGWU, which had sunk to a membership of a mere 40,000 workers in early 1933, rose to 200,000 in a few months.

Lewis believed that what he achieved in the mines could be achieved elsewhere, and that an unprecedented opportunity which might never arise again existed for the AFL to organise the mass-production workers. Throughout the 1930s he was at the forefront of the drive to tackle head-on the bastions of the open shop, to wrest economic power from the oligopolists by bringing unskilled workers into industrial unions which, by organising all the workers in a particular industry, could challenge national corporations. At first sight Lewis's role was a surprising one. He had presided over the collapse of his own union in the 1920s, and had unsuccessfully tried to protect the mineworkers by supporting stabilisation measures for the industry as a whole. A mixture of corruption, physical force, and Red-baiting had enabled him ruthlessly to suppress radical challenges to his own authority and to maintain autocratic control of his union. But the union he controlled was essentially a paper organisation. The miners were among the most militant of American workers in 1931 and 1932, but that militancy was not directed by John L. Lewis but by organisations like the Communist National Miners Union. The UMW simply did not have the strike or relief funds to sustain any strikers. What Lewis did have was a keen sense for the levers of power and a single-minded determination to exploit favourable situations. From 1933 to 1935 he impatiently prodded the AFL Executive Council to launch an organising drive in the mass-production industries and he championed the idea that workers in those industries form industrial unions.

The president of the AFL, William Green, had long recognised the need for industrial unions. AFL craft unions, like the Carpenters, were prepared to organise workers with different skills if their jobs affected the strategic position of their own craft. The AFL

Executive Council, however, deferred to the cautious conservatism of men like Arthur Wharton of the Machinists and John P. Frey of the Metal Trades, who jealously protected the exclusive jurisdiction given them by their international union charters over all workers of their particular skill. Wharton and Frey regarded the Federal Labor Unions which the AFL had finally sanctioned in the auto, rubber, and electrical goods industries simply as holding operations until the members of those federal locals could be parcelled out to the appropriate craft union. By the AFL convention in 1935 at Atlantic City Lewis recognised that the AFL would never commit adequate resources to organise the mass-production industries. In November he therefore founded the Committee for Industrial Organization (later the Congress of Industrial Organizations) to do what the AFL had signally failed to do.

Initially Lewis and the UMW *were* the CIO. Aside from Hillman and Dubinsky, the other founder members represented weak and small unions like the Hatters and the Oil Workers. Lewis entrusted his own lieutenants, Adolph Germer, Powers Hapgood, and Philip Murray, to run the organising drives in autos, rubber, and steel. The UMW bankrolled the Steel Workers' Organizing Committee. Lewis, a Republican who had supported Hoover in 1932, decided that the CIO drive needed the protection of the federal government, protection that could only be secured by the re-election of Franklin Roosevelt. He founded the Labor Non-Partisan League to support Roosevelt and committed CIO funds and organisers to the Democratic campaign. The UMW committed almost $600,000 to the re-election drive. Lewis personally negotiated key settlements with General Motors and United States Steel. Until he failed to persuade labour voters to support Republican presidential nominee Wendell Willkie in 1940, Lewis personified the new-found power of the labour movement.

The forces unleashed by Lewis seemed irresistible during most of 1936 and 1937. In 1936 the United Rubber Workers successfully struck Goodyear at Akron; SWOC organisers stormed through Pennsylvania signing up members and campaigning for Roosevelt; and sitdown strikes erupted in the auto industry at the end of the year. The sitdown strike seemed to solve a persistent dilemma for the unions. Unions could only overcome the fear and suspicion of the majority of the workers if they could mount a successful strike, but a successful strike was impossible if they did not have the support of a majority of workers. The sitdown strike enabled a small minority of workers to halt the production of an entire company by occupying a single strategic plant. A successful strike would then bring the rest of the workforce into the union.

The single most important confrontation took place in January and February 1937. Not only did the United Automobile Workers take on General Motors, the market leader in the auto industry and probably the largest manufacturing corporation in the world, but it did so in Flint, Michigan, a town completely dominated by GM where the UAW local had only 122 members in early 1936. The tactic of the sitdown was crucial to UAW success. By taking over Fisher Body Number 1 plant, which contained the dies for GM's 1937 models, a small number of workers paralysed the whole corporation. GM's production of cars fell to a mere 150 a week and in February the company capitulated and agreed to bargain with the union. Chrysler backed down shortly afterwards.

The UAW membership rose from 98,000 in February to 400,000 by the summer. In the aftermath of Flint, United States Steel, the country's first billion-dollar corporation, its largest steelmaker, and a relentless foe of unionisation, settled with Lewis without a strike. In rubber, a March strike brought a settlement with Firestone, Goodrich signed a contract in March 1938, and US Rubber in August the same year. In electrical goods, RCA and General Electric negotiated collective bargaining agreements in 1937 and 1938. Defeats in Little Steel and textiles halted the CIO's momentum, but it had for the first time unionised the heart of America's manufacturing industry. John L. Lewis, in the words of his biographers, had moved labour 'from the fringe of the economy to its core'.

2 Rank-and-file militancy

The change in government attitude and the shift in union leadership, however, are not a sufficient explanation of the labour breakthrough of the 1930s. Neither change was unambiguous and, as historians increasingly emphasised in the late 1960s and 1970s, both were linked to militant action by the workers themselves.

Historians and social scientists faced a paradox. The 1930s more and more seemed a heroic golden age of labour activism. Workers seemed to be part of an anti-capitalist mass movement: industrially militant, tackling employers head-on in ferocious strikes; politically radical, responding to Communist and Socialist leadership, and acting as a powerful force for social justice in the Democratic Party. Yet the post-war unions seemed so passive, complacent, and conservative. Union leaders appeared to accept the existing economic system and the employers' prerogatives: they fought for better wages and fringe benefits for their members, but within an ordered system of contract negotiation. They eschewed strikes except at the termination of contracts and, indeed, disciplined wildcat strikers themselves. Contract negotiations and union officials were increasingly remote from rank-and-file union members. Unions led by highly paid career officials were more and more bureaucratic, undemocratic, and sometimes corrupt. In the Cold War the unions were staunchly anti-Communist, accepted the liberal consensus values of American capitalism, supported the Vietnam War, and opposed the student and minority group radicals of the 1960s.

The fate of two of the unions that had been the cutting edge of labour radicalism in the 1930s seemed to typify this paradox. The United Mine Workers, which had championed the cause of industrial unionism so vigorously, became reluctant to threaten the fragility of the mining industry by aggressive wage demands or by insisting on rigorous safety standards. Rank-and-file opinion was smothered in a union which became ever more autocratic in Lewis's last years as president. Ageing union officials were increasingly unaccountable. The union's pension fund was scandalously mismanaged. Ultimately Lewis's successor as president solved the problems of a reform challenge from the discontented rank and file by ordering the murder of his rival in the presidential election. The United Automobile Workers which had boasted one of the most democratic union constitutions became a bureaucratised and staunchly anti-Communist giant under Walter Reuther. Its once independent locals lost power to the centralised authority of the international union. Internal debate and controversy which had always threatened to spill over into anarchic factionalism was stifled by the overwhelming power of propaganda and patronage wielded by the union leadership. Its expert negotiators won increasingly generous wage and welfare benefits for its members,

but contracts were imposed on the membership, grass-roots democracy in the locals atrophied, and the union failed to represent the
continued alienation felt by the workers on the assembly lines.
When that alienation bubbled over into wildcat strikes in the 1970s
UAW officials themselves broke up picket lines to force their
members back to work.

Radical historians offered a simple explanation to resolve this
paradox. A potentially revolutionary mass movement of industrial
workers had been defused by corporate liberals in the New Deal
and the business world. Far from stimulating workers' protest and
union organisation, the New Deal, supported by the more sophisticated elements of the corporate élite, acted to limit the damage
done by rank-and-file militancy and to contain protest by channelling it into safe and responsible trades unionism.

Such an analysis with its emphasis on rank-and-file protest,
rather than on government policy and union leadership, as the
decisive force in the struggle has plausibility. The ambiguous
government attitude, the irrelevance of the Wagner Act to some of
the major organising gains, the spontaneity of worker discontent,
and the role of political radicals in the breakthrough, all add some
credence to the revisionist interpretation.

The commitment of the New Deal to the union cause was by no
means wholehearted. Many New Dealers, including Roosevelt,
Secretary of Labor Perkins, and the leaders of the NRA, had what
might be called a 'progressive' attitude to industrial relations – if
employers provided reasonable working conditions, workers
would not need unions. The NRA was expected to remove the
sources of industrial conflict, not to stimulate it. NRA leaders
were taken aback when worker demands for union recognition
unleashed a wave of strikes in the summer of 1933. The establishment of the National Labor Board in August was an *ad hoc* move
to prevent those strikes disrupting the recovery drive. The employers' most effective device for thwarting 7a was the formation
of company unions: in steel alone there were over 90 company
unions in 1934, compared to 7 in 1932. NRA administrators Hugh
Johnson and Donald Richberg believed that such unions, which
made a mockery of independent collective bargaining, were
consistent with 7a. Both men were opposed to the principle of
majority rule and exclusive representation laid down in the
Reading Formula and reiterated in NLB and NLRB rulings. Their

alternative – proportional representation – played into the hands of employers, who could divide and rule their workforce in piecemeal negotiation and favour their company unions. Roosevelt appeared to side with Johnson and Richberg rather than his Labor Boards. In the settlement to the auto industry dispute which he personally dictated in the spring of 1934 he came down in favour of proportional representation: a settlement which was entirely congenial to the anti-union auto manufacturers and which effectively sanctioned company unions.

Given these attitudes, it is not surprising that the Labor Boards under the NRA found it so difficult to enforce their pro-labour rulings. When determined employers decided to resist 7a, there was little that could be done to stop them. When the National Labor Board settled a strike at Weirton Steel, Ed Weir allowed the workers to vote only for the company union in the representation elections. At Budd Manufacturing the management simply refused to hold the NLB-ordered election. In neither case did the NRA Compliance Division remove the Blue Eagle from the recalcitrant firms. The authority of the National Labor Relations Board during the NRA was undercut by the existence of autonomous labour boards for autos, textiles, and steel and the reluctance of either the Compliance Division or the Justice Department to prosecute NLRB cases.

Roosevelt could claim little credit for the Wagner Act of 1935, which remedied so many of those weaknesses. The need to close the loopholes revealed in the operation of the NRA Labor Boards was felt most keenly by Senator Wagner. Wagner had come to the United States in 1886 when he was nine. His German parents soon returned home but Wagner stayed to enter City College and become a lawyer. Drawn into local Democratic politics, Wagner represented a new breed of machine politician in Tammany Hall. Well educated, Wagner eschewed corruption and sought instead to benefit his lower-income constituents by social welfare legislation. In his first term as a state legislator Wagner shared a room with young Assemblyman Al Smith. Tammany boss Charles F. Murphy soon made Wagner and Smith majority leaders of the state Senate and Assembly. Both soon found themselves investigating the appalling Triangle Shirtwaist Factory fire of 1911 when 146 women workers were killed in a New York sweatshop. Thirty years later Wagner could still win a bet by remembering the exact date and hour the fire started. The two Tammany progressives piloted through the legislature 54 of the 60 bills they proposed regulating factory conditions.

Wagner went on to sit on the New York Supreme Court and was elected to the United States Senate in 1926. His friend Smith became gradually less enamoured of economic reform and government regulation. Wagner by contrast became the epitome of the urban liberalism which under the New Deal sought to provide economic security for lower-income groups. There was scarcely a piece of New Deal industrial and welfare legislation that did not bear Wagner's imprint. He had been an early supporter of large-scale public works spending; he was largely responsible for the labour standards provisions of the Industrial Recovery Act; he masterminded the passage of the National Labor Relations Act; as an early advocate of unemployment insurance he sponsored the Social Security Act; he doggedly won legislative backing for low-cost public housing in the face of presidential indifference. Few senators have seen as many of their ideas put on the statute book; but few senators have been as hard-working, constructive, and well informed as Wagner. Running through all Wagner's thinking was not just concern for social justice but also a conviction that the American economy could not operate at its fullest capacity unless mass purchasing power was guaranteed by government spending, welfare benefits, and the protection of workers' rights. Wagner continued to fight for these ideas as the tide turned against the New Deal; he strove to fill the gaps in the new social security system by pushing first for health insurance, then, during the war, for a federalised social security system. He sought legislation that would guarantee full employment after the war. It was fitting that his final speech in the Senate in 1947 was a passionate defence of his labour relations act against the Republican Taft-Hartley bill, which planned to curb labour's powers.

The ideas in the 1935 National Labor Relations Act were Wagner's, in collaboration with the frustrated officials of the NLRB. Neither Roosevelt, his Secretary of Labor, nor the NRA leaders showed any enthusiasm. With little help from the administration, Wagner almost single-handedly brought his act to a vote. He was able to exploit the perception of many congressmen that the 1934 election results showed a pro-labour swing in public opinion and an apparent collapse in the prestige of the business community. Only when the Senate Labor Committee favourably reported the bill did Roosevelt privately agree not to hinder Wagner's efforts. Only when eventual passage in both houses seemed inevitable, and the Supreme Court invalidation of the NRA left him bereft of policy options, did Roosevelt throw his weight behind the Wagner Act as a piece of legislation to which he then assigned 'must' status – the highest priority. Thus, the New Deal's commitment to labour was belated and cautious.

The two key settlements in the labour breakthrough of the 1930s occurred outside the framework of the Wagner Act. It was not the law which guaranteed the union victory at General Motors and US Steel but the simple exercise of union muscle at a strategic moment in an economic upswing. Both settlements took place before the Supreme Court had declared the Wagner Act constitutional in the Jones and Laughlin case (April 1937). In neither instance could the unions have gone to the NLRB since neither the UAW nor SWOC had signed up a majority of the relevant workers. Indeed the key to both settlements was that the unions were given time to sign up the necessary members during which the management promised not to negotiate with other representatives.

What determined the CIO's success at both GM and US Steel was not the law, which neither employer recognised, but the unions' ability to exploit the employers' need to maintain production at a time of economic recovery. Between 1932 and 1936 GM had quadrupled its car and truck sales. 1936 was a boom year, as it was for all car firms. GM's pre-tax profits from its motor vehicle division were $163 million compared to a $7 million loss in 1932. To meet the expected increased demand in 1937 GM invested millions to reorganise production. With such an investment, GM could not afford a long strike, especially as the Flint strike so tied up production that, instead of 15,000 cars a week, GM was producing 150. Seeing its rivals taking over its market share, GM had little choice but to negotiate a settlement. Similarly, US Steel did not want to lose out on prospective recovery. Its chairman, Myron Taylor, knew that US Steel was targeted for a strike at its Carnegie–Illinois complex: after the success of the Flint sitdown he knew how effective a strike led by the well-funded and well-organised SWOC might be. He also knew that US Steel was losing its competitive edge to smaller firms that produced lighter strip and sheet steel and that these firms would be only too anxious to see US Steel take on the unions. These considerations, not the Wagner Act, led Taylor to horrify his fellow steel executives by signing an agreement with Lewis.

The historian has to be impressed by the spontaneous surges of worker militancy, translated into strike action and mass organisation: rank-and-file militancy that, far from being orchestrated by union leaders, often prodded hesitant leaders into action. John L. Lewis made the strategic decision to capitalise on 7a and launch the major organising drive in coal in the summer of 1933, but his organisers, like Van Bittner in West Virginia, reported that the miners were organising themselves in any case. As John Brophy recalled, there was 'a different feeling among the miners everywhere. They seem to feel that they are once more free men.' During the NRA, workers flocked into unions in some of the most unpromising and inhospitable places for organisation. Few industries were more determinedly open shop than steel yet not only did the membership of the old, ineffectual Amalgamated Association rise tenfold and the rank and file revolt against the leadership of Mike 'Grandmother' Tighe, but even the company unions established by the steel companies revolted against their employers. Some 40,000–50,000 rubber workers streamed into Federal Locals in the summer and fall of 1933 at meetings 'something like a cross between a big picnic and a religious revival'.

Nowhere were the forces of local and state governments more firmly set against labour than in the southern Piedmont, yet the United Textile Workers grew from 15,000 members to 270,000 in under a year. Its new members clamoured for strike action and in September 1934 300,000 textile workers stayed out. Employers who believed that in North Carolina they had eradicated the bacillus of unionisation at Gastonia in 1929 were astounded when all the mills in Gaston County were closed by the strike on the first day. There were also powerful rank-and-file movements against corrupt and cautious maritime unions like the International Longshoremen's Association and the International Seamen's Union.

1934 as a whole brought a great explosion of unrest: 1,856 stoppages involving almost a million and a half workers. In particularly bloody conflicts, workers across the community mobilised to support the Electric Auto-Lite workers in Toledo, the truckers in Minneapolis, and the longshoremen in San Francisco. In 1935 it was reports of the strength of rank-and-file feeling and their support for industrial unionism, together with their distrust of the AFL, from Adolph Germer in Toledo, Akron, Cleveland, and Detroit that pushed Lewis into forming the CIO. Among these workers, the sitdown was a particularly strong manifestation of local and spontaneous strike action: 48 sitdowns in 1936 involved 88,000 workers and 477 in 1937 involved almost 400,000 workers. The key Goodyear strike in 1936 started with a sitdown that the United Rubber Workers' leaders did not know about. The UAW simply could not keep the lid on the agitation that spilled over into spontaneous sitdown strikes in autos towards the end of 1936. The sitdowns threatened to jeopardise the planned assault on GM and forced union organisers rapidly to adjust their schedule and bring forward the strike call. The euphoria created in Detroit by the success at Midland Steel and Kelsey Hayes, together with the triumph at Flint, led autoworkers to form unions faster than the UAW could send them organisers. Throughout 1937 this rank-and-file discontent to the embarrassment of union leaders led to a rash of sitdowns to settle grievances on the job after contracts had been signed. In steel, Philip Murray was pushed into the premature and ill-fated confrontation with Little Steel by pressure from members who were chafing at the bit.

What caused this pent-up rage to explode was not just the wage cuts and unemployment brought about by the Depression but accumulated old resentments against arbitrary employer power and job insecurity: management's autocratic use of the power to hire and fire, the unrestrained supervisory day-to-day control of foremen, the pace of work, and dangerous conditions all aroused smouldering hostility. The arbitrary power of foremen to hire and fire led to favouritism and corruption, and enabled the foremen to act as petty tyrants on the shop floor towards workers who knew their jobs depended on the foremen's grace and favour. In the automobile and rubber industries, the foremen's leverage over the workforce was increased by the annual lay-offs that took place when car models were changed. On the docks, longshoremen depended for their employment each day on the whim of the labour agent at the degrading early-morning shape-up when he casually allocated the day's available work. What the unions wanted was a seniority system to determine lay-offs and rehiring, and on the docks a union-controlled hiring hall. Unrestrained supervisory power led to other daily humiliations: the arbitrary retiming of jobs to lessen incentive payments for piecework, the speeding up of assembly lines, the stretch-out in the textile industry, and work rules in factories that gave workers no respite against the incessant demands of the machines. Grievance procedures and control of the speed of assembly lines were therefore key union demands in the 1930s.

Such resentments had been voiced in the 1920s but worker protests had been sporadic and unofficial: for example 'quickie' strikes and job actions in the car industry. Ethnic loyalties, rural and peasant backgrounds combined with welfare capitalism and repression to deter working-class action. What the Depression did was to offset the effects of these counterbalances. Desperation in many cases overcame fear; any loyalty to welfare capitalist employers disappeared as schemes of welfare capitalism were abandoned by employers in the face of declining profits and burgeoning unemployment; the ties of ethnic loyalties and conservative backgrounds were overridden by the demands of economic crisis and need. Thus, Polish and Ukrainian first-generation peasant immigrants working in a Detroit auto plant transferred their deferential allegiance from the employer to the union. Notoriously individualistic Appalachian migrants in the same plant decided to assert their personal grievances under the union banner. Steelworkers in Steelton, Pennsylvania, who had for so long substituted ethnic enthusiasm for class identification, now joined SWOC. French-Canadian textile workers in Rhode Island found their traditional loyalty to the local Catholic employer élite badly shaken by the Depression and so joined the Belgian skilled workers in the union. Thousands of individual and collective decisions like these fuelled the union breakthrough and gave it its strength and passion.

Finally, there could be no denying that political radicals played an important role in channelling this rank-and-file militancy. British labourite Matt Smith led the Mechanics Educational Society of America in the unprecedentedly successful strike of tool and die workers in the auto industry in 1933. The success of the Auto-Lite strike in Toledo was made possible by A. J. Muste's Workers Revolutionary Party, which organised the unemployed into the Lucas County Unemployed League in support of the strike. The Trotskyite Dunne brothers and Farrell Dobbs controlled Teamsters local 544, which dictated the Minneapolis truckers' strike. Harry Bridges, the Australian leader of the San Francisco longshoremen, was a Communist sympathiser who had earlier tried to organise longshoremen into the Communist Maritime Workers International Union. When John L. Lewis organised the coalfields and later sent organisers into the mass-production industries, he turned to socialists like John Brophy, Adolph Germer, and Powers Hapgood, whom he had bitterly opposed in the 1920s and had driven from the UMW. Socialists played key roles in Detroit auto parts locals and the Reuther brothers were prominent in the Flint sitdown.

Above all it was the Communists who had the money, discipline, and full-time workers that other radical groups lacked. Earlier Communist organising efforts had been handicapped by conflicting directives from Moscow: first to capture AFL unions, then to build Red unions of the unorganised. The Comintern's decision in 1935 to advocate a Popular Front with all left-wing forces in the face of the Fascist threat in fact postdated a decision by American Communists to abandon doomed dual unions like the Autoworkers Union and the MWIU. The way was open for Communist participation in the mainstream of American labour organising. Despite their failures in the 1920s, many of which were self-inflicted, the Communists brought from their experience in the 1920s and the Depression strengths that were invaluable in the late 1930s. In the auto industry, not only had the Communists consistently stressed the importance of industrial unions and of organising mass-production workers, but shop-floor nuclei of Communist workers, with their Communist shop papers, had articulated with unequalled sharpness the day-to-day grievances of the auto workers. Communist organisers in textiles and coal mining had demonstrated great ability transforming rank-and-file discontent into militant strike action, even if they could not continue the transformation into long-term union organisation. Above all, Communists gained prestige by their willingness to enter the most forbidding territory in an effort to represent the most unpromising groups of unorganised workers: Harlan County coal miners, California farm labourers, Alabama sharecroppers. They gained similar kudos for their efforts to organise the unemployed.

It was this unrivalled organising experience and commitment of men who had often started in the old Industrial Workers of the

World which left Lewis and the CIO no option but to enlist their aid. Communists were prominent at both the national and local levels. In the CIO's national office Len deCaux edited the CIO News and Lee Pressman was general counsel, first of SWOC, then of the CIO itself. Sixty full-time SWOC organisers were Communists. In the auto industry Communists led by John Anderson directed the Midland Steel strike and Communists were at centre stage in the Flint sitdown. Wyndham Mortimer had originally directed the organising drive in Flint and was the only UAW official present at the final negotiations. His successor as director of the Flint campaign, Roy Travis, and the man handling publicity, Henry Kraus, were both party members, as were three of the key members of the strike committee inside Fisher Body Number 1 plant. The Communists brought an indispensable source of funds, a flair for publicity, and a disciplined ability to organise the essential outside support and provision of supplies for the strikers. Their role was not so prominent in the rubber workers' drive but in electrical goods crucial UE locals in General Electric and Westinghouse had traditions of Communist union organisation and the union 'pioneers' had similar radical backgrounds.

3 The limitations of rank-and-file militancy

This emphasis on rank-and-file militancy is a salutary corrective to any tendency to see American workers in the 1930s simply as passive victims, acted upon by government, employers, and union leaders. But rank-and-file militancy on its own does not sufficiently explain labour's breakthrough under the New Deal. Without the necessary government and community backing, rank-and-file militancy did not in itself bring success. Nor can New Deal labour policy be neatly pigeonholed into a 'corporate liberal' device to defuse a revolutionary mass threat. Nor did the grass-roots agitation actually signify the existence of a radical popular anti-capitalist mass movement.

First, the Wagner Act and the attitudes of employers, both to the Act and to unionisation in general, give the lie to any sophisticated strategy of containment on the part of the corporate élite. The Wagner Act passed in 1935 at a time when union activity was collapsing, not challenging the existing order. Far from a capitulation to labour pressure, the Act was seen by its sponsors as a means of rescuing trades unions. Nor was the Act supported by leaders of the American business community. On the contrary, business leaders were uniformly hostile to it. Indeed, Howell John Harris has convincingly demonstrated that businessmen in the 1930s were desperately anxious to oppose independent unions and were prepared to go to almost any lengths to achieve their ends. 'Responsible' unionism may in the long run have served the interests of corporate capitalism, but the corporate capitalists at the time did not think so. Some employers were belligerently determined to resist any form of unionism, even after the Wagner Act was declared constitutional. Senator Robert La Follette Jr's committee on Civil Liberties amply documented the lengths to which employers like the Harlan County coal operators and the Republic Steel management were prepared to go in order to thwart the unions. Republic Steel in 1937 bought 10 times more gas guns and 26 times as many shells as the Chicago Police Department. Other companies, like Goodyear and International Harvester, simply refused to bargain meaningfully when inescapably confronted with unions. Yet others, like General Motors, realistically made the best of a bad job. Forced by economic circumstance to accept unions, they adopted a hard-nosed aggressive bargaining posture. Still others, perhaps the majority, had no clear-cut policy.

One searches in vain for sophisticated 'corporate liberals'. There were isolated examples. Gerard Swope at General Electric happily allowed UE to win local bargaining elections and then signed an industry-wide contract with the union. Cyrus Ching also welcomed URW organisation of US Rubber. But leaders such as these, who saw positive advantages in a stabilised and orderly system of industrial relations and therefore welcomed unions and co-opted them, were very much the exception. Most executives regarded the unions as, at best, a necessary evil and, at worst, an unmitigated disaster.

Not surprisingly, therefore, the genesis of the Wagner Act owed little to the ideas of corporate liberalism, little to any idea on Roosevelt's part to contain militancy, and indeed little to the ideas of labour leaders. Robert Wagner, his advisers, and the NLRB bureaucrats who decisively established the framework of the Act had two overriding aims: first, that labour organisation should enable workers to gain a more equitable share of the national income than they had received under the NRA, second, that a model of industrial relations should be established along the lines of the impartial arbitration provisions in the New York needle trades. The first aim would ensure a more widely dispersed purchasing power, which Wagner and others believed was a pre-condition for genuine economic recovery. The second aim would create the sort of labour relations that Wagner was familiar with in New York and which academics trained in problems of labour relations both advocated and participated in. Neither corporation executives of large-scale, dispersed operations, nor national union leaders, wanted such a system.

The Wagner Act and changing government policy did make a tangible contribution to labour gains in the 1930s. The NRA years, when government support was perfunctory at best, vividly demonstrated that rank-and-file militancy was not enough on its own to defeat the employers. Worker militancy, though real, was ephemeral. It was stimulated to a large extent by the hopes aroused by Roosevelt and the NRA. For example, the same miners who flocked to join unions in western Kentucky in the summer of 1933 had been described as totally quiescent only months earlier: 'As far as western Kentucky is concerned there is no sign of organization. Now . . . you could not organize a baseball team.' Everywhere, workers might sign up in droves, but they would not remain in unions when their lack of economic leverage, government support, or a responsive union leadership dashed their hopes. Federal Locals in the car industry sprang up overnight; within months there would often be no trace of their existence. The enthusiastic recruits to the textile union rapidly disowned their union allegiance when the September 1934 strike was defeated. New members in rubber and steel fell away when the AFL was so unresponsive to their industrial needs.

The Act itself did make a difference, even if some of the major union gains in 1936 and 1937 took place outside its jurisdiction and represented the potency of rank-and-file strength and favourable economic circumstances. The Act to a large extent protected the unions against recession and a counterattack by employers. The 1937–38 recession drastically cut into the membership rolls of unions like the UAW and severely restricted improvements in contracts that could be negotiated. But, in contrast to earlier economic downturns, the unions were not wiped out. They survived as sole bargaining agents to take advantage of the upturn when it came. Similarly, the National Labor Relations Board ultimately broke the resistance of recalcitrant employers like the Harlan County coal owners, Little Steel, and Henry Ford. NLRB decisions, and the possibility of losing lucrative defence contracts, ultimately forced these hostile employers to recognise unions, when the efforts by the unions themselves had been fruitless. In general, the Wagner Act made unions less vulnerable to the catastrophic effects of a premature failed strike. Previously, unions found themselves pushed by their members' impatient demands into ill-timed confrontations with employers. Once defeated, the unions often collapsed. Now, union leaders could more easily resist grass-roots pressure for a premature strike, and, if they were forced into an early strike, defeat was a setback but not fatal. The union lived to fight another day.

A further crucial protection to the unions, which was linked to the change in government attitude, was the change in community sentiment towards unionisation. Such a change had tangible manifestations in the election of pro-labour local and state officials, the mobilisation of community resources in support of, rather than against, the strikers and a general perception that traditional employer anti-union tactics could no longer be tolerated. As early as 1933 a New York *Times* reporter in the coalfields marvelled that 'the operators offered no resistance. . . . Shopkeepers in the coal camps hailed the union organizers with an almost evangelical fervour, supplied them with gasoline for their shabby cars, and gave them a life in the work of organization.' In 1934 the successes at Toledo, Minneapolis, and San Francisco owed much to the support strikers received from the wider community and the great difficulty the employers had in using strikebreakers. The conflicts in the auto industry in 1937 emphasised the change. In Flint, for example, it was not simply Governor Murphy's refusal to use the National Guard on behalf of the company that thwarted General Motors. GM used the traditional tactic in company towns of funding a 'back to work' movement of allegedly loyal workers, the Flint Alliance, only to find that the community at large in Flint, particularly the women, were mobilised in support of the strikers. Similarly, GM was inhibited from using the armed muscle it had acquired for this eventuality, by the unfavourable publicity it received from the carefully-timed releases of the La Follette committee, which revealed just how much the company had spent on espionage in the previous three years. Chrysler, facing a sitdown in its Dodge plant in Hamtramck, was confronted by a mayor and three members of a five-member council who had campaigned on a promise not to use troops against the strikers. In the same community, management in a traditionally anti-union auto parts plant studied by Peter Friedlander felt increasingly isolated and doubtful of their ability to resist the union, unaware in fact of just how vulnerable and fragile the particular local was.

The importance of favourable community sentiment was dramatically highlighted by the difficulties organisers faced when such support was not forthcoming. The United Rubber Workers could counter the activities of the Akron Law and Order League when striking at Goodyear in Ohio because the League received no significant community backing. When the URW tried to organise Goodyear in Gadsden, Alabama, union organisers were simply beaten up and run out of town by vigilantes and a hostile police force. The well-financed Textile Workers Organizing Committee, masterminded by Sidney Hillman, abjectly failed in its efforts to break into the southern textile communities. By the spring of 1939 only 7 per cent of southern millhands were signed up. Union organisers for example, took one look at Gaston County in North Carolina, realised their cause was hopeless in the face of united employer, middle-class, press, and church opposition, and moved on to what they thought might be more favourable locations. They did not find them in the southern Piedmont.

The final qualification to a revisionist interpretation of the labour breakthrough is more precisely to define both the dimension and the nature of the rank-and-file militancy which has loomed so large in the recent historiography. Concentration on the great and violent clashes and emphasis on the role of political radicals obscures the fact that militancy was directed essentially at limited, trades union gains, not at political revolution or a fundamental change in the economic system.

The militant mood of the workers was relatively short-lived. Not only was the 1933–34 upsurge ephemeral, but the later dramatic gains in 1937 were followed by a remarkable fall-off in dues-paying by the newly signed-up workers. Walter Reuther's UAW Local 174 fell from 14,000 dues-paying members to 4,406 in a year. The SWOC had to mount pickets to collect dues in the steel mills. At the height of unrest in 1937 only a small minority of workers went on strike – 7.2 per cent of employed workers – and strikes represented only 0.043 per cent of time worked. Small numbers of workers were responsible for many of the decisive victories: the great surges in rubber, steel, and auto union membership came *after* strikes had been won and contracts signed. The core of militant activists, 'spark plug' unionists or leadership cadres, was always small and not representative of the mass workforce. In the car industry, Peter Friedlander has argued, it was skilled and semi-skilled workers from native or old immigrant backgrounds or the more urbanised and cosmopolitan of the second-generation Eastern European immigrants who were the activists. In the electrical goods industry, Ronald Schatz has shown, union pioneers tended to be British and old-stock migrants, usually from radical family backgrounds: long service and highly-paid skilled workers who had been pushed down into semi-skilled occupations during the Depression.

These leaders gained support from the mass of workers essentially to remedy shop-floor grievances. Militancy was directed towards the contract, higher wages, seniority, and grievance procedures, and control of the speed of production. What the workers were seeking was control of the shop floor, not control of the means of production or a role in wider management policy-making. It was true that workers, after contracts were signed, often used their shop-floor power to secure immediate redress from supervisors, rather than through the formal grievance procedure. But job actions and wildcat strikes did not necessarily have wider radical implications. In the auto parts plant studied by Friedlander wildcat strikes were conducted by groups of young Poles, high-school drop-outs who formed neighbourhood gangs. Their solidarity was effective, but their goals were immediate and specific: their job actions were not intended to build a power base for political radicalism.

As the politically radical militant leaders had to acknowledge, the ordinary mass of new immigrant, newly organised workers were loyal and enthusiastic supporters of Roosevelt and the Democratic Party. The radicals served the cause of trades unions far better than trades unions served the cause of the radicals. Communists and Socialists were effective and gained support because they were good organisers. Indeed, Communist Party membership gains came disproportionately from the ranks of trades union officials who saw the party as the most aggressive force for industrial unionism. As good union organisers, the radicals tended to subordinate their wider political aims, not only because of the Popular Front tactics of the party, but also because of their realistic awareness that the workers they were recruiting to unions were a good deal more conservative. Time after time, veteran Communist and Socialist organisers of the 1930s lamented self-critically their failure to inculcate radical political values in the workers they were so successfully organising into unions. Socialist organisers like the Reuther brothers increasingly found that their goals could be just as well won within a labour-dominated Democratic Party. Communist organisers found themselves vulnerable, well before the anti-Communist hysteria of the post-war years, to Red-baiting attacks from within their unions. That support for them was essentially for their role as good unionists was illustrated by the way that support evaporated, if the issue of their Communism was posed in purely political terms. Thus, rank-and-file workers supported the expulsion of SWOC Communist Party organisers and the elimination of Communist officeholders from the UAW.

This limited and precisely circumscribed rank-and-file militancy partly explains the later conservative and bureaucratised nature of the trades union movement. The union development was not simply the result of a self-serving bureaucratic plot by union officials, or a sophisticated move by corporate liberals. The UMW and the United Steel Workers did not suddenly become centralised and non-democratic. The mass of workers, even in the auto industry, though loyal to their unions, were essentially passive supporters of activist leaders. It was only for a small group of workers that the union became the centre of their day-to-day existence. For others, ethnocultural ties continued to complement union membership. Unionism did not become the mechanism for a class-based, anti-capitalist movement. Given the return eventually of prosperity and given the essentially pragmatic goals of rank-and-file militancy, it is not surprising that workers, while remaining in their unions, should maintain other loyalties and remain committed to essentially individualistic goals.

4 'Responsible' unionism

Radical historians, disillusioned by the later behaviour of trades unions, may in retrospect have romanticised the rank-and-file agitation of the 1930s and vastly overestimated the cohesion and farsightedness of the corporate élite in the United States. But it is difficult to deny that the end product of New Deal labour policy was a stable industrial relations system which revolved around conservative and 'responsible' unions that operated within an agreed consensus of capitalist values. The very limitations of rank-and-file militancy, just outlined, help explain that result, but a number of other factors served also to check and whittle away the apparent labour power of the late 1930s and channel unionism into moderate and acceptable forms: the exigencies of war-time mobilisation, the policies of government agencies, conservative political reaction, and realistic management strategy.

To mobilise the economy for pre-war defence preparedness, and later for war-time production, and eventual reconversion to a peace-time footing, the government largely relied on securing the cooperation of the business community. It brought businessmen to Washington to staff the planning agencies, relied where possible on voluntarism rather than controls, and offered mouth-watering incentives to industry. Labour representatives never wielded the same power, but the government did establish a National Defense Mediation Board and a National War Labor Board, on which labour was represented, in order to settle disputes in defence industries. Labour leaders offered their wholehearted cooperation in the war effort; their zeal was only exceeded by the superpatriotism of the Communist Party, which would not then tolerate any worker obstacles to the war against Hitler once Germany invaded Russia in June 1941. Labour's cooperation was rewarded. The carrot of defence contracts dangled in front of Little Steel and Ford helped force them to grant union recognition; the NWLB was able to impose a 'maintenance of membership' formula in its settlements that consolidated union membership gains and effectively established union security; the NWLB also forced firms to move beyond the passive granting of union recognition to sitting at the negotiating table and entering into genuine bargaining.

But this protection came at a price. Labour agreed to wage controls and a 'no strike' pledge. As a result, both in the pre-war period and during the war itself, unions were confronted with the problem of wildcat strikes by their own members, resentful of wage controls and spiralling living costs and frustrated by their inability to have shop-floor grievances remedied. John L. Lewis in the UMW used such militancy and the miners' strategic position to break down wage controls and restore free collective bargaining in the coal industry. Other union leaders, committed to the war effort and the Democratic administration, felt compelled to quash wildcat strikes. As a result, workers lost a good deal of their independent power on the shop-floor. Increasingly, shop stewards lost the power to demand from management the settlement of complaints on the spot. Instead they became simply referral agents, who passed on complaints to be dealt with through the established and long-winded grievance procedures.

A further price unions had to pay for government protection was increasing federal dictation of the parameters of collective bargaining and restrictions of their freedom of action. The NLRB, once it had restrained the worst excesses of employer anti-union practices, saw its task as one of even-handedly promoting stable and orderly industrial relations. To that end, it more and more curbed union-worker autonomy and rights. It prescribed appropriate bargaining units, prevented workers leaving existing bargaining units or unions, widened the definition of workers who had no protection under the Wagner Act, and specified unfair practices by workers which would deny them the protection of the Act. The NWLB, under the influence of its public members, dictated the terms of contracts and set precedents for the post-war world. Unions tended to agree to no-strike clauses in contracts. Tight and specific grievance procedures leading to impartial arbitration lessened the chance of unions wresting more favourable interpretations of the contract through job actions. The NWLB's widening of the sorts of subjects that the contract covered led to contracts becoming far more technical, and removed negotiations even further from the comprehension of the ordinary union member. Reinforcing this move towards a professionalised and orderly system of industrial relations was the work of the War Labor Board in creating a labour relations bureaucracy. These officials were available after the war to man the stations of the new system by providing the necessary impartial arbiters, fringe benefit specialists, and labour lawyers.

Union leaders had to go along with these restrictions because the unions definitely needed the government protection that went with them. They needed protection against both a conservative political counterattack and a management determined to recapture managerial prerogatives which they believed they had lost during the 1930s and the war. Hostility to unions, especially after the alleged surrender of the rule of law to sitdown strikers, was a central theme of the conservative coalition of southern Democrats and Republicans that wielded such influence in Congress after 1937. Southerners, anxious to attract investment by offering a cheap and docile labour force, farm groups balking at the increased costs caused by wage demands, and powerful business interests combined into a potent constituency to put backbone into conservative congressmen. In the late 1930s the coalition attempted to emasculate the Wagner Act, constantly harassed members of the NLRB, and attempted through the House Un-American Activities Committee to expose Communist influence in both the Labor Board and the unions. Anti-Communism was a useful stick with which to beat wildcat strikers. During the war wage demands and strikes could be dismissed as selfish and greedy betrayals of the fighting men overseas.

In 1943 Congress passed the Smith-Connally War Labor Disputes Act, which gave the president power to seize strike-bound plants, made it a crime to encourage strikes in such plants, provided for a 30-day cooling-off period and a majority vote for strike action in other plants, and outlawed union contributions to political campaigns. The great surge of strikes in 1945–46 prompted a host of anti-union proposals which were finally pared down and consolidated in the Taft-Hartley Act of 1947. Under the Act the unfair labour practices of employers specified in the Wagner Act were now complemented by unfair union practices like the secondary boycott and jurisdictional disputes; the president was given the power to seek an 80-day cooling-off period if strikes threatened the nation's health or safety; unions were made liable for their members' illegal actions; the union shop had to be approved by secret ballot and could be prohibited by state 'right to work' laws; unions were forbidden to make election campaign contributions; if they desired NLRB protection they had to file detailed financial statements with the Board and also affidavits that their officers were not associated with the Communist Party.

To employers, Taft-Hartley redressed the pro-union bias of the Wagner Act and represented the successful conclusion of a sustained propaganda drive by the National Association of Manufacturers. Such determined management policy ultimately shaped the emerging industrial relations system. Management did not view war-time developments as necessarily disciplining workers into 'responsible' modes of behaviour; employers believed, rather, that the war had further eroded their managerial prerogatives. Union security appeared to restrict their right to hire and fire while the exigencies of war-time production weakened their control of production on the shop floor. The imperative war need to maintain production, combined with profits guarantees that made cost concerns relatively unimportant, led to a slackening of shop-floor rules. Employers could only see more threats to their management rights in the threat of unionisation of foremen and in Walter Reuther's demands in the General Motors strike of 1945–46 that GM's pricing policy was a legitimate subject of collective bargaining and contract settlement. (Reuther argued that GM could afford a 30 per cent wage increase without resorting to an inflationary price increase.)

In a competitive post-war world, management wanted to retain its powers to increase production and control costs, and it wanted to contain industrial disputes by restricting strikes simply to the periods after contracts had terminated. Employers like GM recognised that unions could no longer be eliminated but that a hard-nosed, and increasingly expert, negotiating strategy could successfully reaffirm traditional management prerogatives, if at the expense of the concession of liberal fringe benefits. Unions to a large extent accepted this trade-off. Few union leaders showed any interest in the sort of involvement in management decision-making envisaged by Reuther in his 1945 demands. Industrial relations did not become strike-free but conflict was increasingly stabilised and predictable, contained to the period after contracts had ended. Unions concentrated more and more on securing wage increases and liberalised fringe benefits, rather than on improving shop-floor working conditions.

5 The labour achievement

The labour movement emerged from the New Deal and the war years in a position of unprecedented strength but with its role precisely circumscribed. Leaving management to manage, the role of unions was not to give workers increased control over their jobs, but to fight for higher wages and improved fringe benefits in a well-ordered system of industrial relations. The apparent strength of the labour movement hid other weaknesses as well. Union power was concentrated in mining and the manufacture of consumer durables: sectors of the economy that were not going to expand in the post-war years. Whereas unionised industries like coal and steel were to see a sharp decline in their labour force, the service sector of the economy was to grow, emphasising union weakness in the service, white-collar, and public sectors. Similarly, unions were strong in the industrial North-East, a region about to enter a period of relative decline, and weaker in booming California and the South. The industrialising and urbanising South in particular would steadfastly maintain its traditional hostility to unions.

But the achievement of the New Deal years should not be belittled. A system of orderly industrial relations was a vast improvement on the historically unrestrained and arbitrary exercise of employer power. Unions gained for American workers wage increases and benefits far in excess of anything that even the enlightened minority of welfare capitalists had been prepared to contemplate. Workers' control of their workplace may not have been as great as the champions of wildcat strikes and shop stewards would like to have seen, but shop-floor conditions were dramatically better than those imposed by tyrannical foremen and supervisors. In the 1960s and 1970s the role of the unions may have been far from what radical intellectuals desired, but throughout the post-war years the unions were the single most powerful and consistent voice for bread-and-butter liberalism; the most determined and influential pressure group favouring the extension of the broad social welfare goals of the New Deal. The labour unions were in the forefront of the fight, not only for the interests of their own members, but also for the extension of civil rights, social security, and minimum wage protection to all the most disadvantaged members of society.

It is not clear that alternative strategies would have yielded better results. Given the hostility of employers to the whole idea of unions, no matter how responsible unions might be, it is unlikely that more militant union demands for a change in the economic system, for greater power on the shop floor, and for a greater say in management, would have succeeded. Non-cooperation during the war, for example, would surely have laid the unions open to gleeful and unrestrained congressional and employer vengeance. There is no evidence that divorce from the Democratic Party and support for a labour party would have brought anything other than political oblivion. In view of the apparently limited goals of the workers themselves and the realities of the political environment, union leaders did well to carve out for themselves the independence and the power that they did.

4
Parity and Poverty: Agriculture

In 1933 the plight of farmers was of more immediate concern to New Deal policy-makers than the problems of industrial workers. Farmers still constituted 30 per cent of the nation's workforce. Farm pressure groups commanded far more attention in Washington than did trades union leaders. Farm politicians in the South and West were Roosevelt's earliest and strongest supporters both in the Democratic Party and amongst progressive Republicans. Their demands for immediate action to rescue farmers from rock-bottom prices and from crushing indebtedness were endorsed vociferously by businessmen whose success in insurance, banking, and the mail-order business depended on farm prosperity. As Roosevelt took office, the militant Farmers' Holiday Association in the Midwest was calling for a national farm strike if relief legislation was not forthcoming. This compelling need to do something about agriculture enabled Secretary of Agriculture Henry Wallace to persuade Roosevelt to keep Congress in session after the emergency banking legislation had been enacted.

The New Deal responded to this agricultural crisis with a combination of production controls, government payments, and price-support loans. These policy tools, consolidated in the Second Farm Act of 1938, would serve as the basic instruments of American agricultural policy until the 1970s. The New Deal as a result regulated the daily economic lives of millions of farmers to an unprecedented degree – destroying some of their crops, telling them what they could and could not grow, providing an alternative source of credit. As Gilbert Fite has commented, 'The Roosevelt administration gave more direct help to farmers than to any other economic group or class of businessmen'.

Farm policy-makers however had more ambitious aims than simply to restore farm income. In the long run New Deal planners wished to place American agriculture on a more efficient footing by eradicating high-cost uncompetitive production. Thus, New Dealers battled to combat soil erosion, to take the worst land out of production, and to resettle the displaced farmers. The Bureau of Agricultural Economics was transformed into a central planning agency for agriculture to achieve the goal of enabling every American farmer to grow what was best for his soil, his available machinery, and the market conditions.

New Deal farm policy had a further aim: to rescue those who were permanently poor in the rural economy, however prosperous that economy might be. This first great federal government assault on rural poverty worked initially through the relief agencies and then the Resettlement Administration. Loans and grants were made to poor farmers and cooperative communities established to enable some of them to start a new life. These programmes were centralised in 1937 in the Farm Security Administration, which supervised the resettlement projects, made the rehabilitation loans and grants to the poorest farmers, and loaned money to enable tenants to purchase their own farms.

In the 1960s and 1970s historians became both less sympathetic to, and less interested in, Roosevelt's farm policy. As the farm population dramatically declined, farm policy seemed less important. As awareness of world hunger intensified, the destruction and restriction of crops in the 1930s seemed more reprehensible. As the farm programme became more expensive and a small number of agribusinesses became its main beneficiaries, it was harder to see the New Deal as a worthy effort to aid millions of farmers. Revelations of cotton subsidy payments of over $1.5 million a year in the 1960s to the Delta Pine and Land Company of Mississippi did little to commend the New Deal origins of such programmes to radical historians at a time when the full extent and horror of rural poverty was being once more uncovered. Historians in the 1970s amply documented the failures of the New Deal to aid sharecroppers and migrant farm labourers.

New Deal farm programmes in fact were neither as effective as the policy-makers hoped nor as culpable as later critics contended. The consequences of the immediate and necessary aims of securing agricultural recovery precluded to a large extent the successful attainment of the longer-term planning and social justice goals. In addition, alternatives that were radical, workable, and politically acceptable were simply not available in the 1930s. As a result, despite the dramatic nature of the rural depression and the government response, the New Deal was marginal to the major developments – the flight from the land, mechanisation, and the consolidation of small farms into larger holdings – that were to revolutionise American agriculture in the next 50 years.

1 Agricultural recovery programmes

In the search for agricultural recovery, two policies – the direct control of farm production and price-support loans to farmers – distinguished New Deal farm programmes from those of Herbert Hoover and also served as the main components of post-war American farm policy. The evolution and implementation of both those policies depended very much on the particular circumstances of the economic emergency of 1933.

Schemes of agricultural relief put forward and implemented before 1933 failed because they did not tackle the problem of overproduction. McNary-Haugen legislation passed by Congress provided for a guaranteed price for the portion of a crop domestically consumed, while the surplus would be sold at the world price. Irrespective of whether or not the surplus could be disposed of in that way, there was no incentive for growers to reduce their production. Hoover's alternative policy, the encouragement of cooperatives by the Federal Farm Board, offered marginal savings in cost and efficiency, but no inducement to the farmer to cut back production and thus boost prices. The purchase of surplus cotton and wheat by the Farm Board was offset by the failure of prices consequently to rise, thus the surplus eventually had to be put back onto the already glutted market. As a last resort, the Farm Board vainly exhorted farmers voluntarily to curtail their crops.

As a result, while industry cut back production 42 per cent between 1929 and 1933, farmers only reduced their crops by 6 per cent. The problem was that neither voluntarism nor compulsion seemed feasible. No individual farmer was voluntarily going to cut back his production unless he had some guarantee that his neighbour would also do so. Otherwise, he had no certainty that supplies overall would be cut and prices raised. On the other hand, compulsion seemed to involve impossible enforcement procedures. A massive bureaucracy or police force would surely be necessary to regulate the production of millions of individual farmers.

The beauty of the Voluntary Domestic Allotment Plan, put forward by M. L. Wilson, an economist at Montana State College, was that it combined voluntarism, positive incentives for farmers to cut their acreage, and a mechanism for effective enforcement. Under Wilson's scheme, the government would pay farmers who agreed to reduce their acreage. A farmer was perfectly free to refuse to participate and would share in any rise in price, but would not receive any government payment. The farmers themselves would enforce the scheme by checking that their neighbours had complied with their acreage cuts.

Wilson had become convinced in the 1920s of the need to control production from his own experience in wheat farming in Montana and by a visit to Russia. Even with the most modern farming techniques, Wilson could not lower costs enough in Montana to make wheat farming profitable, if there was overall overproduction. In any case, a visit to the Russian wheatlands convinced him that the United States would never lower costs sufficiently to compete with the economies of scale possible in the Soviet Union. He regretted that the Land Grant Colleges and his fellow agricultural economists still devoted their time to the task of improving productivity, making two blades of grass grow where one grew before, rather than to the crucial problem of how farm commodities could be sold at a reasonable price. In the long run, he believed that with the right information the structure of American agriculture could be adjusted so that farmers could plan their production to suit market conditions. In the short term, Wilson was absolutely certain that farmers had to be induced to cut their production. He set about vigorously lobbying farm editors, politicians, and businessmen in favour of his Domestic Allotment Plan. His most important converts were Rexford Tugwell of the Brains Trust and Henry A. Wallace, who was to become Secretary of Agriculture.

Few men had a more profound understanding of the problems of agriculture than Henry A. Wallace. He was a plant geneticist who pioneered the use of hybrid corn, a statistician, and editor of *Wallace's Farmer*. His father was Secretary of Agriculture under Harding: the young Henry never forgave Hoover for blocking his father's proposals for farm relief. In the short run Wallace was prepared to see farmers cut back production because they were merely following the example of industry, where monopolies, along with the forces of economic nationalism, had sabotaged the economy of abundance.

Wallace was often portrayed as a naive, eccentric mystic: religion certainly influenced his thinking and inspired his imagery. Wallace was, however, an eminently practical agriculturalist who surrounded himself with tough-minded, but liberal, administrators like Paul Appleby. Wallace exploited the planning and statistical strengths of his department and gave full rein to 'service intellectuals' to improve the quality of farm policy-making. No member of the Roosevelt administration better understood the contribution science and technology could make to the transformation of the economy. His deep moral convictions, his exposure to the full impact of rural poverty, and the Keynesian ideas of his economic advisers gave him by the end of the 1930s a vision of a full-employment economy. Economic democracy, which originally for Wallace meant the involvement of farmers in decision-making, involved by 1940 the regulation of monopolies, the protection of labour's rights, and the guarantee of economic security for the urban poor. The creation of such a society would also solve the farmers' problems by dramatically increasing their market.

It was Wallace's thorough-going liberal vision which led Roosevelt to impose him on a reluctant Democratic Party as the vice-presidential nominee in 1940. As vice-president Wallace continued to preach for a liberal domestic and international order but found himself in a bitter public bureaucratic struggle with Jesse Jones over economic warfare. In 1944 Roosevelt abandoned him and agreed to Harry Truman as his running mate in order to pacify party professionals and southern conservatives. He did appoint Wallace as Secretary of Commerce in 1945, but the Senate stripped Wallace of the department's lending agencies.

In the post-war world Wallace saw his liberal international order threatened by international cartels and militarism in the United States. He feared excessive business domination of the Truman administration. As one of the few politicians who understood the scientific arguments about atomic energy, he realised the futility of relying on an American nuclear monopoly. Truman sacked him in September 1946, and in 1948 Wallace ran as the Progressive

Party's presidential candidate. He protested the growing power of big business, the acceptance of inevitable conflict with the Soviet Union, and denial of black civil rights in the South. Red-baited and race-baited, the Progressive Party collapsed. In later years Wallace returned to his first concerns – food production, plant experimentation, and the development of a national farm policy.

Wallace and Tugwell, convinced of the need for production control, persuaded Roosevelt in 1932 of the practicality of M. L. Wilson's Domestic Allotment Plan. Roosevelt in turn insisted to doubtful farm leaders gathered in Washington in March 1933 that the Domestic Allotment Plan be a central feature of any farm bill.

The Agricultural Adjustment Act, however, provided for other options in addition to the allotment plan. Like so much legislation in the first Hundred Days, the Farm Act did not mandate a single detailed programme. Rather, the Act was a piece of enabling legislation that gave the Secretary of Agriculture discretion to choose from a number of alternative policies. Aside from entering agreements with growers of basic commodities to pay them to reduce their acreage, the Secretary could also negotiate marketing agreements by which processors would pay farmers a minimum price for their produce; he could give cotton growers the option of buying government stored cotton in return for cutting production and could subsidise agricultural exports. Finally, the president was given the power to inflate the currency by purchasing silver. The farm programme was to be self-financing, funded by a tax on the first processing of agricultural commodities, and the overall aim was to raise farm income to parity, i.e. to establish the same relationship between the prices farmers paid and the prices they received as existed in the so-called golden age of American agriculture between 1909 and 1914.

The eclectic nature of the Act was emphasised by the appointment of George Peek to head the Agricultural Adjustment Administration, which was to carry out the farm programme. Peek was no supporter of the Domestic Allotment Plan. The combative former business partner of Hugh Johnson had been a leading advocate of McNary-Haugenism. He viewed marketing agreements and export subsidies as the key to raising farm income. But the men who headed the crucial production divisions of the AAA – M. L. Wilson himself for wheat, A. G. Black for corn-hogs, J. B. Hutson for tobacco, and Cully Cobb for cotton – were firm champions of crop control. These division heads soon assembled advisory committees of farmers that recommended crop control contracts for 1934 and 1935 which were to be at the heart of the AAA programme. Wheat farmers were to reduce production by not more than 20 per cent, cotton planters by 40 per cent, tobacco growers by 30 per cent, and corn-hog producers by 20 per cent.

Such agreements which would control production in the future would do little in 1933 to offset overproduction and lift prices. Other policies had to supplement the control programmes for cotton, wheat, tobacco, and corn-hogs. For other commodities crop control itself was inappropriate. As a result, the destruction of existing production, marketing agreements, export subsidies, and price-support loans were all used in 1933 in the desperate effort to boost farm income.

At the start of the 1933 season the unsold cotton in the United States already exceeded the total average annual world consumption of American cotton. Cotton farmers had also planted 4,000,000 more acres than they had in 1932. The AAA therefore saw no alternative than to pay cotton farmers actually to destroy some of the cotton they had already planted in 1933. Farmers were to be either paid to plough up cotton, or they could take an 'option' on an equivalent amount of cotton from government stocks. Growers destroyed 10.5 million acres of cotton and the price of the 1933 crop rose to over 10¢ a pound compared to 6.5¢ in 1932. The cash value of the crop was $114 million more than it otherwise would have been, the growers received nearly $112 million in rental payments and probably a further $48 million as a result of the cotton option purchases.

There seemed little immediate problem with the 1933 corn crop, which, because of the declining price of corn and the drought, was one of the smallest since 1900. But low corn prices had stimulated the production of hogs at a time when the consumption of pork was falling and the storage of tank pork was increasing. Hogs born in 1933 would cause a massive oversupply of pork in twelve to sixteen months' time. The AAA therefore decided to buy and slaughter 6,000,000 piglets. The processors had difficulty in handling that number of carcasses because of NRA restrictions on hours, but they did manage to kill 8.5 million little pigs. Hog prices didn't rise but the government purchase brought a 10 per cent increase in income for hog producers.

The AAA ploughed up no other crop than cotton, nor did it slaughter any livestock but pigs. Drought reduced the wheat crop to the smallest since 1896 and obviated the necessity of destroying it, even if the existing excessive carry-over of wheat was scarcely dented. Production control for 1934 was still a pressing issue since winter wheat would be planted in the autumn of 1933. The income of wheat farmers for 1933 was supplemented by three devices: benefit payments under the 1934 control agreement, the subsidising of the export of 28,000,000 bushels from the Pacific North-West (mainly to China), and the purchase of 16,000,000 bushels by the Farm Credit Administration to be used to feed the poor. This programme did little to raise wheat prices in 1933. However, in November government benefit payments eventually arrived in the wheat belt. Together with the government purchase scheme, they dampened the political dissatisfaction that had led the prairie state governors to demand a more drastic farm programme, fixing the prices of licensed growers.

Marketing agreements were an alternative means of raising prices in 1933, pending acreage reduction in the future. They were also a means of raising prices of commodities that were not suited to production control.

The Tobacco Section, while it laid plans for reducing cigarette tobacco acreage in 1934 and 1935, attempted to negotiate a marketing agreement with the tobacco companies by which the cigarette manufacturers would guarantee leaf prices for the 1933 crop. When the companies refused, the Tobacco Section simply had to hope that the prospect of a small crop the next year would lift 1933 prices. The Section's hand was strengthened by angry growers in eastern North Carolina who forced the markets to close. The Tobacco Section then launched an immediate campaign to sign up growers to reduce their future crops and reopened negotiations with the manufacturers.

Since leaf costs were a relatively small part of the cigarette manufacturers' costs, the companies were willing to pay a price approaching parity for the 1933 crop. What they were not pre-pared to do was concede demands from the Consumers Counsel and the Legal Division of the AAA that they should open up their books to the government and submit cigarette price rises to detailed government control. The AAA was reluctant to back down before processors who competed so little in the purchase of tobacco leaf and who made such handsome profits, but the growers desperately needed the money the manufacturers were offering, and the government was in no position to carry out its threat of taking over the tobacco industry under licence if the companies refused to sign. The consequences of the agreement that was reached were dramatic. The flue-cured tobacco crop brought in almost three times as much as in 1932. In no other major commodity were the benefits of the New Deal in terms of prices and cash receipts so spectacular. 'The flat country', reported a North Carolina newspaper, 'is no longer flat.'

The disagreements over the tobacco agreement highlighted the disagreements between Administrator George Peek and the staff of Frederic Howe's Consumers Counsel Division and Jerome Frank's Legal Division. To Peek, the sole aim of marketing agreements was to raise farm prices, he was not worried about price rises that the processors might pass on to consumers. To the young lawyers under Howe and Frank, who had little practical knowledge of agriculture, the attitude of the processors simply confirmed their radical suspicions of business. They were reluctant to sanction a suspension of the anti-trust laws under the agreements unless they were offered the chance to inspect the processors' books in order to protect consumers and to discipline the businessmen into socially responsible behaviour. To Peek, however, such demands were simply the first stage in a drive by 'collectivists' to socialise American industry.

Negotiations therefore for a marketing agreement with meat packers to benefit livestock producers (including hog farmers) simply failed. The meat packers were not prepared to submit to the Secretary of Agriculture for approval in advance plans for allocating market shares or fixing prices, nor were they going to let Legal Division radicals look too closely at their profits by having access to their books. Similar disagreements plagued the negotiation of milk marketing agreements. By the end of 1933 only a small number of dairy farmers were benefiting from the agreements. In any case the structure of the milk industry forced the abandonment of a marketing agreement. The industry was too fragmented: separate agreements had to be negotiated for over 200 different marketing areas or milksheds, and small retail outlets, like grocery stores, disagreed fiercely with individual producer-distributors over the proposed milk prices. To make matters worse, the failure at the time to curtail milk production led to a drastic fall in butter and cheese prices.

The obstruction and sabotage by the AAA lawyers, which Peek believed undermined his efforts to negotiate marketing agreements, finally led him to resign in December 1933. His exasperation with the Legal Division was shared in fact by advocates of production control. M. L. Wilson recalled that 'Jerome Frank had nothing to do with farmers, knew nothing about farmers, knew nothing about their folkways or anything of that kind'. Only Alger Hiss among the radical urban lawyers managed to maintain good relations with production division heads. But Peek's resignation nevertheless left the champions of controlled production, led by the new administrator, Chester C. Davis, firmly in control of the AAA.

The production control advocates by this time had another policy to supplement the Domestic Allotment Plan. Price-support loans from the Commodity Credit Corporation were to underpin the farm programme for the next 50 years, but they came into existence almost by accident in 1933 after the main outlines of the commodity programmes had been drawn. In September, southern politicians demanded action to satisfy cotton planters who complained that, while cotton prices were falling after an initial speculative boom, they were paying higher prices, caused by the National Recovery Administration, for goods they needed to buy. Roosevelt, using the Reconstruction Finance Corporation, established the Commodity Credit Corporation and authorised a loan of 10¢ a pound on cotton. This was a 'non-recourse' loan. Planters could store the cotton; if prices rose above 10¢ they could repay the government, if not they simply kept the money they had been lent. In November Roosevelt faced similar pressure from corn-belt politicians. Midwestern farmers asked for government price-fixing to match prices of industrial goods fixed under the NRA. The governor of North Dakota threatened to embargo the movement of grain from his state. The Farmers' Holiday Association called for another farm strike. Roosevelt therefore authorised the Commodity Credit Corporation to lend 45¢ a bushel on corn.

These innovative programmes launched by the New Deal depended for their political and administrative success on the consent of the farmers themselves. A radical departure from traditions of limited government intervention, such as the Domestic Allotment Plan, had to be sold politically as what the farmers, rather than some faceless New Deal bureaucrat, wanted. To implement such policies quickly in an economic emergency required the active cooperation of the farmers. The voluntary nature of the programme and its dimensions demanded that it be administered not by an army of officials sent down from Washington but by the local farmers. The policy-making and administrative producers which the AAA used in the short-term emergency were to have unanticipated consequences for farm policy in the long term.

The foremost justification in winning over Congress to the Farm Act in 1933 was that its programmes were what the farmers wanted. The legislation appeared to have emerged from a meeting of farm leaders on 10 March. In fact, none of the major farm organisations had previously favoured the Domestic Allotment Plan; they endorsed it because they were desperate for government aid. As Rex Tugwell recalled, 'They – the leaders of the farm organizations – met on the train on their way from Chicago to Washington and when they arrived they presented us with a memorandum which asked us to do what we already had done'. Edward O'Neal and the Farm Bureau in particular decided to offer wholehearted support to the AAA not out of conviction of the need for the Domestic Allotment Plan, but out of the hope that close links to a successful government programme would revive their flagging membership and finances, especially in the South.

AAA programmes were voluntary: their success depended on the cooperation of farmers traditionally hostile to government interference. In the 1920s such seemingly innocuous and worthy schemes as tick eradication had led to the dynamiting of dipping vats by individualistic farmers. In formulating particular commodity programmes, the AAA was at pains to stress that the ideas would have to come from the farmers themselves: J. B. Hutson told tobacco growers, 'Don't expect us to sit in Washington, devise a plan and say here it is . . .'; Henry Wallace told corn-hog producers, 'The wheat program had been asked for by the wheat growers . . . if the corn-hog farmers wanted a program they would have to ask for it'.

The problem for the AAA was that, with the exception of cattle and milk, none of the commodities was represented by an effective producers' organisation. The AAA to a large extent had to create advisory committees of farmers for each commodity. Not surprisingly division heads turned to people they already knew or who were recommended by Extension Service directors. These farmers were likely to be more substantial farmers and also sympathetic to the idea of production control. All the evidence suggests that the AAA deliberately created and fostered these committees and pressure groups, in part to provide detailed technical expert advice on policy implementation but largely to provide legitimacy for policies which AAA officials intended to carry out in any case. It is significant that the well-organised cattle and dairy producers resisted AAA demands for production control. The pressure groups which the AAA created or institutionalised in 1933 might be controlled by the AAA then, but they would not always be so easily led in the future.

To put production controls into operation the AAA had to act quickly. In order to destroy cotton before the harvest, over a million farmers had to sign contracts in three weeks. Wheat farmers had to be signed up to reduce their acreage before they planted winter wheat in September. Tobacco growers had to be signed up in less than three weeks so that markets could reopen and protect perishable leaf. To reach individual farmers, explain the brand-new programmes to them, and persuade them to sign contracts, the AAA had little alternative but to turn to the one organisation that had employees in every rural county – the Extension Service, which through its county agents brought the benefits of agricultural experiments and research from the Land Grant Colleges to the farmers.

These county agents were to serve as the local administrators of the control programmes. In the South the agents initially chose county and community committees of farmers to help them run the cotton and tobacco programmes. In the wheat and corn belts the agents served as secretaries of Production Control Associations of participating farmers who elected their own local committees. Chosen or elected, these committees were made up of men of influence, anyone who was the 'outstanding man from a community'. The sort of farmer who could afford the time to serve on such committees was unlikely to be a small farmer, a tenant, or a sharecropper. He was much more likely to be a large farmer or a farmer-businessman-politician. There rural élites sold the programmes to the farmers with the aid of the massive literature from

Washington, the support of local newspapers, and the endorse-ment of state politicians. The committees carried out the time-consuming tasks that operating the early farm programme re-quired: they estimated the previous production and acreage of farms which often did not keep records, they measured the contracted acreage, they checked that the required acreage had been ploughed up or left fallow, they distributed the government payments.

Because of local administration the early production control programmes ran remarkably smoothly. The fears of some Exten-sion Service directors that their agents would become unpopular in their new regulatory roles proved unfounded. On the contrary, they made contact with more farmers than ever before and derived new power from their role in the distribution of government largesse. In the major areas of most commodities, most growers agreed to cooperate. The sign-up figures were remarkable – the incentives of Wilson's Domestic Allotment Plan seemed to work. Over three-quarters of the cotton acreage was covered by the first sign-up; 95 per cent of flue-cured tobacco farmers signed up; over 89 per cent of the wheat base period acreage was contracted in Kansas, Montana, and the Dakotas; for corn 93 per cent of the base acreage in Iowa and 98 per cent in South Dakota was signed up. There were hitches of course. Local committees tended to accept higher estimates of previous production than the county figures in Washington indicated was possible and contracts had to be delayed and adjusted. In some areas vigilante violence 'per-suaded' some farmers to cooperate. Rental and benefit payments were sometimes slow to reach farmers. There would always be complaints of favouritism. But, given the size of the task it is difficult to see how any other method of administration could have worked as well. Nevertheless, giving such power in the programme to local élites had serious consequences for the rural poor.

Having launched the initial control programmes, the AAA's main problem in 1934 and 1935 was drought in the western states. The most serious drought in 70 years of water recording not only reduced wheat production drastically but severely depleted feed grains so that cattlemen were desperate for government aid. Ranchers, who had refused to allow beef to be a basic commodity in 1933, now pressured Congress to bring beef cattle under the protection of the AAA. They agreed to reduce breeding cows by

20 per cent by 1937; in return the government purchased drought cattle for either slaughter or shipment to the East. By 31 January 1935 the government had purchased 8.3 million head of cattle.

The drought was of course a most effective means of crop control. As a result, the wheat and corn programmes were not threatened in those years by the substantial number of farmers who did not sign contracts and instead increased their production. Cotton and tobacco farmers, however, determined that the small number of non-signers should not wreck their programmes, persuaded Congress to pass compulsory control legislation whereby the sale of cotton and tobacco by farmers who had not signed contracts would be taxed punitively. Otherwise, modifications to the control programmes which were the mainstay of the AAA were slight. The emphasis towards the end of 1935 was on ironing out some of the more obvious inequities in contracts that the growers could sign for 1936–39.

That farmers did want to continue the programmes was clearly indicated by overwhelming votes in referenda in 1935. Wheat farmers voted six to one to continue, corn-hog producers eight to one, tobacco farmers over nine to one, and cotton planters nine to one. Their enthusiasm was not matched by the justices of the Supreme Court. In January 1936 the Court held in the Hoosac Mills case that agricultural production was a local matter for state rather than federal regulation, and that the processing tax had illegally expropriated money from one group to benefit another. Farmers reacted angrily to the declaration that the Agricultural Adjustment Act was unconstitutional.

To circumvent that decision, the Department of Agriculture hurried through Congress the Soil Conservation and Domestic Allotment Act. Drawing on the existing soil conservation programme, farmers would be paid for reducing their acreage of soil-depleting crops and for increasing their acreage of soil-conserving crops or adopting certain soil-conserving practices. Since soil-depleting crops were cash commodities like cotton and wheat, this Act was a thinly veiled attempt to perpetuate production control. It was inevitably an inadequate substitute since the payments that could be made out of congressional appropriations as incentives to reduce acreage were much smaller than the rental and benefit payments that had been made possible by processing tax revenue under the first Farm Act. In 1936 the lack of incentive did not matter since bad weather kept crops small but 1937 was the first drought-free summer in the West since 1929. When it became clear that the stimulus of good prices, the absence of effective controls, and the onset of good weather would lead to record crops in 1937, congressional spokesmen for corn, wheat, and especially cotton called on Roosevelt for renewed price-support loans from the Commodity Credit Corporation. Roosevelt authorised these loans only on condition that Congress promised to pass a permanent and comprehensive substitute for the first Agricultural Adjustment Act at its next session. In February 1938 Congress did finally pass a second Farm Act, eight months after legislation had first been introduced.

Secretary of Agriculture Henry Wallace had favoured an Ever Normal Granary scheme with voluntary production controls and relatively low price-support loans. Surplus crops in good years would be stored to ensure good supplies in bad crop years. Cotton and tobacco farmers and the Farm Bureau favoured instead rigid production controls and high price-support loans. Other farm groups and the House Agriculture Committee, however, disliked compulsory controls. In the end, Wallace and the House committee had to concede. If there were to be high price supports, Wallace had to agree to tight production controls, otherwise huge stored surpluses would pile up as in the days of the Federal Farm Board. Confronted with the overproduction of 1937, the House committee had to acknowledge that it would be too expensive to secure the necessary acreage reduction by voluntary means.

Under the 1938 Farm Act, the Commodity Credit Corporation would offer non-recourse price-support loans on stored crops. These were to be mandatory in the case of cotton, wheat, and corn if prices in those commodities fell below a certain level. In addition, parity payments could be made if prices fell below 75 per cent of parity. As for production control, voluntary control through acreage allotments would continue under the soil conservation programme. But if supplies for a particular commodity were excessive, compulsory control would be imposed if two-thirds of farmers agreed in a referendum. In such cases, marketing quotas would be proclaimed and any sale in excess of an individual quota would be heavily taxed.

The late passage of the Act and the complexity of its provisions led to considerable administrative confusion and farmer resentment. County committees had so much to do that they had little chance satisfactorily to explain the programme to farmers. Calculations of allotments and quotas were now designed to be fairer to smaller farmers than the simple calculation of past production, but complicated and ill-understood calculations simply left farmers suspicious of favouritism. And there was simply not enough time: application forms for price-support loans for wheat farmers did not arrive with county committees until early August; many tobacco growers went to market without knowing their individual quotas and found that they had unwittingly produced more than their quota on the acreage allotment given them under the soil conservation scheme. Farmers expressed their resentment at the polls: in the Midwest Republicans gained in the mid-term elections, two Democratic senators who had been sponsors of the Farm Act, James Pope of Idaho and George McGill of Kansas, were defeated. In flue-cured tobacco, growers who had overwhelmingly voted in favour of quotas in March 1938, defeated them for the following year in the December 1938 referendum.

The inescapable facts of overproduction and the disruption of markets caused by the European war that began in September 1939 forced farmers to accept production control. The wheat programme operated between 1938 and 1940 without compulsory controls, but whereas most stored wheat in 1938 and 1939 was redeemed by the farmers, in 1940 one third of the crop was stored under loan, and two thirds of that was not redeemed. Quotas were therefore proclaimed and supported for 1941 and 1942. In tobacco, growers produced a record flue-cured crop in 1939 but then found in September that the British buyers who purchased over one third of their best leaf had to withdraw from the markets because of the war. The markets closed. The government agreed to purchase leaf for the British buyers with Commodity Credit Corporation funds, but only on condition that the growers voted to reimpose quotas for 1940. After a whirlwind campaign to secure a favourable vote, the markets reopened and subsequently tobacco growers routinely voted every three years to maintain quotas.

Cotton farmers had little option after the 1937 crop than to stick with compulsory controls. They had produced an all-time record of 18.9 million bales in 1937 and the carry-over was such that in August 1938 there was still over a year's supply of cotton on hand. Controls and loans could do little more than stop prices falling even further. The war made this crisis worse and export markets collapsed but producers were rescued by the later dramatic war-time rise in domestic demand that doubled the price of cotton between 1940 and 1945.

2 The limitations of planned scarcity

The New Deal measures designed to raise farm prices were open to the criticisms that they precluded the rational planning of American agriculture and that they exacerbated the plight of the rural poor. But they were also open to criticisms on their own terms as recovery measures. The policy of planned scarcity – resolving the paradox of want in the midst of plenty by removing the plenty – appeared wasteful and immoral. 'That we should have', said farm leader William Hirth, 'idle and hungry and ill-clad millions on the one hand, and so much food and wool and cotton upon the other that we don't know what to do with it, this is an utterly idiotic situation, and one which makes a laughing stock of our genius as a people.' Surely, said critics then and later, the New Deal was tackling the problem from the wrong end. The problem was not overproduction, but underconsumption. Nor did planned scarcity and production control work. Drought removed the need for production restraint; non-cooperating farmers offset acreage cuts by planting more themselves; increased yield more than made up for acreage taken out of production; artificially high prices lost foreign markets. The evidence of New Deal failure was the large surpluses that had piled up once more by 1940. These would only be eliminated by surging war-time and post-war demand. New Deal farm policy also conferred a position of special privilege on farmers at the expense of other sectors of society: farmers, especially the 'large and already prosperous' farmers, should have been capable of looking after themselves in the free market but were given permanent protection by the government at the expense of the national interest.

The criticism that planned scarcity, tackling the problem of overproduction, was wrong in itself can largely be disposed of in the way that New Deal policy-makers themselves did. Men like Henry Wallace were embarrassed by destroying crops but they saw crop control only as a short-term emergency solution pending the necessary long-term adjustments in agriculture. Few could deny that in the short term the crippling carry-overs of cotton, wheat, and hogs had to be removed. New Dealers were also convinced that in simply raising farm prices they were making a major contribution to general economic recovery in the United States which would eventually increase urban purchasing power and thus in the end eliminate the need for crop controls. Men like Rex Tugwell and Wallace's economic adviser Mordecai Ezekiel believed that the restoration of farm purchasing power was as good a way as any of stimulating overall recovery. The alternative farm policies that were canvassed in 1933 – government guarantees of the cost of production and some form of currency inflation – promised to raise farm prices without controlling production but failed to suggest how urban purchasing power was to be increased to buy unlimited production at increased prices. There was no serious discussion of, and certainly no political mandate for, a policy of subsidising low food prices or drastically altering the system of processing and distribution in order to put the farm surpluses into the hands of the urban poor. Nor did the government have the resources or expertise to take over the processing industries.

Nevertheless, it must be admitted that New Deal farm policy-makers were slow to see that urban demand was the eventual key to farm recovery. They clung to the belief rather that rural demand was the key to industrial recovery. Henry Wallace, one of the most wide-ranging of the New Deal intellectuals, remained for much of the 1930s in Richard Kirkendall's words an 'agricultural fundamentalist'. He moved only under the prodding of his advisors, Paul Appleby and Mordecai Ezekiel, to a broader perception of the need to increase urban consumption. His own concept of the Ever Normal Granary which tried to escape from the constraints of planned scarcity was never really accepted by the rural pressure groups like the Farm Bureau. Even those New Deal programmes which did address the possibilities of surplus distribution to the poor were developed first and foremost out of the needs of the farmer – help to the urban consumer was a by-product. Studies of the Surplus Relief Corporation, established in 1933 to use farm surpluses in the relief programme, and the Food Stamp programme, established in 1939 to enable the poor to purchase food more cheaply, show that the main policy concerns were those of disposing of whatever commodity surplus was on hand rather than those of catering to the need of the relief clients or the poor.

There is even more prima facie evidence to sustain the second criticism that production control simply did not work. Drought certainly reduced wheat and corn production more effectively than did the Domestic Allotment Plan: an estimated 90–95 per cent of the reduction in wheat production in 1934 was due to drought. Improved techniques could increase yields on contracted acreage to offset cuts: the introduction of hybrid corn to 75 per cent of corn-belt farms helped account for the persistent corn surpluses. There was evidence that farmers tired quickly of the rigid constraints of controls as the agricultural economists had predicted. Crop control might be tolerated in an emergency but not when the economic benefits were less dramatic and when efforts to make programmes more suitable increased the complexity of bureaucratic procedures. In the Midwest the non-contracted acreage in wheat almost doubled from 1934 to 1935. When the Farm Bureau demanded the return of strict production controls in 1937 and 1938 there was little evidence of any genuine grass-roots demand for such controls among wheat and corn-hog farmers. When marketing quotas were imposed for wheat in 1941, farmers planted the smallest acreage for twenty years yet produced the largest crop in history. There seemed little the government could do in the late 1930s to prevent the mounting surpluses, particularly in a crop like cotton which was too highly priced to compete on the world market. Only the onset of war-time prosperity and increased demand rescued the farm programme. After World War II governments were reluctant to impose mandatory controls on production and so surpluses piled up in the 1950s. When President John F. Kennedy attempted to solve that problem by reintroducing controls for wheat farmers in 1962, the farmers in a famous referendum on quotas rebuffed the government.

Theodore Saloutos thus concluded that New Deal production control programmes 'can hardly be adjudged a success'. But the proponents of production control had always envisaged it as a short-term necessity pending a wider readjustment of American agriculture. They recognised the likely difficulties of a permanent programme of crop restriction. In the short term increased yields did not invalidate the case for acreage cuts. The great technological breakthroughs in agriculture were largely a phenomenon of the 1940s and 1950s. Until the late 1930s farmers did not have the financial resources to invest in the new fertilisers and chemicals that were to transform production. In any case, marketing quotas under the 1938 Act controlled production not acreage. Equally, artificially high prices did not lose export markets for crops like tobacco and cotton – they had been lost even before the New Deal.

Drought may have made crop control initially unnecessary in the wheat and corn belts, but it was the rental and benefit payments from acreage reduction contracts that enabled farmers in drought areas to survive when their income from their crops was almost wiped out. In South Dakota government payments contributed $27 million towards a farm income of only $55 million in 1934. In the same year such payments were responsible for $37.5 million of North Dakota's farm income of $63 million.

Finally, it was possible in some commodities, notably in cotton and tobacco, to sustain long-term and fairly strict crop control. In both cotton and tobacco farm leaders were convinced of the need for control even before the New Deal: they were grateful for a mechanism like the Domestic Allotment Plan that seemed to make control possible. In other commodities, sceptical farm leaders had to be won over to the idea. Tobacco growers could see that control led to a spectacular price rise; in other commodities the direct impact of control on prices was minimal, benefits came from government payments. Cotton growers both in the 1930s and later knew that government aid, for which control was a precondition, was essential in view of existing carry-overs and their awareness that high-cost American cotton could not survive on the world market. An oligarchical social structure eased the acceptance of the control of cotton production, since decisions by a small number of landlords determined the growers' response. The concentration of tobacco production in a limited geographical area facilitated the necessary educational campaigns and the smooth administrative procedures that lessened the chance of grower resentment of government intervention. By contrast, in the wheat and corn belts, where the family farm still predominated in the 1930s, decision-making was more diffuse and more likely to represent the grievances of individualistic farmers against federal interference.

The criticism that the New Deal created a position of special privilege for agriculture was given credence by the way that farm pressure groups seemed to be able to win from the government ever more generous price supports. Farm policy in post-war America seemed to be determined not by the national interest or indeed even the overall farm interest but by the narrow special interests of particular farmers, who appeared to be wielding more and more political control as they grew ever fewer in numbers. An 'iron triangle' of the commodity pressure group, its representatives on congressional agriculture committees, and sympathetic commodity experts in the Department of Agriculture appeared to perpetuate the favoured position that growers had secured during the New Deal.

It could scarcely be said, however, in the 1930s that the New Deal was fostering a position of special privilege for farmers who did not need help. As Gilbert Fite has emphasised, even in a good year like 1929 there were no really prosperous farmers with the exception of the occasional agribusiness. Van Perkins has pointed out that in 1933 with prices at rock bottom there were no prosperous farmers, large or otherwise. It was only during the war and after, when Congress wanted to ensure that there were incentives to *increase* production, that price-support provisions started to become mouth-wateringly generous. Farmers were virtually guaranteed 110 per cent of parity – or as one critic noted, 110 per cent of heaven.

Nevertheless, the process by which the New Deal secured consent for production controls did pave the way for the excessive power of commodity interest groups. At first, the New Deal had had to create growers' organisations, often from scratch. Pressure groups like the Farm Bureau were so weak that they had to defer in the emergency to AAA experts. The AAA was creating pressure to which policy-makers could respond by doing what they had wanted to do in the first place. If pressure groups made excessive demands, the AAA could veto them. When tobacco growers, for example, in 1935 wished to restrict their crop and raise their prices more than the Tobacco Section of the AAA thought justified, Hutson and Wallace combined to turn down their demands. But there was already evidence, particularly in cotton, that the large planters called the tune in policy formation. Howard Tolley believed that the whole process of consultation had become distorted so that farmers viewed the AAA as simply a mechanism for 'grinding out checks'. Tolley came back to run the AAA in 1936 in an attempt to check this trend. He reorganised the AAA on regional rather than commodity lines in the hope that regional divisions would break down the power of particular commodity interests. The 1938 Farm Act showed how little this effort had halted the shift in the balance of agricultural power. Whereas the 1933 Farm Act had given broad discretionary power to the Secretary of Agriculture to choose from a number of very general policy alternatives, the 1938 Farm Act laid down specific detailed policy instructions for each commodity that left no room for manoeuvre. Farm policy had previously been determined by AAA bureaucrats imposing their will on farmers under the guise of securing their consent. From now on, farm policy would be determined by how much a commodity interest group could persuade its representatives on congressional agriculture committees to accept. An increasingly servile AAA bureaucracy would then implement that policy.

For all the criticisms of farm recovery programmes, they represented a modest success. They doubled net farm income from $2 billion in 1932 to $4.6 billion in 1939. In 6 years the government made direct payments to farmers of over $4.5 billion. Yet in 1939 farm income was only 80 per cent of parity and farm income only reached 1929 levels twice before 1940. Nevertheless, the AAA enabled farmers to survive. The New Deal was essentially a holding operation for a large underemployed agricultural labour force. The farm programmes enabled that surplus labour force to stay on the land at a time when there was nowhere else to go. When urban prosperity created employment opportunities in the 1940s those surplus farmers could then move to the cities in relative security.

Farm recovery programmes also provided the policy tools with which farmers could be guaranteed security in the future. They changed the value system of farmers so that they could organise effectively to take advantage of government intervention. Above all, they removed much of the risk that had made farming previously such a vulnerable occupation. Debt adjustment by local committees and the refinancing of farm mortgages by the Farm Credit Administration substantially removed the burden of indebtedness and banished the pervasive fear of foreclosure. Soil conservation, flood control and irrigation, rental and benefit payments, and later crop insurance for wheat enabled farmers to survive appalling drought conditions. Per capita farm income in 1939 was still only 37.5 per cent of non-farm income but the changes of the New Deal did ensure that farmers who stayed on the land and benefited from the dramatic price rises of World War II operated in a much more risk-free environment than before 1933.

3 Planning to modernise rural America

Recovery had been the immediate goal of farm policy-makers and production control had been a short-term expedient. Agricultural economists like M. L. Wilson and Howard Tolley had more ambitious aims to adjust American agriculture on a long-term basis so that each American farmer would be able to utilise his full productive capacities to produce the sort of crops that best suited his soil, size of farm, degree of mechanisation, and prevailing market conditions. The reform of agriculture through planning in the interests of efficiency was the New Deal's ultimate aim.

To a large extent production control ran counter to these aims. As a means of planning crop-control programmes were crude and inefficient. They tended to freeze agriculture into the pattern existing either in the base period 1929–33 or in the parity period 1909–14. Crop control perpetuated the existing relationship between large and small farms, between landlord and tenant, between different crops, irrespective of changes in patterns of consumption, and between efficient and inefficient farms.

New Deal rural planners believed government intervention could be much more constructive. They planned to reorder agriculture and to reverse the traditional exploitative, individualistic attitude to the land. To achieve such far-reaching goals, they sought to use the same devices employed to implement production control. The planning was not to be imposed by fiat from Washington: the farmers themselves in a revived local democracy of farmer committees would voluntarily utilise the technical knowledge and advice of New Deal experts. As Commissioner of Indian Affairs John Collier noted:

New Deal planned government in a changed relation to the

'grass-roots'. That relation was not one of authority, nor except in minor ways was it a subsidy. It was the transfer of knowledge, of technical assistance, and of a man-nature orientation to the people acting voluntarily, autonomously, in old and newly-formed local groups, towards aims which were national, and also world-wide.

The short-term priority was to rescue and restore land that had been ravaged by intensive, careless farming and eroded by droughts, wind, and flood. The dust storms highlighted the urgency of the task. One single duster on 11 May 1934 removed 300 million tons of top soil. Nationally, an estimated 332 million acres were affected by wind erosion in 1934. A survey of twenty counties in the heart of the Dust Bowl in 1936 concluded that 97.6 per cent of the land suffered from the effects of erosion, with 53.4 per cent affected to a serious degree.

A host of New Deal agencies tackled this problem, with pioneering enthusiasm. As Alastair Cooke noted, 'The New Deal's symbolic worker had a firm jaw and a will . . . to take up contour plowing late in life'. Some of this activity to rescue the land reflected Roosevelt's personal initiative. In 1933 he established the Civilian Conservation Corps where unemployed youngsters from the cities would work in rural camps on projects supervised by the Departments of Agriculture and the Interior. He also pushed through, against the scepticism of many professional foresters, the plan to plant a 2,000-mile Shelterbelt of trees down the middle of the United States.

Of more immediate concern to farmers was the Taylor Grazing Act of 1934, under which the Secretary of the Interior restricted the entry of cattlemen to the public range in the West to prevent overgrazing. Also in the West, the Bureau of Reclamation carried out irrigation projects to rescue arid lands in the Great Plains and to open up desert lands further west.

At the same time the Soil Erosion Service organised demonstration projects to show farmers the benefits of terracing and contour ploughing, of planting cover, wind-resistant crops, and of turning land over to pasture. Reorganised under the crusading Hugh Hammond Bennett in 1935, as the Soil Conservation Service, it offered more positive cash inducements to plant soil-covering, rather than soil-depleting crops. Soil conservation could not simply be an individual farmer's responsibility. Any farmer could see his land damaged by the inaction of his neighbour. Eventually farmers were organised into over 2,000 soil-conservation districts in which, after referenda, they could impose conservation practices on other farmers.

The rural planners wanted to do much more than restore the fertility of the American soil. Too many farmers, economists in the Bureau of Agricultural Economics believed, were farming submarginal land that could never be profitable. They argued that the government should purchase and take out of production the 75,000,000 acres of land which they had surveyed as submarginal and resettle 450,000 farm families on more suitable land. The Resettlement Administration established communities where re-settled farm families could live in model housing, benefit from cooperative services, and farm under expert supervision.

On the Great Plains a presidential committee mapped out a coordinated plan for the region's future. According to *The Future of the Great Plains* the government would purchase and control large tracts of range land. Conservation and irrigation projects would protect farmers if the farmers organised themselves into cooperative grazing associations and soil-conservation districts. Credit would be available to farmers following approved conservation practices to enable them to consolidate their holdings into units large enough to be economically viable. Tax reform, local government reform, and the creation of a regional coordinating agency would provide the effective political structure to supervise this regeneration of the Plains.

The Tennessee Valley offered a model for such coordinated regional development. During World War I the government had built a dam at Muscle Shoals, Alabama, to produce cheap power for nitrate manufacture. Throughout the 1920s progressives in Congress led by George W. Norris of Nebraska fought to prevent the government selling off Muscle Shoals to private power companies and fertiliser manufacturers. Roosevelt's general interest in public power and conservation and his personal knowledge of the devastating effect of erosion in the South led him to champion a precedent-shattering Tennessee Valley Authority in 1933. The TVA was to revitalise one of the most deprived and backward regions in the nation. A series of dams would not only prevent the annual spring floods which washed away the top soil but also provide the cheap power to fuel diversified small industry. Dispossessed farmers could live in model communities or resettle on farms made viable by cheap fertilisers, the best soil conservation techniques, and the best efforts of agricultural educationalists.

If the New Deal could rescue one of the nation's most depressed regions, it could perhaps rescue one of the nation's most depressed rural groups – Native Americans. With Harold Ickes's backing, the new Commissioner of Indian Affairs, John Collier, planned to reverse the traditional policy of assimilation, the long history of white exploitation, and the corrupt paternalism of the Bureau of Indian Affairs. Collier aimed both to restore tribal self-government, modernise the Indian economy, and yet enable Indians to recapture and sustain their traditional culture.

In the long run, the agricultural economists also hoped to eliminate two of the major structural flaws of commercial agriculture: high-cost production and inadequate demand. They recognised that high-cost American farmers, particularly cotton planters, could not compete indefinitely on the world market. By the end of the war the Bureau of Agricultural Economics had developed plans to phase out the more expensive producing areas and subsidise the farmers' transition to diversified farming. The Bureau also demonstrated that if every American family consumed an adequate diet American farmers would have to increase, not curtail, production. Some steps were taken to stimulate urban consumption through the Federal Surplus Relief Corporation and a Food Stamp programme. Later under President Truman, Secretary of Agriculture Charles Brannan proposed to end price supports to farmers and replace them with subsidies, which would guarantee farmers a continued protected income, but would also result in low-priced food for the urban consumer.

How were farmers to be persuaded to make the necessary shifts in production and land-use? How were they to be persuaded to grow not only what was best for their own soil and labour needs, but also what was best in terms of national and international markets? The Program Planning Division of the BAE would lay down national guidelines. County land-use planning committees, elected by the farmers themselves, would draw up the appropriate plans which would reflect the particular circumstances and needs of their own counties. These local planning committees were to be the ultimate expression of 'grass-roots democracy'.

The rural planners scored some short-term successes, particularly in soil conservation. Yet their grander goals of a more rational and efficient agriculture were elusive. They proved more successful in identifying problems than in solving them. Sometimes their interventions had unanticipated consequences. Other plans had to be sacrificed to war-time necessities. Many of their more ambitious ideas were foiled by the unremitting opposition of some of the farm organisations who had benefited so much from the AAA. The mechanisms of 'grass-roots democracy' proved incapable of securing the major adjustments in agriculture that the planners wanted.

The efforts of the Soil Conservation Service undoubtedly rescued the land of the Dust Bowls and the Great Plains. But, as Donald Worster has shown, soil-conservation techniques were sold to Dust Bowl farmers as a means of enabling them to grow wheat again. As a result, Dust Bowls recurred in the 1950s and 1970s. The grandiose visions of *The Future of the Great Plains* came to nothing. As the weather improved in the later 1930s there was little pressure on Congress to make the appropriations needed to implement the report. If the aim of the Report was to persuade farmers to 'lower their expectations' as Richard Lowitt describes it, it failed. Great Plains farmers showed no signs of altering their basically expansionist, exploitative attitude to farming, especially with war-time pressure to increase production. Further west, water projects opened the way for large-scale farming and industrial expansion during the war.

Reform of land use was ultimately piecemeal and fragmentary. The federal government only purchased 11.3 million acres of the 75 million acres targeted nationally for withdrawal from production. New Deal communities resettled only 10,000 farm families of the 450,000 that the planners wanted to move. Farmers did not want to move; they did not want to stay in the resettlement communities, which never attracted congressional support and were sold off during the war.

The efforts to eliminate agriculture's broader structural flaws were doomed by the opposition of conservative farm organisations, in particular the Farm Bureau. The Farm Bureau's revival in the 1930s was due almost entirely to its association with AAA recovery programmes, especially in the South. It had little sympathy with the urban consumer. New Deal efforts to stimulate urban demand had in any case a low priority: the Surplus Relief and Food Stamp programmes were primarily designed to remove the surplus and help the farmers rather than to encourage urban consumption. But the Farm Bureau nevertheless thought the Bureau of Agricultural Economics too sympathetic to both the urban consumer and the rural poor and influenced Congress to divest the BAE of its national planning role during the war. The Farm Bureau resolutely argued that the job of government was simply to guarantee the farmer a good price in the market place: farmers did not want a demeaning subsidy. Its representatives rejected any plan after 1945 that would have subsidised a move away from cotton production. Later the Farm Bureau successfully opposed the subsidies and cheap food policy of the Brannan Plan.

The New Dealers did persuade Americans to treat the soil better. The various conservation programmes had some effect. The Civilian Conservation Corps at its peak in 1935 had over half a million men enrolled in over 2,000 camps. The young men reforested denuded slopes, cut woodland breaks to prevent forest fires, built roads to give better access to the forests, demonstrated soil conservation to farmers, and worked on irrigation and flood-control schemes. The CCC was one of the most popular New Deal agencies – even the cantankerous 'Cotton Ed' Smith called it 'the most marvellous piece of legislation that has been enacted during the present Administration or any preceding Administration'. Urban congressmen whose unemployed constituents enrolled and rural congressmen whose constituents welcomed the camps both endorsed it. Yet attempts to make the agency permanent failed. Congressmen acknowledged that there was enough conservation work to be done to justify its permanence, but the CCC was jettisoned during the war when its relief function was no longer needed.

The Shelterbelt worked despite the critics' ridicule. Eighty per cent of the 220,000,000 trees planted survived. Surveys even indicated that rainfall in the neighbouring counties increased, even if the Belt was too far to the east to have much impact on the Dust Bowls.

At the local level, Farm Bureau opposition was instrumental in killing off planning committees. The Farm Bureau saw these committees as a challenge to the influence exerted over farmers in many areas by its ally, the Extension Service. Local county planning committees largely failed, even without Farm Bureau hostility. The county was too large a unit for genuine participation by the farmers, but too small for effective planning. Few farmers were interested enough to vote in elections: in some cases turnouts were reported to be so low as to be 'farcical'. No committee could represent both dominant community values and the less privileged members of the rural community. Efforts to give the committees a war-time role in planning increased food production were resisted by the Farm Bureau.

The Farm Bureau therefore found some instruments of 'grass-roots democracy' too democratic and sought to destroy them. The Tennessee Valley Authority, like the AAA, showed how interest groups could alternatively appropriate those same instruments of 'grass-roots democracy' for their own ends.

The multipurpose aims of the TVA – flood control, agricultural regeneration, and cheap power – were reflected in the members of its first Board of Directors: the chairman, Arthur E. Morgan, a flood control engineer; H. A. Morgan, a long-time agricultural educationalist; and David Lilienthal, a young lawyer from the Wisconsin Power Commission. Arthur E. Morgan had a compelling vision of an 'integrated, social and economic order'. The model town of Norris built by the first dam served as the epitome of the balanced order which Morgan hoped to establish in the valley – a small town with vernacular housing, a cooperative barn and store, and a small woodworking store. But Morgan's ideas often seemed vague and archaic – promoting handicrafts and self-help cooperatives using scrip – as well as paternalist. But his cause was doomed less by his desire to 'uplift' Valley residents and impose change on them than by his willingess to work in cooperation with, rather than against, private utility companies, like Commonwealth and Southern under Wendell L. Willkie. The utilities bitterly resented the legislative authority given to TVA not only to produce but also to transmit and distribute electricity. The companies alternated between negotiation and litigation in their efforts to destroy the TVA. Arthur E. Morgan's desire to conciliate set him on a collision course with his fellow directors and ultimately with Roosevelt, who dismissed him in 1938.

As a result it was H. A. Morgan and David Lilienthal who shaped the TVA. H. A Morgan, responsible for fertilisers and agricultural development, sought to revitalise farming through the time-honoured Extension Service way of cooperating with local community leaders – the Farm Bureau and the county agents. Lilienthal, responsible for power development, sought to distribute cheap TVA electricity to municipal power systems and rural cooperatives. By any standards their achievement at the TVA was impressive. The high dams, engineered and constructed by TVA's own workforce, ended the annual threat of flooding and provided a huge source of electricity. TVA power lines reached right through Tennessee and into large parts of Mississippi and Alabama. Local power companies reduced their rates and found to their surprise that demand increased. In the Valley itself 75 per cent of the farms were electrified in 1945 compared to 2 per cent in 1933. In the south-eastern states TVA was extremely popular, cementing the allegiance of local congressmen to the New Deal.

But the achievement was costly. 'Grass-roots democracy' was a powerful protective ideology as it was with the AAA. Lilienthal aggressively popularised the notion. But cooperation with established rural groups meant working with the Extension Service and the AAA and ignoring the Soil Conservation Service and the Farm Security Administration. Rural development served the needs of the more substantial, rather than the poorer farmer. The TVA also conformed to local racial norms and largely excluded blacks.

There was little 'grass-roots democracy' about the operation of the power programme. Its increasing success did benefit farmers but it also brought rapid industrialisation. Among the TVA's first customers were the chemical company Monsanto and the Aluminum Company of America. By 1947 there were manufacturing plants in all 212 of the Valley's counties. Unlike the CCC and the land-use planning committees, the TVA successfully developed a war-time rationale. It alone could generate the electricity needed by Alcoa and the atomic research establishment at Oak Ridge. The TVA played a crucial role in the South's post-war take-off into self-sustaining economic growth. Arthur E. Morgan's vision was rapidly obliterated. In 1947 Norris was sold off to a private real estate developer. By the 1970s the TVA was a giant power company assailed by environmentalists and consumers alike.

The TVA was also exceptional. The plan to establish seven 'little TVAs' in 1937 which would coordinate the development of other river basins floundered in Congress. Private interests were alert to halt any repetition of the TVA experiment. As an exercise in regional planning the TVA had benefited from a number of special circumstances: the Valley was an isolated region, in desperate need of help, whose regeneration appeared to offer no threat to any other region; the need to do something about the Wilson Dam at Muscle Shoals had ensured long public debate before 1933; Roosevelt's personal interest put ambitious plans on the statute book in 1933 when Congress was unlikely to demur and when the relevant state governments were too weak to challenge a supra-state regional authority. These conditions were not replicated elsewhere.

One of the TVA's first customers was a rural cooperative from Alcorn County, one of the poorest counties in north-eastern Mississippi. So successful was the introduction of electrification to the county's farmers that the cooperative was able to pay back its loan from the TVA in less than half the contracted repayment period. Crucial to its success was low-cost financing from the Electric Farm and Home Authority, established in conjunction with the TVA, which enabled the farmers to buy cookers, water heaters, and refrigerators. The success of the Alcorn cooperative paved the way for a full-scale New Deal commitment to what the *Progressive Farmer* described as the 'power revolution'. The New Deal set out to electrify rural America through cooperatives funded by the Rural Electrification Administration, set up first under the WPA in 1935, then as a permanent independent agency in 1936.

Only one in ten farmers had electricity in 1930. Over half the farmers in the Far West were linked up but only a small minority in the Midwest or South had electricity: less than 1 per cent of farmers in Mississippi. Private-utility companies argued that the cost of providing a rural service to isolated farms was prohibitive and that farmers' consumption of electricity would be too small to make a service viable. But electricity was not an optional luxury for farmers. Its absence complemented low incomes as the major explanation of the low quality of rural life. The lack of running water, outdoor privies, and the poorly stored food led to poor health, particularly in the South. The lack of labour-saving devices shaped the drudgery of domestic life. The lack of electric power inhibited mechanisation and diversification.

The REA demonstrated that loans to farmer cooperatives were financially viable and the farmers surprised the electricity industry with the demands they made for electric appliances. Nevertheless, the REA had to overcome formidable opposition from private utilities. The power companies used sympathetic lawyers and Extension Service officials to discourage farmers from applying to the REA for assistance; state power commissions friendly to the utilities hamstrung cooperatives; the companies built 'spite lines' alongside proposed REA lines or 'skimmed the cream' by serving the most financially attractive customers and leaving the rest to the REA. But the REA persisted. For every rural customer the private utilities chose to serve, the REA linked up three farm families. By 1939 417 cooperatives served over a quarter of a million rural households. By 1945 rural electrification had reached 40 per cent of American farms. With the 'power revolution' came increased leisure, better health, and the elimination of much of the tedium and drudgery of farm life. Electrification also made possible the post-war diversification of agriculture, notably in the South, where chicken brooders enabled farmers to abandon cotton for poultry after 1945.

New Deal plans for the poorest rural Americans, the Native Americans, were as far-reaching as they were for the Tennessee Valley. Roosevelt and Ickes's choice as Commissioner of Indian Affairs, John Collier, had vigorously defended Indian rights and lambasted federal government policy in the 1920s. Among the Pueblos of New Mexico Collier had found the maintenance of traditional values which he had vainly sought in the immigrant communities of New York during his time as a social worker. Collier aimed to bring the benefits of education and scientific knowledge within reach of every Indian, at the same time as he encouraged the preservation of traditional culture. Under the Indian Reorganization Act of 1934 he halted the allotment and alienation of Indian land which had so eroded the Indian land base since 1887. Surplus lands that had not been allotted to individuals could now be controlled by the tribes. Referenda amongst the Indians themselves would lead to the establishment of new tribal corporations which would govern Indian resources and have access to a $10 million revolving credit fund to help modernise the Indian economy. Collier's vision was as heady and thorough-going as Arthur E. Morgan's. Enlightened experts would replace corrupt white officials; the restoration of traditional Indian culture would supplant the goal of assimilation; democratic self-government would end Bureau paternalism.

Collier accomplished much. He ended the policy of individual allotment and added 7.4 million acres to the Indian land base. He eliminated much of the petty corruption and high-handedness of Bureau officials. Anthropologists and social scientists came in to evaluate his programme and recommend changes. To replace the old boarding schools, he set up day schools where 'progressive' teachers could instil a renewed pride in their old Indian culture. He encouraged the revival of ancient dances previously discouraged as heathenism, restored small herds of buffalo, and promoted the sale of Indian arts and crafts. He protected religious freedom and restored Indian civil liberties. Improved medical services eliminated trachoma on the reservations and battled against tuberculosis. To achieve all this, he utilised a wide range of the alphabet agencies. The CCC, the Civil Works Administration, and the Works Progress Administration provided emergency employment; the PWA built schools and hospitals; the Subsistence Homesteads Division resettled landless Indians; the Resettlement Administration bought additional land; the Soil Erosion Service ran demonstration land-use projects.

Yet the long-term impact of these efforts were negligible. New Deal relief alleviated Indian distress: yet the Indians remained poor. The New Deal only partially introduced a wage economy. Indian land-use practices remained largely unchanged. Collier was unable to institutionalise the New Deal. After the war federal government protection and special services were discontinued in return for a once-and-for-all cash settlement of Indian claims. Twelve tribes whose self-government had been so carefully nurtured by Collier voted to accept termination.

Conservative opposition in Congress and the impact of the war accounted for many of Collier's problems just as they negated other rural plans. Western congressmen, including liberals like Burton K. Wheeler of Montana and Elmer Thomas of Oklahoma, favoured the traditional aims of assimilation. Wheeler later resented Collier's efforts to lobby Indians on behalf of Supreme Court reform. The Indian Affairs Committees in Congress offered a ready sounding-board to critics of Collier, both white and Indian. In 1945 congressional appropriations for the Indian Bureau were $3.6 million less than in 1932.

The war also disrupted the Indian New Deal. Fifty per cent of the population left the reservation for jobs in the defence industries or the armed services. The Bureau lost personnel to the war effort: Collier himself was diverted to the War Relocation Agency and its camps for Japanese-Americans. Indian projects fared badly in the competition for appropriations with war-related plans.

Nevertheless, Collier's attempt to combine planning, community-building, and 'grass-roots democracy' suffered from its own internal contradictions. Collier's view of tribal unity and community cohesion had been shaped by his experience with the Pueblos, who had a tight social structure, a highly-organised religious hierarchy, and had escaped the effects of allotment. Elsewhere, there was far less unity and commitment to traditional values. As an Indian observer of the Dakota Sioux noted, the divisions could be endless: 'Full bloods versus mixed bloods; progressives versus conservatives, Protestants versus Catholics; Radicals versus Holdfasts; Democrats versus Republicans; Collier versus Bureau; chiefs versus Council; Sons of Chief versus sons of other chiefs . . .'

The tribe was not necessarily the appropriate unit for self-government. Some tribes occupied huge reservations scattered across four states; others had no reservations; some reservations were shared by many tribes; the Flathead Reservation in Montana was shared by two tribes speaking mutually incomprehensible dialects. Critics noted that the clan or the village, rather than the tribe, served as the real focus of authority for Indians. Tribal self-government sometimes fuelled factionalism: at other times it was rejected by a cultural conservatism which found democracy and majority rule alien concepts.

Indians who might have taken the lead in organising tribal governments were sometimes the most suspicious of Collier's plans. They themselves were the beneficiaries of the assimilation policy which Collier was trying to reverse, often educated at the boarding schools the Commissioner was trying to close down. They feared that he was trying to make them 'return to the blanket'. They complained, for example, that the new day schools were not concentrating on teaching the reading and writing of English – the skills which were essential to success in modern American society.

To win over such sceptics would take time. Time was essential to the task of community building and establishing viable democratic institutions. But time was not what Collier had. Immediate planning needs often collided with the need to win over Indian acceptance of new ideas. To unlock the credit resources necessary for the regeneration of the Indian economy, Indians had to agree in referenda to reorganisation. Yet in the economic emergency of 1933 and 1934 Collier and his officials had little time for the educational task of winning over Indians to the wisdom of tribal self-government: certainly not the time to establish the patiently-built consensus which characterised decision-making amongst the Navajos.

Even more crucially, Collier was convinced that the immediate reduction of the Navajos' herds of sheep and goats was essential to the rescue of the Navajo land, severely eroded by overgrazing. But the livestock slaughter imposed vigorously in 1933 and 1934 not only initially reduced many smaller herds below a viable minimum but also seriously underestimated the Navajo cultural attachment to their livestock. As a result, in the referendum, the Navajo, the largest single tribe, rejected reorganisation. In the long-run the live-stock programme over-shadowed the many-faceted programmes which assisted the Navajos. As a result in 1942 one observer noted, 'Most of the individual spirit is broken, and with this has come a sociological problem to the reservation which will not be solved in many years'.

Planning for rural America was therefore largely partial, piecemeal, and fragmentary. Efforts to reorder American agriculture were thwarted in part by pressure groups which the AAA had done so much to promote, in part by the war, which lessened the need for change and provided a rationale for eliminating inessential programmes. But ultimately government rationalisation of agriculture faced an insoluble dilemma. To be effective, planning had to be coercive. Coercion might be acceptable to farmers in the short term, but not in the long-term timetable envisaged by the planners. Planning by consent on the other hand could only be effective if there were demonstrable short-term benefits to the farmers. But the sort of benefits New Deal planners were seeking were long-term adjustments. Planning for the distant future did not sufficiently engage the farmers' interest to make grass-roots democracy work. Wider economic forces, not governmental plans, would eventually rationalise and modernise American agriculture.

4 The assault on rural poverty

In recent years the New Deal has been criticised less for its failure rationally to plan American agriculture than for its failure to tackle successfully the problem of rural poverty. Not only was the New Deal's belated assault on rural poverty an inadequate response, critics argue, but its recovery programmes actually made the plight of the rural poor, particularly the tenants and the sharecroppers of the South, worse.

Of the three major groups of the rural poor in the United States one group – those farmers who lived on submarginal land and often did not participate in the commercial farm economy – were little affected by commodity programmes of the New Deal; neither did the rural poverty programmes significantly improve their lot. The main benefit they derived from the New Deal came from direct relief payments. This extra income, the lack of economic opportunity anywhere else, and the farmers' reluctance to move meant that they tended to stay where they were in the Ozarks, the Appalachians, and the cut-over regions of the Great Lakes. The other two groups – southern tenants and sharecroppers and migratory farm labourers, of whom the most important were working on the factory farms of California – shared similar experiences, first as workers unexpectedly affected by the farm recovery programmes, then as surprisingly militant protesters and ultimately as major targets of the rural poverty programmes.

Both sharecroppers and migratory labourers were economically and politically powerless. The former were often black, usually voteless, and their dependence on landlords was sanctioned by both law and community and racial norms; the latter were migrants, usually Mexican and employed seasonally on the factory farms precisely because they were low-paid, impotent, and docile successors to the Chinese. Whether in the tenant shack or in the labour camp, the living conditions of these rural poor mirrored an income that scarcely attained bare subsistence levels.

Neither group benefited initially from New Deal policies: in the South tenants were discriminated against in the allocation of rental and benefit payments, frequently cheated even out of what they were due to get, and often evicted in defiance of the AAA's cotton contract; in California fruit and vegetable growers had responded to the Depression with savage wage cuts but they showed no signs of restoring those wages when New Deal-inspired prosperity returned. The cotton growers of the San Joaquin Valley whose income from the cotton contract went up by 150 per cent in 1933 refused to grant a wage increase to their workers.

In both the South and California the dispossessed were driven to radicalism by desperation, sometimes spurred by rising expectations aroused by the New Deal: in the South some joined the Communist-led Alabama Sharecroppers Union and later the Socialist-led Southern Tenant Farmers Union, in California many joined the Communist-led Cannery and Agricultural Workers Industrial Union. Both the STFU and the CAWIU succeeded in overcoming the potential tensions of a racially mixed membership. Both had initial success: the STFU with a successful picking strike in 1935, the farm labourers in California with 37 strikes in 1933 involving over 47,000 workers which won wage increases of up to 100 per cent.

Both unions, however, ultimately fell victim to the inherent difficulties of agricultural unionism but above all to the violent repression by southern planters and Californian growers. Mass terrorism, sanctioned by local law enforcement officials, kidnappings and assaults of union organisers, the mass eviction of tenant farmers and strikers, and finally in California, the prosecution of Communist leaders under the criminal syndicalism statutes, combined to smash the unions. The STFU had virtually collapsed by 1938, save for a roadside demonstration of evicted tenants in the Missouri boot heel in 1939. The CAWIU had already collapsed with the arrest of its leaders in 1934.

The response of the New Deal was initially unsympathetic. The Cotton Section of the AAA was staffed by Southerners with backgrounds in the Extension Service who shared the landlords' paternalistic attitude to 'shiftless' tenants. They regarded the sharecropper agitation as Communist-inspired, relied on the word of the landlord-dominated local committees that no tenant problem existed, and suppressed critical investigations by outside observers. In California, George Creel for the NRA manifested that early New Deal confidence that unions would be unnecessary once the source of industrial relations conflict – poor working conditions – was eliminated. He attempted to impose wage increases, but not union recognition, on the San Joaquin Valley cotton growers in the great strike of 1933 and to persuade employers to treat their workers more fairly and thus undercut unions. Pelham Glassford, appointed by Frances Perkins as special labour conciliator for the Imperial Valley, tried to win the confidence of the employers by bitterly attacking Communist union leaders and refusing to protect their civil liberties. Too late did he realise that once the employers had smashed the unions they had no intention of making the sort of reforms in working conditions that he thought essential.

The rural poor suffered from the failure of national farm policy-makers to understand that agricultural relations on southern plantations and on western factory farms were not the same as relations on the family farms of the Midwest. Thus it was wrongly assumed that the raising of farm prices in both the South and California would be translated into increased income for those at the bottom of the rural ladder, that local committees of farmers would produce genuine grass-roots democracy in the South, and that farm labourers in California did not need the protection of the Wagner Act.

New Dealers were fearful of offending powerful political interests in both the South and California. The need for southern congressional support clearly limited AAA policy regarding sharecroppers. In 1935 urban liberals from the Legal Division attempted to force landlords to keep their tenants on the land. When Chester Davis sacked them, Wallace had either to acquiesce in the purge or make way for someone more acceptable to the southern Democrats. The cautious response to STFU complaints from Arkansas was in large part prompted by a desire to avoid offending majority leader Joe Robinson of Arkansas in an election year. Robert La Follette's civil liberties committee, which came into existence as the specific result of the sharecroppers' plight, did not investigate conditions for fear of jeopardising the committee's congressional appropriation. In California, the power of agribusiness was such that even a sympathetic New Deal official like Gardner Jackson had to admit in 1935 that it was 'politically fatal to take up the question of these workers in the field'. The local power of the employers' association, Associated Farmers, meant that both relief and WPA policies in the state forced farmworkers off the relief rolls throughout the 1930s to satisfy the seasonal labour demands of the factory farms, even though the government admitted that the wages paid were criminally low.

There was a belated New Deal response to the plight of the rural poor. But the poverty programmes at best offered only partial solutions and their implementation failed even to provide that. The goal of the Farm Security Administration, which coordinated the poverty programmes in 1937, of individual small farm ownership through purchase loans to tenant farmers was anachronistic when efficient agriculture demanded larger units, capitalising on mechanisation, particularly in cotton. In any case, funds were woefully inadequate and could satisfy only 1 in 22 applicants. The programme was also run cautiously, 'skimming the cream' and aiding those among the rural poor best able to help themselves.

The more radical programme of resettlement communities and the cooperative services that went with them failed not simply because of conservative opposition, but because the individual farms were too small and too expensive to allow farmers much hope of ever purchasing their own farms and the turnover of clients was consequently discouragingly high. The major programme of the FSA – the rehabilitation loans and grants to poorer farmers – all too often failed in the daunting task of turning poorly educated small farmers into efficient producers. In California, the FSA's goal was also to tackle the more extreme symptoms of poverty rather than to alter the position of the farm labourers in relation to their employers. FSA labour camps did provide model housing and community facilities, but those camps were reserved for the migrants from Oklahoma and Arkansas rather than the non-white majority of farm labourers who were already in California. The model camps also in a sense subsidised the employers who no longer had to furnish those particular workers.

This indictment of the New Deal treatment of rural poverty needs to be qualified. First, the AAA was by no means responsible for all the displacement of tenant farmers in the 1930s. In any case fewer left the land in the South in the 1930s than in either the 1920s or the 1940s. Of those who did leave, many were displaced by low prices before 1933. To the extent that the New Deal rescued cotton agriculture, it may have even kept tenants on the land. On the other hand in the western cotton states there is no doubt that mechanisation made possible by New Deal profits did spark the exodus to California.

In belatedly tackling the problem of rural poverty, New Dealers were not responding to, or attempting to defuse, radical protest.

To a large extent it was the New Dealers themselves who first discovered the plight of the rural poor. It was the relief officials of the Federal Emergency Relief Administration who unexpectedly confronted large rural relief demands in 1933 and it was their initiatives that led to the establishment of the Resettlement Administration. New Deal policy-makers were fully aware of the need for more money, of the inadequacy of the individual small farmer goal, and of the need for more supervision of FSA clients. What they hoped was that they could launch the programme with all its faults in 1937 and improve it later.

As in so many other New Deal programmes, the opportunity to make improvements later never came. As with rural planning, so with rural poverty, the Farm Security Administration came up against the power of the farm pressure groups who had so much benefited from the AAA programme. At the local level in the South, FSA programmes for all their inadequacy threatened the traditional patterns of dependence in the rural communities. Landlords and merchants were worried by the existence of alternative sources of credit and advice, particularly to black tenants. Southern conservative politicians and the Farm Bureau responded to these alarms and combined effectively to kill off the Farm Security Administration during the war.

5 Limited options

The limitations of New Deal farm policy are clear. Analyses of the distribution of agricultural spending by Leonard Arrington and Don Reading show that on a per capita basis New Deal benefits went to those states, like the cattle states of the West, that had lost farm income dramatically after 1929 rather than to those states, like the southern states, that were permanently poor. This emphasis on agricultural recovery largely precluded the attainment of the New Deal's other goals of rationalising American agriculture by planning or of eliminating rural poverty. The need for the consent of the farmers to introduce the radical departure of production control led to a process of policy-making that created or bolstered rural pressure groups that would later become conservative opponents of New Deal goals. These groups in the long-run fostered the special interest of particular commodities, were unsympathetic to planning, and relentlessly hounded the FSA. The need to implement crop control put the local adminis-tration of the farm programme into the hands of local élites who did little to protect tenants and sharecroppers.

It is difficult to see how these constraints of localism and voluntarism could have been avoided. In the economic emergency of 1933 the emphasis of almost everybody was on immediate relief and recovery. The existence of rural poverty was acknowledged only by a small group of rural sociologists; the fate of the tenant farmers was simply not considered when the AAA and the commodity programmes were launched in 1933. To make crop control work the cooperation of large farmers was needed, other-wise a voluntary programme would fail and the New Deal had neither the mandate, the constitutional authority, nor the bureaucracy to impose a compulsory programme. Throughout the New Deal the political pressure on the farm programme was to increase, not diminish, the importance of local administrators.

The supposedly radical options that the New Deal failed to choose were in fact either unworkable, politically impossible, not wanted by the farmers themselves, or open to the same objections as New Deal policies.

Huey Long, one of the most radical critics of the New Deal, particularly of the failure to help the rural poor, had advocated a cotton holiday, a total ban on cotton production in 1932. Aside from practical questions of enforcement, how were tenant farmers to survive with no cash income coming in? Planned scarcity on such a scale would have led to massive tenant displacement.

In 1933 the radical remedies were to guarantee the cost of production and currency inflation. Both were schemes purely designed to help the commercial farmers, both were over-generous to the farm sector, neither did anything to help urban consumer purchasing power, and neither did anything to help the rural poor. Critics who have argued that a straightforward free market approach would have secured the necessary adjustments in American agriculture more quickly and avoided the long-term distortion caused by government programmes, have not offered any suggestions as to how the surplus labour force on the land would have been looked after in the 1930s when there were no urban economic opportunites for that surplus labour to exploit.

Donald Worster has argued that it might have been better to let the Dust Bowl revert to grass rather than encourage farmers to grow wheat there again and restart the damaging ecological cycle. Such a policy, he acknowledges, would again have led to a massive displacement of Dust Bowl farmers. He also laments the failure to eliminate capitalist economic values, which were responsible for the exploitation of the soil in the first place. Yet he stresses how reluctant farmers were to lower their expectations. They wanted a cash income. Both New Deal and radical critics in the 1930s assumed that farmers would have to earn an income from commercial farming.

Pete Daniel, the most subtle and sophisticated analyst of the relationship between government programmes, technological change, and the modernisation of southern agriculture, believes that the New Deal should have systematically upgraded tenant farmers in the South so that they would not later have had to leave the land. He cites approvingly a Federal Emergency Relief Administration experiment rehabilitating tenant farmers in an older form of economic relationships based on barter and growing non-commercial crops. Daniel believes that it was better to survive in poverty on the land than to move to the cities. In contrast to the contemporary city, 'At the center of this [farm] life was a natural harmony – the season of planting, hoeing, harvesting and settlement. It was a primitive way of life, a struggle for survival, but the human race has found grim satisfaction in living as close to the margins of absolute failure as possible.' But most American farmers had been living close enough to absolute failure for too long. They wanted a substantial cash income like other Americans.

Decentralist intellectuals during the New Deal had envisaged a rural America much like Daniel's vision of small, non-commercial farmers. They disliked much of the AAA but the one New Deal agency they championed was the Rural Electrification Administration. Electricity, they believed, would improve the quality of a small farmer's life and persuade him to stay on the land. But what electricity did was to convince farmers they needed a greater cash income to take advantage of all the benefits of a consumer society that they had been denied for so long.

The Southern Tenant Farmers Union suggested a much more radical solution: the resettlement of farmers into collective farms which could take advantage of economies of scale and invest in mechanisation. There is little evidence that any massive resettlement of farmers could be either induced or coerced by government and the experience of resettlement communities raises doubts that more collectively organised farms would have worked. Above all, as the STFU acknowledged, its own tenant members wanted the chance to purchase their own land, not to join a collective farm.

The problems with these alternatives highlight the final constraint on New Deal policy-makers: the pervasive and persistent conservatism of the farmers themselves. Midwestern farmers in the Farmers' Holiday Association did not want a change in the system or permanent government interference; they simply wanted higher prices. Dust Bowl farmers did not want to leave the Dust Bowl, they wanted the chance to grow wheat again. Farmers on submarginal land did not want to be resettled. Farmers in resettlement communities regarded them as temporary stopping places until they could own their own land. Members of the Southern Tenant Farmers Union wanted individual farm ownership, not collective farms. California farm workers, as their Communist leaders conceded, wanted higher wages, not radical political change.

Ironically these farmers did not get their conservative wish because of the major transformation of American agriculture that was to take place, and it was equally ironic that it was a transformation on which the New Deal was to have only a marginal impact. Farms were to be transformed in the next 40 years by unprecedented mechanisation and technological advance, a massive flight from the land, the virtual disappearance of the family farm, the decline in the number of farms, and the vast increase in their size. The New Deal rescued farmers from the worst of the Depression but had little effect on these developments which so dramatically changed the structure of American farming.

5
Doles and Jobs: Welfare

In the absence of any significant economic recovery the most important measure of the New Deal's effectiveness for many Americans would have to be the generosity with which the New Deal aided the jobless and the unemployables. Recognising that private and local relief efforts had been overwhelmed by the sheer extent of the Depression, the federal government, for the first time in 1933, granted money directly to the states for unemployment relief under the auspices of the Federal Emergency Relief Administration. As it became clear that this assistance was not enough, the New Deal tried to provide work relief for as many of the unemployed as possible, first, under the Civil Works Administration and, then, in 1935 under the Works Progress Administration. Such emergency measures did not, of course, tackle the long-term problem of economic insecurity. In 1935, therefore, Roosevelt secured passage of a Social Security Act which provided both insurance against old age and unemployment and federal matching grants to state assistance programmes to the indigent.

Critics have found much wrong with the American welfare state which the New Deal launched. The random combination of federal and state programmes handed down by the New Deal is largely responsible for the ramshackle nature of current welfare provision in the United States. Some have argued that the New Deal welfare policy was not the start of a progressively more liberal acceptance by the government of the welfare society, but rather the bare minimum necessary to contain the threat of radical social disorder: a minimum standard which itself was eroded as the threat diminished, so that a permanent pool of surplus labour was available as prosperity returned. These criticisms seriously underestimate the obstacles facing New Deal policy-makers in the 1930s. In the face of these obstacles in the 1930s over 46,000,000 people, some 35 per cent of the population, at one time or another, received public assistance or social insurance. It was these benefits, the tangible evidence of the New Deal's concern, that did more than anything to cement the loyalty of lower-income voters and disadvantaged minorities to Franklin Roosevelt and the Democratic Party.

1 Direct relief: The Federal Emergency Relief Administration

In contrast to Hoover's reluctance to grant money to the states for unemployment relief, the New Deal in 1933 established the FERA with $500 million to grant, not loan, to the states for relief. $250 million was available as matching funds whereby one federal dollar was put up for three state dollars. $250 million was available as a straightforward grant on the basis of need.

Roosevelt appointed Harry Hopkins to run the new agency. Hopkins came from rural Iowa and was educated at Grinnell College. But for most politicians he epitomised the New Deal's ideals for urban America. Like many New Dealers, he had worked in a settlement house and had then gone on to build up an effective reputation in New York social work agencies until he was finally brought in to run the state emergency relief administration. Hard-drinking, profane, divorced, fond of cigarettes, cards, and the racetracks, Hopkins professed a certain world-weary cynicism, a cynicism which when related to relief and the political process would lead him into trouble with conservative politicians. But he, perhaps more than any other New Dealer, also dreamed of a welfare system in which every American was guaranteed a measure of economic security.

In the first Hundred Days, Hopkins appeared a relatively minor figure, distant from the momentous policy struggles over industrial and agricultural policy. By the end of 1933 he was a key figure in the development of New Deal strategy. His relief programmes were the key to the success of Roosevelt's short-term efforts to alleviate mass distress. He was soon part of the presidential inner circle and in the second term perhaps the most powerful presidential adviser. He was one of the liberal leaders pushing an uncertain Roosevelt towards more extensive social reform in 1935. He played the decisive role in pushing Roosevelt towards the resumption of government spending in 1938 and was intimately involved in the attempted purge of Democratic conservatives that summer. He was a hero to young New Deal congressmen elected in 1934 and 1936: he was the one figure in Washington who could give them the jobs and projects they needed. It was this power – of which Hopkins sometimes too frankly reminded his listeners – together with the mainly urban needs which his policies addressed that made him the symbol for many conservatives of what was wrong and corrupting about the New Deal. One by no means reactionary Georgia congressman responded to an invitation from southern liberal congressmen to attend a meeting addressed by Hopkins by noting that 'If there is one thing for which I have a distinct aversion, it is hearing Mr. Hopkins speak'.

To widen Hopkins's appeal as a potential presidential successor, Roosevelt nominated him as Secretary of Commerce in 1939. Hopkins moved to reassure the business community. But a long fight with cancer meant that Hopkins had to give up any hope of personal political advancement. As he needed nothing from the president, so Roosevelt came to rely on him even more. Hopkins was the man who pulled the strings to ensure Roosevelt's nomination for a third term at the Chicago convention in 1940. During the war he became effectively the President's top foreign policy adviser. He was the crucial go-between between Roosevelt and the other two great Allied leaders, Stalin and Churchill. After Roosevelt's death Hopkins's emaciated frame was a ghostly reminder of the goals of peaceful post-war cooperation between the superpowers which he and Roosevelt believed they had secured at the Yalta conference in 1945.

As a relief administrator, Hopkins combined compassion with tough-mindedness: a combination that characterised the approach of a remarkable staff of relief officials that he assembled in Washington. From the start these relief officials were refreshingly self-critical. Changes in relief policy in the 1930s took place not so much because of outside pressure from militants as from a constantly self-questioning attitude on the part of these policy-makers. It was Hopkins's own officials, for example, who first uncovered the problem of endemic rural poverty in the South and started to devise means of tackling it. It was their own inquiries that highlighted the deficiencies of their own programmes and led to policy shifts like the establishment of the Civil Works Administration. No better example of their receptivity to new ideas from unlikely sources could be found than the initiation of a survey of sunken ships in harbours and round the coast. This scheme under the CWA was suggested by a tramp who walked off the street in Washington into the CWA office and sold the idea to Arthur Goldschmidt, an assistant director. The tramp turned out to be a highly competent ship designer who had not received a commission since 1929.

From the start, speed and flexibility characterised the FERA. Hopkins allegedly spent $5 million within 2 hours of taking office. The need for speed left Hopkins no alternative but to use state agencies to administer relief. There simply was not the time to establish the gigantic federal bureaucracy that otherwise would have been necessary. The FERA staff in Washington which supervised this massive spending programme was never in fact more than 750 strong.

Administration by the states may have been unavoidable but localism caused problems. The distribution of funds plagued the FERA throughout its life. The principle of matching funds tended to penalise the poorer states who could not afford to make the same contribution as richer states. While the national average of relief payments in 1933 was $15.07 a month, in the poorer South it varied from $3.96 in Mississippi to $13.89 in Louisiana. The matching principle was, however, increasingly tempered by direct grants. Thus, although the matching principle penalised the South, direct grants meant that federal money accounted for 90 per cent of relief spending in the southern states, in contrast to an average of 62 per cent in the nation as a whole. Similarly, sparsely populated, drought-ridden western mountain and Great Plains states were the top ten recipients per capita of FERA spending.

All too often, however, it was not an inability to pay but a tight-fisted reluctance to pay that accounted for the lack of state spending. Hopkins spent an inordinate amount of time trying to prod miserly state governments into more realistic appropriations for relief. Some states were hampered by constitutional restrictions or by the fact that legislatures were not in session. More often, however, fiscal conservatism was the cause. Governor C. Ben Ross of Idaho boasted to his constituents that he had outguessed the Washington bureaucrats and kept Idaho relief spending down, while continuing to receive federal grants. Other western states were equally notorious. In the South, states like Virginia and North Carolina which prided themselves on their fiscal soundness refused to jeopardise their balanced budgets to spend on relief. By special pleading and budgetary legerdemain they managed to appease Hopkins. In other states outright hostility to relief was the cause. Georgia did not even furnish its Relief Administration with office space: Governor Talmadge believed that castor oil was the best cure for the poor. In Oregon, Governor Martin believed that no able-bodied unemployed person should receive relief and wished that the needy aged and feeble-minded could be chloroformed. In the face of such intransigence Hopkins's ultimate weapon was to cut off federal funds. He was pushed to do this in the case of particularly recalcitrant states like Colorado, but most of the time it was an empty threat, since both Hopkins and the local politicians knew that the people who would really suffer from a cut-off of funds would be the poor themselves.

The state administration of relief meant wide variations in the competence of the administration. To find the trained personnel to run relief and welfare programmes was a major task. In a city like New York, relief administrators could draw on social workers from many private agencies and could capitalise on the experience and expertise of a massive private charity effort at work relief and the state government's own Temporary Emergency Relief Administration. Consequently, by September 1933 a field investigator could report that 'she found relief administration and adequacy so far ahead of what I had seen in other states that there just isn't any basis for comparison at all'. But in some southern states it was a different matter. In Georgia, relief director Gay Shepperson had to overcome formidable local political and male opposition to appoint trained women as county relief administrators. 'Many counties in Georgia that had never seen a social worker now had one permanently stationed within their borders', notes Michael Holmes. South Carolina and Mississippi were not so lucky. In South Carolina a Washington investigation of the Relief Administration uncovered an administrative nightmare of inadequately supervised, untrained personnel on poor salaries. Nepotism and faulty accounting were not the least of the problems of county administrators who were described as 'conscientious, hardworking, sincere and incompetent'. The absence of social workers in Mississippi meant that trained county relief directors would have had to be imported from outside the state. Mississippi politicians had no intention of tolerating that.

Many of these problems reflected traditional conservative attitudes towards relief and the poor. The Mississippi state director of relief believed that three dollars a week was ample for a relief client. Five dollars was the most that would normally be paid in the state no matter how hard Hopkins's assistant Aubrey Williams tried to convince him that $12 might be appropriate. In Fairfield County, Ohio, homeless relief clients were sent to sleep in the horse stalls of the county fairground. Everywhere applicants for relief were subject to a means test, and, often, humiliation. One of Hopkins's aides visiting a relief office in Phoenix, Arizona, found over 100 people jammed into a small room when the temperature was over 100°, with an overflow crowd waiting for hours in a nearby garage. He fumed, 'When I see the lack of intelligence, not to say common, ordinary human sympathy which characterizes the handling of destitute families in some places, I am ashamed of what we are doing'. In the more bland words of an audit report in New York City: 'Crowded precinct offices, occasional hostile police guards, long waits for interviews, long delays in investigations tend to sap the courage and self-respect of clients'.

No aspect of local relief practice aroused more anger among relief clients than the continued distribution of food orders rather than cash, making the recipients feel like charity cases. As an unemployed man in Pittsburgh complained, 'Does a man's status change when he becomes unemployed, so that, while he was perfectly able to handle money when he had a job, he can't be trusted when he's out of work'. 'I cannot accept', Aubrey Williams announced for the FERA, 'the projecting of nation-wide arrangements on a grocery order as anything but bad and undesirable. I have more confidence in what Mrs. John Smith can do with a five dollar bill.' But Williams often fulminated in vain.

At other times the influence of local farmers and businessmen, who believed that generous relief rates were depriving them of cheap labour, was paramount. In the southern states Hopkins reluctantly had to waive the 30¢ an hour wage rate for work relief and to suspend relief operations altogether in rural counties at harvest. Local racial discrimination was endemic. Blacks in the South, the group most in need of assistance, found it harder to get on the relief rolls and then received less money than whites when they did manage to get on. Southern cities usually paid white clients twice as much as blacks. Atlanta gave out monthly relief cheques of $32.66 to whites and $19.29 to blacks. In some rural black-belt counties black relief payments were as little as 30 per cent of white payments.

The final problem of localism was the unprecedented scope the relief programme gave politicians for political influence and interference. The potential political advantages of filling so many posts and of distributing so much money to the needy were immense and clearly open to abuse. As far as we can tell, Hopkins successfully resisted pressures to politicise relief, although he did have to federalise relief operations in six states where political interference was too blatant. There were plenty of complaints about the political misuse of relief, but on closer examination many of these were simply partisan or factional grievances. In a Republican state like Pennsylvania, Democrats lamented that their opponents were controlling relief. In southern states the non-partisan administration of relief aroused the indignation of local Democrats who assumed that in places like Western North Carolina any non-political appointments were bound to be Republican. Democratic congressmen as a whole resented both the control which state governors exercised over relief and the reluctance of Hopkins to respond to their political imperatives. Their failure to influence Hopkins made them all the more determined to maintain much tighter political control later of the Works Progress Administration.

Aside from the local constraints, the FERA was handicapped by its lack of funds. In 1935 the FERA paid $25 to $29 per family per month, which, as James Patterson points out, was the average pre-Depression *weekly* wage of a regularly employed industrial worker and lagged far behind the $100 or more per month regarded by many as the minimum subsistence level. Yet for all these limitations in 1935 over $3 billion was spent in public relief aid compared to $208 million in 1932. The FERA was largely responsible for this quantum leap and its existence rescued many Americans from the threat of starvation.

2 Work relief: The Civil Works Administration

From the start Harry Hopkins had been unhappy with the stigma attached to the means test and its invasion of relief clients' privacy: 'If we had not become so accustomed, and, in a sense, so hardened to the fact of poverty, we would even now be astounded at our effrontery.' He sympathised with the mounting discontent amongst the unemployed with the humiliating nature of much of the relief that they were receiving under the FERA. Hopkins preferred work relief to direct relief and he was anxious both to expand the number of work relief projects in the FERA and to improve their quality. Work relief, Hopkins believed, should provide proper jobs: it should not be 'make-work'; nor should work relief be considered a penalty imposed on relief clients to reassure hostile conservatives that relief was not subsidising idleness.

Hopkins's commitment to work relief coincided with a pressing crisis in October 1933. Initially, FERA planners had assumed that New Deal economic recovery measures would work quickly and obviate the necessity for relief spending. They made relief appropriations, therefore, only two months at a time. By October, however, it was clear that the recovery programme was not working as they had hoped. Instead the country faced what relief workers described as a 'rapidly onrushing catastrophe of proportions never before experienced or contemplated'. Hopkins and his officials faced the very real question as to how the unemployed would survive the coming winter.

Hopkins's answer was to secure $400 million for a work relief programme, the Civil Works Administration. This was to be a purely federal project. (In fact most state emergency relief administrations became overnight the federally-employed state CWA.) There was to be no means test, workers did not have to come from the relief rolls, and they were to be paid at the wage rates laid down for the Public Works Administration.

The programme was launched with breathtaking speed. On 2 November Roosevelt gave his approval; on 15 November Hopkins outlined his plans to local officials: by 23 November the CWA was paying its first cheques to 814,511 workers. By Christmas 3.5 million were employed. By 18 January 1934 the workforce totalled 4.2 million.

For the federal government directly to employ such a large workforce was an immense managerial task. Projects had to be devised: a job that taxed the ingenuity of some state administrations. Workers had to be hired, equipped, and paid. Two million were transferred from the relief rolls; two million were taken from the nine million workers listed by the National Re-employment Service. Manufacturers, in spite of producing 25,000 wheelbarrows a day, often could not keep up with the demand. The military stepped in: 'We opened up warehouses from World War I', recalled Arthur Goldschmidt. The CWA made 60,000,000 individual payments: at one point the paper and ink to prepare the cheques ran out. Increasingly, Hopkins and state administrators had to bring in engineers and business executives to provide the technical expertise to implement the programme, much to the chagrin both of local social workers and of local politicians. As a result, despite press allegations, the CWA was remarkably free of corruption. Hopkins moved speedily at the first hint of graft and where necessary brought in the Army Corps of Engineers to run troubled programmes.

'We are not', said Hopkins, 'going to permit CWA funds to be used for garbage collection or for cleaning of streets or for snow removal.' The press accused the CWA of employing workers on 'leaf-raking' projects but Hopkins's intent was precisely to avoid that sort of make-work. Inevitably, the bulk of the projects – 95 per cent – were for road building and repairs and for the construction and repair of public buildings. Two million labourers worked on 500,000 miles of roads in record-breaking cold temperatures. CWA workers built or improved 40,000 schools, 3,500 parks, playgrounds and athletic fields, and 1,000 airports.

Despite the emphasis on manual labour, the breadth of projects foreshadowed the later Works Progress Administration. 10 per cent of CWA employees were white-collar and professional men and women. As one historian of the CWA noted, 'It undertook the elimination of chinchbugs in Indiana, the restocking of wild life in Alaska, the construction of a three-ton calculating machine at the University of Pennsylvania, the sealing up of abandoned coal mines, and the compilation and analysis of climatic data from the Soviet Union'. The CWA also provided projects for 300,000 women, employed 3,000 artists to paint murals on public buildings, used 40,000 teachers to teach adult illiterates, surveyed coasts, harbours and historic buildings, and established symphony orchestras in New York and Buffalo.

The wage rates of the CWA were both its greatest source of strength and of weakness. By paying PWA wage rates the CWA was the only work relief programme of the New Deal to pay wages that began to measure up to private industry and to do so without a means test. The wages CWA workers received related to the jobs they performed, not their need. The average weekly wage of $15.04 per person contrasted strikingly with average weekly relief payments before the CWA of $4.25. The stigma of relief had gone as well. As a Chicagoan recalled, 'I hated going to the store with a ticket. Everybody would look at you. Everyone knew you were on relief right away. On CWA there were no tickets to go to the grocery store anymore. My mother bought for cash.' The CWA, noted Bonnie Fox Schwartz, 'restored the productive, wage-earning role of the American workforce'.

Generous wage rates, however, ran up against Roosevelt's budgetary concerns. The high wages meant that the initial $400 million allotment would rapidly be exhausted. When Hopkins went to Roosevelt for more money in early January, because the project would close on 3 February without it, Roosevelt exploded and told Hopkins that he would simply have to make do with what he already had. Although there was some additional congressional funding, Hopkins had to reduce wages and stagger workers in rotation to stretch out his money.

The wage rates also fuelled traditional conservative complaints that relief money kept people from seeking jobs; that CWA wages were creating a shortage of labour for private industry and agriculture. Some complaints came from the privileged, notably the lament that the golf courses in Florida were short of caddies. More substantial, though equally self-serving, complaints came from southern industrialists and farmers. Lorena Hickok, reporting on conditions in the Carolinas for Hopkins, found that wage rates in the textile industry under the NRA codes were lower than the CWA hourly rates. Similarly she reported that South Carolina truck farmers 'charge that CWA has created dissatisfaction among their Negroes. They [the Negroes] all want to be on CWA, working for 30 and 40 cents an hour. Their hearts are no longer in the work on the farms. They are very anxious that this cause of dissatisfaction be removed before farm work really gets under way.' Hickok was in no doubt as to the disingenuous nature of the southern landlords' general complaints:

> During the depression, the paternalistic landlord was hard put to it to 'furnish' his tenants. He was darned glad to have us to take over the job. but now finding that CWA has taken up some of this labor surplus . . . he is panicky, realises he may have to make better terms with his tenants and pay his day labor more, and is raising a terrific howl against CWA.

Cynical about the motives of such critics, Hickok nevertheless found their complaints sufficiently legitimate and vociferous to justify the speedy winding up of the CWA. She herself disapproved of what she saw as an increasingly demanding attitude on the part of the CWA workers who were taking government jobs for granted.

Roosevelt too was fearful that CWA 'will become a habit with the country'. He blanched at the cost of $200 million a month, compared to the $60 million monthly cost of FERA. Pressured by staunch fiscal conservatives like Budget Director Lewis Douglas, he ordered the CWA to be phased out by the spring of 1934. There was considerable congressional pressure to continue the programme and many local relief officials despaired of absorbing the demobilised workforce. But some social workers welcomed the chance to re-establish case work and the criteria of need, rather than efficiency, as the basis for relief practice. Hopkins loyally carried out the decision to terminate the CWA by 31 March.

3 Work relief: The Works Progress Administration

Harry Hopkins constantly emphasised that the poor were just like other Americans, they were not poor because of any distinctive moral infirmity: 'Three or four million heads of families don't turn into tramps and cheats overnight nor do they lose the habits and standards of a lifetime. . . . They don't drink any more than the rest of us, they don't lie any more, they're no lazier than the rest of us.' But Hopkins was concerned that in the long run, government relief would make the poor different, that hand-outs would demoralise relief clients. Instead Hopkins wanted to give the

of removing the stigma of charity or make-work from the assistance given the unemployed.

Unlike the FERA, the WPA was an entirely federal operation. Its state organisations and staff were federal agencies and employees. However, WPA projects required local sponsorship, and different degrees of local efficiency and enthusiasm led to wide variations in the speed of starting up projects. WPA projects for example started up far more rapidly in New York than in Boston and Pittsburgh. In New York City not only did dynamic Mayor Fiorello La Guardia persuade Hopkins to establish a separate WPA unit for the city (the only city in the country so rewarded), but his Commissioner of Public Works, Robert Moses, was ready immediately with blueprints for the city's projects and his powerful influence soon convinced local WPA administrators to add the necessary foremen to make the projects efficient. In Boston, by contrast, Mayor Curley's preference for prestige projects that were too large for the WPA to handle led to many months' delay in putting men to work. In Pittsburgh, a recalcitrant mayor vetoed bond issues, refused to sign promissory notes, and failed to give due notice of bond referenda in an effort to forestall local sponsorship of WPA projects. In Colorado, a quarrel between the governor and the state WPA director held up the start of the works programme for six months.

The most publicised consequence of localism, however, was the involvement of the WPA in politics. To conservative critics, the WPA symbolised the bribery and coercion by which allegedly the New Deal was corrupting the political process. The call for the nonpolitical administration of relief became a rallying cry for conservatives in Congress in the late 1930s. Their suspicions were fuelled by reported statements by Hopkins that the New Deal would 'spend, spend, spend and elect, elect, elect' and by advice from Aubrey Williams to the Workers' Alliance to 'vote to keep our friends in power'.

Few would deny that the distribution of WPA projects and jobs was a powerful political lever, but it was Congress, rather than the New Deal, that first injected politics into the WPA by insisting on the senatorial confirmation of all employees earning over $5,000 a year. As in the FERA, it was the local politicians, not Washington, who brought politics into the administration of relief, and many politicians who benefited were opponents of the New Deal.

North Carolina provided the most striking example. Senator Josiah W. Bailey, arch-conservative critic of the New Deal, illegally secured lists of key WPA personnel in his re-election campaign of 1936 and his henchmen openly solicited campaign contributions in the WPA offices. Within a year of being re-elected with WPA help, Bailey was bitterly denouncing the WPA as a gigantic political machine run by the federal government. In 1936 also the North Carolina director of the WPA was given $25,000 in a brown bag to distribute amongst his workers on behalf of the conservative gubernatorial candidate, Clyde Hoey, in his battle against a liberal pro-New Deal challenger. In 1938 in Kentucky, where the WPA was loudly accused of aiding administration stalwart Senator Alben Barkley, it was in fact supporters of his opponent, Governor 'Happy' Chandler, who were threatening WPA workers with dismissal if they did not vote for Chandler.

The New Dealers, however, were not innocent bystanders in the politicisation of relief. Increased cynicism fuelled by congressional hypocrisy, added perhaps to personal presidential political ambitions, led Hopkins to turn a blind eye to the political activities of local WPAs provided that they benefited New Deal loyalists and did not threaten to embarrass the administration. In Louisiana, Hopkins, under intense pressure from local opponents of Huey Long, allowed a vigorous foe of Long to turn the previously impartial relief administration into an anti-Long agency. Long's opponent was allowed to stay on as head of the WPA despite a report which characterised his record as 'inefficiency from every angle from which a job could be viewed'. When the Long organisation, after their leader's assassination, came to terms with the New Deal, foes of Long in the state were abandoned. The Louisiana WPA now became the plaything of Long's supporters and Washington tolerated a cornucopia of graft and corruption in the WPA until 1939, when the scandals became too blatant to ignore.

The political coercion files of the WPA give ample evidence that loyal city machines were allowed to exert illegal pressure on WPA workers to elect machine-supported candidates. In Illinois, not only did WPA patronage immensely strengthen the pro-FDR Kelly machine in Chicago but WPA workers all over the state were told to back Kelly's candidates in the primaries. In Memphis and Kansas City WPA workers were expected to support the candidates of Boss Crump and Tom Pendergast. Pendergast's Ready-Mixed Concrete Company also grew rich on WPA contracts. Pendergast was given a free hand by the New Deal until an ambitious local politician, Lloyd Stark, was prepared vigorously to attack machine corruption. The New Deal switched sides as his attacks seemed to succeed. In New York, Ed Flynn, the Bronx Democratic boss, systematically used WPA workers in 1938 to help defeat the conservative chairman of the House Rules Committee, John O'Connor. In Pittsburgh, jobs on the WPA were the patronage cement which enabled the Democratic machine to be built. Perhaps one third of Democratic local committeemen were on the WPA rolls at one time. As a thirteenth ward committeman recalled, 'I was laid off from my job as a printer. I got a job as a foreman on WPA. The ward chairman got you the good jobs. Anyone could be a laborer; politics was only needed in key jobs.'

Restrictions on government spending were greater obstacles to adequate relief provision than localism and political interference. Not only could the works programme never cater for all the needy employables, but the WPA could never afford to provide the conditions of work that would have given work relief the same legitimacy as private employment. As a result, Harry Hopkins never succeeded in his heartfelt ambition to remove the stigma of charity or the dole from relief.

When Roosevelt asked for $4.8 billion in 1935, Senator Bob La Follette believed that he needed $9.8 billion to put all the unemployed to work. In 1937 Roosevelt cut WPA spending despite the pleas of governors from the north-eastern industrial states. In 1939 Congress successfully made clear its determination to reduce WPA spending permanently. Hopkins and his associates knew only too well that they did not have the money to carry out their task. They always encouraged pressure groups to lobby for increased relief appropriations. Evidence of Hopkins's recognition of the inadequacy of WPA funding came early. In 1935 he was prepared to allow Wisconsin to go it alone and run its own works programme under Governor Phil La Follette. Washington would help with the funding and Wisconsin would put all its unemployed to work. La Follette's scheme, however, with its controversial provision for scrip payments that could only be redeemed in Wisconsin, was narrowly defeated in the state legislature. Hopkins had to accept that a combination of Roosevelt's personal fiscal conservatism, a persistent optimism about imminent economic recovery, and congressional hostility to the WPA would always prevent adequate funding.

As a result, the WPA could never provide jobs for more than a third of those who needed work in the United States. Between 1935 and 1938 in New York City no more than 40 per cent of the city's unemployed found work in any given month. The remaining employables had to get whatever aid they could from state and local relief agencies. Such aid revealed the same wide variations in levels of assistance from region to region that existed under the FERA. State welfare agencies did become much more professional under federal stimulus in the 1930s, but they remained often deeply imbued with the poor law philosophy. There was ample scope for niggardliness, discrimination against minorities, and rural and business hostility to the very idea of relief. Thus in South Carolina five counties provided no relief assistance at all to needy employables while one community insisted that its reliefers pick cotton or go to jail. In California the legislature clearly expressed its preference for grocery orders rather than cash payments to clients and its intention that no relief should go to aliens.

The need to allocate scarce resources to the most deserving led to the requirement that 90 per cent of WPA workers came from the relief rolls. This regulation meant that workers had to undergo the very degradation that Hopkins had most wanted to avoid: a means test. The rule discriminated against those laid off after 1935 and also made it difficult to employ the number of skilled and supervisory workers necessary to make projects efficient. The need to conserve funds meant that wage levels, unlike the CWA, were never allowed to compete with prevailing wages in private industry, despite the protests of craft unions and local WPA directors. Even when hourly rates were comparable, the number of hours worked was restricted, so that weekly wage totals still fell short. Average wages per recipient were $55 a month but in some areas fell as low as $21. The need to spread the benefits of limited resources meant ultimately that skilled workers could not be employed on jobs commensurate with their skills. More often than not, skilled workers were employed as common labourers, although not all work assignments were as inappropriate as the dispatch of a man with a wooden leg to a New York building site.

The unpredictability of funding meant that money would usually be doled out to state offices on a month-by-month basis. Such hand-to-mouth financing made long-term planning impossible, restricted the type of projects that could be contemplated, and hindered the completion of others. In vain, bodies like the Maine WPA Advisory Committee called for year-long allocations to allow adequate local planning. Sudden spending cuts also meant the arbitrary laying-off of workers, regardless of the quality of work of the individual worker, of the overall level of the economy, and of the availability of jobs in the private sector. The requirement imposed by Congress in 1939, that no WPA worker could be employed for more than eighteen months at a time, further made workers vulnerable to dismissal through no fault of their own. It was these lay-offs that were perhaps the greatest source of discontent amongst WPA workers and led to recurrent strikes and demonstrations. Federal cutbacks also threw sudden and unexpected burdens onto state relief agencies that found themselves confronted with demands for assistance from workers abandoned by the WPA. These burdens were particularly heavy in 1937–38. States had to cope not only with the men laid off during the recession but also with thousands more released by the WPA.

It is not easy to see how these constraints could have been avoided. The effective political pressure in Congress was always for less, rather than more, relief spending. Even in 1935 one vote in the Senate Appropriations Committee had been for a mere $2.8 billion. In 1937 Roosevelt's reduced request for the WPA nevertheless faced bitter opposition from hitherto loyal administration supporters. There was never any likelihood that Congress would vote enough money to put all the unemployed to work at prevailing wages without a means test. Congress wanted consistently to restrict the WPA: to curb the overall spending levels, to make fewer workers eligible for assistance, to increase local sponsorship requirements, and to limit administrative costs. Conservative critics, increasingly powerful in Congress, simply did not want the WPA to provide employment comparable to the private sector for fear that workers would not seek available private jobs.

As a result the WPA never created amongst its own clients a sense that a WPA job was a fully legitimate alternative to private employment. Short hours, low earnings, inappropriate jobs, and constant fear of lay-offs did little to foster the morale of the workers. Renewed pride and self-esteem amongst reliefers remained an elusive goal, despite the cherished ambitions of New Deal policy-makers.

If the WPA failed to create a feeling of legitimacy amongst its own workers, it is not surprising that it was unable successfully to refute the general conservative stereotype that WPA workers were lazy, incompetent, and inefficient. William Faulkner's brother, a WPA engineer in Mississippi, summed these hostile images up in a novel, *Men Working*. To John Faulkner, the WPA irresponsibly encouraged inadequate people to abandon the security of their farm tenancies in mid-season. The superficial lure of WPA wages led these unfortunates to leave their farms without a thought to the crop they were raising and with no idea of the increased costs of urban living. The WPA workforce, he complained, was old and useless, cynically exploited by local politicians and bewildered by lay-offs and rapid changes in government policy. The WPA stripped the workers of whatever vestiges of self-reliance and individual initiative they had and made them incapable of seeking available jobs in private employment.

Such attacks were unfair. It is true that early WPA projects may have been overmanned as workers were hastily assigned to some which did not yet have the necessary tools and materials. But, time and again, independent surveys of the WPA indicated that most projects were economically and efficiently run, bearing in mind the age of the workforce, the rapid turnover of workers which both the administration and Congress wanted, the need to work all the year round, and the desire to use manual labour rather than machines wherever possible. The efficiency of the WPA was boosted by the increasing use of personnel from the Army Corps of Engineers, men who were used to administering large workforces and were on the whole immune to the blandishments of local politics.

The cost-efficiency of the WPA both in rural states like Vermont and in big cities like New York did not, however, impress conservatives in Congress. Opposition to continued government spending, southern rural dislike of spending in northern cities, hostility to the possibility of a permanent relief force dependent on the government, and allegations of waste, inefficiency, and radicalism, combined to erode congressional enthusiasm for work relief. Even the NYA, which had always found a strong ground swell of congressional favour, came under fire from an alliance of economy advocates and lobbyists for the existing vocational schools. For all the efforts of WPA administrators to gear the agency to the war-time needs of supplying trained labour for the defence industries, the war gave congressional conservatives just the excuse they needed to kill off the WPA in 1943 as an unnecessary luxury.

In 1939 Aubrey Williams had expressed the belief that 'What has begun will never be changed . . . I do not think that ever again for any long period will the needy unemployed be subject to the desperate and disgraceful treatment that was characteristic of the poor relief arrangements'. Williams's optimism was misplaced. Government jobs programmes never attracted the legitimacy that many New Dealers assumed would be the consequence of the experience of the 1930s. When Williams's own protégé, Lyndon Johnson, launched the War on Poverty in the 1960s as a conscious effort to complete the unfinished business of the New Deal, a jobs programme did not reappear. It was testimony to the power of the conservative stereotypes of the WPA that it was Johnson himself who implacably refused to countenance the revival of a massive government works programme. It is ironic that Ronald Reagan, whose father was head of the WPA in Dixon, Illinois, remembered the WPA more accurately and affectionately than did Lyndon Johnson. 'Now a lot of people remember it as boondoggles and raking leaves', noted Reagan in December 1981. But that was not correct, he continued. 'Maybe in some places it was. Maybe in the city machines or something. But I can take you to our town and show you things, like a river front that I used to hike through once that was a swamp and is now a beautiful park place built by WPA.'

4 Relief for the artists

The strength and weakness of the WPA were nowhere more sharply highlighted than in the agency's programme for unemployed artists, writers, actors, and musicians. Federal Project One illustrated not only the WPA's capacity to respond boldly and imaginatively to real need, but also the conflicting demands of relief and quality, the inhibiting effect of bureaucracy and spending cuts, the problems of localism, and the long-term failure of the programme to achieve legitimacy in the face of congressional attacks on waste and radicalism.

Artists, Harry Hopkins noted, had been 'hit just as hard by unemployment as any other productive worker'. An estimated 20,000 workers in the theatre were unemployed; one third of Broadway's theatres closed and one half of New York's actors were out of work. Writers struggled as book publishers reduced production of new titles and newspapers closed or merged. One thousand journalists were on the relief rolls in March 1935. Private patronage for the visual arts dried up, and few painters could make their living from their art or their teaching. Black artists were particularly hard hit. The flowering of patronage in Harlem in the 1920s was choked off by the Depression. Musicians had already been hit by technological advance. Records, radio, and the advent of soundtracks in the movies had reduced the demand for live music. 22,000 musicians had been employed playing in movie houses for silent movies in 1926. By 1934 only 4,000 were needed for the motion picture industry. Between 1929 and 1934 the American Federation of Musicians estimated that 70 per cent of formerly employed musicians were unemployed.

The New Deal had responded to the plight of artists even before 1935. In New York, the state relief agency had employed 100 artists painting murals and teaching in settlement houses. In 1933 Edward Bruce, entrepreneur and Treasury silver expert, had crusaded for the formation of a Public Works Art Project to employ artists to decorate federal buildings. Under the CWA 3,479 artists were put to work in this scheme. Later Bruce headed the Section of Fine Art in the Treasury which was responsible in the 1930s for the murals which adorned US Post Offices, sometimes to the shock and bewilderment of their users. Five state emergency relief administrations also employed artists. A small number of actors were employed on the CWA and sent out to entertain enrollees at Civilian Conservation Corps camps. Writers were employed on the white-collar projects of FERA and CWA and some had more specifically been employed on the Newspaper Writers' Project in Los Angeles and on a programme interviewing former slaves in the Ohio Valley.

Such aid was of necessity piecemeal, localised and limited. The numbers of writers and actors involved were small. Writers were usually employed for their clerical not their creative skills. As Arthur Goldschmidt of the FERA puzzled, 'What should writers do as writers?' For artists, Edward Bruce's aim was not primarily to aid needy artists, but to commission works of quality, irrespective of the need of the artist. The Federal Project One of the WPA, established in 1935, was intended to give systematic and comprehensive assistance to unemployed artists. As with other forms of work relief, Hopkins hoped not merely to provide relief for the needy, but to restore their self-esteem and preserve their skills. Separate projects for Theatre, Music, Writers, and Art were established with an initial appropriation of $27 million. In 4 years the Project spent $46 million in assisting the nation's artists.

There were no guidelines or precedents that could suggest how to employ thousands of artists on a national scale. The task was made even more daunting by the need to operate such a programme within the rules and regulations of a relief bureaucracy geared to organising construction projects. Passionate commitment, imagination, resilience, and incurable optimism were the qualities required by the national project directors if the programme was to work. The background of the directors appointed by Hopkins was testimony not only to Hopkins's powers of persuasion, but also to the ability of the New Deal to attract enterprising and creative spirits to jobs in government service.

Hallie Flanagan, an old college friend of Hopkins, came to the Theater Project with a national reputation for her pioneering work with the Vassar Experimental Theater. Study in Russia had convinced her of the importance of relevant theatre and the potential size of the audience that such drama could attract. Art Project director Holger Cahill was a respected museum curator, but he had also been a farm hand, a stowaway, and a deviser of an avant-garde theory of aesthetics known as Inje-Inje. Another man well-known in Greenwich Village intellectual circles was Henry Alsberg. Alsberg came to the Writers' Project from a prosaic post supervising FERA records and reports, but before that he had been a lawyer, a secretary to the US Ambassador to Turkey, a foreign correspondent travelling widely in revolutionary Russia, secretary of the Joint Distribution Committee to aid Russian victims of famine, editor of *Letters from Russian Political Prisoners*, and a dilettante novelist and theatre producer. Nikolai Sokoloff moved from his distinguished directorship of the Cleveland Symphony Orchestra to take charge of the Music Project.

Administrative skills were not necessarily complements to the creative talents these directors possessed. But somehow from scratch they fashioned a formidable achievement. The Art Project yielded 2,566 murals, 17,544 sculptures, and 108,899 easel paintings. For the $7,800 the Project paid Jackson Pollock, it was estimated that he produced $450,000 worth of art. Within a year the Theater Project was employing 11,000 workers in 22 production centres and performing before weekly audiences of 150,000. By 1939 an estimated 30,000,000 people had watched the Project's productions. Touring companies played in remote rural areas, troupes of vaudevillians entertained in schools and hospitals, and groups performed on street corners in New York. Audiences also enjoyed critically acclaimed successes that exploited the talents of the likes of John Houseman, Orson Welles, Joseph Losey, and John Huston: *Dr Faustus, Murder in the Cathedral*, an all-black *Macbeth*, a swing version of the *Mikado*, and an adaptation of Sinclair Lewis's *It Can't Happen Here*. The last opened simultaneously in 21 centres despite the fact that the script was produced after Lewis and the adapter refused to speak to each other. The Writers' Project employed on average between 4,500 and 5,000 workers and produced 276 volumes, 701 pamphlets, and 340 'issuances'. These included guidebooks for every state which John Steinbeck celebrated later in *Travels with Charley* as 'the most comprehensive account of the United States ever got together, and nothing since has approached it'. The project gave Saul Bellow his first job after college, provided material for Nelson Algren's later novels, and gave Richard Wright the time to write *Native Son*. The Music Project set up 38 symphony orchestras, ran jazz bands and madrigal groups, gave free dances in Central Park, and established an all-blind orchestra in Vicksburg, Mississippi.

British poet W. H. Auden thought that 'to consider in a time of general distress, starving artists as artists and not simply as paupers is unique to the Roosevelt administration'. New Deal administrators had wider goals, however, than those of simply alleviating artists' distress. They wanted to make art more American, more accessible to the public, and more democratic. The visual arts in particular were restricted to a small élite and arbiters of taste deferred to European models. Among those who first suggested a government programme for artists, on the contrary, the influence of the Mexican muralists who had celebrated the revolution in their work was strong. PWAP director Edward Bruce constantly exhorted his artists to use wholesome American subjects. Their

work, he said later, gave him 'the same feeling I get when I smell a
sound fresh ear of corn. . . . They make me feel comfortable about
America.' Art Project director Holger Cahill believed that only if
many artists were fully employed would a few great artists emerge.
He had also served in the Newark Museum, which had pioneered
efforts to attract a wider popular audience. The Project's 103
Community Arts Centers were places where the community could
come, see artists at work, attend classes, and see travelling
exhibits. They gave a tremendous stimulus to art in the Midwest
and the South, regions starved of high cultural resources. The
Project's concern about the indigenous American cultural heritage
was exemplified by the Index of American Design, a colossal
project in which artists tried to capture the definitive history of
decorative arts in America by studying and painting the artefacts
of everyday life – furniture and household items, toys, weather-
vanes, tavern signs – anything that contributed to the history of
American design.

Hopkins had chosen Hallie Flanagan to run the Theater Project
because he knew 'something about the plays you have been doing
for ten years, plays about American life'. Flanagan's Vassar
Theater had produced in 1931 *Can You Hear Their Voices?*, a
dramatised documentary based on Whittaker Chambers's account
of the plight of drought-ridden Arkansas sharecroppers. The use
in that show of dramatic vignettes, slides, and loudspeakers
inspired the Theater Project's Living Newspapers. Flanagan
thought 'we could dramatize the news without expensive scenery –
just living actors, lights, music, movement'. The Living Newspapers offered a quick way of providing productions suitable for actors
of varying degrees of skill and experience, as well as making the
theatre relevant to contemporary America. From *The Triple A
Plowed Under* to *Spirochete*, Living Newspapers tackled the farm
problem, housing, public power, flax growing in Oregon, labour
and the courts, and the problems of syphilis. Alongside Flanagan's
commitment to relevant theatre was her desire to create a new
audience for the theatre. Thus, she championed the idea of touring
companies and insisted on the development of children's theatre.

The Writers' Project attempted to capture the folklore and
culture of those groups who failed to leave written records and
whom historians ignored: blacks, ethnic groups, the working class,
and the poor. 'History', said B. A. Botkin, head of the Folklore

Unit, 'must study the inarticulate many as well as the articulate few.' The interview technique enabled the Project to put down on paper 'the grassroots and basic oral culture' of the country for the first time. Fourteen thousand folklore manuscripts provided a wealth of information for future folklore specialists. The Social Ethnic Studies Unit produced material on Swedish Lutherans in New Jersey, Russians in Alabama, Armenians in Massachusetts as well as the more obvious studies of Italians and Jews in New York. For blacks, Sterling Brown carved out the opportunity to get black history and black contemporary living conditions seriously treated in the State Guides. His efforts were part of a wider attempt to record black culture. On the one hand, former slaves in Florida, Georgia, and South Carolina were interviewed about their experiences. On the other, material gathered in the black studies projects in the New York and Chicago ghettos became part of those classic studies, Roi Ottley's *New World A-Comin'* and St. Clair Drake and Horace Cayton's *Black Metropolis*. Parallel to the slave narratives were the life histories constructed from interviews with ordinary working people: 150,000 pages of testimony were gathered, some of which found its way into the *These Are Our Lives*, a vivid portrait, edited by W. T. Couch, of the remorseless impact of poverty on the daily lives of southern millworkers and farmers.

The project most committed to traditional artistic standards was Sokoloff's Music Project. His main aim was to bring classical music of the highest possible standard to the widest audience. But the Project also conducted an educational programme: almost 70,000 Mississippians enrolled in 40 counties and created a booming demand for second-hand pianos. The Project actively encouraged the performance of work by American composers and ran a Composers' Forum Laboratory. Complementing the work of the Folklore Project, Music Project staff scoured the South, returning with 419 12-inch records of black folk songs.

Nevertheless, the arts projects were first and foremost relief programmes and relief aims were bound to conflict with the project directors' desire for quality. Problems immediately arose in the selection of the workforce from the relief rolls. Should the most needy or the most gifted be hired? In some places that choice could be avoided because there seemed to be no applicants: Idaho and North Carolina at first threw up no genuine unemployed writers and the Georgia WPA director doubted that anyone could find twenty actors on her relief rolls. But, at the other extreme, so many actors clamoured for jobs in New York City that auditions had to be swiftly abandoned, and any pretence at selection on the basis of talent disappeared. Naturally many mediocre or incompetent actors were chosen and the Theater Project was particularly plagued by old vaudeville veterans: actors with little talent and even less adaptability. The Atlanta director complained that of 28 'actors' in a single production, only 5 could by any stretch of the imagination be called actors. In Ohio the regional director asked plaintively, 'Is this social work or theater?' For the Writers' Project the problem of selection was exacerbated by the fact that any literate professional could claim to be a writer. And what was the Project to do with a mail carrier who was listed by a social worker as a man of letters? As a consequence, a large number of writers were hired who, even if literate, had no creative skills at all. Typical perhaps was the Kansas staff whose 'idea of writing centered round the split infinitive'. None of the arts projects could have been launched if the requirement that 90 per cent of the workers had to come from the relief rolls had been strictly adhered to. Only the temporary waiving of that regulation enabled project directors to hire the necessary directors, editors, and supervisors.

Bureaucracy, regulations, and red tape did not always lie easily with creative endeavour. Should writers and artists be required to punch a time clock and fulfil production quotas like construction workers? On the whole, administrators thought they should. As a result, a gifted but deaf printmaker had to travel from her home on Staten Island each morning to Manhattan to sign on before returning home to work. Fearful that she might miss the alarm and lose her job, she often stayed awake all night. Outside metropolitan areas, Art Project officials were prepared to let artists work at home. In the cities, however, they were too nervous to do so. In the Writers' Project the New York director experimented by allowing novelists like Richard Wright to work at home, but the experiment came to an abrupt end because of the inability of one of the selected writers to remain sober without the discipline of regular office hours. Some skilled writers cynically lapsed into the easy task of producing a weekly quota of words or resigned themselves to hack drudgery, or gloomily edited appalling manuscripts and confronted unsympathetic superiors. For the

Theater Project, union hourly wage rates severely restricted the number of hours that could be worked each week. Performers were limited to six performances a week and only four hours a day of rehearsal. 'How do you stand it?' enquired Lincoln Kerstein of Hallie Flanagan. 'Requisitions, time sheets, inadequate rehearsal time, inferior pianos and temperament.' As Walter Hart resigned, he wearily summed up the cumulative effect of red tape.

> The best theatrical talent on the project has to spend four-fifths of its time, not in theater work, but in preventing people and orders completely alien to theatrical practice from preventing the exercise of that talent.
>
> Every time a play is produced by the Federal Theater a major miracle has been passed. After passing ninety-five such miracles one begins to tire. . . . Now as the Federal Theater goes into its ninth reorganization within eighteen months, I realize that I am tired – tired of the constant reorganization, tired of the constant changes in rules and regulations, orders, orders and counter-orders. Most of all I'm tired of passing miracles.

Bureaucratic obstacles were symbolised at the local level by state WPA directors. The arts projects were federally operated and funded in order to offset any lack of enthusiasm at the local level, but the cooperation of state WPA directors was essential in the approval of local appointments, the securing of office space, and in the procedures covering requisitions and the relief rolls. State WPA directors were understandably suspicious of projects they could not completely control. They were often impatient with what they regarded as unnecessary projects that interfered with their more important construction projects. The Iowa director was in no hurry to see the arts project start in his state: he wanted everything else launched before letting in the 'tap-dancing units'. In the end, he conceded, he might spare the Theater Project a stenographer, a man who had done 'a good job of keeping records and counting hog carcasses in connection with their farm program'. The California director, Colonel Conolly, assumed complete control of the arts projects in his state: he cancelled theatre productions, opened mail from the national office to theatre personnel, and insisted that no Project employees write directly to Washington.

WPA directors were particularly reluctant to allow the transfer of artists from the relief rolls of another state to their own rolls. In all the projects the consequence was a concentration of workers in Los Angeles, Chicago, and New York. Whereas there was a waiting list of 1,800 for posts in the New York City Writers' Project, in Georgia it was difficult to find enough writers to fill the state's quota. New York accounted for 40 per cent of the painters employed by the FAP in 1938, Georgia only supported one a year. The concentration in a few metropolitan areas was a significant political weakness. Even when actors and painters from New York were transferred or loaned to other projects, the results were not always happy. Actors were sometimes arrogant, sullen, condescending, and uncooperative. Black painters found it difficult to accommodate to local southern racial mores.

Another drawback of localism was the wide disparity in quality and competence between state project directors. The Art Project suffered from a number of status-conscious society ladies, anxious to exploit their patronage by bestowing grace and favours on suitably grateful and deferential artists. Fortunately, the New York project was run by a formidably tough-minded professional. The talents of state directors of the Writers' Project were even more variable. At one extreme was the distinguished novelist Vardis Fisher, who travelled almost every inch of Idaho in his effort single-handedly to produce the first state guide to appear. At the other were the senile director of the Tennessee project and the dictatorial and incompetent director in Missouri, whose sole qualification was endorsement by the Pendergast machine. The latter's arbitrary and paranoid methods eventually provoked a strike by her talented staff. The crucial New York project was run for a time by one-legged poet Orrick Johns, whose administrative weakness was matched only by his lack of discretion. When he attempted to seduce the girlfriend of a disgruntled employee, he was knocked out by the enraged boyfriend. Johns came round to the smell of burning – his wooden leg had been doused in brandy and set on fire. Heavy drinking was a more common problem for the Project than sexual harassment. Henry Alsberg wryly noted, 'If we made it a rule not to hire workers given to drink, we would not have a writers' project'.

Censorship at the local level was a recurring difficulty. Sponsors in Massachusetts, Montana, and New Jersey wanted pro-labour material excised from their State Guides. The New York City WPA director examined murals closely and insisted that circles and hands grasping objects should be removed lest they be mistaken for clenched fists and sickles. The Des Moines Public Library rejected its mural because it would frighten children. Belleville, Illinois, sponsors rejected a painting of Lincoln because his face allegedly resembled Lenin's. The Commissioner of Immigration and Naturalization insisted on changes in the size of rails, the shape of rail ties, and the height of Army officers' boots before allowing a mural of the construction of the Union Pacific and Central Pacific Railroad, to hang in the Ellis Island dining room.

Spending cuts handicapped Federal Project One as they did other WPA programmes, although the art and theatre directors took advantage of lay-offs to weed out some of the hastily hired incompetents. Appropriations always seemed haphazard for the arts projects: at times they seemed to depend on chance conversations between Ellen Woodward, Harry Hopkins, and Mrs Roosevelt. Long-range planning was difficult – thus the Art Project never established the promotion bureau which officials had recognised from the start would be essential adequately to bring their art to the attention of the general public. Cuts in 1937 and 1938 prevented the Theater Project from going ahead with plans to form permanent touring companies and to expand their activities in the Midwest and the South – schemes which might have substantially widened the Project's political base of support. Lay-offs in 1937 in New York City provoked a series of debilitating and highly publicised sit-ins by writers and artists in which local WPA officials were held prisoner. Morale on the New York projects never fully recovered.

In the face of these obstacles, it is surprising that Federal Project One produced work of such high quality. But, like the WPA, the Federal Project failed to become permanent: the Project was unable to establish the legitimacy of government aid to needy artists. Conservative critics always regarded the arts projects, which were more expensive per worker than construction projects, as unnecessary and wasteful. They also regarded the Theater Project in particular as a taxpayer-subsidised propaganda agency for the New Deal. It was inevitable that Hopkins's desire for a 'free, adult uncensored theater' should arouse alarm. As Hopkins himself commented after watching *Power*, 'People will say it's propaganda. Well, I say what of it? It's propaganda to educate the consumer who is paying for power. It's about time that someone had some propaganda for him. The big power companies have spent millions on propaganda for the utilities. It's about time the consumer had a mouthpiece. I say more plays like *Power* and more power to you.' Hallie Flanagan proclaimed that 'Giving apoplexy to people who consider it radical for a government-sponsored theater to produce plays on a subject vitally concerning the governed is one function of the theater.' It is small wonder that conservative senators who found themselves portrayed as mean and unfeeling to the plight of the poor in *One Third of a Nation* were indeed apoplectic.

Investigations to probe for Communism and waste in the arts projects launched by Congress in 1938 and 1939 immensely fuelled conservative criticism. Under rabid anti-New Dealer Martin Dies, the House Un-American Activities Committee in 1939 paraded allegations that membership of a Communist organisation, the Workers' Alliance, was a prerequisite for employment on the Theater Project, that project director Flanagan had Communist leanings, that Communistic plays were produced, that the Writers' Project was infiltrated by Communists, and that material in the State Guides was tailored to the party line. Such charges relied on the dubious testimony of a number of former employees, Flanagan's admiration in the 1920s for Soviet theatre, the paralysing Stalinist-Trotskyite battles on the New York Writers' Project, and the suspicions on the part of opponents of the New Deal of any project material that criticised existing social conditons or championed the cause of labour. The expertise of the Dies Committee was best summed up by Joe Starnes of Alabama, who was determined to track down a particularly dangerous Communist infiltrator, Christopher Marlowe. 'Tell us,' he ordered Hallie Flanagan, 'who Marlowe is so that we can get the proper reference.' Even Starnes was discomfited by the reply that he was a great dramatist at the time of Shakespeare.

The Woodrum Committee in 1939 rehashed these charges and laid out a full bill of other criticisms: that the projects were an unnecessary and expensive boondoggle, that the plays in particular were of little worth and contained salacious material, that when successful, the plays competed with the private theatre, that blacks and whites on the projects worked together and were encouraged to date each other, and that the audiences 'had the appearance of an extremely radical type'. On the floor of the Senate, Robert Reynolds of North Carolina denounced the 'putrid plays' that 'spewed from the gutters of the Kremlin'. Despite the mobilisation of Hollywood stars in support of the projects and the staunch defence of them by a number of usually conservative Republicans like Senator Davis of Pennsylvania, it was clear that the arts projects could not hope to escape unscathed from the congressional hostility to relief spending. In 1939 Congress ordered the Theater Project to be wound up and the other projects to continue only on the state level, as long as they found local sponsors. The other projects carried on in subdued fashion until 1943.

The legacy of the arts projects was mixed. Much of the drama and most of the State Guides received critical acclaim. The collection of slave narratives would be a major source of new directions in slave historiography in the 1960s and 1970s. The FAP helped a generation of American artists to achieve real international recognition. No one could deny that the arts had been made more accessible to the American public. In established artistic centres like New York, new audiences were attracted from the black ghettos, the working class, and the schools. In other areas which had been artistic wastelands, the New Deal introduced performing arts for the first time.

Yet much of the achievement was not exploited. A junk dealer acquired several bales of Art Project canvasses from a New York surplus property warehouse for 4¢ a pound and acquired in the process several paintings by Mark Rothko and Jackson Pollock. The plates of the Index of American Design languished unconsulted in the National Gallery basement. The Writers' Project life histories lay largely ignored in the Library of Congress. For every community arts centre that was supported by private citizens once the Art Project ended, many more closed down. As a cultural administrator in a midwestern city noted a quarter of a century later, 'I see no evidence of the project ever having been here'. Six of the WPA orchestras led to the establishment of permanent local orchestras but most did not. Hallie Flanagan's dream of a national theatre was unrealised.

For twenty years after the demise of the arts projects, opponents of government aid to the arts successfully repeated the criticisms levelled at the WPA's efforts: the arts were too expensive to support, other priorities were far more important, government aid would produce intolerable controls, support for the arts was a local and private, not a federal government, function. Even supporters of government assistance were anxious to avoid 'the deplorable standards of the WPA arts projects'. Just as the WPA jobs programme was not the model for the poverty programmes of the 1960s, so the arts projects were not the model for government support of the arts which finally came in the 1960s. The National Endowment for the Arts established in 1965 was very different from the bold and comprehensive experiment of the WPA in the 1930s.

5 Long-term help: The Social Security Act

If the constraints of federalism and fiscal conservatism limited the New Deal's short-term efforts to relieve the plight of the unemployed, those same constraints hindered Roosevelt's attempt to protect the long-term economic security of the population through a social security programme.

From the start of the New Deal Roosevelt had been committed to protect the individual against the vicissitudes of old age and unemployment. He had spoken in favour of unemployment insurance as governor of New York; his Secretary of Labor, Frances Perkins, accepted her cabinet post only after Roosevelt promised to introduce a social security system; when separate congressional proposals for unemployment insurance and for assistance to the needy aged surfaced in 1934, Roosevelt announced the establishment of a Committee on Economic Security to prepare a comprehensive social security system. The Committee's recommendations for unemployment and old age insurance and for federal aid to state assistance programmes for the old, blind, and dependent children were eventually largely accepted by Congress in 1935.

Roosevelt considered himself the author of the phrase, usually attributed to Sir William Beveridge, 'cradle to grave' security. But the Social Security Act of 1935 fell a long way short of that ambitious goal. A sympathetic historian like William Leuchtenburg noted that 'In many ways the law was an astonishingly inept and conservative piece of legislation'. A critic like Barton J.

Bernstein dismissed the Act as merely '[b]uilding on the efforts of the states during the Progressive Era'.

Bernstein's judgement exaggerates the success of welfare advocates before the New Deal. During the Progressive Era social workers and social scientists had indeed pushed for measures of social insurance and for assistance particularly to defenceless and needy groups. The reformers had before them the European example where measures of state-sponsored insurance against injuries at work, sickness, old age, and unemployment were common before 1930. In the United States reformers made little headway in persuading states to enact model legislation. They did secure passage of workmen's compensation laws in most states. But employers were prepared to acquiesce in workmen's compensation as a cheaper and more predictable alternative to litigation. It certainly did not serve as an entering wedge for other forms of social insurance. 'Rather it solidified', noted Roy Lubove, 'the opposition of private interests to any further extension of social insurance.'

Reformers were not merely handicapped by the hostility of conservative business interests to social insurance. Reformers themselves were uneasy about positive state intervention and were fearful of raids on the public treasury. There was no competent, non-partisan welfare bureaucracy to reassure them. The provision of Civil War pensions seemed to confirm their fears that federal government welfare spending would not be rational and efficient but would be susceptible to open-ended expansion, pushed ever upwards as party politicians bid for the support of a particular interest group. Organised labour suspected the benevolence of state intervention and the motives of middle-class reformers. The experience of Britain and Germany in the 1920s confirmed the fears of many. Mass unemployment shifted their schemes of unemployment compensation away from insurance principles to the provision of unemployment benefits – the dole – irrespective of the workers' insurance contributions.

Reformers therefore made little progress. In the 1920s attention shifted to non-statist alternatives: the private provision of pension and welfare benefits for their employees by 'welfare capitalist' employers. Only a fifth of large corporations offered formal welfare schemes. Few of them could afford to sustain even those schemes under the impact of the Depression. No more than

116,000 workers were covered by voluntary unemployment insurance in 1931. In 1932 only 15 per cent of the industrial workforce were covered by private pension plans. At the federal government level there was a tiny bureaucracy administering grants-in-aid to states to provide vocational rehabilitation for injured workers and to try to lessen rates of infant and maternal mortality. But in 1929 Congress discontinued grants for maternal health care and the Depression made vocational rehabilitation irrelevant since there were no jobs for the rehabilitated workers.

The lone success for social insurance advocates before the New Deal was the passage in Wisconsin of an unemployment compensation law in 1931. But the intent behind the Wisconsin law was not so much to provide benefits to the unemployed as to prevent unemployment in the future. The scheme imposed a payroll tax on employers which diminished as the employers' individual reserve funds built up. The employers' liability to pay unemployment compensation was limited to their own workers. They would therefore have an incentive to avoid laying-off workers. This distinctively 'American' plan of unemployment insurance aimed to promote rational and efficient economic order. But 25 states considered unemployment compensation bills in 1933 and rejected them all.

Reformers had had a little more success in providing categorical assistance at the state level for those in need who could not look after themselves. By 1934, 28 states offered pensions to the needy aged, 24 to the blind, and 45 to single-parent, female-headed families (Aid to Dependent Children). But only 400,000 old people out of some 6.6 million in need received state old age assistance at an average of $16.21 a month. In 1931, 93,280 out of possibly 3.8 million needy female-headed families received assistance under an ADC programme. Only a quarter of the states actually contributed to their ADC programmes: the remainder left mothers to the moralistic mercy of local government funding and administration.

The Depression produced a radically different political climate favourable to social insurance. Economic disaster eroded some suspicions of the positive state. Even the American Federation of Labor abandoned voluntarism and acknowledged the need for unemployment insurance. Further, old people were organised into a visible pressure group for the first time. In the 1920s the

Fraternal Order of Eagles, alarmed at the cost of looking after its older members, had pressed for state pension laws. In 1927 Abraham Epstein had formed the American Association for Old Age Security. During the Depression Francis Townsend, a retired Californian doctor, organised thousands of clubs to call for pensions of $200 a month to be paid to those over 60, provided they spent them within a month. At the same time, a small number of businessmen, conscious of the collapse of their own welfare schemes under the weight of the Depression, began to advocate compulsory insurance programmes. Men like Gerard Swope of General Electric and Marion Folsom of Kodak saw the advantages of forcing their competitors to absorb higher welfare costs. Finally, social insurance offered a means of economic stabilisation: old age insurance might prompt early retirement; unemployment insurance might deter lay-offs, increased assistance to the dependent, the old, and the unemployed would increase mass-purchasing power.

These Depression-induced developments did not compel Roosevelt and Frances Perkins to introduce social security legislation. Organised labour was not very interested in social insurance in 1935; bills sponsored by the Townsend organisation were overwhelmingly defeated in Congress; few businessmen shared Swope and Folsom's enthusiasm for social security. But these developments had removed some obstacles and increased potential support to the point where Roosevelt and Perkins might hope to succeed.

The goals of economic stabilisation, the pressure of social insurance advocates, the model of private pension plans, and the existence of state assistance programmes shaped the Social Security Act of 1935. The Act provided for both insurance and assistance programmes. Under the insurance provisions, unemployment compensation was to be provided by the states, prodded by tax incentives from the federal government. Ninety per cent of a federal payroll tax on employers would be offset if they contributed to an approved state scheme of unemployment compensation. Old age insurance on the other hand was to be a purely federal programme. Employers and workers would contribute to a federal fund that would provide earnings-related retirement pensions. Categorical assistance was to continue to be a state responsibility, bolstered by matching funds from the federal government.

Washington would provide $1 for $2 spent by the states on the needy, aged, and blind. For aid to dependent children, three state dollars would be matched by one federal dollar.

The limitations of the Act were glaring. Federal-state operation of unemployment compensation was bound to lead to wide variations in benefits and eligibility requirements. States anxious to attract industry kept contributions and benefits low. Mobile workers were frequently not covered. The principle of matching assistance funds meant as usual that eastern industrial states, being wealthier, offered more generous payments than poor rural southern states. ADC payments in 1939 ranged from $8.10 per month in Arkansas to $61.07 in Massachusetts. Ten states had not even joined the programme at that point and at least two-thirds of eligible children in the states that did participate were not covered. The federal government set no minimum standard for benefits under the assistance programmes.

At their best, social security benefits were inadequate. Under the assistance programmes, limits on the federal contribution of $18.00 for the elderly and the blind and $12.00 for ADC took away incentives from the more generous states. The national average ADC payment in 1940 was only $32.10 per month per assisted family. The most common unemployment benefit was a maximum of $15.00 a week for 16 weeks. The maximum pensions paid under old age insurance was $85.00 a month.

In addition, those who needed help most were excluded. Employees in small firms, agricultural labourers, and domestic servants were exempt from unemployment compensation. Domestic servants and agricultural labour were excluded from old age insurance. The Committee on Economic Security had recommended that these two groups should participate in the old age insurance programme but Secretary of the Treasury Henry Morgenthau persuaded Congress that they should be initially left out. The task of collecting their contributions, he argued, would stretch the Treasury's resources. As a result, women and blacks were disproportionately excluded from social security coverage.

Old age insurance was to be funded entirely by employee and employer contributions: the federal government made no contribution from general tax revenues. As a result, the opportunity for a substantial redistribution of income through social security taxation was largely missed. Passionate supporters of old age benefits like Abraham Epstein believed that only government contributions would ensure adequate pensions for the elderly; other reformers saw social security taxation as an opportunity for substantial income redistribution; Keynesian economists favoured government contributions as a means of boosted compensatory government spending. But the insurance scheme retained its entirely contributory character: workers themselves bore the burden of providing their own pensions. In addition, contributions were unnecessarily high at the start. The original plan had been for contributions to rise gradually from 0.5 per cent of the payroll in 1937–41, to a maximum of 2.5 per cent of the payroll in 1957. People would start receiving pensions in 1940 even though they had not paid in full contributions. In fact, all those who paid in pensions before 1957 would receive more in benefits than they paid in. The scheme could afford this since the government would still be collecting more money than it was disbursing because of the relatively few retirements. But by 1965 it was predicted that the programme would be running a deficit which was calculated to reach $1.4 billion by 1980. When Roosevelt realised how many people would be benefiting on more than a strictly contributory basis, he insisted that the scheme be financially self-sufficient until 1980. Contributions were therefore raised to an intial 1 per cent of the payroll in 1937 and would reach 3 per cent in 1949. Not only did these taxes create an unnecessarily large reserve fund of $50 billion rather than the $14 billion originally envisaged, but the collection of social security taxes in 1936 had a severe deflationary impact which contributed to the recession of 1937–38.

Finally, there was no provision for health insurance. The Committee on Economic Security delayed its report on health insurance until after the Social Security Act had been passed, for fear of endangering the Act as a whole by stirring up the opposition of doctors and private insurance companies.

The limitations of the Act were substantial and contributed to the jerry-built structure of the modern American welfare system. Nevertheless, the explanation of the Act's failings did not simply lie in the conservatism of New Dealers. A persistent faith in localism, congressional constraints, the need to safeguard the programme in the future, and the expectation of future improvement, as well as fiscal conservatism accounted for its failings.

Rex Tugwell and Jerome Frank had argued on the Committee

on Economic Security for a purely federal programme of unemployment compensation. At times the Committee was convinced, but it eventually came down in favour of the federal-state system. Not only were there real doubts about the constitutionality of a federal scheme, but there were important practical considerations. Unemployment compensation was uncharted territory in the United States, there was no ready and competent federal bureaucracy to launch it. As Felix Frankfurter told Edwin E. Witte, the Technical Director of the Committee on Economic Security, 'Yes, the Federal Government is *too big* for most things. . . . Don't let the Doctrinaires or those who know not the problems of national administration have their own way.'

Scepticism about national competence was not the only concern that directed experts like Witte towards a federal-state solution. Witte, a Wisconsin academic and a protégé of John R. Commons, sympathised with the preventive approach of Wisconsin's existing unemployment insurance legislation with its provision for individual employer reserve funds. But formidable critics of the Wisconsin scheme like Epstein, Isaac Rubinow, and the Ohio Commission on Unemployment argued that employer reserves were inadequate to cope with mass unemployment: they favoured a centrally pooled fund financed by both employer and worker. Advocates of the Wisconsin scheme, however, naturally did not want to see their own patiently-nurtured scheme aborted by federal legislation. A state system of unemployment compensation in which the federal government offered incentives to states to participate, but which left the states themselves to choose which scheme they wanted, seemed a practical solution.

Witte told one critic who was lamenting the absence of national standards in the unemployment insurance plan that 'Many members of Congress seem to think that we have altogether too many standards'. There was certainly no pressure in Congress for a national scheme: what pressure there was in congressional committee hearings and debate was repeatedly for less, not more, federal presence in social security. The original provisions for categorical assistance included a minimum standard of 'reasonable subsistence compatible with decency and health'. But Harry Byrd of Virginia led other Southerners to eliminate even this vague requirement which they feared would be a federal lever to interfere in state provision of assistance to blacks.

Despite the ease with which the final Act passed, social security was politically vulnerable. There was no great congressional commitment to social insurance. The one compelling pressure on congressmen was to do something for old people in order to alleviate pressure from the followers of Dr Townsend. Yet, in both the House Ways and Means Committee and the Senate Finance Committee, old age insurance came within a hair's breadth of being eliminated from the bill. Without that old age provision, the bill itself would have been doomed. It was the fragility of the consensus behind social security which made Roosevelt favour both a purely contributory scheme of old age insurance and payroll taxes for unemployment compensation. He wished to protect the system from congressional depredations in the future. As he recalled, 'These taxes were never a problem of economics. They were politics all the way through. We put these payroll contributions there so as to give the contributors a legal, moral and political right to collect their unemployment benefits. With those taxes in no damn politician can ever scrap my social security program.' Roosevelt never wavered in his determination to maintain the contributory insurance principle. The ideology of insurance, rather than assistance, was the protection that guaranteed popular and congressional support in the future.

Piven and Cloward have argued that 'the relief system created by the Social Security Act of 1935 in the United States was administered for more than two decades to ensure that as few of the poor as possible obtained as little as possible from it. The principle of "less eligibility" was reflected in statute policy and day to day practice.' But the intentions of the New Dealers were not so grudging or restrictive. They were instituting a welfare system, not in response to the threat of disorder or even, with the exception of the organisation of old people, radical political action, but as a progressive first step towards a more liberal welfare provision. Their overriding goal was to get a social security system started: improvements could be made later. What the New Dealers did not realise was the first steps would all too often be last steps. Frances Perkins had acquiesced in the exclusion of agricultural labourers and domestic servants because she believed that it would be a simple matter to include them later once the programme was working. But whereas Secretary Morgenthau had advocated their exclusion for purely administrative reasons, Congress favoured leaving them out so that farmers need not pay contributions for their workers. Coverage would not be extended to excluded groups until 1950.

The social security system went into operation remarkably smoothly. By 1937 all states had approved unemployment compensation laws. By 1939 they had all provided old age assistance programmes. States, of necessity, had to reorganise and professionalise their welfare departments to cope with their new responsibilities. At the federal level, the administrative task of launching old age insurance was enormous: some 26,000,000 social security applications had to be processed, accounts established and cards issued, without the aid of a computer. 202 regional offices held the data. The central card index occupied an acre of floor space. For the first time the federal government had a significant social welfare bureaucracy of over 12,000 people.

6 Sickness and slums

In 1943 Roosevelt sent Congress the last two reports of the National Resources Planning Board which Congress had voted to abolish. Its report, *Security, Work and Relief*, listed nine basic guarantees that the American citizen should possess under a New Bill of Rights. These included the right to adequate shelter and decent medical care. Such guarantees were an integral part of welfare provision in industrialised European countries but were conspicuously absent in the welfare state which the New Deal fashioned. The New Deal failure to provide health insurance and low-cost housing graphically demonstrated the cautious nature of reform, the powerful vested interests, and the misplaced optimism which restricted the New Deal's efforts to provide economic security for American citizens.

Campaigns during the Progressive Era to introduce health insurance at the state level had foundered on labour indifference, employer hostility, and the vigilant opposition of commercial insurance companies. These companies so successfully stirred up grass-roots opposition amongst doctors that the American Medical Association was forced by its membership to reverse its 1917 endorsement of the principles of health insurance. In the 1920s doctors even opposed private group schemes designed to enable middle-income Americans to prepay their medical expenses. The doctors refused to countenance any interference by a third-party with their right to determine what fee to charge the patient.

The Depression exposed the inadequacy of the nation's system of health care. Health resources were inequitably distributed even for those who could afford to use them. Rural areas, inner cities, and the South all suffered. Excessive specialisation amongst doctors created a shortage of competent general practitioners. Private hospitals faced financial crises and even middle-income Americans found medical costs too high. In 1933, 1 in 20 Americans was admitted to a general hospital; the nation's total medical costs exceeded $2.3 billion; yet only 6 per cent of the population had any insurance to pay their medical bills.

New Deal agencies made scattered efforts to help. FERA sometimes paid directly for medical care for needy clients; the WPA sponsored public health programmes and surveyed national health needs. The Resettlement Administration and the Farm Security Administration made loans to their clients to participate in cooperative medical schemes with local medical societies. By 1943 over half a million people in 88 counties in 43 states took part in these government-inspired cooperatives.

Reformers believed that such scattered piecemeal initiatives were no substitute for compulsory national health insurance. Roosevelt's proposals for social security appeared to offer the chance for a comprehensive solution to the provision of affordable medical care. The Technical Committee on Medical Care drew up for the Committee on Economic Security proposals for health insurance on the same lines as the federal-state pattern of unemployment compensation. Employers would receive tax credits if they contributed to an approved state scheme of health insurance. Supplementary appropriations from general revenues would help states provide adequate medical services for the lowest-income groups. Supporters of health insurance took comfort from the apparently cooperative attitude of some doctors who feared that the AMA's absolutely unyielding anti-insurance stance would be counterproductive. But the Medical Care Committee's efforts to convince Edwin Witte, Frances Perkins, and the president that health insurance was politically feasible were unavailing. Instead the firestorm of opposition raised by the AMA convinced Witte and Perkins that immediate recommendations in favour of health insurance might jeopardise passage of the entire social security bill. The Committee on Economic Security therefore delayed making any recommendation on health insurance. Its caution seemed justified when the House Ways and Means Committee even deleted health insurance from the list of topics which the newly established Social Security Board might study.

'How can social workers', asked one reformer in 1937 summing up their plight, 'expect the President and the Congress to act on controversial issues in the face of such vociferous and politically powerful opposition to health insurance, if there is no organized expression of public opinion in favor of it?'

One solution was to add health insurance to other health demands which already had organised support. After a conference on a National Health Program in 1938, designed to build up public support, health insurance was added to increased spending on public health, maternal and infant hygiene, and hospital construction as part of a legislative health care package introduced by Robert Wagner.

Another tactic was to wait for public support of health insurance to grow as people saw the rest of the social security programme go into operation smoothly. Public opinion polls early in World War II seemed to indicate widespread popular support. Alarm at the poor physical condition of many recruits and the experience of government medical care for servicemen during the war seemed to confirm the desirability of health insurance. In 1943 Wagner introduced legislation for health insurance on a national, not federal-state basis. Roosevelt endorsed the idea in 1944. Truman made it one of his first demands for domestic reform in 1945, campaigned vigorously in its favour in 1948, and tried to get health insurance enacted in 1949.

The optimism of health reformers was misplaced. Most parts of the coalition pushing for increased federal health care provision – the Public Health Service, the Children's Bureau, and hospital administrators – soon distanced themselves from compulsory health insurance. They preferred to concentrate on increasing federal sponsorship of medical services rather than tackle the controversial issue of how individuals would pay for health care. As for organised public opinion, no lobby in favour of insurance could possibly match the seemingly limitless financial war chest of the American Medical Association, which employed skilled public relations consultants to put over its remorseless campaign against socialised medicine, government regimentation, and second-rate health care. In 1950 the liberal Committee for the Nation's Health spent $36,000 campaigning for health insurance; the AMA spent $2.25 million to oppose it. It was not, as Monte Poen has wryly concluded, a fair fight. In 1951 Harry Truman had to acknowledge the impossibility of defeating the AMA and supported, instead, health insurance for the aged under social security. In 1965 Lyndon Johnson finally put these proposals for the elderly on the statute book as the Medicare programme.

Public support for health insurance had not simply been swamped by the AMA's campaign, the pressing need for health insurance had been eroded by the success of voluntary private health insurance. Voluntary group schemes to prepay hospital costs (with the Blue Cross symbol to indicate that the scheme met Hospital Association guidelines) mushroomed from 200,000 members in 1933, to 1,000,000 in 1937, 4,000,000 2 years later, and 30,000,000 in 1948. Such schemes excluded low-income families and the unemployed and did not meet the cost of medical services. But their success substantially lessened the crucial middle-class support of health insurance.

In 1937 Roosevelt described one third of the nation as ill-housed. A year later he promised that the administration was 'launching an attack on the slums of this country which must go forward until every American family has a decent home'. The problem of inadequate housing was real enough. A Real Property Survey by the CWA estimated that a third of urban dwellings were substandard. But the New Deal made only token efforts at slum clearance and the building of low-cost government housing. As a result, public housing, which as Kenneth T. Jackson notes was 'the standard extension of the welfare state' in other industrialised countries, was never a significant part of the American response to urban poverty.

Housing reformers during the Progressive Era had concentrated on improving the regulation of inner-city housing – improving housing codes and insisting on their more stringent enforcement. To build new houses for the poor, they put their faith not in government construction but in limited-dividend housing corporations. But only New York had passed enabling legislation by 1932.

Even the stimulus of Reconstruction Finance Corporation loans for that year could not obscure the conclusion of a 1938 report that the housing corporation 'while successful for people two or three degrees above slum dwellers economically . . . did not meet the need of the people for whom it was originally intended'. By contrast, governments in both Britain and Germany in the 1920s had built a million homes and the Netherlands housed one fifth of their population in government-owned housing.

The New Deal's first concern in 1933 was homeowners in danger of losing their homes. Desperate to stem the rising tide of mortgage foreclosures (running at a thousand a day in March 1933) the Home Owners' Loan Corporation refinanced threatened mortgages. Between July 1933 and June 1935 the Corporation came to the rescue of one in ten of the nation's owner-occupiers, aiding over one million homeowners. Borrowers were also able to pay back their mortgages over a longer period, usually twenty years instead of the customary five.

The government also wanted to revive sagging demand for new private houses. The construction industry had only started 93,000 new houses in 1933 compared to almost 900,000 a year in the 1920s. The Federal Housing Administration, established under the National Housing Act of 1934, insured private lending agencies who made long-term mortgage loans for the construction and sale of new housing. FHA support encouraged lenders to reduce the downpayments they required, lengthen the repayment period, and lower the interest rates they charged. Housing starts rapidly rose to over half a million in 1940 and in the next 40 years the percentage of Americans owning their homes increased by almost a third. The unanticipated result was a further stimulus to suburbanisation at the expense of the inner cities. FHA-backed loans were for newly-purchased single family homes, rather than for the renovation of existing property or the building of housing for rent. The FHA insured loans predominantly for white borrowers and steered clear of blighted inner-city areas. Their policies excluded, for example, half of Detroit's districts and one third of Chicago.

The stimulus to provide housing therefore did little to solve the problem of urban slum-dwellers. One estimate suggested that 65 per cent of new houses built between 1929 and 1938 cost over $4,000, a price only a quarter of non-farm families could afford. To housing reformers the only answer for the urban poor seemed to be the construction of low-cost government housing.

The New Deal's most ambitious attempt at housing construction – the construction of whole new Greenbelt communities just outside big cities – offered little hope, however, to the urban poor.

The Greenbelt programme at least recognised that Americans wanted to work in the cities. Its realism contrasted starkly with the ill-fated Subsistence Homesteads scheme of 1933 to resettle urban dwellers in communities based on subsistence agriculture and part-time work in light industry. The aim of the Greenbelt programme was to disperse the urban working population out of the overcrowded inner city into planned, congenial 'new town' environments where residents would be democratically involved in community decision-making.

The programme never began to fulfil the ambitious goals of its main supporter, Rex Tugwell, whose Resettlement Administration supervised it. Substantial local real-estate opposition and congressional resentment of socialistic regimentation ensured that only three out of nine projected communities were built. The programme also suffered from its own contradictions. Sites were chosen outside cities which had already gone a long way to eliminate the problems Greenbelt communities aimed to solve – cities with steady growth, diversified industry, enlightened labour policies, and above-average wage levels. The cost of building quality housing quickly and the need to make the project self-liquidating dictated rent levels that were out of the range of low-income tenants. The need to ensure the selection of appropriate clients led the government to hold on to ownership of the homes in defiance of the politically powerful and popular ideals of individual home ownership. The government could not afford to build enough homes to support a population large enough to justify expensive community services. The rapid turnover of young tenants thwarted the government's ideals of active community participation by the residents.

Greenbelt communities had little relevance to slum-dwellers on relief. Social workers and urban politicians saw no alternative but for the government itself to clear slums and build low-cost houses in their place. Under the National Industrial Recovery Act, the Housing Division of the Public Works Division built its own low-cost housing projects. But under Harold Ickes's cautious leadership, the Division built only 21,709 units of public housing in

50 projects between 1933 and 1937.

Local opposition, as well as Ickes's caution, often delayed projects and the cost of both land and house-building put the rents even of the small number of units that were built outside the reach of many low-income families. In Boston the PWA project at Old Harbor Village, authorised in 1933, did not open until 1938. Local real-estate interests and the city council blocked PWA efforts to purchase land and exempt it from municipal taxation. When finally constructed, no one on relief could afford the rents. Tenants had to have permanent jobs, not even WPA workers were eligible. As Charles H. Trout noted, there was no point in 'the truly poor and the non-Irish' applying. In Charleston, South Carolina, a conservative newspaper editor commented that only 'negro economic royalists' could afford the rents on the PWA project. In Cleveland Christopher Wye has shown that not only did the PWA perpetuate residential segregation but that within the ghetto the projects displaced low-income blacks and built apartments that only middle-income blacks could afford.

Disappointed by the PWA's lack of progress, Robert Wagner introduced legislation in 1935 for the permanent provision of low-cost housing. The senator from New York sought to eliminate slums, increase mass-purchasing power by reducing what the poor spent on housing, and boost the construction industry. It was not until 1937 that Roosevelt put his full weight behind Wagner's proposals for a United States Housing Authority which would loan money to local housing authorities to establish low-cost housing projects and would make annual grants to help meet the interest payments. Roosevelt had only limited enthusiasm for the scheme; he seemed to have difficulty visualising the full dimension of the urban housing problem; he displayed far more sympathy with 'back-to-the-land' proposals and with programmes aimed at increasing home ownership. A sceptical Congress insisted that the new Authority would only have $0.5 billion as distinct from $1 billion. To curb New York and other north-eastern cities, legislators also required that no more than 10 per cent of USHA funds could be spent in a single state and that loans to the local authorities could only cover 90 per cent of project costs.

Within 18 months 221 local Housing Authorities had been established under enabling state legislation. But only 117,755 units of public housing were built under the 1937 Act. Local real-estate interests often foiled modest New Deal goals. Referenda enabled middle-class taxpayers to defeat plans to establish local authorities. Complacent civic leaders often refused to acknowledge the existence of slums in their communities.

So, despite conservative fears the 1937 Act was not the entering wedge for massive public housing projects. Republican opposition to 'the cutting edge of communism' combined with rural southern hostility to an essentially urban programme prevented further public-housing appropriations after 1939. Only in 1949 did the acute post-war housing shortage finally prompt Congress to authorise another 810,000 units of public housing. Urban liberal Democrats at that time found allies among northern urban Republicans and southern senators, newly aware of their states' rapidly expanding cities, in order to overcome rural and real-estate opposition.

Lack of local enthusiasm, however, congressional second thoughts, and the private home-building spree of the Affluent Society ensured that under half the target of public-housing units, 356,203, were built in the next fifteen years. Low-cost housing in the United States therefore never attained public legitimacy and met only a small part of the poor's housing needs. Instead, public housing, in contrast to European countries, served further to isolate and stigmatise the poor, creating the end result that New Deal welfare policies had expressly set out to prevent.

7 The welfare revolution

New Dealers received some unpleasant surprises from the welfare state they fashioned in the 1930s. They expected government jobs programmes and social insurance to banish forever the degrading spectre of public assistance based on a means test for most of the poor. Social insurance would eventually provide protection against the ordinary insecurities of age, disability, ill-health, and joblessness; a repetition of mass unemployment would be countered by works programmes; the need for public assistance would wither away. Instead, the WPA never achieved sufficient legitimacy to ensure that its emergency employment programmes would serve as a model for tackling future recessions. Social insurance programmes tended to benefit middle-income Americans at the expense of the poor. The poor had to rely on the continuation, not disappearance, of assistance programmes whose inadequacy was magnified by state-to-state variations. The New Deal legacy served to perpetuate the traditional distinction that reformers had tried to obliterate between the deserving and undeserving poor. Deserving, responsible individuals were protected by their contributions to social security: the undeserving and helpless received welfare.

Similarly, New Deal initiatives in health insurance did not lead to increased medical protection for the poor but provoked the mushrooming of private health-care plans for middle-income citizens. New Deal housing policies, far from eliminating slums and rejuvenating the inner-city, fostered middle-class suburban sprawl.

Policy-makers in the 1930s had believed they were taking crucial first steps towards ever more progressive and generous welfare standards. But whereas other countries went on to make social security more comprehensive and to raise national standards of welfare provision, in the United States it proved extremely difficult to launch further programmes, extend coverage, and establish national minimum standards. Reform had mainly to be limited to adding incremental benefits to existing programmes.

These limitations owed much to the obstacles posed by congressional conservatism and local constraints. The federal government lacked the necessary bureaucracy to launch a national emergency relief programme in 1933. No Congress in the 1930s was likely to make the semi-permanent commitment to the level of spending necessary for the WPA to care for all the unemployed. The decision by the Committee on Economic Security not to go for a national scheme of unemployment compensation and assistance provision seems reasonable in the light both of constitutional doubts and of congressional moves to remove or dilute what federal standards there were in the Social Security Act. The decision to delay the introduction of health insurance in order to protect the rest of the social security package seems prudent in the light of the subsequent ferocious AMA assault. Roosevelt's insistence on a purely contributory old age insurance scheme did protect social security from future congressional depredations and guaranteed it the crucial middle-income constituency backing that other poverty programmes lacked.

The obstacles were real enough. Yet there was never to be a

better opportunity to impose national standards or introduce health insurance. The demonstrable weakness of existing welfare provision, the demonstrable need of so many constituents – and their organisation into visible pressure groups – created a unique, if fleeting, political opportunity. Apocalyptic conservative fears of disorder could for a brief moment be exploited to achieve substantial, if non-revolutionary, change. It is possible that the New Deal compromised too much in anticipation of opposition.

To a certain extent, also, the president and his advisers reaped what they sowed. Roosevelt's fiscal conservatism, as well as congressional caution, cut off the CWA and prevented the adequate funding of WPA. The New Deal's priority to save homeowners and encourage the construction industry, together with Roosevelt's lack of interest in low-cost housing, delayed the passage of housing legislation until the conservative opposition to northern, urban-oriented reform was beginning to take its toll. The protective insurance ideology of social security locked the system permanently into a regressive scheme of payroll financing. Roosevelt's reluctance to envisage government contributions to old age insurance, his opposition to using federal funds for assistance on a non-matching basis, and the determination of social security administrators to maintain the insurance principle may have protected the programme from conservative assault. But these commitments also inhibited liberal and Keynesian proposals from 1939 onwards for establishing national minimum standards to ensure adequate public assistance programmes and launching flat-rate pensions to moderate the anti-poor bias of social security.

Nevertheless, for all its undoubted faults, the New Deal had revolutionised the provision of welfare in the United States. In 1930 the states had spent $9 million on categorical assistance. In 1940 they disbursed $479 million. In 1935 there were no unemployment compensation payments. In June 1940 they totalled over $480 million. In the same year the government paid out the first pensions under the old age insurance scheme. The federal government, for the first time on any significant scale, was directly making benefit payments to individual clients. However imperfectly, the New Deal had provided the United States with a welfare state which, as James Patterson has concluded, 'responded with a level of public aid scarcely imaginable in 1929'.

6
Partial Realignment: Politics

The New Deal represented an immense electoral and legislative achievement. Roosevelt was elected president four times. No previous president had dared challenge the tradition that opposed third presidential terms: anxious conservatives ratified the 22nd amendment in 1951 to ensure that no subsequent president would do so. The peak of FDR's election victories was attained in 1936 when he lost only the states of Maine and Vermont in his landslide victory over Republican Alfred M. Landon. Unlike later landslide victories by Nixon and Reagan, Roosevelt's success was a party as well as a personal triumph. His New Deal fashioned the Democratic Party into the new national majority party, the party with the most registered voters, and the party that customarily controlled Congress. The Democrats have never entirely relinquished that status.

Roosevelt enjoyed almost unparalleled success in Congress. In the century and a quarter since the Civil War, only the radical Republicans in 1867 and Lyndon B. Johnson between 1964 and 1966 have passed as much substantial reforming legislation as Roosevelt secured between 1933 and 1936. Not only was Congress persuaded to pass laws that fundamentally altered the relationships between government, the economy, and the individual, but Congress also vested extraordinary powers in the executive branch. Eventually, these powers were carefully limited and defined, but in the early days of the New Deal Congress willingly delegated vast, unencumbered authority to the president.

Despite this success, Roosevelt had hoped for more. In 1932 he had told Rex Tugwell, 'I'll be in the White House for eight years. When those eight years are over, there'll be a Progressive Party, it may not be Democratic, but it will be Progressive.' In November 1936 Roosevelt won 60.4 per cent of the popular vote and the

Democrats in Congress increased to record totals of 76 seats in the Senate (against 16 Republicans) and 331 in the House (against 89 Republicans). The scene seemed set for the major political realignment envisaged by Roosevelt. He had surely created an avowedly liberal Democratic Party which would extend the benefits of the New Deal to the one third of the nation that he identified in his January 1937 inaugural as 'ill-housed, ill-clad, and ill-nourished'. Yet within twelve months Roosevelt could secure no legislation from the special session of Congress he called in November. The momentum of the greatest domestic reform movement in American history had been decisively checked by conservative forces in Congress, who inflicted a series of major defeats on Roosevelt in 1937 and 1938. For the next 25 years those conservative forces would be in a position to ensure that no major extension of the New Deal would take place. The realignment that Roosevelt had achieved was not what he expected it would be. The New Deal had created a schizophrenic Democratic Party: on the one hand, a northern urban wing, backed by organised labour, lower-income voters and blacks, pushed for liberal reforms; on the other, a conservative southern wing, entrenched in Congress in alliance with the Republicans, was determined to block any advance of the New Deal along urban liberal lines.

Roosevelt made a sustained effort in 1938 to resurrect his liberal dream. Invoking his right as head of the Democratic Party 'charged with the responsibility of carrying out the definite liberal declaration of principles set forth in the 1936 Democratic platform', the president intervened in the Democratic primaries, attempting to purge leading conservatives, notably Senators 'Cotton Ed' Smith of South Carolina, Millard Tydings of Maryland, and Walter George of Georgia. The purge failed. A measure of that failure was Roosevelt's recognition that it would be impossible for the party to nominate any genuine liberal in 1940 except himself. This depressing realisation of the limitations of his political success played a major part, along with the war that broke out in Europe, in his decision to defy tradition and run for a third term.

This political failure was important for the overall achievement of the New Deal. So many of the limitations in New Deal programmes were the result of constraints imposed in Congress. Time and again in matters of urban and regional planning, rural poverty and social security, New Dealers concentrated on launching programmes with admitted imperfections in the belief that flaws could be eradicated and omissions rectified later. Time and again, those first steps proved to be last steps. When New Dealers set about expanding and improving their reforms they found themselves checked by the bipartisan conservative coalition.

Both liberal contemporaries and some later historians have faulted Roosevelt for his failure to create an unambiguously liberal Democratic Party, for his failure to achieve a complete party-realignment on clear-cut ideological lines. In politics, as in policy, they argue, Roosevelt sacrificed long-term goals for short-term expediency. The constraints of the emergency, the power of localism, and the fundamental conservatism of the electorate in fact sharply restricted the president's room for manoeuvre. The nature of the political alternatives to the New Deal in the 1930s also cast doubts on the potential for more radical and thorough-going political action. There simply did not exist the ground swell of radical opinion that could have sustained either more liberal policies or a more far-reaching political realignment.

1 The new Democratic Party

Roosevelt strove to project an image that was above party and above class. His rhetoric in the early New Deal stressed national unity, interdependence, and class harmony rather than class conflict. He welcomed support from progressive Republicans and independents. He played down the use of the word Democrat in the 1934 and 1936 election campaigns. He delighted in presidential, avowedly non-political trips round the country to inspect New Deal projects. Trips like his August 1936 inspection of drought-affected states in fact served a highly political purpose. As one North Dakota Republican wryly acknowledged, 'Roosevelt has traveled across our state three times and has sewn it up. Most of our Republican candidates do not even know where North Dakota is.' FDR aroused a personal loyalty and popularity that has been approached among modern American presidents only by Eisenhower and Reagan. The pictures of the president in tenant shacks, the crowds jammed into cities to hear him on the campaign trail, and the mail that flooded the White House all testify to the strength of that popular, personal identification with Roosevelt.

The nature of New Deal rhetoric did change a little after the initial euphoria of national cooperation. Roosevelt welcomed the hatred of the wealthy and they reciprocated in kind. But FDR's more strident approach of 1935, and after, was less a politics of class than a 'politics of ostracism'. The president's appeal was still intended to be all-embracing – only the small group of the super-rich were to be excluded. The cross-class, cross-regional nature of the landslide victory of 1936 testified to the success of this approach.

Yet the ultimate political impact of the New Deal was to create a more precisely delineated, sharply focused, class-based Democratic Party. The core of the Democrats' new status as the national majority party was the support of voters in the northern cities.

In 1920 the twelve largest cities in the country gave the Republicans a plurality of 1,540,000 votes. That plurality fell away slightly in 1924, and in Al Smith's campaign in 1928 the Democrats achieved a plurality of 21,000 votes. The Depression and the New Deal confirmed that turnaround. In 1932 those twelve cities gave Roosevelt a 1,791,000 margin, and almost doubled that in 1936. Those cities became increasingly important to Democratic victory nationally. In 1936 Roosevelt ran well everywhere. But from 1940 as the urban population expanded and as Roosevelt's appeal elsewhere diminished, urban majorities became decisive. The twelve largest cities alone provided sufficient margin for Democratic victory in 1940, 1944, and 1948.

This urban appeal was increasingly a class-based appeal. Lower-income voters, often recent immigrants and their children, supported Roosevelt and the Democrats. Again the movement of these voters to the Democrats had been taking shape before the New Deal. Al Smith's campaign in particular had consolidated much ethnic and Catholic support for the Democrats, and newer immigrants and their families were the fastest-growing section of the electorate. But Roosevelt and the New Deal cemented this Democratic allegiance. As John Allswang has shown, there was a very high correlation in the urban North-East between Democratic voting in the 1930s and the density of population in counties, the percentage of urban and foreign-stock residents, the rate of unemployment, and the absence of eighteen- and twenty-year-olds in college. The explanation is simple enough. If ethnocultural impulses pushed lower income new-stock voters away from the old stock, Prohibitionist Republican Party towards the Democrats between 1910 and 1930, economic need in the 1930s hastened that shift. The New Deal brought desperately needed income to the urban poor – increased relief payments when local resources were exhausted, jobs on the CWA and WPA, opportunities for young men to get away to CCC camps, slum-clearance, and low-cost housing projects. The New Deal also gave recognition to newer ethnic and cultural groups. The president worked closely with prominent Catholic politicians and encouraged the efforts of social welfare Catholics like Father John A. Ryan. There had only been four Catholic cabinet members before 1932: Roosevelt appointed James Farley and Thomas Walsh to his first cabinet. One in four New Deal judicial appointments was Catholic, in contrast to one in twenty-five in 1920. The Catholic hierarchy and the National Catholic Welfare Conference responded enthusiastically. No longer did the Democrats acknowledge only Irish support. For the first time Italians featured prominently in federal appointments. Similarly Jews were unprecedentedly visible both in New Deal posts and amongst Roosevelt's closest circle of advisers. By 1940 Jews of all economic backgrounds had become overwhelmingly Democratic.

City machine politicians were quick to respond. They had been the most loyal of Al Smith's followers, but that loyalty was rapidly transferred to Roosevelt. If patronage was the life-blood of city machines, the New Deal provided a blood transfusion. The local administration of New Deal programmes, which was placed in the hands of established city politicians, gave the machines unprecedented patronage opportunities. In addition, the federal government was providing just the sort of services – jobs, relief, recognition for their constituents – on a formal basis, that the bosses had traditionally provided on an informal basis. They soon realised that the alliance with the federal government was the key to their own local political power. Far from sounding the 'Last Hurrah' of the machines, the New Deal consolidated the power of some and helped create the power of others. In Chicago, where Mayor Anton Cermak had finally pulled together the feuding ethnic groups behind the Democratic banner on the eve of the New Deal, his successor Edward Kelly strengthened the machine's hold on the city's voters with relief payments, WPA jobs, and great public works projects. In Pittsburgh in 1934, the local Democrats used the Roosevelt appeal to wrest control of the city from the Republicans. As the New York *Times* commented, 'The proverbial man from Mars might indeed get the notion that it is Mr. Roosevelt himself who is running for Mayor of Pittsburgh'. Once in power, the city Democrats used the WPA to build up a machine. The vote for the Democratic candidate for mayor in 1936 bore the closest correlation to the number of individuals on the WPA rolls per ward. WPA jobs were the key to enlisting local Democratic workers: most ward committee men served as WPA foremen or supervisors at some time. As one ward worker summed it up, 'We all got into politics to get a job because we were unemployed'.

City bosses now needed a liberal Democrat in the White House to safeguard their local fortunes. It was no coincidence that the one-time champions of Al Smith were in the forefront of those demanding that Roosevelt run for a third term. But the machine politicians saw the federal government as more than just a convenient provider of jobs. The New Deal opened their eyes to the possibility that the federal government, rather than the notoriously unresponsive state governments, might be able to help solve their intractable education, health, and housing problems. If the New Deal liberalised machine politicians, machine politicians also helped liberalise the New Deal. Urban demands and urban problems were now placed on the Democrats' agenda.

The loyalty of lower-income urban voters to the New Deal was reinforced by the emergence of organised labour as a key element in the new Democratic Party. There was a high correlation in northern states between counties with high percentages of workers in manufacturing industry and Democratic voting. Earlier nonpartisanship by trades unions was replaced by aggressive support for the New Deal both by the leaders of the new industrial unions and their members. Organised labour became a crucial source of finance, of political organisers, and of votes for the Democrats.

CIO leaders supported the New Deal in gratitude for past actions, the passage of the Wagner Act, and, in anticipation of future favours, the safeguarding of their planned organising drives in the mass-production industries. They correctly surmised that employers would not be able to turn to the federal government for assistance in beating off the union challenge. In 1936, therefore, CIO leaders formed the Labor Non-Partisan League to back

Roosevelt and contributed 10 per cent of the Democratic campaign finances. At the state level, unions sought the election of governors like Frank Murphy in Michigan and George Earle in Pennsylvania who could be relied on not to use the National Guard to help employers break strikes. At the local level, unions needed mayors and councilmen who would not cut off welfare payments to strikers, would restrain the local police, and would not enforce anti-picketing ordinances.

Blue-collar workers were amongst the most devoted admirers of the president. Grateful for welfare benefits, jobs, and social security, they responded to the president's rhetoric for the more equitable distribution of wealth, gloried in the enemies he made, and identified with a man they believed understood their problems. Roosevelt convinced them, as one southern millworker noted, that he 'is the first man in the White House to understand that my boss is a son of a bitch'. As with city machines, the important contribution of unions and their leaders was to mobilise this rank-and-file loyalty to Roosevelt. In both 1944 and 1948 labour's role in getting the vote out was crucial to Democratic victory.

No group of lower-income voters shifted allegiance more dramatically in the 1930s than blacks. Blacks in the northern cities had traditionally voted for the Republican Party, the party of Abraham Lincoln and emancipation, rather than for the Democrats, the party of Southerners and white supremacy. Whereas other lower-income urban voters shifted to the Democrats in the 1920s, northern blacks for the most part remained loyal to the Republicans. As late as 1932 an estimated two-thirds voted for Herbert Hoover. In Cincinnati's black ward, for example, only 29 per cent voted for Roosevelt.

In the mid-term elections of 1934 there was already a shift to the Democrats in cities like St Louis, Kansas City, and Chicago, where the local Democratic bosses made an effort to woo black support. In 1936 that shift was massive and permanent. Gallup polls estimated that 76 per cent of northern blacks voted for FDR; at least 60 per cent of the black vote in every northern city except Chicago went to the president; in Cincinnati's black ward he now gathered over two-thirds of the vote.

This transfer of black allegiance to the Democrats was important because migration from the South increased the potential number of black voters by 400,000 in the northern cities during the decade and the numbers of blacks registered to vote doubled. The shift was indispensable to long-term black civil rights gains. As the northern cities became ever more important for Democratic presidential victories and as blacks flocked to those cities in the 1940s and 1950s, so black political leverage over national Democrats sharply increased. As early as 1941 Roosevelt issued Executive Order 8802, aimed to end discrimination in the defence industry and the armed services, in order to avert the threatened March on Washington led by A. Philip Randolph. In 1946 Harry Truman established a presidential commission on civil rights to satisfy black protest against post-war racial violence. In 1947 and 1948 he endorsed that commission's liberal findings. These were early and vivid instances of the power of black political leverage which would later help bring civil rights legislation in the 1960s.

Yet what had Roosevelt done for blacks in the 1930s to justify this change in political loyalty? Few aspects, after all, of the New Deal have been more severely criticised than its failure to aid blacks. Roosevelt did little for black civil rights. Anxious not to upset the sensibilities of the southern congressmen who controlled the destiny of his general legislative programme, Roosevelt introduced no civil rights legislation. There was no challenge to segregation in the South and no attempt to enable blacks to vote there. The president took an equivocal stand on the one clear civil rights issue of the decade – the anti-lynching bill introduced in 1934 to combat the rapid increase in lynching by holding local law-enforcement officials responsible and liable to punishment. He clearly denounced lynching as murder, but he never endorsed the anti-lynching bill as a piece of 'must' legislation. Consequently in 1934 and 1935 the bill failed to reach the floor of the House; in 1938 it was filibustered to death in the Senate.

To the extent that the New Deal in general failed to protect the poor, blacks as the poorest section of the population were disproportionately affected. The failure to bring recovery left 25 per cent of black workers in many cities unemployed on the eve of American entry into the war. The exclusion of agricultural workers and domestic servants from the NRA, social security, and minimum wage-maximum hours legislation excluded 70 per cent of black workers. The lack of success in aiding tenants and sharecroppers in the cotton South hit hardest the 70 per cent of southern black farm operators who were tenants. The inadequacy of the low-cost housing programme penalised black ghetto-dwellers. Conversely assistance to homeowners, farm owners, and traditionally racist trades unions meant little to blacks.

The New Deal specifically sanctioned discrimination against blacks. At times, this reflected the racist attitude of New Deal administrators at the top in Washington, particularly in the main recovery agencies of the early New Deal. Hugh Johnson dismissed a black woman investigating black complaints against the NRA because he believed that it was preposterous that a black should investigate such complaints. NRA codes directly and indirectly perpetuated existing discriminatory practices. Similarly, the Cotton Section of the AAA was headed by southern whites sympathetic to white landlords and scornful of black tenants. An important relief agency like the Civilian Conservation Corps was run by a conservative Southerner, Robert Fechner, who made little effort to open up CCC oportunities to blacks. At other times, New Deal discrimination occurred at the local level. Programmes in the South were run by whites sympathetic to the cultural norms of the communities in which they lived and worked. They ran programmes on a segregated basis, routinely paid less in benefits to blacks than to whites, and often excluded blacks from participation altogether.

Yet this gloomy picture underestimates the change in status and perception of black rights as an issue for New Dealers in the 1930s. While New Deal agencies may have discriminated against blacks in the South, they provided blacks with greater assistance than they had ever received before, especially from state governments. State and local welfare agencies had essentially ignored black needs before 1933; any assistance from New Deal relief agencies was therefore a bonus. The Public Works Administration spent proportionately more on projects for southern whites than for southern blacks, yet it spent four times as much on building black schools and hospitals between 1933 and 1936 as had been spent by governments in the previous 30 years.

The New Deal improved as time went on. The agencies that were most important for blacks were increasingly headed by men sympathetic to their cause like Harold Ickes at the PWA, Harry Hopkins at the WPA, and Will Alexander at the Farm Security Administration. Ickes insisted on equal wage rates for black workers and imposed minimum quotas for blacks on PWA projects. The FSA made tenant purchase loans in proportion to the black population in the South, albeit not in proportion to black need. Even the CCC, which had operated a lily-white enrolment policy in many southern counties, had an 11 per cent black enrolment by 1938. What most determined the transfer of black political allegiance was the efforts of Harry Hopkins and Aubrey Williams to eradicate discrimination in the WPA. In the northern cities their efforts were on the whole successful and it was of course the northern cities in which blacks could vote. The percentage of blacks on the WPA rolls in most northern cities was three to five times the black percentage of the population. In 1939 an estimated 1,000,000 black families depended on the WPA for their livelihood. Tangible economic benefits and rational self-interest accounted for the black switch to the Democrats. As the songs and slogans reminded black voters, 'Abraham Lincoln Is Not A Candidate In The Present Campaign', 'Let Jesus lead you and Roosevelt feed you', 'Roosevelt you're my man. When the time come, I ain't got a cent. You buy my groceries, and pay my rent. Mr. Roosevelt, you're my man.'

New Deal liberals, often prompted by the rapidly learning Mrs Roosevelt, soon realised that general economic assistance to the poor was not enough, that blacks had to be specifically targeted. Many of the racial limitations of the New Deal were revealed by the government's own field investigations. New Deal officials were accessible to black critics and frequently co-opted them into the administration to try to solve the problems they highlighted. Together with the expansion of the federal bureaucracy, this attitude helped appoint blacks to lower-level federal jobs in unheard-of numbers. A black cabinet of officials monitored the New Deal's racial progress. Through the remarkable black South Carolinian educator Mary McCleod Bethune and her friendship with Mrs Roosevelt, black critics often had access to the president himself, an access that helped offset the limitations of both his own and his staff's commitment to civil rights.

The New Deal itself was therefore one of the forces that made civil rights a substantial political issue. New Deal liberals were part of what Harvard Sitkoff has identified as a developing civil rights coalition of the black civil rights organisations, the radical left, organised labour, and intellectuals. The contrast with the previous decade was stark: in the 1920s the Republicans had taken the black vote for granted; both Communists and Socialists argued that black problems would be solved once capitalism had been abolished, little could be done specifically for blacks until then; skilled trades unions excluded blacks; sociologists, biologists, and psychologists sanctioned racism as intellectually respectable; civil rights organisations languished, losing members by the thousands.

The radical left in the 1930s took perhaps the first steps to change this picture. Communists targeted blacks as potential recruits: the party's defence of the convicted Scottsboro boys from 1931 put it in the forefront of the white defence of black civil rights. The Socialists took up the cause of black tenant farmers in the South. CIO organisers came to realise that the organisation of black workers was essential if organising drives amongst unskilled workers were to succeed. Intellectuals more and more stressed environment rather than race as the cause of differential achievement. The NAACP bounced back in membership and its newly created Legal Division began to win landmark decisions before the Supreme Court.

The New Deal both responded to and contributed to this coalition. Even in the segregated South, where the New Deal was so reluctant to upset established politicians and local custom, there were stirrings of change. New Deal farm programmes, by giving blacks the vote in crop control elections and by offering alternative sources of credit, gave rural blacks some increased living space and lessened their dependence on white landlords. In some southern cities emboldened blacks launched voter registration drives. The New Deal showed to black leaders in the South the potential of federal solutions to black problems. In the 1930s federal programmes were largely directed at economic problems but for the first time since Reconstruction black leaders saw some hope that in the long run the federal government could be invoked to offset their local political powerlessness.

More visible than the recognition given to blacks was the recognition the New Deal gave to women. In 1940 a banquet organised by the Women's Division of the Democratic National Committee featured 70 women at its speakers' table who held high positions either in the federal bureaucracy or the Democratic Party. The prominence of Eleanor Roosevelt and the first female cabinet officer, Secretary of Labor Frances Perkins, was matched at a lower level by women like Mary Harriman Rumsey, chairman of the NRA's Consumer Advisory Board, Ruth Bryan Owen, Minister to Denmark, and Ellen Sullivan Woodward, Assistant Administrator of the WPA, as well as by women in more traditionally female posts, like Katherine Lenroot at the Children's Bureau and Mary Anderson at the Women's Bureau in the Department of Labor. However, just as the New Deal has tended to be downplayed in the history of black civil rights, so the 1930s was until recently ignored in women's history since it was not a decade of agitation on avowedly feminist issues such as the Equal Rights Amendment. In fact women played a more substantial role in government and politics then than at any time before or since. As Molly Dewson, first full-time director of the Women's Division of the Democratic National Committee, recalled, 'In three years Roosevelt had set a new trend. At last women had their foot inside the door. We had the opportunity to demonstrate our ability to see what was needed and to get the job done while working harmoniously with men.'

The success of women in the early years of the New Deal was the achievement of a remarkable network of women bound together by ties of friendship, common experience, and shared ideas, 'a cordial interlocking group of minds' as Frances Perkins herself described them. A generation born in the 1880s, New Deal women were usually college-educated and had often gone into social work at a time when social work training had not yet been professionalised. Participants in the suffrage movement and World War I relief activities, they were prominent in voluntary associations like the National Consumers League and the Women's Trade Union League which did so much to keep social reform issues alive in the 1920s. Like black leaders, who in the 1930s placed a higher premium on securing adequate economic assistance than on securing civil rights, this network, while conscious of its special role as women, ultimately placed a higher priority on social reform than on women's issues. Thus, most of them opposed the ERA for fear that it would jeopardise the protective legislation they had for so long striven to achieve.

Their success owed much to Mrs Roosevelt. She provided a dynamic role model and gave the women's network in the New Deal unrivalled visibility and prestige, special access to the president, and an insistent voice to champion their social welfare causes. No First Lady had been as independent and as public a figure as Mrs Roosevelt. Radio broadcasts, a newspaper column, a weekly press conference for women reporters, and a relentless schedule of trips inspecting New Deal projects gave her a unique profile. The crippled president had used her as his 'eyes and ears' when he was governor of New York: he still paid close attention in the White House to her reports on conditions around the country. She sponsored White House conferences on consumers and the NRA, the emergency needs of women and camps for unemployed women, all of which prompted action which her female friends had sought in vain from hitherto unresponsive government agencies. She put forward strongly her own views and those of her liberal friends on social welfare, women's concerns, and black civil rights. She could also secure appointments with the president for spokesmen, particularly black leaders, who otherwise found their way to Franklin D. Roosevelt blocked by white Southerners on his staff, Marvin McIntyre and Steve Early, who controlled the president's schedule.

This prominent role was an unlikely one for a woman who had what one cousin described as 'the grimmest childhood I had known'. Rejected by a mother who told her she was ugly, repeatedly let down by a much loved but tactless father, she was orphaned by the age of 10 and brought up by stern, forbidding aunts. Liberation came with schooling in England and social work in New York, but marriage to debonair Franklin Roosevelt trapped her into a conventional women's domestic role. A domineering mother-in-law did not even allow her to take charge of that domestic sphere.

World War I gave the chance to escape into war welfare work. Her husband's affair with Lucy Mercer made her determined never again to be so dependent. His polio gave her even greater opportunity to carve out a distinctive political niche for herself. In the 1920s she developed close contacts with other women reformers in the League of Women Voters, the National Consumers League, and the Women's Trade Union League. She also developed powerful emotionally rewarding friendships with activists like Nancy Cook and Marion Dickerman, who joined her in establishing a cottage and craft factory on the Hyde Park estate. She became a national political figure in her own right in the Democratic Party, playing a leading role in women's campaigns in the 1924 and 1928 presidential campaign. She was in a unique position to articulate the growing liberalism of younger New Dealers on welfare and black civil rights. Franklin D. Roosevelt always listened to, even if he occasionally wearied of, her insistent, uncompromising demands. One reason Roosevelt listened was that he took women seriously. As governor of New York he had grown accustomed to working with talented and forceful women.

Nor was the story over for Mrs Roosevelt when her husband died in 1945. Appointed by Truman as a delegate to the United Nations, she was responsible, more than anyone, for the eventual acceptance of the Universal Declaration of Human Rights. She was a rallying point for liberal New Dealers in Democratic politics and a passionate champion of Adlai Stevenson in the 1950s. She continued to call politicians to account on black civil rights and women's issues till her death in 1962.

Mrs Roosevelt constantly prodded Postmaster General Jim Farley, the New Deal's chief patronage dispenser, to find posts for women. Her pressure was matched by the tireless efforts of Molly Dewson, who was determined that women should be rewarded for their contribution to the 1932 victory. She claimed to have had a part in over 100 appointments ranging from Frances Perkins's cabinet post to the appointment of three women to mark airstrips for the Aeronautics Board. Above all, however, the opportunity for women came from the exigencies of the Depression. The emergency agencies of the New Deal needed their social work skills and the social welfare reforms of the 1930s drew on their expertise in consumer affairs, protective legislation, low-wage industries, and social security.

Molly Dewson's foremost priority had been the appointment of Frances Perkins to a cabinet post. Perkins herself exemplified the career pattern of that generation of female reformers who contributed so much to both progressivism and the New Deal. Educated at Mount Holyoke, she worked in settlement houses in Chicago before doing graduate work in New York, where she served as local secretary of the National Consumers League. Her knowledge of working conditions in the city made her a formidable witness before the commission investigating the Triangle Shirtwaist Factory fire and an effective lobbyist for protective legislation at the state capital, Albany. She found her concerns shared and her causes helped not only by Al Smith but also by the more traditional Tammany politicians. Smith appointed her to the state Industrial Commission in 1919, and made her chairman in 1922. Perkins never lost her loyalty to Smith and spent the last years of her life working on his biography and trying to unravel the mystery of the split between Smith and her own patron, Franklin Roosevelt.

Roosevelt made Perkins his Industrial Commissioner in New York and then his Secretary of Labor in Washington, against the wishes of the American Federation of Labor. She presented Roosevelt with a full agenda of social welfare reforms and the president appointed her knowing that she would always remind him of his commitments to welfare reform. As chairman of the Committee on Economic Security she pulled together the proposals for social security legislation. She later pushed through the minimum wage-maximum hours legislation of 1938.

Yet she was peripheral to much of the New Deal. She administered no great New Deal programme. She failed to have the National Labor Relations Board placed in her department. She was caricatured in the press either as a weak woman in a harsh male world of strikes and unions or as a naive sentimentalist who believed that a social revolution would come if all Southerners wore shoes or as an innocent dupe who refused to deport Australian-born radical union leader Harry Bridges. She had little role to play in the mobilisation of the war effort and she was unceremoniously removed by Harry Truman in 1945.

Nevertheless, she served as a constant symbol to the president of the need for social reform; she reorganised and professionalised a notoriously corrupt Department of Labor; and played a major role in the formation of the American welfare state. After the war she served on the Civil Service Commission, wrote the most perceptive of all the memoirs of Roosevelt, and introduced a new generation of students at Cornell to the stories of the New Deal.

Molly Dewson was determined that women should now be an indispensable part of the new Democratic Party. The Reporter Plan which she devised used 15,000 women, particularly in the Midwest and West, to educate women about New Deal issues. These reporters, together with 10,000 state and county leaders and 60,000 precinct workers underpinned the important contribution the Women's Division made to the 1936 landslide. But whereas black political leverage increased from the 1930s onwards, women's political influence did not. Unlike blacks, women were not an easily identifiable voting bloc. The remarkable network of New Deal women grew old: their influence declined as the momentum for social reform in the late 1930s slowed. When the war came, women failed to advance to the higher levels of government despite their vital contribution to the war effort. Whereas their social welfare expertise had been perceived as invaluable in combating the Depression, their skills were not seen as essential for tackling the problems of war-time mobilisation.

New Deal women placed the cause of welfare reform and economic assistance above women's rights. In a hostile environment, they defended women's work by stressing its contribution to preserving the family. They secured jobs for women on relief programmes that tended to perpetuate stereotypes of women's domestic and service role. These understandable strategies nevertheless inhibited the development of an explicitly feminist ideology which might have sustained women's political activity after the Depression.

Nevertheless, during their period of influence, women had joined with other new forces in the Democratic Party to promote a wide range of social reform. The reforms that benefited lower-income voters, organised labour, and blacks needed to be consolidated and extended. A new agenda for the Democratic Party had been defined by the New Deal, raising the minimum wage, extending social security, protecting trades unions privileges, and securing black civil rights. This essentially urban and liberal agenda, however, would be anathema to an increasingly powerful rural, small-town coalition of southern Democrats and Republicans in Congress.

2 Success and failure in Congress

Roosevelt had a number of advantages to exploit when he called Congress into special session in March 1933. The Democrats enjoyed healthy majorities in both houses: 311 to 116 in the House, 60 to 35 in the Senate. They confronted a Republican opposition that was split between a progressive wing prepared to support many New Deal measures and a stand-pat conservative faction for whom the New Deal was anathema. Congressional leadership was in the hands of skilled and experienced southern Democrats. There was little that was radical about Senate Majority Leader Joseph T. Robinson of Arkansas or House Majority Leader (soon to be Speaker) Joseph W. Byrns of Tennessee. Key committee chairmen like Senator Pat Harrison of Mississippi at the Senate Finance Committee or Bob Doughton of North Carolina at the House Ways and Means Committee showed little understanding of or sympathy with the broader aims of the New Deal. They were most at ease when they could interpret New Deal measures as the legacy of Wilsonian reform. But they were all loyal party men, anxious to build a legislative record and personally friendly to Roosevelt, whose nomination most of them had supported in opposition to the hated Al Smith. While the president often tried their patience to the limit with preemptory demands for the passage of extraordinary and complex legislation, he also established a warm and easy personal rapport with them and never underestimated their almost limitless susceptibility to presidential flattery. Leadership positions and committee chairmanships constrained them to support the president more often than they offered them the opportunity to obstruct.

These advantages did not guarantee success. Roosevelt enjoyed them for most of his presidency, not only between 1933 and 1936. His success in 1933 was helped by the dire nature of the economic crisis which persuaded bemused congressmen to hand over power and responsibility to any leader willing to accept them. On a more prosaic level, the traditional patronage available to any new administration was vastly increased by the proliferation of emergency agencies. The prospect of these jobs was a juicy carrot to dangle in front of congressmen, especially since most of them were not filled until the end of the Hundred Days.

Neither crisis nor patronage sufficiently explain why Congress was prepared to yield so much of its independence: constituency pressure pushed Congress into line with the New Deal. Nowhere was this more important than in the South, where Democratic congressmen were prepared for at least three years to support measures which violated their traditional beliefs in limited government and individualism. Whatever their ideological convictions, southern congressmen, both leaders and rank and file, were acutely aware of the desperate need of their constituents for relief from rural devastation. The South received less per capita from

New Deal expenditures than other regions. Yet New Deal spending was more crucial for Southerners than for others. Because of the poverty of southern states, federal relief spending was more important than in less disadvantaged areas. The impact of farm credit, benefit payments, and increased farm prices was dramatic in a region where rural poverty was endemic. The demand of their constituents for assistance, and their gratitude for what the New Deal gave them, meant that few southern congressmen dared to oppose the New Deal.

The importance of constituency pressure was illustrated by those Southerners who did oppose the New Deal from the start. Blind senator Thomas P. Gore from Oklahoma believed that the New Deal sapped individual initiative: he was defeated in the 1936 Democratic primary. The Virginian senators Harry F. Byrd and Carter Glass consistently voted against what they saw as the New Deal's unsound finance, its unconstitutional infringement of states' rights and individual economic liberty, and its insidious weakening of individual resolve. Not only, however, was their political position impregnable because of the power of the Byrd machine, but the low level of political participation in Virginia excluded from the political process those who most needed New Deal aid. Their state had in any case escaped the worst ravages of the Depression. Senator Josiah W. Bailey of North Carolina shared the Virginians' distaste for the new federal experiments and he voted against the Agricultural Adjustment Act and the Bankhead Cotton Control Act. Yet Bailey had been elected in 1930 on a platform of party loyalty defeating an incumbent who had deserted the party in 1928. Additionally, he was soon aware of the immense popularity of the farm programme which he had vilified in front of his tobacco-growing constituents. As a result, his diatribes against the New Deal were relegated to his private correspondence or reserved for measures which Roosevelt had not identified as 'must' legislation. Few politicians more self-righteously proclaimed their independence of popular whim, yet were more finely attuned to constituency sensibilities. Until Bailey was safely re-elected in 1936 he was publicly obsequious to the president.

Together with Millard Tydings of Maryland, these senators were the core of the Democratic opposition to the New Deal in 1933 and 1934. They were joined in the House by no more than twenty or so representatives who regularly voted against key New Deal measures. After 1934 these critics were joined by other Democrats as the sharp edge of the Depression was blunted. Some congressmen found different constituency pressures to respond to which allowed them more readily to vote their convictions. Hostility to the New Deal from businessmen who made important campaign contributions gave them pause. Thus Senator Walter George began to listen more to the complaints of Coca-Cola and the Georgia Power and Light Company than to the enthusiasm of Georgia cotton farmers. 'Cotton Ed' Smith, chairman of the Senate Agriculture Committee, already mistrustful of New Deal intellectuals and bureaucrats, heeded the power companies in South Carolina and opposed the holding companies legislation. Old-style conservative, business-oriented, northern Democrats, like Royal S. Copeland of New York or the new House Rules Committee chairman, John O'Connor of New York, allowed their opposition to the New Deal to surface. Some, like Senators Peter Gerry of Rhode Island and Ed Burke of Nebraska, were now safely elected until 1940.

Nevertheless, New Deal legislation continued to pass Congress in 1935 and 1936. Administration victories in 1935 on holding companies and taxation, both of which provoked substantial congressional revolts, were ultimately costly. On the one hand, Roosevelt's threats of veto and his refusal to compromise over the utilities measure provoked thinly-veiled congressional resentment of presidential whip-cracking. On the other, his cavalier despatch of ill-prepared tax legislation late in the summer sorely tested congressional patience, particularly that of an angry Senate Finance Committee chairman Pat Harrison. Yet despite the increased suspicion with which congressional leaders viewed the ultimate purposes of the New Deal, only 19 Democratic senators had voted against more than one key New Deal measure and only 61 House members had deserted consistently on key votes.

Following the 1936 election triumph, the stage was set for a further burst of New Deal reform when Roosevelt sprang on a surprised Congress a proposal to increase the number of Supreme Court judges by as many as six. The president would have the power to appoint an extra judge for every judge over the age of 70 who refused to retire. This ingenious plan was initially presented by FDR as a measure merely to help an overburdened court carry out its business more efficiently. This pretence was soon dropped and the real purpose – to produce a more amenable Supreme Court – was explicitly acknowledged.

Four aged conservatives on the Court, in combination with either Chief Justice Charles Evans Hughes or Associate Justice Owen Roberts, had savaged New Deal legislation. Their decisions against the Railroad Retirement Act, the NRA, the AAA, and a New York State minimum wage law severely restricted the government's right to regulate the economy under the commerce clause, to tax and spend for the general welfare, and to interfere with freedom of contract. The Court appeared to be creating a constitutional no-man's-land between state and federal government where neither government could exercise effective regulatory power. What made this threat from the Court more alarming at the start of 1937 was that it had yet to hand down rulings on the Social Security Act, the Wagner Act, and challenges to the power of the PWA and the SEC. Negative rulings on the constitutionality of these pieces of legislation would rip the heart out of the New Deal and destroy any hope of extending New Deal reform on the lines of Roosevelt's Second Inaugural.

Roosevelt had been unable to change the complexion of the Court. There had been no deaths or retirements during his first term. The more fervent New Dealers believed that the four conservatives were not only refusing to retire, but also refusing to die, in order to continue to restrain the New Deal. The Court-packing plan, as critics called it, offered the president the opportunity to safeguard both present and future reform by a simple legislative act. The proposal appeared to offer both speed and certainty, in contrast to alternative proposals for a constitutional amendment or legislation restricting the review functions of the Court.

The Court plan was greeted with predictable outrage by conservative Republicans and those Democrats like Glass and Bailey already thoroughly alienated from the New Deal. Their apocalyptic denunciations left Roosevelt unmoved. He expected that popular opinion, which had just elected him to a second term with a landslide vote, would in time force doubtful congressmen into line in support of the bill. He was wrong. He suffered his worst political defeat, which, in William Leuchtenburg's words, served to 'blunt the most important drive for social reform in American history'.

The opposition of the New Deal's bitter enemies would not have defeated the Court reform plan. Roosevelt indeed strove to make the issue one between the people and his reactionary and partisan opponents. He was unable to do so because his opponents skilfully refused to allow the issue to be identified in this way.

Conservatives formed an effective, well-financed pressure group – the National Committee to Uphold Constitutional Government – which appeared to demonstrate that there was widespread distrust of the president's alleged drive for dictatorship and his blatant disregard for traditional American liberties. Targeting twelve wavering senators, the Committee mobilised enough evidence of public opinion to persuade eight that they could safely afford to oppose Roosevelt.

Conservative Republicans on the whole kept their more reactionary spokesmen quiet and allowed Democrats to make the running against Court reform, so that Roosevelt could not whip up party loyalty by labelling the opposition as merely partisan. Similarly, conservative Democrats pushed progressive Burton K. Wheeler of Montana to the forefront of their fight on the Senate Judiciary Committee against the plan. Wheeler had been one of the first politicians to endorse Roosevelt for the presidency and had been his leading lieutenant in the utility holding company fight. In 1924 he had run for the vice-presidency on the Progressive Party ticket, on a platform which called for control of the unbridled power of the Judiciary. But Wheeler felt insufficiently appreciated by the president and was especially angered by the distribution of patronage in his state to National Committeeman J. Bruce Kremer, one of his arch enemies. While Wheeler was suspicious of big business, such as the Anaconda Mining Corporation in his own state which Kremer represented, he was also hostile to big government and big labour. He threw himself wholeheartedly into the Court fight.

Roosevelt's faith that an emerging public opinion would slowly force congressmen into line was undermined by the failure of pro-New Deal interest groups to lobby enthusiastically for Court reform. Both organised labour and groups like the Farm Bureau did have a vested interest in a more sympathetic Supreme Court, but this long-term interest was offset by more immediate concerns: the great unionisation drives in the mass-production industries and the need to secure a second Farm Act to replace the original

Agricultural Adjustment Act. The urgency of the issue was further diminished by the handing down of Supreme Court decisions in favour of a state of Washington minimum wage law and the Wagner Act. In addition, one of the conservative judges, Willis Van Devanter, announced his retirement. The administration might still have been rescued by a compromise measure. Senate Majority Leader Joseph Robinson, who had been promised the next vacancy on the Court, was determined to secure a Court reform bill if it killed him. It did. His fatal heart attack finished any hopes of Court reform.

In the long run, Roosevelt's ideas won the day. The judges he was able to appoint during his remaining year as president vastly expanded the power of the federal government to regulate the economy, promote social welfare, and defend civil rights. But that long-term victory was of little use if New Deal reform could not pass Congress in the first place. The Court-packing defeat was important, although not decisive, in the development of a bipartisan conservative coalition that would stalemate Roosevelt's reforming efforts.

Senators who for the first time had openly opposed Roosevelt on Court reform were more prepared to stand up against the president again; not only had their first excursion into independence been successful but they also did not appear to suffer electoral retribution, particularly in 1938. Resentment of high-handed White House attempts to pressure congressmen, which had always been lurking beneath the surface, now came out into the open. When Roosevelt twisted arms to elect Alben Barkley to succeed Joseph Robinson as Majority Leader, his narrow victory over Pat Harrison of Mississippi was almost worthless. Conservative Democrats and Harrison's many friends felt no obligation to follow Barkley, even less to follow the president. The Court plan also gave apparent substance to the charges of dictatorship that the opposition had always levelled at Roosevelt. These were charges given greater salience by contemporary developments in Germany and Italy and were fully exploited by the National Committee to Uphold Constitutional Government, which used them to defeat Roosevelt's modest and reasonable plans to reorganise the executive branch of government. Court reform united the Republicans. Most western progressive Republicans deserted Roosevelt on Court reform: the plan confirmed their worst suspicions about the statist designs of the New Deal, suspicions they could now share with their more conservative colleagues. Finally, the Court proposals prompted the first occasion of informal bipartisan cooperation to defeat a New Deal measure. Conservatives from both parties met daily for lunch to plan their strategy to defeat Court-packing.

Many of the same senators met at Senator Bailey's instigation in November 1937 to draft a statement of principles with which they hoped to attract and unite conservatives of both parties. The recession that autumn convinced them that New Deal remedies had been tried and found wanting. While the Roosevelt administration hesitated, the conservatives grasped the opportunity to restate traditional policy prescriptions. The restoration of business confidence, which alone would bring economic recovery, would only come if government ceased its interference with private enterprise. The Conservative Manifesto laid down the preconditions for the return of that confidence: the repeal of anti-business taxes and the reduction of the tax burden, the primacy of the balanced budget, the restoration of states' rights, and the strict maintenance of the right of property and the rights of capital.

In addition to their victory over Court reform conservatives in Congress had further reason to be heartened by developments in 1937 and 1938. In 1937 Roosevelt had faced substantial revolts over relief spending and sitdown strikes, had seen his bill for minimum wages and maximum hours locked in the House Rules Committee, and had made no progress with his plans to reorganise the executive branch of government. In November he summoned a special session to tackle a farm bill, the minimum wage bill, executive reorganisation, and an extension of regional planning along the lines of the TVA to other river basins. The special session gave him nothing and in 1938 his plans for executive reorganisation and taxation were defeated.

Nevertheless, conservatives did not always call the tune. A Housing Act and the Bankhead-Jones Farm Tenancy Act passed in 1937 and in the following year not only did the Farm Bill and the Fair Labor Standards Act eventually pass, but Congress also overwhelmingly approved the president's new spending programme which he unveiled as his answer to the recession. Conservatives did not have the votes to defeat New Deal proposals which offered tangible benefits to important elements of the New Deal coalition.

Farm price supports were in 1938, and would continue to be, irresistible to rural representatives. Housing and minimum wage legislation mobilised support from organised labour and urban politicians. Spending on relief and public works at a time of continued high unemployment and on the eve of the 1938 elections appealed to too many constituents for the conservatives to be successful. Conversely, executive reorganisation, like Court reform, and tax revision were not issues that seemed to offer immediate gains to New Deal pressure groups. On issues where New Deal forces were aroused, like the Fair Labor Standards Act, conservatives had to try to prevent the issue coming to a vote by bottling them up in the House Rules Committee where they enjoyed a bipartisan majority.

The necessary votes came, however, with the 1938 elections. Roosevelt failed in his efforts to purge conservative Democrats. While he made no attempt to defeat a number of invulnerable conservative incumbents, he did attempt to secure the defeat of five conservative Senate opponents of Court Reform: Guy Gillette of Iowa, Frederick Van Nuys of Indiana, as well as George, Smith, and Tydings. Roosevelt also worked to beat Rules Committee chairman John O'Connor. Only O'Connor was defeated. The 1938 primaries showed that liberal incumbents could be re-elected with presidential backing – like Claude Pepper of Florida or Alben Barkley of Kentucky – but that the president could not transfer his personal popularity to other candidates and defeat well-entrenched conservative incumbents. The message for congressmen was that it was possible to defy the president and be re-elected.

The greater boost in conservative strength came from the general elections in 1938. Republicans gained eight seats in the Senate and increased their representation in the House from 89 to 169. In the Senate it now only needed 23 Democrats to join the Republicans in order to defeat the administration while in the House the defection of only 50 Democrats could put the New Deal in trouble. The 1939 Congress confirmed this conservative strength. Relief spending was slashed and proposals for spending on self-liquidating public works and housing were defeated. A hostile House launched investigations of the WPA and the NLRB by bitter opponents of the New Deal, Clifton Woodrum and Howard Smith of Virginia, and continued to sanction the search by

Martin Dies's Un-American Activities Committee for Communists in the government. Stalemate had been reached between the conservatives and the administration. The conservatives did not have enough votes to dismantle or repeal New Deal legislation: but they did have enough votes to prevent further New Deal reform. Roosevelt had little choice but to accept his impotence, albeit with an ill-will, since he needed congressional support for his foreign policy initiatives. A *modus vivendi* had to be established with the conservative Southerners since they were some of the most internationalist and pro-British senators.

The bipartisan conservative coalition was not a monolithic bloc. Party loyalty prevented more than informal cooperation. The numbers and personnel of the coalition varied from issue to issue. Numerically its consistent core was the Republican opposition. Conservative congressmen were also more likely than their liberal counterparts to represent rural areas. But what gave the coalition its strength and distinguished it from the early days of the New Deal was the central role of the southern Democrats. Those pre-1936 critics of Roosevelt – Byrd, George, Glass, Tydings, Bailey, and Smith – were still the heart of the conservative cause. By the end of the decade half the southern senators consistently voted against the administration. In the House at least 20 but sometimes as many as 70 Southerners were prepared to defy the president. Eugene Cox of Georgia and Howard W. Smith of Virginia were the decisive link men with new Minority Leader Joe Martin in bottling up New Deal measures in the Rules Committee.

Senators like Glass and Bailey and congressmen like Cox and Smith hated the New Deal passionately and had seen the Court-packing episode as final confirmation of Roosevelt's undemocratic and un-American designs. Their bitter mistrust of the president was however shared by few southern politicians; most southern congressmen indeed had been prepared to acquiesce in Court reform; Gallup polls suggested that the South was the one region where a majority supported the president on the issue. Most southern congressmen continued to acknowledge the president's popularity in their districts and continued to be grateful for the New Deal farm programmes. Loyal New Deal politicians like Claude Pepper, and Hugo Black's successor in Alabama, Lister Hill, continued to be elected in the South.

The crucial defection of hitherto loyal Southerners in Congress from the New Deal occurred not because of apocalyptic concerns about the future of the Republic prompted by Court-packing but a more restrained concern about the direction of the non-emergency New Deal. Influential southern leaders like Senator Jimmy Byrnes of South Carolina had enthusiastically backed the New Deal in the economic emergency of 1933; they would always remain grateful for the assistance that relief and recovery programmes brought; they were happy too to support the regulation of distant eastern bankers and financiers. But in 1937 many thought that the emergency was over; cotton and tobacco had after all been largely rescued. Instead, the non-emergency New Deal seemed oriented not to the South but to the North and to the cities. Minimum wage legislation threatened to erode the competitive advantages enjoyed by low-wage southern industry; housing legislation primarily benefited northern cities; relief spending would mostly be spent in the North and threatened to create a permanent army of the unemployed on welfare rolls in the North. Within the South, the New Deal seemed to threaten traditional patterns of dependency. The position of employers was being challenged by organising drives by the New Deal-backed CIO. The position of landlords was being threatened not only by relief programmes which might lessen the surplus labour available but also by rural poverty programmes which helped tenant farmers. The traditional political power exercised by county seat, small-town, rural élites was being undermined by alternative sources of credit, union organisers, WPA officials, and new voters.

Nowhere was this threat to traditional patterns of dependency greater than in race relations. The New Deal had been extremely cautious and deferred to southern sensibilities on race. Racism certainly did not dictate opposition to the New Deal. Two of the most violent Negrophobes in Congress, Theodore Bilbo and John Rankin, were amongst the New Deal's most ardent supporters; the New Deal's programmes for cotton and its commitment to rural electrification and public power ensured that. But in the late 1930s conservatives increasingly invoked the racial spectre to whip up support. Some, notably Carter Glass, justified their opposition to Court reform by arguing that its supporters wanted 'the repeal of every statute and ordinance of segregation'. (As it turned out, his fears of what a liberalised Supreme Court might do for black civil rights were entirely justified.) Others like 'Cotton Ed' Smith and

Bailey deplored the success of the northern Democratic Party in winning over the black vote. Catering to that vote would lead the party to 'the upmost depths of degradation' and threaten the 'mongrelisation of the American race'. But it was what was happening to southern blacks that alarmed them most. Southerners perceived a subtle increase in black assertiveness and they knew whom to blame. As one southern white crudely summed up their fears, 'You ask any nigger in the street who's the greatest man in the world. Nine out of ten will tell you Franklin Roosevelt. That's why I think he's so dangerous.' This fear of outside interference in race began in the 1940s to encompass a fear of outside interference in economic matters as well and helped solidify and increase southern congressional suspicion of the New Deal.

The consequence of the creation of this schizophrenic Democratic Party was what James MacGregor Burns described as the 'Deadlock of Democracy'. To win presidential elections, the Democrats had to espouse urban liberal policies which would attract the lower-income voters of the northern cities. Once in power, however, Democratic presidents for years could deliver little more than symbolic reform: the conservative coalition in Congress spearheaded by southern Democrats ensured that liberal national Democratic Platform promises had little chance of being kept. Deadlock would remain until John Kennedy's assassination and Lyndon Johnson's landslide victory of 1964.

3 Obstacles to party realignment

This half-way realignment seemed to political scientist Burns a great missed opportunity to create an ideologically clearly defined Liberal Party. Roosevelt, he argued, could have ended the deadlock of democracy. Instead, he made concessions to conservatives in Congress, especially southern leaders, which strengthened their position; he failed to encourage rank-and-file liberal organisation in Congress behind his programme; above all he failed to encourage New Deal support at the local level. 'He ignored the possibilities for the future of a voting alignment of great strength: one composed of less privileged farm groups, masses of unorganized or ill-organized industrial workers, consumers, Negroes, and other minority groups.' 'He did not', Burns continued, 'try to build up a solid organized mass base for the extended New Deal that he projected in the inaugural speech of 1937.' He failed in particular to build up pro-New Deal factions in state politics by directing patronage and recognition to these vigorous new elements in the party. 'Roosevelt as party leader, in short, never made the strategic commitment that would allow a carefully considered, thorough and long-term attempt at party reorganization.'

Roosevelt's political failure epitomised for Burns the overall weakness of Roosevelt's presidency. He was too much the fox, not enough the lion. Too often, according to Burns, the president went for short-term tactical advantage that precluded the attainment of longer-term strategic objectives. James Patterson has argued that the obstacles to the realignment desired by Burns were formidable. He argues that Roosevelt's opportunistic policy of helping progressive non-Democrats in some cases, sustaining liberal Democratic factions in others, and working with established conservative forces in yet others, was about the best that could be expected. The evidence supports Patterson's contention that the forces of localism were too great to have been overcome, even by a more forceful, systematic policy. Established conservative politicians were too entrenched to be ignored; assisting progressive non-Democrats would not necessarily have brought long-term success; building up local pro-New Deal factions depended on the right sort of local politicians being available and identifiable; the raw material of an electorate clearly demanding more liberal action simply did not exist.

There is no doubt that New Deal programmes offered massive opportunities for political influence. Not only did the proliferation of new agencies vastly expand the number of routine patronage positions available for distribution, but local politicians were bound to look hungrily at the relief and works programmes which offered jobs and money to their hard-pressed constituents. Many of the supporters of the New Deal complained bitterly that this potential was wasted, that Roosevelt and his advisers allowed this patronage to fall into the wrong hands. In 1936 a young liberal pro-New Deal candidate in North Carolina angrily told Democratic National Committee chairman and Postmaster General James Farley, 'With a few exceptions ... those who control and direct the Party machinery [in the state] are either outright against the

President or very indifferent towards his election, . . . yet the New Deal is continuously recognizing known anti-New Dealers as its spokesmen in the state'. The candidate, Ralph MacDonald, would have been even more angry if he had known that the full weight of the state director of the WPA was being illegally thrown behind the campaign of his conservative gubernatorial opponent (see Chapter 5).

Nevertheless, Roosevelt did positively intervene in local politics. He did not simply work with established political organisations, no matter how conservative or corrupt, even though that would have been the preferred policy of his campaign manager, Jim Farley.

Against the wishes of local Democrats, Roosevelt did help progressive politicians who were not Democrats. In Wisconsin, Philip La Follette, despairing of recapturing control of the Republican Party and dismayed by the conservatism of local Democrats, had formed a Progressive Party to contest the 1934 elections. He persuaded his brother Robert to stand for re-election to the Senate as a Progressive. Roosevelt endorsed Robert and made no moves to assist local Democrats. When the Progressives swept to power in the state and Philip La Follette became governor, Roosevelt agreed to let him set up his own work relief programme and appointed a Progressive to run the Wisconsin WPA.

In Minnesota, Governor Floyd Olson of the Farmer-Labor Party, who proclaimed his vision of the 'cooperative commonwealth' and advocated widespread public ownership, held the hopes of many of those who favoured a national third-party in the early 1930s. Roosevelt actively encouraged those local Democrats who were prepared to work with Olson, the liberal Protestant Scandinavian faction, and ignored the conservative Irish Catholic faction.

In New York City, feisty former Republican congressman Fiorello La Guardia ran for mayor in 1933 as an independent. Roosevelt secretly backed him against both the Democratic Tammany machine candidate and its reform challenger. The president cooperated enthusiastically with the successful La Guardia in public works projects and relief spending and created a separate WPA for New York City, the only city in the country to be recognised in that way. La Guardia was able to build a formidable independent political organisation relying not only on the Italians,

who had hitherto been ignored, but also on the newly formed
American Labor Party, which allowed disaffected local Democrats
who were loyal New Dealers to vote for La Guardia and
Roosevelt.

In Nebraska, Republican George Norris, the man most responsible for keeping Muscle Shoals under public control, was
endorsed by Roosevelt when he ran as an independent in 1936.
Roosevelt consistently gave Norris whatever patronage and all the
flood control projects in Nebraska that he wanted.

Roosevelt was also prepared to intervene within the Democratic
Party to try and create or bolster liberal pro-New Deal factions,
and sometimes to insist on the nomination of progressive candidates. Michigan Democrats, who needed campaign assistance
from the president more than he needed their help, were given an
ultimatum in 1936 to nominate Frank Murphy for governor.
Roosevelt was also ready on occasion to use patronage against
conservative Democrats. As A. Cash Koeniger had shown, Roosevelt was even willing to try to undermine the Byrd machine
in Virginia, directing patronage to the two anti-Byrd congressmen
and to the state's pro-New Deal governor, James H. Price who had
defected from Byrd's state machine. The New Dealers were also
prepared at times to challenge corrupt Democratic organisations.
Roosevelt used not only the independent La Guardia but the boss
of the Bronx, Ed Flynn, to undermine Tammany. He backed
Lloyd Stark in his bid to defeat the Pendergast machine in Kansas
City and even encouraged Charles Edison's fight to free New
Jersey from the grip of the notorious Hague machine in Jersey
City. In Louisiana, although some agencies like the Resettlement
Administration were politically neutral, most patronage was
directed to opponents of Huey Long. The patronage plums in the
state – Collector of Internal Revenue, federal judges, federal
attorneys, federal marshals – went to candidates endorsed by the
anti-Long leaders. Eventually both the ERA and the WPA in the
state were run in an overtly anti-Long style.

There were, however, major obstacles to more systematic
intervention by Roosevelt. In the emergency of 1933 when
Roosevelt's influence and the leverage given by patronage were at
their greatest he had little alternative but to work with the
established southern congressional leadership. The patronage and
recognition that southern conservatives like Joe Robinson re-

ceived undoubtedly strengthened their local political position. When Robinson complained about the hellish task of ramming through New Deal legislation, Carter Glass noted that the road to hell in his case was lined with post offices. But when the New Deal's priority was the passage of relief and recovery legislation, it would have been politically suicidal for Roosevelt to try to undermine the Southerners' status. The president would have been slapping in the face those who had backed him for the nomination and who were loyally, and often enthusiastically, supporting his programme. The whole New Deal would have been jeopardised for some hypothetical long-term political gain.

Aiding progressives outside the Democratic Party was not an unqualified success. On the one hand, western progressive Republicans were not reliable supporters of the New Deal; on the other, partisan problems with local Democrats were often insoluble.

Western progressive Republicans may have been scornful of their own party's reactionaries and may have enthusiastically backed many New Deal measures before 1936, but they remained an individualistic and egotistical group, intensely suspicious of professional Democratic Party politicians like James Farley. Their dislike of organised labour, their distaste for the increasingly urban orientation of the New Deal, and their deep hostility to the extension of state bureaucratic power meant that they rapidly deserted Roosevelt after 1936. It was not simply their fervent isolationism that drove men like Hiram Johnson of California, William Borah, and Gerald Nye into the anti-Roosevelt camp.

Where western progressives remained supporters of the New Deal, the relationship between their continued support of the New Deal and long-term political realignment was complex. In Wisconsin, local conservative Democrats were infuriated by New Deal backing for the La Follettes and the Progressives. Denied what they considered their just and long-awaited patronage rewards, these Democrats became even more conservative. As a result it was even less likely that the La Follettes would ever go over to the Democrats. One consequence was that Philip La Follette was defeated in 1938, squeezed out by the two traditional parties. His brother was unwilling to undertake the task of local political organisation and the Progressive Party collapsed. By 1946 Robert La Follette was back in the Republican Party to be defeated by Joe McCarthy in the primary. By that time, the liberalisation of the

Democratic Party, seemingly moribund in the 1930s, had finally taken place. Voting for the Democrats in post-war Wisconsin correlated with the Progressive vote of the 1930s.

New Deal support of George Norris in Nebraska eventually ended in Republican success. Norris was staunchly independent and refused to organise his own party. Local Democrats split into three groups: a conservative faction, hostile to Norris, supported conservative senator Ed Burke and was willing to work with the Republicans; a New Deal faction backed Norris; and a radical faction endorsed the Townsend movement. The result was conservative Republican success in 1942.

Even in Minnesota cooperation with the Farmer-Labor Party did the New Deal little good in the short run. The ineffectiveness of Olson's successor, Elmer Benson, the split between the farmer and labour elements of his party, bitter factional divisions over the issue of Communist infiltration and the revival of the Republican opposition under liberal Harold Stassen led to an overwhelming Republican triumph in 1938. It would take another ten years before a liberalised Democratic Party, which had absorbed the Farmer-Labor Party, would recapture state power.

Conversely, in New Mexico, where Roosevelt was bitterly criticised for *not* backing progressive Republican Bronson Cutting, the short-term consequences were favourable to the New Deal. Patronage and the gratitude of his constituents for farm and drought relief benefits made Dennis Chavez, who defeated Cutting, a loyal administration supporter in the Senate. In the state Clyde Tingley controlled an urban- and labour-based liberalised Democratic Party. New Mexico Democrats may admittedly have been corrupt, but then most politicians in New Mexico were.

The third element which made more systematic efforts at party realignment difficult was the difficulty of intervening in struggles within the Democratic Party.

The obstacles facing attempts to build up pro-New Deal factions were perhaps most obvious in the unsuccessful efforts by Roosevelt to purge conservatives in the 1938 primaries. It was impossible with very little planning simply to transfer the popularity of the president to a local candidate. But by 1938 there had been a general conservative reaction to the New Deal. The obstacles to local intervention were equally daunting earlier when the New Deal was riding the crest of the wave of popular acclaim.

Conservatives often refused to allow themselves to be identified as anti-New Dealers. Before 1936 few Democrats seeking election admitted to be anything other than enthusiastic New Dealers. Even in the 1938 primaries, the targets of the purge were at pains to point out their undying support for the president and the large number of New Deal measures that they had supported.

National issues were not always the salient ones at the local level. Studies of local congressional elections suggest that primary battles were rarely fought on an ideological pro- and anti-New Deal basis. Personality clashes and factional disputes frequently led to supposedly loyal New Dealers fighting each other in Democratic primaries: S. Davis Wilson against George Earle in Pennsylvania, Burnet Maybank against Olin Johnston in South Carolina, E. W. Marland against Josh Lee in Oklahoma.

The New Deal had great difficulty in reaching down to the local level and finding candidates who were genuinely liberal yet at the same time commanded local political strength. Again, the failed 1938 purge highlighted the difficulties of finding electorally attractive liberals to challenge conservative incumbents. The challengers selected by Roosevelt in Georgia and Maryland had impeccable liberal credentials but no local organisation. Lawrence Camp, the state director of the WPA in Georgia, was a political neophyte ill-equipped to callenge the established strength of either Walter George or the other contender, Eugene Talmadge. Congressman David Lewis, for all his work on the Social Security Act, was old, colourless, and had little strength in Maryland outside his own congressional district. Even in South Carolina, where Governor Olin Johnston upheld the New Deal cause, his four years in the governor's mansion had brought him powerful political opposition as well as support.

In Virginia, the liberal base for New Deal intervention was similarly flimsy. There was no opposition to the Byrd machine for the New Deal to cultivate until 1935 and 1936 when the two congressmen and Lieutenant-Governor Price deserted the machine. By 1938 one of the congressmen had been defeated and Price as governor was thwarted in his hope for reform aspirations by the conservative legislature. Senators Byrd and Glass were as firmly entrenched as ever.

In Indiana, the handsome Paul McNutt seemed to offer both the liberal determination and the organisational strength that

Washington was looking for. McNutt as governor had combined progressive reforms on taxation, pensions, and labour with a tightly controlled political organisation, funded by salary deductions from state employees. But when Roosevelt attempted to purge conservative Senator Van Nuys in 1938, the pragmatic McNutt read the signs of rural discontent with the WPA and the urban New Deal, concluded that Van Nuys could not be beaten, and therefore supported him in 1938 and another conservative candidate in 1940.

In California conservative and moderate local Democrats with the president's ear – notably Senator McAdoo and defeated gubernatorial candidate George Creel – persuaded Roosevelt not to endorse novelist Upton Sinclair, the surprise winner of the 1934 primary. Sinclair's plan to end poverty in California would have turned over idle factories and farms to the unemployed for production for use. This idea attracted a wave of support in a state where the Depression had spawned an unusually large number of barter and self-help cooperatives. But it is not clear that Roosevelt's backing would have saved Sinclair's gubernatorial campaign in November 1934. Republican and conservative Democrats successfully combed the former Socialist's voluminous writings for material to wage a hysterical Red-baiting campaign. A third-party progressive candidate took votes away from Sinclair, equal to the Republican margin of victory. Sinclair made no attempt to placate moderate and liberal Democrats and soft-pedalled the old age pension issue whereas his Republican opponent endorsed the Townsend Plan. The record of a liberalised Democratic Party when it finally captured the statehouse in 1939 under Culbert Olson suggested the difficulties of pinning too much faith on Californian liberals. The party was fatally divided over government spending, relief policy, labour rights, and Communist infiltration in a state where powerful business and large-scale farming interests were all too ready to exploit such divisions.

Louisiana demonstrated in extreme form the difficulty of identifying genuine liberals at the local level from distant Washington. In 1933 Roosevelt and Farley cut off patronage to Huey Long after a barrage of complaints from Long's opponents that the senator and his associates were unfit to govern. The opponents were able to get a hearing for their complaints because they were established politicians with long-standing ties with Jim Farley, with southern members of the cabinet, and with congressional leaders. In addition, five anti-Long congressmen had thrown in their lot with the New Deal rather than Long. But Roosevelt was certainly not fostering embryonic New Deal liberalism in Louisiana with patronage. Long with some justice complained that the New Deal was rewarding 'the most rebuked, repudiated, conscienceless characters known to either the public or the private life of Louisiana or of any other state'. The beneficiaries of the New Deal's largesse were either old-time, routinely corrupt political bosses or aristocratic élite reformers. Both were irredeemably conservative on economic and social welfare issues. They had jumped on the New Deal bandwagon because Roosevelt offered them both the issue and the means with which to challenge Long. When the New Deal later made peace with the Long organisation after the senator's assassination in 1935, most of Long's opponents showed their true colours by becoming outspoken conservative opponents of New Deal economic regulation.

The final obstacle to long-term goals of party realignment was the conservatism of the electorate. There simply was not the raw material with which to fashion the sort of realignment on ideological grounds that political scientists have dreamed of.

In the northern, urban, and industrial states the potential for realignment was clear. We have already examined the interaction of New Deal welfare programmes, the needs of lower-income constituents, and the self-interest of urban machine politicians. The result was to cement the allegiance of new immigrant voters to the Democrats, win over blacks, and create a powerful pressure group for the expansion of the New Deal towards a permanent welfare state. Even under these favourable circumstances, the success of the New Deal realignment was not immediate and complete. Democratic hegemony did not necessarily replace Republican hegemony: the 1930s often paved the way for a period of two-party competition between the Democrats and a liberalised Republican Party. Nor did old-style conservative Democrats in the North disappear overnight. Rural, small-town interests continued to be important in the Democratic Party in states like Indiana, Ohio, and Illinois. There was a time-lag in many northern states in the liberalisation of the party. It was often the 1940s before 'issue-oriented' liberals took over from 'patronage-oriented' regular politicians.

The extension of the New Deal on liberal lines was not always wanted in the rest of the country. The midwestern farm belt, the western mountain states, and the South had all benefited immensely from the New Deal and had shown their gratitude by unprecedented support for Roosevelt and the Democrats through the 1936 elections. But in contrast to the northern industrial states the voters in these regions, once the worst of the Depression was over, did not want to push to sustain and expand the New Deal.

John Allswang's county-by-county voting analysis has charted how the rural Midwest swung towards the Democrats in gratitude for the benefits of the New Deal farm programme, but he noted not only that votes for Roosevelt did not always extend to a partisan commitment to the Democrats at the congressional level, but also that after 1936 the rural counties shifted back to the Republicans. Kansas, for example, received more wheat payments than any other state; its oil and livestock producers received crucial government aid. In 1936 its farmers received almost four times as much in benefit payments under the Soil Conservation and Domestic Allotment Act as those in any other state. In 1936 Roosevelt carried the state against its own governor, Alf Landon; the Democrats won the governorship and a Democrat came close to beating Senator Arthur Capper. But two years later, George McGill, an enthusiastic supporter of the new Farm Act, was defeated by a Republican in his bid for re-election to the Senate and the Republicans recaptured the governorship. As Frances Schruben noted, 'Kansas's attachment to the New Deal was only temporary'.

In neighbouring Nebraska the New Deal had been the salvation of the state. In the short term, massive AAA and relief payments offset the effects of five summers of drought; in the long term, the development of the state's water resources secured its farming future. In the 1936 elections Roosevelt and George Norris received appropriate support. But Norris, who believed that FDR had done more 'for the farmer of this great middle west than any president ever had', was appalled to find that as agricultural prosperity returned in the late 1930s and early 1940s Nebraska farmers detested the New Deal and hated the president. Farm programmes that had been their salvation now seemed burdensome and restrictive and the urban New Deal seemed no longer to be responsive to their needs. The defection of these farmers paved the way for Norris's defeat in 1942 and the long-term triumph in the state of a particularly conservative brand of Republicanism.

The hold of the New Deal on the electorate of the mountain West and the South was equally tenuous. No areas of the country benefited from the New Deal as much as these two regions. Because of the expanse of public lands and because of droughts in the 1930s, western states received more per capita from New Deal spending than any other states. In the South the farm programme undoubtedly rescued the region from disaster and government spending was an indispensable supplement to the income of a poverty-ridden region. Federal aid became the largest source of income for the state of Mississippi in the 1930s and remained so until 1972. The resulting popularity of the New Deal among southern and western voters meant that it was almost a *sine qua non* for politicians in both regions to support the New Deal before 1936. But in the West there were neither the lower-income ethnics nor the powerful organised labour pressure groups to push for an extension of FDR's programmes. After 1936 even apparently enthusiastic New Dealers like Burton Wheeler and Joseph O'Mahoney of Wyoming began to desert the liberal cause. All the studies of mountain states agree that while the 1930s saw a Democratic and liberal upsurge, the New Deal did not permanently change these states' long-term political configurations. States' rights philosophies and traditions of individualism survived the New Deal largely intact despite the federal largesse the states had received. Utah was a possible exception where the election and re-election of Senator Elbert Thomas gave the Democrats a foothold in that centre of Mormon Republicanism.

Roosevelt was optimistic about liberal prospects in the long term in the South. 'I know the South', he assured Socialist leader Norman Thomas, 'and there is a new generation of leaders in the South and we've got to be patient.' His confidence was not without basis. Younger Southerners who came to serve in New Deal agencies in Washington like Clifford and Virginia Durr, Aubrey Williams, Frank Graham, Clark Foreman, and Will Alexander soon learned to throw off the stifling gradualism and paternalism that had characterised southern racial liberalism. There were Southerners in Congress who were, as John Sparkman described himself, TVA liberals, even if their fervour did not necessarily match the aggressive economic liberalism of Hugo Black of

Alabama, whom Roosevelt appointed to the Supreme Court in 1937. Social scientists at the University of North Carolina at Chapel Hill provided the data which underpinned the TNEC's *Report on Economic Conditions of the South* in 1938 which Roosevelt used to describe the South as 'the Nation's number 1 economic problem'. The report laid out a liberal agenda for the region that was taken up by the newly formed Southern Conference for Human Welfare. Southern poverty could be eliminated with federal help through the creation of mass-purchasing power. Rural poverty programmes, minimum wage legislation, and the extension of social security would have to be buttressed by the extension of economic and political democracy in the region through the abolition of the poll tax and the protection of the civil liberties of union organisers. As in the North, there was also a time lag in the impact of the New Deal on southern politics. Younger politicians were elected in the 1940s who advocated liberal economic programmes which appealed to the disadvantaged of both races and who played down the race issue. Even in Mississippi, the election of Paul Johnson in 1939 heralded a decade which saw the greatest advances in social welfare programmes. War-time prosperity meant that the state could for the first time afford to participate in many welfare programmes.

Southern New Dealism was, however, a frail flower. Groups like the Southern Conference for Human Welfare never developed a mass base. Liberals were always vulnerable on the race issue which conservatives increasingly emphasised after the late 1930s. Southerners returning from Washington often found themselves ostracised because of their racial views. State governments acted to eliminate the region's poverty not by raising mass-purchasing power but by the traditional remedy of seeking low-wage industry through tax concessions and the attractions of a cheap and docile (non-union) labour force. Growth of that sort did not challenge traditional patterns of race relations. Most politicians in the South did not see the non-emergency New Deal as the solution to their problems: they distrusted a federal government geared to northern cities and organised labour. Given the absence of black voters in the South, the failure of organised labour, and an electorate that still excluded many lower-income whites, there were simply not the pressures for change that the New Deal could exploit to shake the power of the southern conservatives. A

long-term strategic commitment to party realignment and the
systematic direction of New Deal patronage could not have altered
that.

4 The political alternatives

The nature of the political alternatives to Roosevelt in the 1930s
and the strength of support for supposedly more radical options
also raises doubts about the existence of a genuinely radical
ground swell that Roosevelt could have exploited to sustain a more
far-reaching political realignment.

The challengers to Roosevelt for the Democratic nomination in
1932 certainly did not offer a radical alternative. Governor Ritchie
of Maryland, Speaker John Nance Garner, Al Smith, and Newton
D. Baker offered little more than the repeal of Prohibition and a
commitment to a balanced budget as solutions to the nation's
problems. Their conservatism reflected the conservatism of the
politicians elected to Congress and to the statehouses during the
Depression. Even when electors voiced dissatisfaction with established politicians they turned to men who colourfully denounced
the rich and the financial centres of power but who offered
conservative remedies for economic ills.

No better evidence of the electoral context of politics of the
1930s can be found than the conservatism of the men elected as
governors. Only two governors, Philip La Follette in Wisconsin
and Floyd Olson in Minnesota, ran administrations that were to
the left of the New Deal. Even here recent studies of their
governorships have stressed the moderation of their policies. For
all the Farmer-Labor Party's platform commitments to public
ownership, Olson's regime yielded substantial but conventional
reforms in welfare and taxation. Olson played down the issue of
public ownership and his legislature displayed little enthusiasm for
collectivist measures. La Follette's radical tone obscured, as John
Miller has noted, his 'essentially moderate actions' committed as
he was to a balanced budget and pay as you go taxation. A handful
of governors like Herbert Lehman in New York, George Earle in
Pennsylvania and Frank Murphy in Michigan enacted 'Little New
Deals' in major northern industrial states but the majority of
governors were, as James T. Patterson describes them, 'nobodies,

moderates, undramatic, yawn-inspiring men with legislative programmes as pedestrian as they were unhelpful'. Federal largesse
was accepted as a means of balancing the budget; new federally-
inspired obligations were an excuse to impose regressive taxation.

In the first flush of enthusiasm for the New Deal, the response of
the states was often in the hands, even in northern industrial
states, of men who had not been elected with a New Deal
mandate, like Governor Joseph Ely of Massachusetts, or conservative Republican legislatures, as in Pennsylvania. The Democratic governor of Colorado, Ed Johnson, later described the New
Deal as 'the worst fraud ever perpetrated on the American
people'. Even later governors who sponsored 'Little New Deals'
were often opportunists who lacked a genuine commitment to
reform. Eurith D. Rivers of Georgia promised a New Deal but he
was simply an office-hungry former ally of Gene Talmadge. His
trusted adviser recalled that the governor-elect called him one
morning shortly after his election in 1936 with a problem: 'I got
elected because I said I was going to provide for an old age pension
and a lot of other welfare programs, but I don't know a damned
thing about it. How about fixing me up a welfare program.'

In the northern, urban, industrial states which offered the most
fruitful soil for reform, it still required a combination of particularly favourable circumstances to put state reforms on the statute
books. In New York, as Robert Ingalls has shown, a Little New
Deal needed not only the state's wealth and urban base, but also a
tradition of progressive governors, strong liberal pressure groups,
radical agitation in New York City, and, finally, the decisive
leadership of Herbert Lehman. This combination produced welfare, health, housing, and labour legislation which represented a
genuine attempt by the state government to guarantee its citizens
as a matter of right a minimum standard of living. Yet at the same
time, in Ohio, a combination of rural representatives and spokesmen for the business community sustained Democratic governor
Martin Davey in his steadfast refusal to recognise the relief and
welfare needs of the unemployed or the unemployables. Even in
Michigan and Pennsylvania the 'Little New Deals' of George Earle
and Frank Murphy were short-lived – they fell foul of Democratic
factionalism and the Republican revival of 1938.

It is not surprising in this context that most of the time the New
Dealers defended themselves against attacks from the right, not

the left. Their rhetoric was geared not to refute charges of insufficient radicalism but to rebut charges that they were subverting American traditions of democracy and individualism. The complaint that the New Deal was un-American recurred: at first, there were charges that the ideas behind the New Deal were socialistic or communistic, later came charges that Roosevelt sought European-style dictatorial power, finally, with the formation of the House Un-American Activities Committee came charges that members of the Communist Party with a loyalty to a foreign power were infiltrating the government.

The right found ready bogey-men in the administration. Initially, the target was Tugwell. His admiration of Russian economic planning was taken to be responsible for the master-plan which lay behind New Deal programmes and their sovietisation of the American economy. Then, the target was Hopkins. His profligate spending, critics argued, aimed to subvert the very soul of the republic, corrupting the very foundation of politics and demoralising millions of individual welfare recipients.

The seriousness with which New Dealers felt obliged to respond to these charges was in part a reflection of the financial resources and the prominence in the press of their right-wing critics. Editorials crackled with fears for the safety of the republic. The formation of the Liberty League in 1934 gave prominence to the criticism of wealthy conservative businessmen, like John J. Raskob, Jouett Shouse, and the Du Ponts, and to disaffected conservative northern Democrats, like Al Smith. The founders of the League had been previously associated with the Association Against the Prohibition Amendment. Their aim then had been to lighten the tax burden on business through liquor taxes: now, New Deal deficits, business regulation, taxation, and labour legislation posed a much greater threat than Prohibition to their concepts of states' rights and limited government.

The publicity given to the Liberty League's onslaughts and the defection of prominent Democrats appeared to strengthen the Republican Party. In fact, the League increased the tension between the conservative GOP Old Guard who saw no merit at all in the New Deal and the moderate faction associated with Senators Charles McNary and William Borah who were prepared to embrace large chunks of the New Deal. The moderates in the party appreciated the danger of allowing Roosevelt to portray their party as the representatives of reaction, wealth, selfishness, and greed. But the lure of well-financed all-out attacks on the New Deal was difficult to resist. The party's candidate in the 1936 presidential election, Alf Landon, who was himself a New Dealish governor of a drought-ridden state, allowed his campaign to be overshadowed by strident attacks on all the New Deal stood for.

The Republican Party debacle in 1936 should not obscure the continued strength of the party. As William Allen White, the Kansas newspaperman, had noted after the 1934 midterm setbacks, 'Parties do not die from the top but from the roots, and the roots of the Republican Party in the East and the Mid West are still full of courthouse sap'. Roosevelt delighted in attacking the GOP as the party of callous reaction, but he was accutely aware of the potential threat the party could pose in 1936. He had feared a Republican campaign that accepted the social goals of the New Deal but lambasted waste and inefficiency. Democrats had also feared an opposition campaign focused on the very real increased tax burden on ordinary Americans. The Republicans' basic strength was shown by the party's rapid revival in 1938 and 1940. In 1938 Republicans won seven out of nine governorships in the Midwest as well as substantially recovering their position in Congress. In 1940 presidential nominee Wendell Willkie attracted an additional 5,000,000 voters to the party. The Republicans had hit on a potentially effective way of challenging the New Deal: as the momentum for economic recovery faltered they could reactivate traditional party loyalties in the Midwest and West, at the same time they could liberalise their image and broaden the party's appeal in the industrial East. Unity was nonetheless difficult to maintain. While the party was not as Janus-faced as the Democrats, it was still difficult to keep the eastern and western wings in tandem. The old factional splits in some ways had reversed themselves. Whereas once the western progressive battled the eastern Old Guard, now a liberalised eastern wing faced an increasingly conservative western right.

The perceived threat posed by the right in the 1930s accounted for the abandonment of radical attempts to form a third party to contest the 1936 elections. Since 1929 intellectuals and academics, despairing of the conventional policies of the two major parties and convinced that Marxism had no American appeal, had argued that the only hope for tackling the problems of the unequal distribution of national resources was the creation of a genuinely liberal independent third party. The League for Independent Political Action, founded by John Dewey, had attempted to organise a national third party in 1932. Rebuffed by leading progressives and other liberal groups, the League had to jettison the idea of nominating a national presidential candidate and endorsed instead Socialist Norman Thomas. Confident that the New Deal would be ineffective, the LIPA sanctioned the formation of a Farmer Labor Political Federation in 1933 that sought a 'Cooperative Commonwealth with a scientifically planned economic system, based on social control of the means of production'. The Federation pinned its hopes on existing third-party strength in Wisconsin, Minnesota, and Washington State and planned in 1935 to exploit discontent with the inadequacy of the New Deal. In July 1935 the American Commonwealth Political Federation was launched to build a third party for 1936 calling for 'production for use instead of for profit'. The movement faltered because of the inherent difficulties of organising a third national party. As Philip La Follette's short-lived National Progressives of America would find later, it was difficult to develop grass-roots organisations in states outside the home base. The ACPF also failed to attract substantial support from organised labour and was fiercely divided over the issue of Communist infiltration. Nevertheless, the key element in the third-party failure was the fear expressed by the leading politicians whom the third party sought to enlist, notably Floyd Olson, of a corporate-financed triumph by the right that would lead to a fascist-style takeover by big business. For Olson, as for the La Follettes, Roosevelt was the only realistic alternative to a 'fascist Republican'. By the late 1930s the prime movers in the third-party movement like Alfred Bingham of *Common Sense*, Paul Douglas, the University of Chicago economist, Thomas Amlie, the Wisconsin Progressive congressman, and Howard Y. Williams of the Minnesota Farmer-Labor Party had all become Democratic supporters of Roosevelt.

Marxist alternatives were available in the 1930s but neither the Communists nor the Socialists developed any electoral base. Both lacked popular support and both struggled with the dilemma of whether to cooperate with, or to attack, the New Deal.

A generation later in Cold War America it was easy to explain the failure of the Communists in the 1930s. The party had no indigenous base: it was simply the tool of the international conspiracy directed by the Soviet Union. Party policy, the argument continued, simply reflected the Moscow line; first, the party refused to work with any liberal or social democratic groups, who were denounced as social fascists; then, in 1935, came an abrupt shift to a Popular Front strategy which involved working with all the previously vilified progressive groups, including New Dealers; the Nazi-Soviet pact of 1939 then prompted the denunciation of progressive hero Roosevelt as a dangerous warmonger. Followers of the Communists were naive dupes. Their causes, notably black civil rights, were an exercise in cynical manipulation. Intellectuals who were attracted to the party during the apparent collapse of capitalism saw the error of their ways after the show trials and purges and the pact with Hitler.

This traditional view fails to comprehend the genuine grass-roots appeal of the Communists during the New Deal that sprang from their willingness to champion causes and people whom established politicians avoided. The Communists were prepared to fight for the welfare rights of the unemployed and courageously to struggle for the most subjugated groups of workers like the southern textile hands, Harlan County coal miners, and California farm labourers. They took up the case of nine black alleged rapists at Scottsboro when the NAACP was reluctant to get involved. They were a central element in all black protest activity in Harlem in the 1930s. Black intellectuals were impressed by the party's genuine interracialism. The party's efforts for blacks were not merely a cynical exercise. As Harvard Sitkoff has concluded, 'the positive effect of the left's involvement in racial matters outweighed the negative'. The party was a key component of the civil rights coalition that made black civil rights part of the liberal agenda. Similarly, Communists played a major role in the great labour organisational breakthrough of the late 1930s. Their success came from the fact that they were skilled labour organisers and, as union leaders, they delivered what their members wanted. The Communists were a routine part of Popular Front protest in the late 1930s: in the unions, in the organisation of WPA workers, and in the civil rights and peace movements.

Nor were American Communists only blind followers of the Moscow line. The move towards a Popular Front with other liberal groups dictated by the seventh and final Congress of the Comin- tern in Moscow in 1935 was actually anticipated by American Communists. A front organisation of the party like the Interna- tional Labor Defense was already cooperating with non- Communists in the defence of the Scottsboro boys. In both labour and the organisation of the unemployed the American party had abandoned its policies of exclusion.

The consequence was certainly the 'Heyday of American Com- munism'. The party had only 7,000 members in 1930, in the summer of 1939 its membership was approaching 100,000. Harvey Klehr suggests that between 200,000 and 250,000 people were party members at some time during the 1930s. Thousands more took their lead from the party without affiliating with it.

Nevertheless, Communist strength was circumscribed. Fratricid- al struggles as party functionaries attempted to keep on the right side of the latest Moscow line could be devastating. The vicious assaults on other left-wingers before 1935 left scars that the soft words of the Popular Front era could not entirely eradicate. Later, the Nazi-Soviet pact was a blow from which the party never fully recovered, even during the height of the Grand Alliance during World War II.

The turnover of membership was rapid. 60,000 people joined the party between 1930 and 1934, yet party membership in 1934 had only risen to 26,000 from 7,000. Although the party held on to more members during the Popular Front years, people still left the party quickly. In 1937, 30,000 new members were recruited but 14,000 were still lost. Life in the party was tough and time- consuming. Only the most dedicated stayed.

Finally, the insoluble dilemma for the Communists was that attacking Roosevelt was a dismal failure, but supporting him left the party with few long-term benefits. Before 1935 the party's isolated efforts clearly failed: dual unions collapsed, successes among the unemployed were small-scale and temporary. After 1935 the Popular Front tactics were much more effective but the beneficiaries were not the party but the groups they were helping, the trades unions and the Democrats. To be successful, Commu- nists had to keep a low profile, but a low profile did not bring party success. Union organisers for example lamented that their undoubted success in signing up union members was not matched by a political success in winning recruits to the Communist Party. The workers they organised rewarded them by fanatical loyalty to Roosevelt.

The Socialists were even less visible in the 1930s than the Communists. While Socialist Party membership rose during the Depression to 20,951 in 1931, by 1937 it had collapsed to 6,500. Its presidential candidate, Norman Thomas, polled 884,781 votes in 1932, three times the 1928 figure. Four years later he secured only 187,342 votes, the lowest figure since 1900. The party suffered from internal splits: at first between the conservative Old Guard and the younger progressives and militants, then, after the collapse of the Old Guard, between the progressives and the Trotskyites. The party lacked a working-class base. As Robert McElvaine notes, while its leader Norman Thomas 'was besieged with invitations to speak at forums, to college groups, to radical organizations, or even to some religious bodies, requests from labour organizations were sparse'. Thomas might complain that Roosevelt had enacted many of the reforms the Socialists had called for in 1932, but therein lay the Socialists' dilemma. To the extent they emphasised long-term radical goals, they enlisted no support; to the extent they stressed immediate reforms, potential supporters preferred to back Roosevelt. The party's insistence on opposing Roosevelt electorally did not help them. Throughout the decade Socialists deserted the party for the Democrats who seemed increasingly to be meeting their needs. Politicians like Andrew Biemiller in Wisconsin or Upton Sinclair and Jerry Voorhis in California or union leaders like David Dubinsky, Leo Krzycki, and the Reuther brothers all found that the new orientation of Roosevelt's Democratic Party fulfilled in practice their political and union goals.

A far more potent alternative to the New Deal was offered by Father Charles Coughlin, Doctor Francis Townsend, and Senator Huey Long. They brilliantly exploited the old political techniques of the stump, the new techniques of the radio and the mass mailing list, and new political constituencies of the unorganised and the old. They capitalised on the inadequacies of New Deal reform in 1934 and 1935, offered comprehensive indictments of Roosevelt's policies, and promised sweeping reform alternatives. An analysis of their policies and their popular support suggests however that both their strength and their radicalism were overestimated.

Detroit Catholic priest Charles Coughlin had attracted large audiences for his radio sermons in the late 1920s on CBS attacking Communism, birth control, and Prohibition. When he started preaching on the Depression and began to excoriate Herbert Hoover his audience dramatically increased. He received an average of 80,000 letters a week and $5 million a year from his listeners. His analysis of the Depression was simple: international bankers and Wall Street were starving the nation of money. The solution was the revaluation of gold, the remonetisation of silver, and the creation of a publicly-owned central bank. He was at first an outspoken supporter of the New Deal, although he bitterly criticised the AAA. When devaluation failed to bring about the anticipated inflation, he more and more stressed the importance of remonetising silver, and the treasurer of his radio League of the Little Flower had large holdings of silver futures.

Disillusioned by the lack of inflation, spurred by the need to find lively new topics for his weekly broadcasts, Coughlin became ever more hostile to the New Deal, which he complained was run both by Communists and by bankers. The 'government of bankers, by the bankers and for the bankers' was condemned at one and the same time for failing to nationalise the banks and for sovietising the economy. In November 1934 he formed the National Union for Social Justice which called for nationalised control of banking, credit, and currency, nationalisation of public utilities and natural resources, fairer taxation, and fairer rewards for farmers and labourers. He moved uneasily between bitter diatribes against the New Deal and praise of Roosevelt personally, an acknowledgement that many of his followers were loyal both to the president and himself. Roosevelt, aware of the potential power of a priest who could unite rural fundamentalist Protestants and urban Irish Catholics, treated Coughlin warily. Coughlin's pulling power appeared all the greater when he campaigned successfully for the defeat of the proposal for the US to join the World Court. Roosevelt granted Coughlin occasional recognition and met him both at the White House and at Hyde Park, but he made no substantive concessions on policy. He discouraged overt attacks on the radio priest, sent Catholic emissaries like Frank Murphy and Joseph P. Kennedy to try to soften Coughlin's opposition, and supported the effort of liberal Catholics like Father John A. Ryan to persuade the Catholic hierarchy to silence him. As long as

Archbishop Gallagher of Detroit backed his priest, these efforts were unavailing. Eventually in December 1935 Coughlin himself initiated the final break with the administration, coming out explicitly against not only the New Deal but the president himself.

Dr Francis Townsend was a relatively unsuccessful Long Beach doctor who saw at first hand the effects the Depression had on old people, wiping out their savings and highlighting the pitiful inadequacy of whatever small fixed incomes they were lucky enough to have. He had identified one of the major unorganised groups of the pre-Depression poor and suggested a dramatic remedy for their plight: a monthly pension of $200 which would be financed by a transaction tax of 2 per cent. Since the pension would have to be spent within 30 days, it would generate general economic recovery by injecting massive purchasing power into the economy. Naturally, old people liked the idea of a large pension which, in the national interest, they would have to spend. They flocked to a national network of Townsend clubs. The *Townsend National Weekly* brought in profits of $200,000 a year through advertising, particularly the marketing of patent medicines. The doctor himself received 2,000 letters a week by September 1934. The presence of fanatical Townsendites in their constituencies concentrated the minds of congressmen considering the Social Security Act, and made them even more disposed towards supporting old age insurance and old age assistance. In fact, the Social Security Act did not buy off Townsend and his followers. As late as 1938, 40 Republican congressmen were estimated to owe their election to their endorsement of the revolving pension plan. The willingness of traditional Republican voters in the West to support Townsend highlighted a central element of his appeal – the appeal to patriotism and to traditional Protestant morality.

The most powerful threat to the New Deal came from Huey Long. Long had come to power in Louisiana by combining an appeal to poor white farmers with bitter denunciations of Standard Oil and the conservative oligarchy of the state, and with vitriolic personal abuse of his opponents. This was a familiar route to power in the one-party South: candidates who could rely neither on campaign wealth from conservative economic interests nor on the endorsement of local power brokers had little alternative but to mount colourful personal campaigns which would arose the voters.

What made Long unusual was that once in power he did not

shelve his reform rhetoric or substitute an appeal to racial prejudice for substantive reform. Nor did he let himself be tied down by a conservative legislature. Instead, Long transformed his campaign promises into legislative reality when he became governor in 1929. His large-scale spending programmes on roads and education dragged the state's road system out of the mud and dramatically improved schools. Schoolchildren received free textbooks; an innovative night-school programme targeted adult illiterates; Louisiana State University was upgraded into a major regional university. He brought improvements to the training of doctors, to the state's hospitals, to the prisons, and to the mental asylums. A state income tax and a substantially increased severance tax on oil were enacted in the teeth of corporate opposition.

The record was impressive by the standard of any southern state government in the 1920s and 1930s. By the standards of a reform demagogue with reform pretentions like Theodore Bilbo, Long's achievement represented a stunning expansion of state government services. And it was enacted during the Depression when most other southern governors sought not to spend money but desperately looked for means of retrenchment. The key to Long's success was his ability to transform the ephemeral personal support of his 1928 victory into a powerful and permanent political organisation. Not only was he able to fight off a determined drive by conservative opponents to impeach him in 1929, but he went on to achieve virtually dictatorial power in Louisiana. By 1931 he was able to go off to Washington as a senator and still exercise day-to-day control of the governor's office and the state legislature. Contemporaries often likened Long to a European fascist dictator, yet his power was based on the familiar tools of American machine politics: patronage, corruption, electoral fraud, and violence. Long simply used these weapons more systematically and ruthlessly than any other American politician. But as with other machine politicians, the ultimate source of his power was his popular support: in return for the services he provided, Louisiana voters gave him enthusiastic and loyal backing.

As a senator, Long always aroused the interest of the curious and the media. From the start, he reiterated his fundamental thesis that a maldistribution of wealth was the cause of the nation's difficulties. A major redistribution of that wealth was the only remedy that would sufficiently restore mass-purchasing power to bring back economic recovery. His ideas culminated in the 'Share Our Wealth' scheme which he launched in February 1934. Long visualised an America in which every family would have an allowance of $5,000 to establish a home and would be guaranteed an annual income of at least $2,500. No personal fortunes would exceed $5 million and no income exceed $1.8 million a year. Annual capital levies and income taxes would bring about this redistribution of wealth.

By 1934 Long was a bitter opponent of Roosevelt. He had not always been so. In 1932 he had found congenial company in the small group of progressive dissidents in the Senate who challenged the conservative orthodoxy of the leadership of both parties. He supported Roosevelt for the Democratic nomination, probably played a decisive role at the convention in keeping the wavering Mississippi delegation in line and campaigned effectively for FDR in the western farm states. In the first Hundred Days he supported the New Deal when it spent money, agreed to currency inflation, and protected smaller banks, but opposed it when bankers and businessmen appeared to wield too much influence or when measures were deflationary. When at the end of the Hundred Days Roosevelt made it clear that Long would not be receiving federal patronage, Long was free to become increasingly vehement in his denunciations of the New Deal. Few aspects of New Deal policy escaped his vitriol: the business domination of the NRA, the scarcity economics of the AAA, the plight of tenant farmers, the feebleness of the Social Security Act, and the inadequacy of the New Deal's efforts to redistribute 'concentrated bloated pompous wealth'.

Coughlin, Townsend, and Long had much in common. They all came to hate Roosevelt bitterly and they all addressed real problems and real New Deal failings: the insufficiency of economic recovery, the plight of the old, and the uneven distribution of wealth. But the solutions they offered scarcely constituted a radical challenge to the New Deal from the left. They offered instead glib panaceas designed to reassure the discontented that the dramatic benefits that they were promising could be achieved without radical or painful change.

They advocated delusively simple solutions – currency inflation and changes in the tax structure – which could be put into effect without the creation of a massive bureaucratic state apparatus. But their solutions could not bring the results which they promised. Coughlin's remonetisation of silver would do nothing for urban workers, the rural poor, or the old. The benefits Long envisaged from dissolving a few fortunes could not materialise since there were not enough millionaires and too many poor. To ensure that each family received a $5,000 allowance, no family would be able to retain more than $7,000 in wealth (compared to the $5 million Long would allow). An annual income of $2,500 per family could only be achieved if no family retained more than $3,000 of its annual income (compared to the $1.8 million Long would allow). The pensions Townsend envisaged could be no more than $50–$75 a month on a 2 per cent transaction tax. The tax itself would have been profoundly regressive, reducing the income of most workers by half.

They all hated the extension of bureaucracy and state power by the New Deal. Yet they all advocated schemes that would have dramatically increased state power. Coughlin envisaged a gigantic central bank. Long conceded the necessity for a vast corporation to supervise the sharing of wealth. Townsend's transaction tax would have been a bureaucratic nightmare and an army of officials would have been needed to police the spending of the monthly pensions. They condemned the New Deal for not doing enough for farmers and the poor, yet at the same time denounced the AAA and the welfare programmes for doing too much.

They were not anti-capitalist. Their targets were distant Wall Street financiers and men of great wealth like the Rockefellers, not local employers or small-town bankers, merchants, and landowners – the élites who constituted the economic and social power structure at the local level. Even Long's highway and educational reforms in Louisiana were consistent with business progressivism. It was not coincidence that they all accused Roosevelt of Communism. The strength of their appeal lay not in a pitch to the people at the bottom of the pile in America – the tenants and sharecroppers, blacks, the urban unemployed, industrial workers – but to more substantial citizens who had been laid low by the Depression. The homeowner threatened by foreclosure, the farm owner-operator paralysed by debt, the small-town merchant unable to fight off the chain stores, the old people whose savings had been wiped out by the slump, the small businessman unable to cut costs like his competitors – these were the people who welcomed the promise of

Long, Coughlin, and Townsend to solve their problems without destroying their traditional individualistic values.

Radical or not, they were appealing to a formidable constituency. How strong a threat did they pose to the New Deal? Long's forays outside his own state, his network of Share Our Wealth clubs, and a poll conducted for the Democratic National Committee in 1935 suggest considerable strength for Huey Long before he was assassinated in September 1935. The fate of the Union Party backed by Coughlin and Townsend in 1936 raises doubts about the popular appeal of all the demagogues.

Long's barnstorming campaigns on Roosevelt's behalf certainly convinced Jim Farley of Long's appeal in 1932 in the northern plains states. The ecstatic receptions given Long at the Farmers' Holiday Association conventions in Iowa in 1934 and 1935 testified to his continued appeal to western farmers. Long himself was confident that he could take Iowa by storm at any time. In the South he had demonstrated his power to invade conservative strongholds in 1932 when he launched a successful whirlwind campaign in Arkansas, the home of Majority Leader Joe Robinson, a particular target of Long's ridicule. Long's campaign almost single-handedly won the Senate seat for the hitherto unregarded Hattie Caraway, widow of the former senator. In Mississippi and South Carolina established politicians were wary of tangling with Long for fear of his potential appeal to their voters.

The network of Share Our Wealth clubs, 27,000 of them with perhaps 8,000,000 members, suggested national, not just southern and western strength. The clubs at the very least constituted a superb mailing list. The evidence suggests that, where the clubs were more than that, their activity and strength were the result of unauthorised activity by local entrepreneurs anxious to use the Share Our Wealth movement for their own particular ambitions. The clubs were an opportunity for sharp-eyed operators to make money by selling material which they had received free from the Long organisation. Similar local problems plagued the National Union for Social Justice and the Townsend clubs.

More substantial testimony to Long's support came in the poll conducted by Emil Hurja in 1935 for the Democratic National Committee. The poll suggested that at that time Long would pick up 12 per cent of the vote as a third-party candidate in a presidential election. The poll was taken by Jim Farley to indicate that Long might poll as many as 6,000,000 votes in 1936: a performance that might throw the election to the Republicans. Hurja's poll was hardly sophisticated; it was also taken well over a year before the presidential election at a time when the New Deal appeared to be floundering. But the pollster did use basic sampling techniques, and his results revealed that Long drew support equally from urban and rural areas and that he received backing from all regions, though less so in the north-eastern and mid-Atlantic states.

The polls suggested that Long could capitalise on the support of the followers of Coughlin and Townsend and it was the prospect of a coalition of the demagogues that alarmed leading New Dealers. After Long's death, Coughlin and Townsend joined Gerald L. K. Smith, Long's Share Our Wealth successor, in endorsing the Union Party candidacy of William Lemke. The derisory showing of the Union Party in 1936 is not a very satisfactory indication of the threat Long might have posed Roosevelt. Lemke, a congress-man from North Dakota, had 'the charisma of a deserted tele-phone booth', recalled Gerald L. K. Smith. The Union Party made no headway in the cities where Hurja's polls suggested significant Long strength, and Lemke made no headway in Long's own region, the South. The campaign did show, however, the difficulty of turning clubs like the Share Our Wealth clubs and the Townsend clubs into effective political forces; the powerful per-sonal jealousies between the demagogues were clearly revealed. But the most important source of weakness that the campaign revealed about the demagogues was their inability to offset the appeal of Roosevelt himself and the very tangible benefits that the New Deal provided for farmers and lower-income voters. What Alan Brinkley has argued for Long was true of Coughlin and Townsend as well. Apart from a small core of fanatical supporters, the demagogues' support was essentially 'soft'. Their support may have been widespread but it may not have been intense. What the demagogues found, like other dissident politicians in the 1930s, was that though they hated Roosevelt, their followers did not necessarily do so. As with the Communists and the Socialists, the demagogues found that Roosevelt inspired great loyalty amongst their potential supporters and that the benefits of the New Deal, however inadequate, were sufficient to attract the loyalty of lower-income voters.

5 The conservative restraints

Roosevelt was unable to fulfil his 1932 prediction to Rex Tugwell of creating a fully fledged liberal party to bequeath to his successor. The reforming thrusts of the new Democratic Party of lower-income northern voters were parried by the continued power of conservative Southerners and Republicans. But the evidence does not suggest that a bolder policy by the president would have given him more scope for radical action. In 1933 he had little option but to work with the existing congressional leadership and in doing so he undoubtedly bolstered the power of conservative Southerners who would eventually turn against the non-emergency New Deal. Even if Roosevelt had handled Congress better at the time of the Court-packing episode he would have been unable to do much to stem the conservative tide, especially after the recession of 1937–38.

His ability to reshape the Democratic Party was sharply restricted by the forces of localism. Even when Roosevelt made the effort, it was difficult successfully to transfer presidential popularity to identifiably liberal candidates at the local level. What ultimately constrained the president was the conservatism of ordinary Americans in the 1930s. The responses of politicians in the South and West, the performance of state governors, the revival of the Republican Party, the fate of Marxist radicalism, the individualistic and anti-statist ideology of the dissident demagogues all powerfully suggest that there was no constituency waiting at the grass-roots for more radical action than Roosevelt offered. Despite the Depression and despite the limitations of the New Deal most Americans continued to elect politicians who wanted the New Deal to do less, not more.

Conclusion: Unanticipated Consequences

The deficiencies of the New Deal were glaring. As the 9,000,000 unemployed in 1939 testified, the policies for industrial recovery did not work. The NRA failed to inject additional purchasing power into the economy. The commitment to deficit spending was belated and half-hearted. Neither through taxation nor through anti-trust prosecution was the Roosevelt administration able to break up the economic power of large corporations or to redistribute wealth. The New Deal's support for the countervailing power of trades unions was ambivalent. Roosevelt was a late convert to the Wagner Act and the Act itself was less responsible for the great organisational breakthrough in the mass-production industries than was the militancy of the rank-and-file workers.

In agriculture, crop reduction and price-support loans could not eliminate surplus production. The New Deal was unable to stimulate urban demand and absorb farm overproduction, nor did it solve the problem of too many people living on the land. Recovery programmes offered little to marginal farmers, share-croppers, and farm labourers. The ambitious plans to solve the problems of rural poverty were largely still-born.

Spending on direct relief was always inadequate both under the FERA and later by the states. Too often relief perpetuated traditional and degrading attitudes towards welfare recipients. Work relief never reached more than 40 per cent of the unemployed. Spending constraints meant that WPA jobs were never invested with the legitimacy and dignity that New Dealers had hoped to impart. The social security system excluded many who needed help most, paid for benefits from the earnings of the beneficiaries, penalised the old and dependent in poorer states, and made no provision for health insurance. For the urban poor, the failure to develop a significant low-cost government housing programme left the worst problems of the inner city untouched. For the poor who were black, the New Deal did little. It enacted no civil rights measures and sanctioned continued discrimination and segregation in its programmes.

It is equally easy to replace this bleak catalogue of New Deal failure with a positive assessment of its success – the more so when New Deal activism is contrasted to the inaction of the federal government under Hoover.

In contrast to Hoover's vain exhortations to keep wages up, the NRA put a statutory floor under wages, checked the downwards deflationary spiral, and halted the relentless erosion of labour standards. Together with direct federal public works expenditure, the NRA seemed to prevent matters from getting worse and, through 1936, government intervention in the economy paralleled, if it did not cause, modest but definite recovery. A stabilised banking and securities system, eventual deficit spending, and protected labour standards gave hope for ultimate orderly recovery. The New Deal's acceptance of organised labour may have been halting but the attitude of the state to labour was effectively reversed. No longer were the forces of government automatically arraigned against trades unions. Rank-and-file militancy could not succeed without government protection. The Wagner Act and the change in government stance disciplined the most anti-union employers and protected the great gains of 1936–37 against economic downturn and employer backlash.

In contrast to Hoover's vain exhortations to reduce acreage, the voluntary domestic allotment plan gave farmers positive incentives to cut production. The benefit payments, farm credit, and debt adjustment all provided farmers with the tangible assistance that the Federal Farm Board had failed to give. The votes of farmers both in crop control and the 1936 elections were striking testimony to their perception that the New Deal had rescued commercial farmers both large and small, and almost all farmers were commercial farmers. In the 1980s, as American farmers once more face drought and foreclosure, the New Deal's achievement for agriculture recaptures some of its lustre. While the resettlement projects and tenant purchase loans of the Farm Security Administration may have 'skimmed the cream' of the rural poor, rehabilitation loans and grants did reach many of the 'submerged third' of the rural population. For all its defects, the FSA nevertheless was effective enough to arouse the fear of conservative politicians in the South.

The Depression had exhausted private, local, and state resources for relief before 1933. Hoover had bitterly resisted the remedy of direct federal grants. New Deal welfare programmes gave the unemployed money and jobs. The lasting loyalty of lower-income voters to Roosevelt expressed their appreciation of the very real and essential benefits they received. The Social Security Act created insurance for the old and unemployed which had existed nowhere in the public sector before and only minimally in the private sector. The Act initiated a quantum leap in the provision of assistance to the old, the blind, and dependent children. The Act might not have been rounded out in the way New Dealers hoped, but the interlocking and contributory system launched in 1935 did ensure that Congress would not lightly abolish it. The New Deal welfare programmes provided direct assistance to perhaps as many as 35 per cent of the population. It bequeathed a commitment to a minimum level of social welfare from which successive governments have never been entirely able to escape.

The political realignment that these welfare measures helped shape ensured that the measures needed to tackle urban poverty would in the future be a part of the liberal Democratic agenda. Similarly, the demands of blacks would now be pushed on the national Democratic Party by the developing civil rights coalition which included New Deal liberals. The shift in political allegiance by blacks in the 1930s bore witness to the genuine assistance they had received in the northern cities from relief and WPA programmes. Despite continued discrimination and segregation, southern blacks received assistance on a scale that surpassed anything they had been granted by any state or private sources. Farm programmes lessened the bonds of dependency of tenants and sharecroppers on white landlords, and the ferment of activity in Washington gave southern black leaders new hope that the federal government might eventually be the source of their salvation.

To lament the New Deal's deficiencies or to celebrate its achievements has only limited utility. Instead, what is needed is an examination of the relationship between reforms instituted by the New Deal and the longer-term developments of American society. What needs to be explained therefore is why New Deal reforms had such unanticipated consequences. The business-warfare-welfare state that America eventually became was not the intentional construct of New Dealers. Much New Deal policy had been designed to curb the power of the key corporations that became so firmly entrenched after 1945. The advocates of social security had envisaged the withering away of assistance programmes not the mushrooming of welfare rolls. Those advocates expected to enact national health insurance in the future: they live instead to see the explosion of private medical insurance plans.

In the 1940s and 1950s Americans fled from the land. Yet in the 1930s rural planners had aimed to keep people on the land. New Dealers aimed to eradicate slums, regenerate the inner cities, and revitalise small towns. Yet their housing policies fostered suburban sprawl.

These unexpected developments were not the result of a plot in the 1930s by a corporate capitalist élite. New Deal reforms were not corporate liberal reforms designed to extend the hegemony of large-scale business over the economy and to defuse the threat of radical protest.

Banking and securities reforms may have stabilised credit and the stock exchange but they were opposed by the very businessmen who ultimately benefited from them. The NRA may have been the brain-child of trade association spokesmen, but few members of the corporate élite positively supported it: most regarded the NRA as a reform to be endured. When the NRA did not bring recovery, a few businessmen saw the virtue of working with it to limit the damage it could do but most fervently hoped for its demise.

Nor did corporate élites support New Deal labour reforms. These reforms did not represent a sophisticated strategy of containment of trades unions by the business community. The Wagner Act may have led to conservative and responsible unionism, but businessmen in the 1930s did not foresee the benefits of such a stabilised industrial relations system. On the contrary, many went to great lengths to try to forestall independent unions. At best, some grudgingly accepted the inevitable, but even they were determined to make no substantive concessions.

Nor does the evidence support the argument that the New Deal welfare measures were designed to ward off the threat of disorder by the unemployed and the poor. Perceived need identified by welfare workers and the political opportunity to act, not the threat of violence, explains the genesis and development of welfare policies. New Dealers did predict increased radicalism in due course if no steps were taken to improve the lot of the poor. The threat of disorder was also a useful spectre to raise before the eyes of conservative politicians. But, if anything, the New Deal stimulated rather than defused disorder. Demonstrations by the unemployed were mostly unavailing efforts to prevent cuts in New Deal benefits.

Some limitations of the New Deal were nevertheless self-imposed; some of its wounds self-inflicted. Roosevelt never pretended that his aim was anything other than to save and preserve capitalism. The consequences of banking and securities reform were conservative precisely because Roosevelt wanted to restore conservative investment practices. His anger at the business community sprang not from an anti-business philosophy, but from his irritation at the ingratitude of the group for whom the New Deal had done so much. This commitment to basic capitalist values made it all the more damaging that he failed to embrace early enough a compensatory fiscal policy. Such a policy might have brought the recovery he sought without disturbing the basic structure and value system of capitalism. The policy was intellectually available and the spending alternative was clearly presented to the president, particularly at the end of 1936. Instead, Roosevelt opted for policies that, first, starved many of his agencies of the funds needed to attain their social justice goals and, then, hastened recession in 1937–38, thereby immensely strengthening the conservative opposition that thwarted so many of the wider-ranging purposes of New Deal reform.

Roosevelt and the New Dealers were also handicapped by the contradictory or ambiguous vision of the America that they were seeking to create. Ultimately most of them believed that economic recovery would come from the revival of private enterprise, yet their convictions and political sensitivities inhibited them from wooing the business community wholeheartedly. There was no unanimity on the future industrial structure of the country. Some New Dealers continued to regard large corporations as efficient and inevitable businesses which should accordingly be regulated; others believed they should be broken up.

The New Deal consolidated an urban liberalism that frankly

recognised the desirability of an increasingly urbanised America. Yet Roosevelt himself was reluctant fully to accept that vision, and his lack of sympathy for urban dilemmas in part accounts for the inadequacy of the 1937 Housing Act. Roosevelt and others yearned to move people back on to the land yet the Department of Agriculture knew that there were actually too many people on the land. Planners in Agriculture were never entirely certain of their goals: were they to hasten the modernisation and rationalisation of farming, or were they to try to increase the numbers of small owners and enable them to stay on the land?

The fear of social security administrators that generous assistance programmes might undermine social insurance prevented the development of an adequate and comprehensive welfare programme.

Many New Dealers were fully conscious of these inconsistencies and acknowledged their reform limitations. Frances Perkins was once described by a friend as 'a half-loaf girl: take what you can get now and try for more later'. New Dealers were not blind to the failures of their own programmes: they had a practical appreciation of political constraints and hoped to refine and improve programmes in due course. Perkins herself was under no illusions about the weaknesses and gaps in the social security system. The Bureau of Agricultural Economics was fully aware of the long-term limitations of planned scarcity and of the need to stimulate urban consumption. No one had a shrewder perception of the damage spending constraints imposed on work relief than Harry Hopkins.

They were remarkably accessible to their critics. In part, accessibility reflected the still manageable size of the federal government. Sharecroppers from Arkansas could travel through the night to Washington, sit down in the early morning outside the Secretary of Agriculture's office, and actually talk to Henry Wallace when he came in to work. In part, accessibility reflected the lack of dogmatic certainty amongst New Dealers. Even the arbitrary Hugh Johnson responded to a shouting match with Leon Henderson by inviting him in to head the Research and Planning Division. When Will Alexander and Frank Tannenbaum exposed the consequences of the collapse of cotton tenancy, they were brought in to draft the Bankhead-Jones bill and to work in the Resettlement Administration. Even when the experience of critics was less happy – when for example Jerome Frank and the liberal reformers were purged from the AAA after the reinterpretation of the cotton contract – they were not cast aside. They went on to work in more congenial parts of the New Deal experiment – in Justice, the Labor Department, at the NLRB, or at the SEC.

Many of the problems that the New Deal found intractable were problems first uncovered by the New Dealers themselves. The existence of a permanently poor rural population in the South was not a problem much recognised by agricultural economists or farm policy-makers in 1933. It was a problem exposed by FERA workers who found an unexpected demand for relief in rural as well as urban areas. Their initiatives led to the assault on rural poverty through rehabilitation loans and resettlement communities. The full dimensions of the needs of the cities and the possibilities of federal action were first laid out by the National Resources Committee in their 1937 report *Our Cities: Their Role in the National Economy*. The TNEC identified in 1938 the needs of the South. The Great Plains Committee partially mapped the problems of the West in *The Future of the Great Plains*. Field studies for the relief agencies first highlighted the health and educational deficiencies of both rural and urban America and the particular plight of the young and women.

The New Deal was not static, it improved over time as deficiencies in existing programmes were exposed and new problems identified. Nowhere was this clearer than in its treatment of blacks. The ignorance of even sympathetic liberals like Eleanor Roosevelt mirrored at first the indifference with which the NRA and the AAA regarded blacks. Slowly she and others became aware that black problems could not be eradicated by generally targeting poverty. As a result of their perception of the special needs of blacks, agencies like the PWA, the WPA, and the Farm Security Administration pursued racial policies that had changed significantly from the white preoccupations of 1933.

Nevertheless, the first steps the reformers took too often turned out to be last steps. Their hopes of a more suitable distribution of wealth, of permanent emergency employment agencies, of a comprehensive welfare state, of coordinated planning and control of the nation's physical resources, and of a full-scale assault on rural poverty were dashed. Sometimes this failure was the result of missed opportunities. The New Dealers' pragmatism may have been self-limiting. As R. Alan Lawson noted, 'Practicality can be treacherous. It urges compromise but may be used against compromise by deeming some evils too firmly rooted for practical reform to touch.' It was undoubtedly prudent not to challenge the American Medical Association, for example, over national health insurance in 1935 in order to safeguard the Social Security Act itself. But in the future, the times were even less opportune to take on the AMA. For so many New Deal reforms, if the opportunity was not grasped in 1935, it would never present itself again.

Liberals were impatient with Roosevelt's lack of a thoroughgoing vision of reform and the administration's lack of valour, but the New Deal was more often restricted by external constraints imposed by the political and economic environment: the lack of a sufficient state apparatus, the strong forces of localism, the great difficulty of policy-making in an economic emergency, and entrenched conservative leadership in Congress.

The structure of the federal government of the early 1930s was inappropriate to centrally-directed radical reform. There was simply not the 'state capacity' in Washington to manage central planning of the economy. Even if the political mandate for coercive overhead planning had existed in 1933, the government had neither the information with which to devise planning policies nor the bureaucracy with which to implement them. By the time the government had acquired the necessary information, the political opportunity to impose such plans had long gone, if it had ever existed. Nor was there a disinterested welfare bureaucracy capable of administering a national relief scheme or launching a purely federal social security system. The Department of Agriculture possessed a federal bureaucracy which had acquired considerable information about American farms. But even there neither crop control nor long-term planning could have been implemented without vesting crucial power in local committees of the farmers themselves.

The political constraints on centralised planning or purely federal programmes were formidable. Hostility to big government was not the preserve simply of conservative reactionary opponents of the New Deal. Suspicion of centralised federal authority governed the attitude of midwestern progressives, dissident demagogues, decentralist intellectuals like the Southern Agrarians, and many New Dealers themselves.

The forces of localism were in themselves a powerful check on New Deal aspirations. Not only were many New Deal programmes operated by state government agencies, but everywhere New Deal programmes were run by local officials who might defer more to local community sentiment than to directives emanating from Washington. Local administration of the farm programme put power in the hands of the local rural power structure and discriminated against the rural poor. Even the FSA found it difficult to overcome the tendency of its local officials to defer to local custom. Local administration of relief often allowed free play to the miserly and conservative prejudices and self-interest of local businessmen and farmers. Everywhere, local administration tended to countenance and perpetuate racial discrimination. The local role in the social security system gave rise to vast discrepancies in coverage and benefits. The intentions of the 1937 Housing Act were often defeated by local real estate interests that prevented the creation of local housing authorities. The formation of local REA cooperatives was thwarted by the ability of power companies to build 'spite lines' to cream off the best business. Everywhere the pressure in Congress was to increase, not decrease, local involvement in the administration of New Deal programmes and to assert wherever possible state, not federal, control in order to safeguard entrenched local interests.

In any case some New Dealers saw positive virtues in such localism. They wanted to resurrect grass-roots democracy, to foster citizen participation. Local committees of farmers ran the AAA programmes, guided the TVA, advised on farm debt adjustment, land-use planning, and farm credit loans. The inhabitants were meant to govern Subsistence Homestead projects and Greenbelt towns. The REA operated through local cooperatives, the Soil Conservation programme through self-governing soil conservation districts. The aim of Indian reorganisation was to give self-government to the tribal councils. But this democratic vision was only partially successful. In the first place New Deal experiments in community building and participatory democracy were almost entirely rural in orientation. New Deal relief and welfare programmes made no attempt to draw on the tradition of urban community organisation that came from the settlement houses or the social unit experiment in Cincinnati. This social unit experiment in 1917 was an urban variant of the rural land-use planning committees – local community residents formed representative committees that met with a parallel committee of representatives from social service agencies. This was not a route taken in the 1930s. It would be the 1960s before urban welfare policy with Community Action Programs took up that approach again.

Post-war social scientists were quick to point to the drawbacks of participatory democracy in the rural areas. Sometimes grassroots democracy meant capitulation to local interest groups. At other times, interest groups destroyed democratic institutions that threatened them. Time and again it was also clear that the grass roots did not want to participate in the way New Deal planners wanted them to. Grass-roots democracy gave local sectional interests a veto over policy designed for the national interest. It is not surprising, given the constraints of localism, that many liberal New Dealers in the 1930s put their faith in enlightened national bureaucracy. Only in the 1960s and 1970s did this faith in federal bureaucracy seem misplaced.

The constraints of localism were compounded by the circumstances of policy-making and implementation in 1933. The economic emergency gave the New Deal vast opportunities to exercise powers that had not been used since World War I. Yet the spectacular exercise of that power for coherent planning required special circumstances, like the power vacuum in the Tennessee Valley in 1933. For the most part in 1933 the emergency, by contrast, severely restricted New Deal options. First, the emphasis was of necessity on recovery, rather than reform. Second, action had to be taken quickly. The banks had to be reopened in a week. NRA codes had to be drafted very quickly to provide an immediate boost to purchasing power. Relief money had to be distributed and spent at once. Millions of farmers had to be signed to contracts in weeks, not months.

Given both the lack of existing 'state capacity' in Washington and the constitutional doubts on coercive government regulation, the New Deal had to rely on the consent of those being regulated to put recovery programmes into operation quickly. To reopen the banks required the cooperation of local bank officials and reliance on their information and good faith. The cooperation of businessmen who possessed a monopoly on information about their industries was essential if codes were to be drafted and administered. There was no alternative to the administration of the AAA by the Extension Service and local committees of farmers. Relief programmes had to be run by state government agencies. So it was that the New Deal fostered interest groups that in the long run obstructed its reforming designs. Thus, businessmen distorted the intent of the NRA and severely limited its ability to raise mass-purchasing power. Grass-roots democracy in agriculture facilitated the creation of commodity interest groups that pressed for ever more generous price supports in their own particular interest. The AAA also promoted the revival of a farm pressure group like the Farm Bureau Federation which ultimately turned against the New Deal's efforts to help the rural and the urban poor.

The circumstances of 1933 contributed to another major constraint on the New Deal: the power of the conservative opposition in Congress. The New Deal had to work with the existing congressional Democratic leadership in 1933 to secure the speedy passage of its essential recovery legislation. The recognition that the New Deal gave and the patronage it distributed undoubtedly bolstered the position of southern congressional leaders. Loyal congressional support for the New Deal was replaced by scepticism and mounting hostility about the direction of the non-emergency New Deal. As Roosevelt moved to complete the unfinished business of the New Deal in attacking urban and rural poverty, so he found it increasingly difficult to take Congress with him.

It is difficult to see how Roosevelt could have avoided this opposition from southern conservative Democrats and Republicans. He had achieved a partial political realignment. But the elimination of the southern conservative wing of his party would have required a much more systematic commitment that would have to have started in 1933 when his first priority was on immediate recovery. Even a more systematic commitment to realignment would probably have foundered on the unreliability of progressive non-Democrats, the refusal of conservatives to allow themselves to be portrayed as opponents of the New Deal, the difficulty of identifying from Washington genuine liberals with local political strength, and the difficulty of fighting local elections on national issues.

Congressional conservatives had effectively checked the expansion of the New Deal by 1940. What created, however, the political economy of modern America was the impact of the dramatic social changes unleashed by World War II on the 'broker state' unwittingly created by the New Deal.

World War II was the juggernaut that ran over American society. The war opened up for the first time for the majority of Americans the possibility of affluence rather than subsistence. For city dwellers, full employment and high wages offered the chance that, once private construction resumed after the war, they might be able to own their own homes and move to the suburbs. For farmers, war-time prosperity suggested that at the end of the war they might be able to enjoy the consumer goods – refrigerators, radios, and air conditioning – that rural electrification was making available to them. During the war 75 per cent of the population paid federal income tax: testimony to their affluence, not to legislative intent.

For businessmen, the war opened up undreamt-of profitability, restored leaders of large corporations to public esteem and respectability, and removed most threats of government regulation. For trades unions, the war forced management for the first time to sit down with them and bargain meaningfully. It established the parameters of post-war industrial relations. The war, not the New Deal, transformed rural America. High prices made possible mechanisation, investments in fertiliser and scientific farming, and consolidation into larger farms. Full employment gave the excess agricultural labour force the chance to dash gratefully to the new industrial jobs.

For blacks, the labour shortages in the defence industries and the armed services eventually broke down some discriminatory barriers and had some belated impact on the levels of their unemployment. As they flocked to the southern and northern cities, their political leverage increased. Urban migration in the South was an essential precondition for the development of the modern civil rights movement. The war similarly created new jobs for women, although it took longer for women than for blacks to translate new economic opportunity into increased consciousness and political gains. For the South, military spending during the war and Cold War, first on defence then later on space also, was the catalyst that sparked the region's take-off into self-sustaining economic growth. This growth would eventually draw most of the remaining rural population away from the cotton fields, reverse the traditional migration out of the region, and help facilitate the breakdown of traditional patterns of race relations. In the West, the defence industries on the coast once again attracted the migration that had been such a feature of the 1920s. The Depression, despite the extensive migration of the Arkies and Okies, had curtailed that population shift. From 1940 that expansion westwards would never again be slowed.

Seen through the lens of the war, the New Deal's overall function appears as a holding operation for American society: a series of measures that enabled the people to survive the Depression and to hold on until World War II opened up new opportunities. Industrial recovery programmes checked the deflationary spiral and yielded modest recovery that enabled businessmen to survive to enjoy dramatic war-time profits. Relief and welfare measures allowed the unemployed to struggle through until the war brought them jobs. Farm programmes enabled an underemployed labour force to stay on the land until the war created the urban demand which would absorb the surplus farm production and the industrial jobs which would absorb the surplus population. The plight of the poorest one third of the nation largely remained the New Deal's unfinished business.

The Office of War Information told Roosevelt that the American people's post-war aspirations were 'compounded largely of 1929 values and the economics of the 1920s, leavened with a hangover from the makeshift controls of the war'. This survey highlighted the ultimate constraint that circumscribed the New Deal's achievement: the underlying conservative response of the people themselves to the Depression. Middle-income Americans may have had more sympathy with the poor and the jobless in the 1930s than before or after. Workers may have exhibited greater class solidarity in those years. But more striking is the pervasive and persistent commitment to self-help, individual liberty, localism, and business-oriented individualism.

Businessmen, who had extracted many concessions from government, worked to end government regulation. Farmers, who had been rescued by massive government subsidies and price supports, argued that they wanted a fair price in the market place. Dust Bowl farmers, whose plight had been caused in part by their passion to plant wheat, wanted to grow more wheat. Submarginal farmers and tenant farmers wanted to own their own land, despite chronic rural overpopulation. The unemployed, having suffered from the collapse of the economic system, wanted another job, not a change in the system. Industrial workers, despite the unprecedented economic disaster, wanted a union contract and some rights on the shop floor, not control of the means of production. Mississippians, who had been rescued by unprecedented federal aid, stressed their steadfast commitment to states' rights. Westerners, who received more largesse than anyone else, proceeded again to elect conservative Republicans. Traditional values survived the Depression and the New Deal with great resilience. In the end, the New Deal was essentially a holding operation for American society because in the democratic, capitalist United States that was what most Americans wanted it to be.

Bibliographical Essay

Introduction

Two older studies of the New Deal which are still worth consulting are Basil Rauch, *The History of the New Deal* (Creative Age Press: New York, 1944) and Denis Brogan's unduly neglected *The Era of Franklin D. Roosevelt: A Chronicle of the New Deal and Global War* (Yale University Press: New Haven, 1952). The standard conservative denunciation of the socialistic trends of the New Deal was Edgar E. Robinson, *The Roosevelt Leadership, 1933–1945* (J. B. Lippincott: Philadelphia, 1955). The revolutionary changes brought by the New Deal were celebrated in Carl Degler, 'The Third American Revolution', in *Out of Our Past: The Forces that Shaped Modern America* (Harper & Row: New York, 1959, second edn., 1970), pp. 379–413, and Mario Einaudi, *The Roosevelt Revolution* (Harcourt, Brace: New York, 1959). Einaudi praised 'the most important attempt in the twentieth century to affirm the validity and the central role of the political instruments of democracy in facing the crisis of our times'. Sympathetic accounts of the New Deal from a liberal perspective which were nevertheless critical of Roosevelt and his advisers were Eric Goldman, *Rendezvous with Destiny: A History of Modern American Reform* (Knopf: New York, 1952), Rexford G. Tugwell, *The Democratic Roosevelt* (Doubleday: New York, 1957) and James MacGregor Burns, *Roosevelt: The Lion and the Fox* (Harcourt, Brace: New York, 1956). Goldman criticised New Dealers for being too casual about the morality of their methods; Tugwell regretted the lost opportunities for injecting greater discipline into the American economy; Burns regretted that Roosevelt had been attracted by short-term political gains at the expense of the long-term strategic goal of creating a genuinely liberal Democratic Party.

The climax of liberal approval of the New Deal's achievements were Arthur M. Schlesinger Jr's three volumes in *The Age of Roosevelt: The Crisis of the Old Order*; *The Coming of the New Deal*; and *The Politics of Upheaval* (Houghton Mifflin: Boston, 1956, 1958, 1960) and William E. Leuchtenburg, *Franklin D. Roosevelt and the New Deal, 1932–1940* (Harper & Row: New York, 1963). Neither author was uncritical: Leuchtenburg in particular noted that the Roosevelt Revolution was only a halfway revolution which excluded from its benefits many who needed help most. Nevertheless, both had impeccable liberal credentials: Schlesinger as a founding member of the Americans for Democratic Action, Leuchtenburg as a former full-time ADA official. Schlesinger celebrated both Roosevelt's genius and the New Deal's pragmatism: 'In the welter of confusion and ignorance, experiment corrected by compassion was the best answer'. Leuchtenburg praised Roosevelt for almost revolutionising the agenda of American politics, for creating a more just society by recognising groups which had been largely unrepresented, and for establishing a sounder basis for eventual economic recovery. At a time when there were few specialist monographs, both authors displayed a remarkably sure touch in identifying the critical issues at stake in the most diverse New Deal activities. Both demonstrated an enviable mastery of a vast range of archival material. No one is ever likely to match the richness of Schlesinger's dramatic narrative. No one is ever likely to produce a better one volume treatment of the New Deal than Leuchtenburg's.

Radical disillusionment in the 1960s soon produced sharp critiques of the New Deal. The most notable of these were Howard Zinn (ed.), *New Deal Thought* (Bobbs-Merrill: Indianapolis, 1966), pp. xv–xxxvi; Paul Conkin, *The New Deal* (Routledge & Kegan Paul: London, 1968) and Barton J. Bernstein, 'The New Deal: The Conservative Achievements of Liberal Reform', in *Towards a New Past: Dissenting Essays in American History* (Pantheon: New York, 1967), pp. 263–8. See also Brad Wiley, 'Historians and the New Deal' (Radical Education Project: Ann Arbor, n.d.) and Ronald Radosh, 'The Myth of the New Deal', in *A New History of Leviathan: Essays on the Rise of the American Corporate State* (E. P. Dutton: New York, 1972), pp. 146–87. Jerold S. Auerbach vigorously rebutted the New Left case in 'New Deal, Old Deal, or Raw Deal: Some Thoughts on New Left Historiography', *Journal of Southern History* 35 (1969), pp. 18–30.

Most New Left critiques have been essentially extended essays. There has been no attempt to establish a full-length interpretation of the New Deal and corporate liberalism. The nearest to such a treatment is Gabriel Kolko, *Main Currents in Modern American History* (Harper & Row: New York, 1976), pp. 100–56.

Arthur Schlesinger's three volumes had by 1960 taken the New Deal up to 1936. As yet no fourth volume has appeared. Frank Freidel's definitive biography of Roosevelt came to a halt in 1956. It took Freidel a further seventeen years to advance Roosevelt's career the eight months from the 1932 election to the end of the Hundred Days; see Frank Freidel, *Franklin D. Roosevelt*: vol. I *The Apprenticeship*; vol. II *The Ordeal*; vol. III *The Triumph*; vol. IV *Launching the New Deal* (Little, Brown: Boston, 1952, 1954, 1956, 1973). It became increasingly difficult for historians interested in Roosevelt and the view of the New Deal from Washington to absorb the large numbers of specialist monographs on particular New Deal agencies and case studies of the execution of government programmes at the local level. The book which isolated and identified this historiographical shift away from policy-making clashes in the capital was James T. Patterson, *The New Deal and the States: Federalism in Transition* (Princeton University Press: Princeton, 1969). I have attempted to digest the plethora of published and unpublished local case studies that followed Patterson's book in 'The New Deal and the Localities', in Rhodri Jeffreys-Jones and Bruce Collins (eds.), *The Growth of Federal Power in American History* (Scottish Academic Press: Edinburgh, 1983), pp. 102–15. John Braeman reviewed some of the earlier specialist monographs in 'The New Deal and the "Broker State": A Review of the Recent Scholarly Literature', *Business History Review* 46 (1972), pp. 409–20. Subsequent general treatments of the New Deal which stressed both its limitations and the constraints within which reformers operated include Otis L. Graham Jr, 'Years of Crisis: America in Depression and War, 1933–1945', in William E. Leuchtenburg, *The Unfinished Century: America since 1900* (Little, Brown: Boston, 1973), pp. 357–459, Richard S. Kirkendall, *The United States, 1929–1945: Years of Crisis and Change* (McGraw-Hill: New York, 1973) and Barry D. Karl, *The Uneasy State: The United States from 1915 to 1945* (University of Chicago Press: Chicago, 1983), pp. 80–181.

The free-market case against the damaging consequences of

New Deal statism was most eloquently expressed by Milton Friedman, *Free to Choose: A Personal Statement* (Harcourt Brace Jovanovich: New York, 1980). Intellectuals on the right in the 1970s found the emphasis on New Deal limitations misguided. Intellectuals on the left found the explanation of those limitations which had been offered by New Left critics unsatisfactory. Neo-Marxists, notably Theda Skocpol in 'Political Response to Capitalist Crisis: Neo-Marxist Theories of the State and the Case of the New Deal', *Politics and Society* 10 (1980), pp. 155–201, find 'corporate liberalism' an unconvincing concept when applied to the 1930s. The ultimate consequences of the New Deal might have been helpful to corporate capitalists but, they note, empirical case studies failed to show a vanguard of enlightened capitalists promoting New Deal measures. The failure of the New Deal to secure recovery before 1941 also casts doubt on the notion that the state or state managers automatically and inherently acted to serve the interests of corporate capitalism.

As yet, the social history of the inarticulate many has not been absorbed into general New Deal historiography. But Robert S. McElvaine's excellent narrative, *The Great Depression: America 1929–41* (New York Times Books: New York, 1984) has two important chapters in which he seeks to examine the 'fundamental shift in the values of the American people': ' "Fear Itself": Depression Life' and 'Moral Economics: American Values and Culture in the Great Depression', pp. 170–223.

Chapter 1

The most compelling personal testimony to the dramatic impact of the Depression on individual lives is contained first in the oral history interviews collected by Studs Terkel in *Hard Times: An Oral History of the Great Depression* (Allan Lane: London, 1970), then in the life histories taken down in the 1930s by the Federal Writers' Project. Selections of these have been edited by Ann Banks, *First-Person America* (Knopf: New York, 1980), and by Tom Terrill and Jerrold Hirsch, *Such as Us: Southern Voices of the Thirties* (University of North Carolina Press: Chapel Hill, 1978). Over 15,000,000 letters from the public survive in the Franklin D. Roosevelt Library. Robert S. McElvaine studied a random sample of 15,000 of these and other letters to federal agencies for a study of working-class reactions to the Depression. His *Down and Out in the Great Depression: Letters from the Forgotten Man* (University of North Carolina Press: Chapel Hill, 1983) contains a selection of these, together with letters to Hoover's relief coordinating committees and to Senator Robert F. Wagner.

Gilbert C. Fite, the doyen of American agricultural historians, provides the best analysis of the general problems confronting American farmers in *American Farmers: The New Majority* (Indiana University Press: Bloomington, 1981), ch. 2. See also Theodore Saloutos, *The American Farmers and the New Deal* (Iowa State University Press: Ames, 1982), pp. 3–14 on the farm crisis, 1918–33. For the particular plight of western farmers after 1929 see Leonard J. Arrington, 'Western Agriculture and the New Deal', *Agricultural History* 44 (1970), pp. 337–53, James F. Wickens, *Colorado in the Great Depression* (Garland: New York, 1979), pp. 219–21, and Michael P. Malone, *C. Benn Ross and the New Deal in Idaho* (University of Washington Press: Seattle, 1970), pp. 37–9. Donald L. Worster brilliantly analyses the cultural and climatic conditions which led sod-busting wheat farmers to create wasteland in *Dust Bowl: The Southern Plains in the 1930s* (Oxford University Press: New York, 1979). For Kansas farmers, see Frances W. Schruben, *Kansas in Turmoil, 1930–36* (University of Missouri Press: Columbia, 1969), pp. 47–51. John L. Shover has provided the definitive study of the angry reactions of midwestern corn and dairy farmers in *Cornbelt Rebellion: The Farmers' Holiday Association* (University of Illinois Press: Urbana, 1965).

For the South, Gilbert C. Fite analyses the fundamental poverty of cotton agriculture in *Cotton Fields No More: Southern Agriculture, 1865–1980* (University Press of Kentucky: Lexington, 1984), pp. 91–138. For the crisis produced by drought in 1930 see Nan Elizabeth Woodruff, *As Rare as Rain: Federal Relief in the Great Southern Drought of 1930–31* (University of Illinois Press: Urbana, 1985); for the crisis produced by overproduction in 1931 and Huey Long's attempt to secure a regional cotton holiday see Robert E. Snyder, *Cotton Crisis* (University of North Carolina: Chapel Hill, 1984). For the consequences of these catastrophes in Mississippi see Roger D. Tate Jr, 'Easing the Burden: The Era of Depression and New Deal in Mississippi' (Ph.D. dissertation, University of Tennessee, 1978), pp. 29–50 and for the parallel plight of tobacco see my own *Prosperity Road: The New Deal, Tobacco, and North Carolina* (University of North Carolina Press: Chapel Hill, 1980), pp. 18–37. The modest, relative comfort of Virginian and New England small farms is shown in Ronald L. Heinemann, *Depression and New Deal in Virginia* (University Press of Virginia: Charlottesville, 1983), pp. 21–6, and Richard Munson Judd, *The New Deal in Vermont: Its Impact and Aftermath* (Garland: New York, 1979), pp. 7–10, 97–103.

The problems of the sick industries of coal and textiles in the 1920s and the vain efforts to stabilise them are admirably explained by James P. Johnson, *The Politics of Soft Coal: The Bituminous Industry from World War I through the New Deal* (University of Illinois Press: Urbana, 1979), pp. 95–134, and Louis Galambos, *Competition and Cooperation: The Emergence of a National Trade Association* (Johns Hopkins Press, Baltimore, 1966), pp. 89–169. John W. Hevener, *Which Side Are You On? The Harlan County Coal Miners, 1931–39* (University of Illinois Press: Urbana, 1978), and Irving Bernstein, *The Lean Years: A History of the American Worker, 1920–1933* (Houghton Mifflin: Boston, 1960), pp. 1–43, describe the desperate response of miners in Harlan County and textile workers in the southern Piedmont.

The sudden collapse of the automobile industry and its impact on Detroit and other Michigan towns is covered by Sidney Fine in both *The Automobile under the Blue Eagle: Labor, Management, and the Automobile Manufacturing Code* (University of Michigan Press: Ann Arbor, 1963), pp. 17–21, and *Frank Murphy: The Detroit Years* (University of Michigan Press: Ann Arbor, 1975), pp. 201–56, Richard T. Ortquist, *Depression Politics in Michigan, 1929–1933* (Garland: New York, 1982), pp. 10–11, and Roger Keeran, *The Communist Party and the Auto Workers' Union* (Indiana University Press: Bloomington, 1980), pp. 61–3.

For corporate development and the impact of the Depression in the electrical goods industry see Ronald W. Schatz, *The Electrical Workers: A History of Labor at General Electric and Westinghouse, 1923–60* (University of Illinois Press: Urbana, 1983), pp. 3–27, 53–61. For the differing timetable of economic disaster in particular cities see Bruce M. Stave, 'Pittsburgh and the New Deal', in John Braeman, Robert Bremner, and David Brody (eds.), *The New Deal*, vol. II *The State and Local Levels* (Ohio

State University Press: Columbus, 1975), pp. 390–2, Joseph J. Verdicchio, 'New Deal Work Relief and New York City, 1933–38' (Ph.D. dissertation, New York University, 1980), pp. 11–14, Charles H. Trout, *Boston, the Great Depression and the New Deal* (Oxford University Press: New York, 1977), pp. 4–9, 25–6, 76–7, Iwan Morgan, 'Fort Wayne and the Great Depression: The Early Years', *Indiana Magazine of History* 80 (1984), pp. 122–45, Roger Biles, 'The Persistence of the Past: Memphis in the Great Depression', *Journal of Southern History* 52 (1986), pp. 183–212, Robert Cotner (ed.), *Texas Cities and the Great Depression* (Texas Memorial Museum: Austin, 1973), David R. Goldfield, *Cotton Fields and Skyscrapers: Southern City and Region, 1607–1980* (Louisiana State University Press: Baton Rouge, 1982), pp. 180–1.

Maurice Leven, Harold G. Moulton, and Clark Warburton, *America's Capacity to Consume* (Brookings: Washington, D.C., 1934) demonstrated how many Americans in 1929 failed to achieve what the authors defined as the minimum requirements for a 'reasonable standard' of living.

Alice Kessler-Harris, *Out to Work: A History of Wage-Earning Women in the United States* (Oxford University Press: New York, 1982), pp. 250–72, analyses the 'curious double message' the Depression sent to women workers. The impact of the Depression and the developments of the 1930s are also covered by Susan Estabrook Kennedy, *If All We Did Was to Weep at Home: A History of White Working-Class Women in America* (Indiana University Press: Bloomington, 1979), pp. 157–80, and Lois Scharf, *To Work and to Wed: Female Employment, Feminism, and the Great Depression* (Greenwood: Westport, 1980). Ruth Milkman, 'Women's Work and Economic Crisis: Some Lessons of the Great Depression', *Review of Radical Political Economics* 8 (1976), argues that the stereotyping of occupations by gender protected female jobs during the Depression. Julia Kirk Blackwelder reinforces this argument but also demonstrates the ethnic base to different rates of female participation in the labour force in 'Women in the Work Force: Atlanta, New Orleans, San Antonio, 1930–1940', *Journal of Urban History* 4 (1978), pp. 331–58, and *Women of the Depression: Caste and Culture in San Antonio, 1929–39* (Texas A and M Press: College Station, 1984).

The extent and structure of permanent poverty in the United States is best described by James T. Patterson, *America's Struggle*

Against Poverty 1900–1980 (Harvard University Press: Cambridge, Mass., 1981), pp. 20–55. For the component groups of the poor: blacks, Raymond Wolters, *Negroes and the Great Depression: The Problem of Economic Recovery* (Greenwood: Westport, 1970), pp. 7–9, 90–4, Harvard Sitkoff, *A New Deal for Blacks: The Emergence of Civil Rights as a National Issue*, vol. 1, *The Depression Decade* (Oxford University Press: New York, 1978), pp. 34–9; the old, Carole Haber, *Beyond Sixty-five: The Dilemma of Old Age in America's Past* (Cambridge University Press, 1983), pp. 108–29, Jackson K. Putnam, *Old Age Politics in California: From Richardson to Reagan* (Stanford University Press: Stanford, 1970), pp. 15–31, Stuart D. Brandes, *American Welfare Capitalism, 1880–1940* (University of Chicago Press: Chicago, 1976), pp. 103–10; the mountain rural poor, J. Wayne Flynt, *Dixie's Forgotten People: The Southern Poor Whites* (Indiana University Press: Bloomington, 1980), pp. 125–61, Woodruff, *As Rare as Rain*, ch. 8; migratory farm labourers, Cletus Daniel, *Bitter Harvest: A History of California Farm Workers, 1870–1941* (Cornell University Press: Ithaca, 1981), pp. 105–40; white and black southern sharecroppers, Flynt, *Dixie's Forgotten People*, pp. 64–91, Charles S. Johnson, *Shadow of the Plantation* (University of Chicago Press: Chicago, 1934), Paul E. Mertz, *New Deal Policy and Southern Rural Poverty* (Louisiana State University Press: Baton Rouge, 1978), pp. 1–19; Indians, David Murray, *Modern Indians: Native Americans in the Twentieth Century* (British Association for American Studies: 1982), pp. 10–13, Donald L. Parman, *The Navajos and the New Deal* (Yale University Press: New Haven, 1976), pp. 3–24, Graham D. Taylor, *The New Deal and American Indian Tribalism: The Administration of the Indian Reorganization Act, 1934–45* (University of Nebraska Press: Lincoln, 1980), pp. 1–16.

Lester V. Chandler, *America's Greatest Depression* (Harper & Row: New York, 1970), provides a sober, thorough analysis of the causes and extent of the Depression. Its international dimension is laid out in Peter Fearon's remarkably concise and lucid, *The Origins and Nature of the Great Slump, 1929–1932* (Macmillan: London, 1979), and in Charles P. Kindleberger's formidable *The World in Depression, 1929–39* (University of California Press: Berkeley, 1973). John Kenneth Galbraith's *The Great Crash* (Houghton Mifflin: Boston, 1955) is a compelling analysis of the stock market collapse. His views resurface every time Wall Street wobbles. Milton Friedman and Anna Schwartz's, *The Great Contraction, 1929–33* (Princeton University Press: Princeton, 1965) is the classic monetarist statement on the causes of the Depression. Peter Temin in *Did Monetary Forces Cause the Great Depression?* (Norton: New York, 1976) attempts to untangle monetary and spending explanations and comes down in favour of a modified spending analysis. Susan Previant Lee and Peter Passell, *A New Economic View of American History* (Norton: New York, 1979), pp. 362–99, offer an accessible summary of the increasingly complex debate and provide full bibliographical references to the technical literature.

For family and ethnic strategies to cope with the effect of unemployment see Winifred D. Wandersee, *Women's Work and Family Values 1920–1940* (Harvard University Press: Cambridge, Mass., 1981), pp. 27–54, John Bodnar, *Immigration and Industrialization: Ethnicity in an American Mill Town, 1870–1940* (University of Pittsburgh Press: Pittsburgh, 1977), pp. 142–4, John Bodnar, *Lives of Their Own: Blacks, Italians, and Poles in Pittsburgh, 1900–1940* (University of Illinois Press: Urbana, 1981), pp. 217–18, 234, Jacqueline Jones, *Labor of Love, Labor of Sorrow: Black Women, Work, and the Family from Slavery to the Present* (Basic Books: New York, 1985), pp. 196–240. Wandersee sums up the literature on the effect of the Depression on family structure and female roles and attitudes in *Women's Work and Family Values*, pp. 103–17. See also Glen Elder, *Children of the Great Depression: Social Change in Life Experience* (University of Chicago Press: Chicago, 1974), and with Richard C. Rockwell, 'The Depression Experience in Men's Lives', in Allan J. Lichtman and Joan R. Challinor (eds.), *Kin and Communities: Families in America* (Smithsonian Institution Press: Washington, 1979), pp. 95–118.

The changing attitudes of private charities and social workers confronted with the magnitude of the Depression are charted in Clarke Chambers, *Seedtime of Reform: American Social Service and Social Action, 1918–1973* (University of Minnesota Press: Minneapolis, 1963), pp. 185–250, and Judith Ann Trolander, *Settlement Houses and the Great Depression* (Wayne State University Press: Detroit, 1975), chs 1–5. There are three excellent case studies of the difficulties faced by private charities and city

governments in coping with mass unemployment: Bonnie Fox
Schwartz, 'Unemployment Relief in Philadelphia, 1930–1932: A
Study of the Depression's Impact on Voluntarism', in Bernard
Sternsher (ed.), *Hitting Home: The Great Depression in Town and
Country* (Quadrangle Books: Chicago, 1970), pp. 60–84, Fine,
Frank Murphy: The Detroit Years, pp. 257–387, Trout, *Boston*,
pp. 50–100.

The alternative models of the response of the unemployed are
provided by Arthur M. Schlesinger Jr, *The Crisis of the Old Order*
(Houghton Mifflin: Boston, 1957), pp. 168, 252, and Frances Fox
Piven and Richard A. Cloward, *Regulating the Poor: The Functions of Public Welfare* (Tavistock Publications: London, 1972),
pp. 45–79. Robert S. McElvaine has provided an excellent survey
of the evidence in his introduction to *Down and Out in the Great
Depression*, pp. 3–32.

Radical action by the unemployed is celebrated in Frances Fox
Piven and Richard A. Cloward, *Poor People's Movements: Why
They Succeed, How They Fail* (Pantheon Books, New York,
1977), pp. 41–91 and viewed more sceptically by Harvey Klehr,
The Heyday of American Communism: The Depression Decade
(Basic Books: New York, 1984), pp. 49–68. See also Roy Rosen-
zweig, ' "Socialism in Our Time": The Socialist Party and the
Unemployed, 1929–1936', *Labor History* 20 (1979), pp. 486–509,
and 'Radicals and the Jobless: The Musteites and the Unemployed
Leagues, 1932–1936', *Labor History* 16 (1975), pp. 52–77, and
Trolander, *Settlement Houses and the Great Depression*, ch. 6.

Bernard Sternsher thoroughly examines contemporary social
science writing in 'Victims of the Great Depression: Self-Blame/
Non-Self-Blame, Radicalism and pre-1929 Experiences', *Social
Science History 1* (1977), pp. 137–77, to explore the psychological
response of the unemployed to the Depression. He shows that the
values of individualism did not necessarily accompany self-blame.
John A. Garraty, *Unemployment in History: Economic Thought
and Public Policy* (Harper & Row: New York, 1978), stresses the
similarity of experience revealed by field investigations of unemployed responses in both Europe and the United States. Of the
American surveys, the most important was by E. Wight Bakke,
who had already investigated the unemployed in Greenwich,
England, in 1931. His *The Unemployed Worker: A Study of the
Test of Making a Living without a Job* (Yale University Press: New

Haven, 1940) stressed the pragmatism of New Haven workers' responses to joblessness. A useful study which attempts to identify class-consciousness among the unemployed on the basis of opinion poll data of 1939 is Sidney Verba and Kay Lehman Schlozman, 'Unemployment, Class Consciousness and Radical Politics: What Didn't Happen in the Thirties', *Journal of Politics* 39 (1977), pp. 291–323.

The bitter opposition to the New Deal which pervades Herbert Hoover's *Memoirs: The Great Depression, 1929–41* (Macmillan: New York, 1952) led conservative Republicans to hijack his presidential reputation and call him one of their own. The *Memoirs* illustrate the dogmatism, the refusal to admit error, the sensitivity to criticism, and the refusal to concede good faith to his opponents which plagued his presidency.

A more sophisticated reassessment of his presidency began from two very different perspectives. Harbinger of the New Left, William Appleman Williams, in *The Contours of American History* (World Publishing Company: Cleveland, 1981), pp. 425–38, stressed Hoover's use of every progressive anti-Depression tool but noted approvingly that he stopped short of the 'syndicalist nation dominated by a coalition of capital and government' that Roosevelt created. Champion of the New Deal revolution, Carl Degler in 'The Ordeal of Herbert Hoover', *Yale Review* 52 (1963), pp. 563–83, noted the positive continuities between Hoover and the New Deal. A sympathetic understanding of the extent of Hoover's activism, together with a full awareness of its limitations, characterised Albert U. Romasco, *The Poverty of Abundance: Hoover, the Nation and the Depression* (Oxford University Press: New York, 1965).

Major re-evaluation of Hoover's record however awaited the opening up of his private papers at the Presidential Library at West Branch, Iowa, in the mid-1960s. Symposia on Hoover led to three notable collections of essays: J. Joseph Huthmacher and Warren I. Susman (eds.), *Herbert Hoover and the Crisis of American Capitalism* (Schenkman Publishing Company: Cambridge, Mass., 1973); Martin L. Fausold and George T. Mazuzan (eds.), *The Hoover Presidency: A Reappraisal* (State University of New York Press: Albany, 1974); and Ellis W. Hawley (ed.), *Herbert Hoover as Secretary of Commerce: Studies in New Era Thought and Practice* (University of Iowa Press: Iowa City, 1981).

There have also been three substantial biographies: Joan Hoff Wilson, *Herbert Hoover: Forgotten Progressive* (Little, Brown: Boston, 1975); David Burner, *Herbert Hoover: A Public Life* (Knopf: New York, 1979); and Martin L. Fausold, *The Presidency of Herbert C. Hoover* (University Press of Kansas: Lawrence, 1985).

All three biographies take Hoover's ideology seriously and sympathetically. Wilson is the most favourable to the president. She sees Hoover as a transitional public leader between obsolete *laissez-faire* economics and monopoly capitalism. Despite his failure, she applauds, like William Appleman Williams, in *Some Presidents: From Wilson to Nixon* (A New York Review Book: New York, 1972), pp. 33–49, not so much Hoover's own policies but his 'prophetic and consistent criticisms of the foreign and domestic policies of the United States from 1933 through the mid-1950s'. Fausold's study is most useful for his discussion of agricultural policy, pp. 49–52, 107–12, and of Hoover's striving for a 'Corporatist Balance', pp. 105–24. David Burner has produced the best single volume on Hoover, combining sympathy for his progressive ideals with a frank appreciation of his political deficiencies, his capacity for self-delusion, and his acquiescence in conservative solutions.

There are important dissents from the revisionist view of Hoover. Conservative Murray N. Rothbard castigates Hoover for intervening too much in the economy in Huthmacher and Susman, *Herbert Hoover and the Crisis of American Capitalism*, pp. 35–8, although he does praise Hoover for finally seeing 'the abyss of fascism' and rejecting the plans of Gerard Swope and Henry Harriman. Elliot A. Rosen in *Hoover, Roosevelt, and the Brains Trust: From Depression to New Deal* (Columbia University Press: New York, 1977), pp. 39–94, 276–302, relentlessly portrays Hoover as a conservative whose 'specific stances . . . promoted the depression'. Arthur M. Schlesinger Jr, in *The Cycles of American History* (Andre Deutsch: London, 1987), pp. 377–87, vigorously resists any reincarnation of Hoover as 'progressive leader . . . master modernizer or . . . profound social analyst'.

On specific aspects of the Hoover presidency, a series of seminal articles by Ellis W. Hawley are crucial to understanding Hoover's ideas about government and its relation to business. Hawley's idea

of Hoover as an 'associational progressive' is developed in Huth-
macher and Susmann, *Herbert Hoover and the Crisis of American
Capitalism*, pp. 3–33, 'Herbert Hoover, the Commerce Secretariat
and the Vision of an "Associative State"', 1921–1928', *Journal of
American History* 41 (1974), pp. 116–40, 'Herbert Hoover and
American Corporatism', in Fausold and Mazuzan, *The Hoover
Presidency*, pp. 101–19, and 'Herbert Hoover and Economic
Stabilization, 1921–1922' in Hawley, *Herbert Hoover as Secretary
of Commerce*, pp. 43–80. In *The Origins of the National Recovery
Administration: Business, Government and the Trade Association
Issue* (Fordham University Press: New York, 1976), pp. 80–180,
Robert F. Himmelberg clarifies exactly why Hoover supported
anti-trust revision in some cases and not in others. James Stuart
Olson, *Herbert Hoover and the Reconstruction Finance Corporation, 1931–1933* (Iowa State University Press: Ames, 1977), sees
the RFC playing a critical role in the transition from voluntarism
to a managed economy. On agriculture, Joan Hoff Wilson,
'Herbert Hoover's Agricultural Policies, 1921–1938' in Hawley,
Herbert Hoover as Secretary of Commerce, pp. 115–47, is crucial to
understanding the far-reaching hopes Hoover held for the Agricultural Marketing Act of 1929. Finally, Craig Lloyd helps explain
what went wrong for Hoover in *Aggressive Introvert: A Study of
Herbert Hoover and Public Relations Management, 1912–1932*
(Ohio State University Press, 1972). Hoover's 'behind-the-scenes
public relations' approach was ideally suited to his public career up
to 1928 but disastrously inappropriate and ineffective for a president in a time of mass economic distress.

As for policy alternatives Hoover rejected: the domestic allotment plan, William D. Rowley, *M. L. Wilson and the Campaign
for the Domestic Allotment* (University of Nebraska Press: Lincoln, 1971), pp. 107–76; the Swope plan, Schatz, *The Electrical
Workers*, pp. 54–8, and Himmelberg, *The Origins of the National
Recovery Administration*, pp. 127–46; on public works and relief
spending, Joseph J. Huthmacher, *Senator Robert F. Wagner and
the Rise of Urban Liberalism* (Atheneum: New York, 1971), pp.
57–86, and Patrick J. Maney, *'Young Bob' La Follette: A Biography of Robert M. La Follette, Jr., 1895–1953* (University of
Missouri Press: Columbia, 1978), pp. 78–108.

Roger Daniels systematically exposes the myths behind the

administration's interpretation of the Bonus Army and the threat it posed in *The Bonus March: An Episode of the Great Depression* (Greenwood: Westport, 1971).

The feebleness of the remedies offered by the conservative Democratic leadership is amply demonstrated by Jordan A. Schwarz, *The Interregnum of Despair: Hoover, Congress and the Depression* (University of Illinois Press: Urbana, 1970). Their determination to stop Roosevelt obtaining their party's nomination is convincingly portrayed in Rosen, *Hoover, Roosevelt, and the Brains Trust*, pp. 26–38, 212–42. Ronald L. Feinman shows the disarray and ideological limitations of progressive Republicanism in *Twilight of Progressivism: The Western Republican Senators and the New Deal* (Johns Hopkins University Press: Baltimore, 1981), pp. 1–32. See also Richard Lowitt, *George W. Norris: The Persistence of a Progressive, 1913–1933* (University of Illinois Press: Urbana, 1971), pp. 487–503. For the conservatism of state governors, taxpayers' revolts, demagoguery, and the balance of local issues in local politics see James T. Patterson, *The New Deal and the States: Federalism in Transition* (Princeton University Press: Princeton, 1969), pp. 3–48, and my own 'The New Deal and the Localities', in Rhodri Jeffreys-Jones and Bruce Collins (eds.), *The Growth of Federal Power in American History* (Scottish Academic Press: Edinburgh, 1983), pp. 104–5, 182.

Roosevelt's credentials to heal the ethnocultural divisions which plagued the Democratic Party in the 1920s are shown in David Burner, *The Politics of Provincialism: The Democratic Party in Transition, 1918–1932* (Knopf: New York, 1968). The standard account of Roosevelt's early life and his governorship of New York remains Frank Freidel, *Franklin D. Roosevelt*: vol. I *The Apprenticeship*, vol. II *The Ordeal*, vol. III *The Triumph* (Little, Brown: Boston, 1952, 1954, 1956). The best description of the Brains Trust comes from the participants: Raymond Moley, *After Seven Years* (Harper & Row: New York, 1939), pp. 1–162, and Rexford Tugwell, in the most impressive of his many books, *The Brains Trust* (Viking Press: New York, 1968). Rosen draws heavily on his work for Raymond Moley in *Hoover, Roosevelt, and the Brains Trust*, pp. 115–211. Rosen also offers the most convincing and critical analysis of Roosevelt's battle for the nomination and the events at Chicago when he came close to losing it, pp. 95–114, 212–75. For the election campaign of 1932 see Freidel,

Franklin D. Roosevelt: The Triumph, pp. 312–71 and Tugwell's lament for lost progressive opportunities in *The Brains Trust*, pp. 267–522. For the interregnum see Frank Freidel, *Franklin D. Roosevelt*, IV *Launching the New Deal* (Little, Brown: Boston, 1974), pp. 3–195. See also Rosen, *Hoover, Roosevelt and the Brains Trust*, pp. 362–80.

Chapter 2

The starting point for any study or the New Deal and industrial recovery must remain Ellis W. Hawley's magisterial, *The New Deal and the Problem of Monopoly* (Princeton University Press: Princeton, 1966). Subsequent scholarship may have supplemented his study or fleshed out additional detail but has done little to alter the basic shape to the policy struggles of the 1930s which Hawley established. He himself summarised his own findings and took notice of other work in a brilliantly concise 'The New Deal and Business' in John Braeman, Robert Bremner, and David Brody (eds.), *The New Deal*, vol. 1 *The National Level* (Ohio State University Press: Columbus, 1975), pp. 50–82. There are two other helpful studies of general recovery policies: Theodore Rosenof's schematic *Dogma, Depression and the New Deal: The Debate of Political Leaders Over Economic Recovery* (Kennikat Press: Port Washington, 1975) and Albert U. Romasco's, *The Politics of Recovery: Roosevelt's New Deal* (Oxford University Press: New York, 1983). Romasco places a salutary emphasis on monetary policy: an emphasis which nevertheless I have not followed in this chapter.

The definitive account of the banking crisis is Susan Estabrook Kennedy, *The Banking Crisis of 1933* (University Press of Kentucky: Lexington, 1973). For subsequent banking legislation see Helen M. Burns, *The American Banking Community and New Deal Banking Reforms, 1933–1935* (Greenwood: Westport, 1974).

The conflict between business self-regulation advocates, planners, and market restorers in the formulation and passage of the Industrial Recovery Act is laid out in Hawley, *The New Deal and the Problem of Monopoly*, pp. 3–52. See also Bernard Bellush, *The Failure of the NRA* (Norton: New York, 1975), pp. 1–29. For the particular role of trade association leaders see Robert F.

Himmelberg, *The Origins of the National Recovery Administration: Business, Government and the Trade Association Issue, 1921–1933* (Fordham University Press: New York, 1976), pp. 181–218, and Louis Galambos *Competition and Cooperation: The Emergence of a National Trade Association* (Johns Hopkins University Press: Baltimore, 1966), pp. 173–202. Edward Berkowitz and Kim McQuaid overstress the positive role of welfare capitalists in launching the NRA in *Creating the Welfare State: The Political Economy of Twentieth Century Reform* (Praeger: New York, 1980), pp. 78–86. For the diversity of planning proposals, their 'faddish' quality, and the lack of any clear proposed mechanism for centralised coercive planning, see Stuart Kidd, 'Collectivist intellectuals and the ideal of national economic planning, 1929–33', in Stephen W. Baskerville and Ralph Willett (eds.), *Nothing Else to Fear: New Perspectives on America in the Thirties* (Manchester University Press: Manchester, 1985), pp. 15–35, Otis L. Graham, *Toward a Planned Society: From Roosevelt to Nixon* (Oxford University Press: New York, 1976), pp. 13–31, and Richard H. Pells, *Radical Visions and American Dreams: Culture and Social Thought in the Depression Years* (Harper & Row: New York, 1973), pp. 43–81. For the recovery programme of Justice Brandeis, see Nelson Lloyd Dawson, *Louis D. Brandeis, Felix Frankfurter and the New Deal* (Archon: Hamden, Conn., 1980), pp. 29–32, 173–6. For the pressure to devalue the dollar and to inflate the currency see Romasco, *The Politics of Recovery*, pp. 67–156. Stanley Vittoz stresses the variety of recovery initiatives and emphasises start-up and share-the-work proposals in 'The Economic Foundations of Industrial Politics in the United States and the Emerging Structural Theory of the State in Capitalist Society: The Case of New Deal Labor Policy', *Amerikastudien* 27 (1982), pp. 369–74.

There is no adequate history of the Public Works Administration. The qualities of Harold Ickes which shaped his performance as Administrator – an incurable suspiciousness, a massive self-righteousness, an inflated sense of self-importance, a limitless susceptibility to flattery, and a fierce combativeness – are best savoured in his own diaries, *The Secret Diaries of Harold L. Ickes*, vol. I *The First Thousand Days, 1933–1936*, vol. II *The Inside Struggle, 1936–1939* (Simon and Schuster: New York, 1953). Graham White and John Maze show how selective the published editions of the diaries were and cast doubt on the reliability of Ickes's version of many events in *Harold Ickes of the New Deal: His Private Life and Public Career* (Harvard University Press: Cambridge, Mass., 1985), but while they may illuminate Ickes's personality, they do not add much to our understanding of the PWA. More helpful is William D. Reeves, 'PWA and Competitive Administration in the New Deal', *Journal of American History* 60 (1973), pp. 357–72.

The ability of businessmen to dominate both the drafting and the implementation of the NRA codes is demonstrated in general by Hawley, *The New Deal and the Problem of Monopoly*, pp. 53–71, Bellush, *The Failure of the NRA*, pp. 30–54, and Peter H. Irons, *The New Deal Lawyers* (Princeton University Press: Princeton, 1982), pp. 26–34. Theda Skocpol and Kenneth Feingold, 'State Capacity and Economic Intervention in the early New Deal', *Political Science Quarterly* 97 (1982), pp. 255–79, highlight the 'virtually complete absence of autonomous capacity to administer industrial planning in the United States policy of the early 1930s'. The consequences in particular industries can be traced in three excellent cases: cotton textiles, Galambos, *Competition and Cooperation*, pp. 202–26, coal, James P. Johnson, *The Politics of Soft Coal: The Bituminous Industry from World War I Through the New Deal* (University of Illinois Press: Urbana, 1979), pp. 150–64, cars, Sidney Fine, *The Automobile under the Blue Eagle: Labor, Management and the Automobile Manufacturing Code* (University of Michigan Press: Ann Arbor, 1963), pp. 44–74. For discrimination in the codes against blacks and the reluctance of NRA officials to acknowledge there was a problem see Raymond Wolters, *Negroes and the Great Depression: The Problem of Economic Recovery* (Greenwood: Westport, 1970), pp. 98–192. For discrimination against women, see Lois Scharf, *To Work and to Wed: Female Employment, Feminism, and the Great Depression* (Greenwood: Westport, 1980), pp. 111–13. Alice Kessler-Harris, *Out to Work: A History of Wage-Earning Women in the United States* (Oxford University Press: New York, 1982), pp. 259–71, demonstrates that nevertheless NRA codes did benefit the lowest-paid women workers who were covered and sometimes, combined with industrial rationalisation, opened up opportunities for low-paid women. The Brookings Institution study of the NRA contains a wealth of information on code provisions, Leverett L. Lyon *et* al., *The National Recovery Administration: An Analysis and Appraisal* (Da Capo: New York, 1972 c. 1935).

The challenge to business domination, the policy stalemate that resulted, and the collapse of the NRA are covered by Hawley, *The New Deal and the Problem of Monopoly*, pp. 72–129, and Bellush, *The Failure of the NRA*, pp. 55–84, 136–75. For the reaction of women and the Consumers' Advisory Board see Susan Ware, *Beyond Suffrage: Women and the New Deal* (Harvard University Press: Cambridge, Mass., 1981), pp. 87–96. For the criticism by midwestern progressives see Ronald L. Feinman, *Twilight of Progressivism: The Western Republican Senators and the New Deal* (Johns Hopkins University Press: Baltimore, 1981), pp. 68–73. For business frustration and intra-industry tensions in industries which did want to see the NRA approach abandoned entirely see Galambos, *Competition and Cooperation*, pp. 227–79, Johnson, *The Politics of Soft Coal*, pp. 195–216, Ian Jarman, 'Harold L. Ickes and United States' Domestic Oil Policy, 1937–1941' (Oxford University: M.Litt. Thesis, 1986), pp. 49–90. For complete business disenchantment with the benefits of government regulation see Fine, *The Automobile under the Blue Eagle*, pp. 141, 410–16, and James E. Fickle, *The New South and the 'New Competition': Trade Association Development in the Southern Pine Industry* (University of Illinois Press: Urbana, 1980), pp. 117–54. For business reaction to excessive codification and bureaucracy see Thomas R. Winpenny, 'Henning Webb Prentiss and the Challenge of the New Deal', *Journal of the Lancaster Historical Society* 81 (1977), pp. 1–24, F. J. Harper, 'The Small Retailer and the New Deal' (Paper delivered at the FDR Centennial Colloquium, David Bruce Centre for American Studies, University of Keele, 23 April 1982), and Ernest B. Fricke, 'The New Deal and the Modernization of Small Business: The McCreary Tire and Rubber Company, 1930–1940', *Business History Review* 56 (1982), pp. 559–76.

The constant problem of enforcing compliance and the final failure to uphold the NRA in the courts is fully elaborated in Irons, *The New Deal Lawyers*, pp. 35–107. Hawley provides the most balanced overall appraisal of the NRA in *The New Deal and the Problem of Monopoly*, pp. 130–46. Hugh Johnson himself sadly sums up his principal errors in *The Blue Eagle: From Egg to Earth* (Doubleday: Garden City, New York, 1935), pp. 295–7. Michael M. Weinstein, 'Some Macroeconomic Impacts of the

National Industrial Recovery Act, 1933–1935', in Karl Brunner (ed.), *The Great Depression Revisited* (Martinus Nijhoff: Boston, 1981), pp. 262–81, argues that not only did the NRA not produce economic recovery but that the codes positively hindered that recovery. The price inflation the NRA induced wiped out any gains that might have resulted from the monetary expansion that began in June 1933. He also suggests however that there was some redistribution of income to labour and some spreading of employment to an increased number of individuals.

The two most important opposing statements of the idea of two New Deals are Basil Rauch, *The History of the New Deal* (Creative Age Press: New York, 1944), pp. 111–39, 156–90, 256–340, and Arthur M. Schlesinger Jr, *The Politics of Upheaval* (Houghton Mifflin: Boston, 1960), pp. 385–423. Otis L. Graham, 'Historians and the New Deals, 1944–1960', *Social Studies* 54 (1963), pp. 133–40 is an excellent survey of the debate. See also William H. Wilson, 'The Two New Deals: A Valid Concept?', *The Historian* 28 (1966), pp. 268–88. Two reasoned attempts to identify what did and did not change in 1935 are William E. Leuchtenburg, *Franklin D. Roosevelt and the New Deal, 1932–1940* (Harper & Row: New York, 1963), pp. 162–5, and Robert S. McElvaine, *The Great Depression: America, 1929–41* (New York Times Books: New York, 1984), pp. 250–63.

There have recently been considerable efforts to pinpoint the exact nature of the impact of Brandeis and Frankfurter. The best of these attempts are Dawson, *Louis D. Brandeis, Felix Frankfurter and the New Deal*, who concluded that 'The New Deal simply did not do what Brandeis and Frankfurter wanted it to do', and Michael E. Parrish, *Felix Frankfurter and His Times: The Reform Years* (The Free Press: New York, 1982), pp. 197–298. Bruce Allen Murphy, *The Brandeis–Frankfurter Connection: The Secret Political Activities of Two Supreme Court Justices* (Oxford University Press: New York, 1982), and Leonard Baker, *Brandeis and Frankfurter: A Dual Biography* (Harper & Row: New York, 1984), add little to our understanding of the New Deal.

For continued interest in planning after the demise of the NRA see Hawley, *The New Deal and the Problem of Monopoly*, pp. 169–86, 270–80, Graham, *Toward a Planned Society*, pp. 45–68, and Rosenhof, *Dogma, Depression and the New Deal*, Ch. 5. For partial planning and efforts to revive the NRA in particular industries see Hawley, *The New Deal and the Problem of Monopoly*, pp. 205–69, Johnson, *The Politics of Soft Coal*, pp. 217–35 and Jarman, 'Harold L. Ickes and United States' Domestic Oil Policy', pp. 91–103. Robert M. Collins, *The Business Response to Keynes, 1929–1964* (Columbia University Press: New York, 1981), pp. 23–52, highlights negativistic business opposition to the New Deal.

The definitive history of the complex efforts to regulate the stock market and control public utility holding companies is Michael E. Parrish, *Securities Regulation and the New Deal* (Yale University Press: New Haven, 1970). Mark Leff unravels the political imperatives behind New Deal tax policy and lucidly demonstrates the limited real, as distinct from symbolic, effects of tax changes in *The Limits of Symbolic Reform: The New Deal and Taxation, 1933–1939* (Cambridge University Press: Cambridge, 1984).

The belated New Deal anti-trust offensive is covered in Hawley, *The New Deal and the Problem of Monopoly*, pp. 404–71, Gene Gressley, *Voltaire and the Cowboy: The Letters of Thurman Arnold* (Colorado Associated University Press: Boulder, 1977), pp. 39–54, and Wilson D. Miscumble, 'Thurman Arnold goes to Washington: A Look at Anti-Trust Policy in the Later New Deal', *Business History Review* 56 (1982), pp. 1–15. For an excellent description of big business's favoured position during World War II, see Richard Polenberg, *War and Society: The United States, 1941–1945* (J. B. Lippincott: Philadelphia, 1972), pp. 5–36, 215–37.

The standard history of fiscal policy in the 1930s is Herbert Stein, *The Fiscal Revolution in America* (University of Chicago Press: Chicago, 1969), pp. 6–168. Stephen W. Baskerville analyses the views of professional economists on spending in 'Cutting loose from prejudice: economists and the Great Depression', in Stephen W. Baskerville and Ralph Willet (eds.), *Nothing Else to Fear: New Perspectives on America in the Thirties* (Manchester University Press: Manchester, 1985), pp. 259–84. He also examines Frankfurter's early role in pushing Keynes's ideas in 'Frankfurter, Keynes, and the Fight for Public Works', *Maryland History* 9 (1978), pp. 1–16. The contrasting views of the Secretary of the Treasury and the chairman of the Federal Reserve Board can be clearly traced in Marriner S. Eccles's own words, *Beckoning Frontiers: Public and Personal Recollections* (Knopf: New York, 1951), pp. 91–323, and

John Morton Blum, *From the Morgenthau Diaries: Years of Crisis, 1928–1938* (Houghton Mifflin: Boston, 1959), pp. 229–451. Dean L. May, *From New Deal to New Economics: An American Liberal Response to the Recession of 1937* (Garland: New York, 1981), is an excellent account of the struggle between Morgenthau and Eccles in the winter of 1937–38 and the crisis of liberal confidence which the recession provoked. For the recession see also Hawley, *New Deal and the Problem of Monopoly*, pp. 383–403, Romasco, *The Politics of Recovery*, pp. 216–40, Leff, *The Limits of Symbolic Reform*, pp. 209–20. Collins, *The Business Response to Keynes, 1929–1964*, pp. 53–112, describes the acceptance by a small but influential group of businessmen of Keynesian ideas. He also provides the best account of the final decision at Warm Springs in 1938 to resume spending. John Kenneth Galbraith with engaging, if unconvincing, self-deprecation describes his own role in shaping the ideas of Henry Dennison and his liberal business friends as well as the triumph of Keynesianism in academic circles in 'How Keynes Came to America', in *Economics, Peace and Laughter* (Houghton Mifflin: Boston, 1971), pp. 43–59, and *A Life in Our Times: Memoirs* (Andre Deutsch: London, 1981), pp. 61–70.

For the inadequacy of the level of New Deal spending for ending the Depression see E. Cary Brown, 'Fiscal Policy in the Thirties: A Reappraisal', *American Economic Review* 46 (1956), pp. 857–79, and Larry Peppers, 'Full Employment Surplus Analysis and Structural Change: The 1930s', *Explorations in Economic History* 10 (1973), pp. 197–210. Ross McKibbin raises doubts about the likely success of more avowedly Keynesian policies both in Europe and America in 'The Economic Policy of the Second Labour Government, 1929–1931', *Past and Present* 68 (1975), pp. 95–123.

For the development of liberal confidence, during the war and after, that the means existed to create a full employment economy see Alonzo L. Hamby, *Beyond the New Deal: Harry S. Truman and American Liberalism* (Columbia University Press: New York, 1973), pp. 3–28, 297–303, and his *Liberalism and Its Challengers: F.D.R. to Reagan* (Oxford University Press: New York, 1985), pp. 28–30, 48, 60–3.

Chapter 3

Much of the best historical writing on the 1930s is to be found in labour history. Here the studies of national policy can be supplemented by history written 'from the bottom up'. Not only are there excellent narrative and analytical accounts of legislative battles, union leadership struggles, and great strikes, but there are also fine case studies of the grievances and responses of ordinary workers.

The rich, dramatic account of labour's struggles by Irving Bernstein, *The Turbulent Years: A History of the American Worker, 1933–1941* (Houghton Mifflin: Boston, 1969), can be complemented by a number of particularly astute interpretative overviews of the decade: David Brody, 'The Emergence of Mass Production Unionism' and 'Reinterpreting the Labor History of the 1930s', in *Workers in Industrial America: Essays on the Twentieth Century Struggle* (Oxford University Press: New York, 1980), pp. 82–172; David Montgomery, 'American Workers and the New Deal Formula', in *Workers Control in America: Studies in the History of Work, Technology, and Labor Struggles* (Cambridge University Press: Cambridge, 1979), pp. 153–80; Melvyn Dubofsky, 'Not So "Turbulent Years": Another Look at the American 1930's', *Amerikastudien* 24 (1979), pp. 5–20; Stanley Vittoz, 'The Economic Foundations of Industrial Politics in the United States and the Emerging Structural Theory of the State in Capitalist Society: The Case of New Deal Labor Policy', *Amerikastudien* 27 (1982), pp. 365–412; Howell Harris, 'The Snares of Liberalism? Politicians, Bureaucrats and the Shaping of Federal Labour Relations Policy in the United States, ca. 1915–1947', in Steven Tolliday and Jonathan Zeitlin, *Shop Floor Bargaining and the State: Historical and Comparative Perspectives* (Cambridge University Press: Cambridge, 1985), pp. 148–91; and Robert H. Zieger, *American Workers, American Unions, 1920–1985* (Johns Hopkins University Press: Baltimore, 1985), pp. 26–61. All these essays subtly weigh the varying degrees of importance of legal change, economic circumstances, union leadership, and rank-and-file pressure in the labour breakthrough.

For successful labour exploitation of Section 7a under the NRA, see Bernard Bellush, *The Failure of the NRA* (Norton: New York, 1975), pp. 88–94, and James P. Johnson, *The Politics of Soft Coal:*

The Bituminous Industry from World War I Through the New Deal
(University of Illinois Press: Urbana, 1979), pp. 166–93. For the
more important failure of the NRA to protect union organisation
in the face of determined employer resistance, see Bellush, *The
Failure of the NRA*, pp. 94–135, Sidney Fine, *The Automobile
under the Blue Eagle* (University of Michigan Press: Ann Arbor,
1963), pp. 142–409, and Louis Galambos, *Competition and Cooperation: The Emergence of a National Trade Association* (Johns
Hopkins University Press: Baltimore, 1966), pp. 230–3, 243–6,
257–68.

The ideas behind the Wagner Act, its passage, and the efforts to
ensure that it withstood challenges to its constitutionality are
covered in Joseph J. Huthmacher, *Senator Robert F. Wagner and
the Rise of Urban Liberalism* (Atheneum: New York, 1971), pp.
190–8, and Peter H. Irons, *The New Deal Lawyers* (Princeton
University Press: Princeton, 1982), pp. 203–89. See also the
exhaustive James A. Gross, *The Making of the National Labor
Relations Board, 1933–1937* (State University of New York Press:
Albany, 1974).

John L. Lewis's seizure of the opportunity to organise mass-
production workers is best followed in the first-rate biography of
the Mine Workers' leader, Melvyn Dubofsky and Warren Van
Tine, *John L. Lewis: A Biography* (Quadrangle New York Times
Books: New York, 1977), pp. 181–386. For the great CIO
breakthrough see: automobiles, Sidney Fine, *Sit-Down: The
General Motors Strike of 1936–37* (University of Michigan Press:
Ann Arbor, 1969), and John Barnard, *Walter Reuther and the Rise
of the Auto Workers* (Little, Brown: Boston, 1983), pp. 18–69;
steel, Bernstein, *The Turbulent Years*, pp. 432–98; rubber, Daniel
Nelson, 'The Great Goodyear Strike of 1936', *Ohio History* 92
(1983), pp. 6–36, 'Origins of the Sit-Down Era: Worker Militancy
and Innovation, 1934–1938', *Labor History* 23 (1982), pp. 198–
225, and 'The Rubber Workers' Southern Strategy: Labor Organizing in the New Deal South, 1933–1943', *The Historian* 46
(1984), pp. 319–38; electrical goods, Ronald W. Schatz, *The
Electrical Workers: A History of Labor at General Electric and
Westinghouse, 1923–60* (University of Illinois Press: Urbana,
1983).

Interpretations which stress the radicalism of rank-and-file
workers and the conservative efforts of government and union

leaders to defuse that threat are Alice and Staughton Lynd (eds.), *Rank and File: Personal Histories by Working-Class Organizers* (Beacon Press: Boston, 1973), pp. 1–8, James R. Green, *The World of the Worker: Labor in Twentieth-Century America* (Hill and Wang: New York, 1980), pp. 133–73, and Frances Fox Piven and Richard A. Cloward, *Poor People's Movements: Why They Succeed, How They Fail* (Pantheon: New York, 1977), pp. 96–180. *Rank and File* contains a vivid set of oral history interviews which highlight both the extent of shop-floor grievances and the political radicalism of local activists.

Rank-and-file militancy has been carefully studied in relation to seniority, work roles, ethnic background, and Depression grievances in Peter Friedlander, *The Emergence of a UAW Local, 1936–1939: A Study in Class and Culture* (University of Pittsburgh Press: Pittsburgh, 1975), John Bodnar, *Immigration and Industrialization: Ethnicity in an American Mill Town, 1870–1940* (University of Pittsburgh Press: Pittsburgh, 1977), pp. 142–9, Gary Gerstle, 'The Mobilization of the Working-Class Community: The Independent Textile Union in Woonsocket, 1931–1947', *Radical History Review* 17 (1978), pp. 161–72, Nelson, 'The Great Goodyear Strike' and 'Origins of the Sit-Down Era', and Schatz, *The Electrical Workers*, pp. 80–164. Bernard Sternsher provides a probing and comprehensive review of the literature in 'Great Depression Labor Historiography in the 1970s: Middle Range Questions, Ethno-cultures and Levels of Generalization', *Reviews in American History* 11 (1983), pp. 300–19.

These studies focusing on the rank and file begin to fill a major gap in New Deal historiography. Much has been written on the aims of policy-makers and intellectuals to preserve the local community and its values. Little has been written on the actual impact of the Depression and the New Deal on individual communities smaller than a big city like Boston. There are no studies to match the classic contemporary sociological studies of Robert and Helen M. Lynd, *Middletown in Transition: A Study in Cultural Conflicts* (Harcourt Brace: New York, 1937), and John Dollard, *Caste and Class in a Southern Town* (Yale University Press: New Haven, 1937). The innovative studies by labour historians are the first steps towards the social history of industrial communities in the 1930s. Rural and small-town communities of the 1930s still await their historians.

Communist activity in the labour movement of the 1930s is no longer treated as a conspiracy to deceive American workers. The most positive assessment of the party's role is Roger Keeran, *The Communist Party and the Auto Workers Union* (Indiana University Press: Bloomington, 1980). Keeran argues that in the car industry 'the communists were legitimate and often outstanding trades unionists and good Communists, and they made an important, even crucial, contribution to building the auto union in the 1930s'. Bert Cochran, *Labor and Communism: The Conflict That Shaped American Unions* (Princeton University Press: Princeton, 1977) is wider in scope, but nevertheless concentrates on the auto workers. His more sceptical assessment of the Communist role is partly shaped by his personal memories of bitter left-wing internecine feuds. Harvey Klehr, *The Heyday of American Communism: The Depression Decade* (Basic Books: New York, 1983), pp. 223–50, relentlessly exposes Communist weakness.

Jerold S. Auerbach, *Labor and Liberty: The La Follette Committee and the New Deal* (Bobbs-Merrill: Indianapolis, 1966), pp. 97–218, graphically illustrates the violent lengths to which anti-union employers were prepared to go and demonstrates the effect of the public exposure of their tactics. Eventual union victories over the most hostile employers – Harlan County coal operators and the Ford Motor Company – are traced in John W. Hevener, *Which Side Are You On?: The Harlan County Coal Miners, 1931–39* (University of Illinois Press: Urbana, 1979), and August Meier and Elliot Rudwick, *Black Detroit and the Rise of the UAW* (Oxford University Press: New York, 1979), pp. 34–107.

The continued difficulty of organising unions in defiance of local community sentiment is most obviously demonstrated in the South, see J. Wayne Flynt, 'The New Deal and Southern Labor', in James C. Cobb and Michael V. Namaroto (eds.), *The New Deal and the South* (University Press of Mississippi: Jackson, 1984), pp. 63–95, and Charles H. Martin, 'Southern Labor Relations in Transition: Gadsden, Alabama, 1930–1943', *Journal of Southern History* 47 (1981), pp. 545–68. Daniel Nelson describes the debilitating, but not fatal, effect of lack of community support in the North in 'The CIO at Bay: Labor Militancy and Politics in Akron, 1936–1938', *Journal of American History* 71 (1984), pp. 565–86.

There is a natural tendency to concentrate on the great dramatic strikes of the 1930s and to focus on the CIO. Robert H. Zieger has patiently built up a broader picture of worker experience during the New Deal looking at two types of union which historians usually dismiss as ineffective. His *Madison's Battery Workers, 1934–1952: A History of Federal Labor Union 19587* (Industrial and Labor Relations Press: Ithaca, 1977) describes an AFL Federal Labor Union which survived. *Rebuilding the Paper Workers' Union, 1933–1941* (University of Tennessee Press: Knoxville, 1982) examines an AFL industrial union whose membership rose from 4,000 in 1933 to 60,000 in 1941 and which eventually saw off its CIO rival. Christopher L. Tomlins also shows how traditional AFL unions revived alongside CIO unions in the late 1930s, 'AFL Unions in the 1930s: Their Performance in Historical Perspective', *Journal of American History* 65 (1979), pp. 1021–42.

Howell John Harris, *The Right to Manage: Industrial Relations Policies of American Business in the 1940s* (University of Wisconsin Press: Madison, 1982), pp. 15–40, emphatically refutes any notion that employers followed a sophisticated corporate liberal strategy in the 30s. His description of management strategies in the war and after in *The Right to Manage*, pp. 41–204, and Nelson N. Lichtenstein's analysis of union strategies, *Labor's War at Home: The CIO in World War II* (Cambridge University Press: Cambridge, 1982), together show how the 1940s decisively shaped the 'responsible' unionism of modern America. See also Harris, 'The Snares of Liberalism', Zieger, *American Workers, American Unions*, pp. 62–136, and James A. Gross, *The Reshaping of the National Labor Relations Board: National Labor Policy in Transition, 1937–1947* (State University of New York Press: Albany, 1981).

In two wide-ranging, authoritative essays, David Brody analyses why labour's bright post-war hopes were dashed, 'The Uses of Power I: The Industrial Background' and 'The Use of Power II: Political Action', *Workers in Industrial America*, pp. 173–257. Christopher L. Tomlins seems to blame state involvement in industrial relations for most of labour's troubles in *The State and the Unions: Labor Relations, Law and the Organized Labor Movement in America, 1880–1960* (Cambridge University Press: Cambridge, 1985). The Wagner Act, he argues, gave workers a 'counterfeit liberty'. Zieger, *American Workers, American Unions*, pp. 137–99, shrewdly analyses labour's strength and weaknesses since 1950 and concludes on a gloomy note on the unions' future in Reagan's America. Graham K. Wilson offers a vigorous, if unfashionable, defence of labour's post-war record in *Unions in American National Politics* (Macmillan: London, 1979).

Chapter 4

In *The Coming of the New Deal* (Houghton Mifflin: Boston, 1958), pp. 27–84, Arthur M. Schlesinger Jr devotes the first section to agriculture, giving farm policy the same high priority New Dealers gave it. In Frank Freidel, *Launching the New Deal* (Little, Brown: Boston, 1973), pp. 83–101, 308–39 the Agricultural Adjustment Act is quite overshadowed by devaluation. Gary M. Walton (ed.), *Regulatory Change in an Atmosphere of Crisis: Current Implications of the Roosevelt Years* (Academic Press: New York, 1979), does not even discuss agriculture – the area where the federal government most directly regulated the daily economic lives of individual Americans. Fortunately declining interest in New Deal agricultural policy has been offset by three first-rate surveys: Richard S. Kirkendall, 'The New Deal and Agriculture', in John Braeman, Robert Bremner, and David Brody (eds.), *The New Deal*, vol. I *The National Level* (Ohio State University Press: Columbus, 1975), pp. 83–109, Theodore Saloutos, 'New Deal Agricultural Policy: An Evaluation', *Journal of American History* 61 (1974), pp. 394–416, and Gilbert C. Fite, *American Farmers: The New Majority* (Indiana University Press: Bloomington, 1981), pp. 40–79. Theodore Saloutos, *The American Farmers and the New Deal* (Iowa State University Press: Ames, 1982), prepared for publication after the author's death, is a slightly disappointing testament to a great farm historian. It contains masterly judgements and much valuable information but it is inevitably patchy, unbalanced, and often confusing.

Richard S. Kirkendall, *Social Scientists and Farm Politics in the Age of Roosevelt* (University of Missouri Press: Columbia, 1967), pp. 11–60, discusses the idea of the agricultural economists who shaped the 1933 Farm Act. M. L. Wilson's particular role in devising the voluntary domestic allotment and selling it to farm politicians and Roosevelt and his advisers is fully covered in William D. Rowley, *M. L. Wilson and the Campaign for the*

Domestic Allotment (University of Nebraska Press: Lincoln, 1971). John L. Shover, *Cornbelt in Rebellion: The Farmers' Holiday Association* (University of Illinois Press: Urbana, 1965), pp. 98–167, discusses the FHA threat of a farm strike in both the spring and autumn of 1933. Van L. Perkins, *Crisis in Agriculture: The Agricultural Adjustment Administration and the New Deal, 1933* (University of California Press: Berkeley, 1969) is the definitive study of the passage of the Agricultural Adjustment Act, the establishment of the individual commodity programmes, and the triumph of the production control advocates. There is no comparable study of any other aspect of New Deal farm policy-making.

The lack of interest in the farm recovery, as distinct from rural poverty, programmes means that for individual commodities we still have to rely on the Brookings Institution studies carried out in the 1930s. The most useful of these are: Joseph S. Davis, *Wheat and the AAA* (Brookings Institution: Washington, D.C., 1935), D. A. Fitzgerald, *Livestock and the AAA* (Brookings Institution: Washington, D.C., 1935), Edwin G. Nourse, *Marketing Agreements under the AAA* (Brookings Institution: Washington, D.C., 1935), and Henry I. Richards, *Cotton and the AAA* (Brookings Institution: Washington, D.C., 1936). These studies led to an evaluation of the AAA which is still relevant, Edwin G. Nourse, Joseph S. Davis and John D. Black, *Three Years of the Agricultural Adjustment Administration* (Brookings Institution: Washington, D.C., 1937), especially pp. 449–79 on 'The AAA Philosophy in the Light of Experience'.

There are more recent studies of the commodity programme. For wheat and corn-hogs, see Michael W. Schuyler, 'Agriculture Relief Activities of the Federal Government in the Middle West, 1933–1936' (University of Kansas: Ph.D. dissertation, 1970), and Don F. Hadwiger, *Federal Wheat Commodity Programs* (Iowa State University Press, 1970). For corn-hogs and cattle, see C. Roger Lambert, 'New Deal Experiments in Production Control: The Livestock Program, 1933–1935' (University of Oklahoma: Ph.D. dissertation, 1962), and 'Southwestern Cattlemen, the Federal Government and the Depression', in Donald W. Whisehunt (ed.), *The Depression in the Southwest* (National University Publications, Kennikat Press: Port Washington, N.Y., 1980), pp. 42–57.

For tobacco I tried to study both national policy-making and local implementation in my *Prosperity Road: The New Deal Tobacco and North Carolina* (University of North Carolina: Chapel Hill, 1980). Pete Daniel, *Breaking the Land: The Transformation of the Cotton, Tobacco and Rice Cultures since 1880* (University of Illinois Press: Urbana, 1985) is a pioneering study of the way in which the impact of New Deal programmes varied according to the degree of technological innovation and mechanisation available to the growers of particular commodities. Gilbert C. Fite offers a characteristically thorough and sensible assessment of the relationship between AAA programmes and change in southern agriculture in *Cotton Fields No More: Southern Agriculture, 1865–1980* (University of Kentucky Press: Lexington, 1984), pp. 120–62. For an example of the local operation of the cotton programme, see Michael S. Holmes, *The New Deal in Georgia: An Administrative History*, pp. 209–69.

There is no authoritative account of the 1938 Farm Act but see Dean Albertson, *Roosevelt's Farmer: Claude Wickard in the New Deal* (Columbia University Press: New York, 1961), pp. 111–17, Christiana M. Campbell, *The Farm Bureau and the New Deal: A Study in the Making of National Farm Policy, 1933–1940* (University of Illinois Press: Urbana, 1962), pp. 111–14, Hadwiger, *Federal Wheat Commodity Programs*, pp. 137–53, Badger, *Prosperity Road*, pp. 144–9 and Donald R. McCoy 'George S. McGill of Kansas and the Agricultural Adjustment Act of 1938', *The Historian* 45 (1983), pp. 186–205.

For Henry Wallace's slow shift from 'agricultural fundamentalism', see Richard S. Kirkendall, 'Commentary on the Thought of Henry A. Wallace', *Agricultural History* 41 (1967), pp. 138–42. For the tentative New Deal steps towards food for the needy, see Charles R. Lambert, 'Want and Plenty: The Federal Surplus Relief Corporation and the AAA', *Agricultural History* 46 (1972), pp. 390–400. Campbell, *The Farm Bureau and the New Deal*, shows how the Farm Bureau capitalised on its links with the AAA and then turned against it. For the politics of policy-making and the strong position of commodity interest groups, see Badger, *Prosperity Road*, pp. 210–19, Grant McConnell, *The Decline of Agrarian Democracy* (University of California Press: Berkeley, 1953), and Graham K. Wilson, *Special Interests and Policymaking: Agricultural Policies and Politics in Britain and the United*

States of America, 1956–1970 (Wiley: New York, 1977).

Richard S. Kirkendall outlines the long-term aims of the New Deal agricultural economists and chronicles the planning efforts of the Bureau of Agricultural Economics in *Social Scientists and Farm Politics*, pp. 63–192. Otis L. Graham Jr shrewdly comments on the limited scope of rural planning in *Towards a Planned Society: From Roosevelt to Nixon* (Oxford University Press: New York, 1976), pp. 35–44.

John A. Salmond, *The Civil Conservation Corps and the New Deal, 1933–1942: A New Deal Case Study* (Duke University Press: Durham, N.C., 1965), is the standard history of the CCC. See also Kenneth E. Hendrickson, 'The Civilian Conservation Corps in the Southwestern States', in Whisehunt, *The Depression in the Southwest*, pp. 3–25.

For soil-conservation efforts in the Dust Bowls and the Great Plains and the more grandiose plans of *The Future of the Great Plains*, see Donald Worster, *Dust Bowl: The Southern Plains in the 1930s* (Oxford University Press: New York, 1979), pp. 183–229, Gary L. Nall, 'The Struggle to Save the Land: The Soil Conservation Effort in the Dust Bowl', in Whisehunt, *The Depression in the Southwest*, pp. 26–41, Richard Lowitt, *The New Deal and the West* (Indiana University Press: Bloomington, 1984), pp. 35–64, and Theodore Saloutos, 'The New Deal in the Great Plains', *Agricultural History* 48 (1969). For the Taylor Grazing Act and irrigation projects in the West see Lowitt, *The New Deal and the West*, pp. 65–96.

Kirkendall, *Social Scientists and Farm Politics*, pp. 165–92, offers a favourable assessment of the local planning committees. Mary W. M. Hargraves. 'Land-Use Planning in Response to Drought: The Experience of the Thirties', *Agricultural History* 50 (1976), pp. 561–82, and Graham D. Taylor, 'The New Deal and the Grass Roots' (University of Pennsylvania: Ph.D. dissertation, 1972), pp. 228–314, emphasised the difficulties faced by these committees. Taylor's dissertation offers a thorough-going analysis of the practical and theoretical difficulties of implementing programmes of grass-roots democracy.

For the more ambitious attempts to eliminate the structural flaws of inadequate demand and high-cost farming, see Kirkendall, *Social Scientists and Farm Politics*, pp. 79–80, 227–32. Allen J. Matusow, *Farm Policies and Politics in the Truman Years*

(Harvard University Press: Cambridge, Mass., 1967), pp. 191–221, describes the failure of the Brannan Plan.

George Brown Tindall, *The Emergence of the New South, 1933–1945* (Louisiana State University Press: Baton Rouge, 1967), pp. 447–57, offers a lucid assessment of the Tennessee Valley Authority. For the general history of the TVA, see Paul K. Conkin, 'The Intellectual and Political Roots', Richard W. Lowitt, 'The TVA, 1933–1945', and Wilmon H. Droze, 'The TVA, 1945–1980: The Power Company', in Edwin C. Hargrove and Paul K. Conkin, *TVA: 50 Years of Grass-Roots Democracy* (University of Illinois Press: Urbana, 1983), pp. 3–85. The conflicts among the directors and with the power companies are detailed in Thomas K. McGraw, *Morgan vs Lilienthal: The Feud Within the TVA* (Loyola University Press: Chicago, 1970), and *TVA and the Power Fight, 1933–1939* (J. B. Lippincott: Philadelphia, 1971). William E. Leuchtenburg discusses the failure to extend the TVA to other regions in 'Roosevelt, Norris, and the Seven Little TVAs', *Journal of Politics* 14 (1952). The debate over the impact of grass-roots democracy within the TVA is carried on in Philip Selznick, *TVA and the Grass Roots: A Study in the Sociology of Formal Organization* (University of California Press: Berkeley, 1949), R. G. Tugwell and E. C. Banfield, 'Grass-Roots Democracy – Myth or Reality?', *Public Administrative Review* 10 (1950), pp. 46–55 and Norman I. Wengert, *Valley of Tomorrow: The TVA and Agriculture* (University of Tennessee: Knoxville, 1952).

For the REA, see D. Clayton Brown, *Electricity for Rural America: The Fight for the REA* (Greenwood: Westport, 1980). For the difficulties of establishing a coherent, planned, national power policy, see Philip Fungiello, *Toward a National Power Policy: The New Deal and the Electric Utility Industry* (University of Pittsburgh Press: Pittsburgh, 1973).

David Murray, *Modern Indians: Native Americans in the Twentieth Century* (British Association for American Studies: 1982), pp. 13–18, succinctly sums up the impact of the Indian New Deal. For John Collier, his hopes and misconceptions, see Kenneth R. Philp, *John Collier's Crusade for Indian Reform, 1920–1954* (University of Arizona Press: Tucson, 1977), pp. 113–213. The difficulties of convincing the largest single tribe of the wisdom of change is shown by Donald L. Parman, *The Navajos and the New Deal* (Yale University Press: New Haven, 1976). The difficulty of the 'grass-roots democracy' approach to Indian reform is fully explored by Graham D. Taylor, 'The New Deal and the Grass Roots', pp. 133–220, and *The New Deal and American Indian Tribalism: The Administration of the Indian Reorganization Act, 1934–1945* (University of Nebraska Press: Lincoln, 1980).

Cletus E. Daniel, *Bitter Harvest: A History of California Farmworkers, 1870–1941* (Cornell University Press: Ithaca, 1981), pp. 141–285, expertly traces the protest of California farm labourers, the inadequate New Deal response, and the violence of the vigilante and police repression.

The southern sharecroppers may have been 'Forgotten Farmers' of the New Deal, but contemporary neglect has been compensated for by the attention of historians since 1965. For the impact of the AAA on the sharecroppers, the indifference of the Cotton Section to their plight, and the purge of those 'urban liberals' who tried to help them, see David E. Conrad, *The Forgotten Farmers: The Story of Sharecroppers in the New Deal* (University of Illinois Press: Urbana, 1965), pp. 40–153, Donald H. Grubbs, *Cry from the Cotton: The Southern Tenant Farmers Union and the New Deal* (University of North Carolina Press: Chapel Hill, 1971), pp. 1–61, Paul E. Mertz, *New Deal and Southern Rural Poverty* (Louisiana State University Press: Baton Rouge, 1978), pp. 20–44, Peter H. Irons, *The New Deal Lawyers* (Princeton University Press: Princeton, 1982), pp. 156–80 and Daniel, *Breaking the Land*, pp. 90–109, 155–83.

The sharecroppers' protest is vividly described by Grubbs, *Cry from the Cotton*, pp. 62–192, and Louis Cantor, *A Prologue to the Protest Movement: The Missouri Sharecropper Roadside Demonstration of 1939* (Duke University Press: Durham, N.C., 1969). See also Jerold S. Auerbach, 'Southern Tenant Farmers: Socialist Critics of the New Deal', *Labor History* 7 (1966), pp. 3–18, and *Labor and Liberty: The La Follette Committee and the New Deal* (Bobbs-Merrill: Indianapolis, 1966), pp. 33–47, and Lowell K. Dyson, 'The Southern Tenant Farmers' Union and Depression', *Political Science Quarterly* 88 (1973), pp. 230–52. H. L. Mitchell recalls his leadership in 'The Founding and Early History of the Southern Tenant Farmers' Union', *Arkansas Historical Quarterly* 32 (1973), pp. 342–69, and *Mean Things Happening in this Land: The Life and Times of H. L. Mitchell, co-founder of the Southern*

Tenant Farmers' Union (Allanheld, Osman: Montclair, N.J., 1979).

The New Deal's discovery of rural poverty, the history of the resettlement communities, and the rise and fall of the Farm Security Administration are covered in excellent monographs: Mertz, *New Deal Policy*, pp. 45–220, Donald S. Holley, *Uncle Sam's Farmers: The New Deal Communities in the Lower Mississippi Valley* (University of Illinois Press: Urbana, 1975), and Sidney Baldwin, *Poverty and Politics: The Rise and Decline of the Farm Security Administration* (University of North Carolina Press: Chapel Hill, 1968). For the bias towards recovery programmes of New Deal agricultural spending, see Leonard J. Arrington, 'Western Agriculture and the New Deal', *Agricultural History* 44 (1970), pp. 337–53, and Don C. Reading 'New Deal Activity and the States, 1933 to 1939', *Journal of Economic History* 33 (1973), pp. 792–807. Donald Worster's alternative vision of what agricultural policy should have done is laid out in *Dust Bowl*, pp. 43, 63, 140–7, 159, 163, 196–7, 242–3. Pete Daniel develops his alternative in 'The Transformation of the Rural South: 1930 to the Present', *Agricultural History* 55 (1981), pp. 231–48, 'The New Deal, Southern Agriculture and Economic Change', in James C. Cobb and Michael V. Namaroto, *The New Deal and the South* (University of Mississippi Press: Jackson, 1984), pp. 37–61, and *Breaking the Land*. For the hopes of decentralist intellectuals, see Edward S. Shapiro, 'Decentralist Intellectuals and the New Deal', *Journal of American History* 58 (1972), pp. 938–57.

Chapter 5

The best overall treatment of New Deal welfare policies is James T. Patterson, *America's Struggle Against Poverty, 1900–1980* (Harvard University Press: Cambridge, Mass., 1981), pp. 37–77, expertly summarised by Patterson himself in *The Welfare State in America, 1930–1980* (British Association for American Studies: 1981), pp. 12–19. Frances Fox Piven and Richard A. Cloward, *Regulating the Poor: The Functions of Public Welfare* (Tavistock: London, 1972), pp. 45–119, see New Deal policy as a minimal response designed to quiet the turbulence of the poor. A remarkable, shrewd, and wide-ranging overview is provided by Theda Skocpol and John Ikenberry, 'The Political Formation of the American Welfare State in Historical and Comparative Perspective' (Paper delivered at the Annual Meeting of the American Sociological Association, 1982), recently published as 'Expanding Social Benefits: The Role of Social Security', *Political Science Quarterly* 102 (1987), pp. 389–416.

There is no full-scale history of the Federal Emergency Relief Administration. Searle F. Charles provides a basic introduction in *Minister of Relief: Harry Hopkins and the Depression* (Syracuse University Press, 1963), pp. 5–43, 66–93. Hopkins himself highlights the issues at stake in *Spending to Save: The Complete Story of Relief* (University of Washington Press: Seattle, 1972 and 1936), pp. 97–107, while the government's own *Final Statistical Report of the Federal Emergency Relief Administration* (Works Progress Administration, Government Printing Office, 1942) provides a mass of data. The reaction of the unemployed to the FERA and the varying quality of local relief programmes are vividly described in Lorena Hickok's regular letters to Hopkins assembled in Richard Lowitt and Maurine Beasley (eds.), *One Third of a Nation: Lorena Hickok Reports on the Great Depression* (University of Illinois Press: Urbana, 1981). The general problems caused by local administration of the FERA are covered by James T. Patterson, *The New Deal and the States: Federalism in Transition* (Princeton University Press: Princeton, 1969), pp. 50–73. Robert P. Ingalls, *Herbert H. Lehman and New York's Little New Deal* (New York University Press: New York, 1975), p. 41, stresses the quality of local administration in New York. For contrasting examples of local miserliness, incompetence, and lack of sympathy for relief clients, see Michael P. Malone, *C. Ben Ross and the New Deal in Idaho* (University of Washington Press: Seattle, 1970), pp. 60–1, Robert L. Heinemann, *Depression and New Deal in Virginia: The Enduring Dominion* (University Press of Virginia: Charlottesville, 1983), pp. 69–87, Thomas Sellers Morgan Jr, 'A Step Towards Altruism: Relief and Welfare in North Carolina, 1930–1938' (Ph.D. dissertation, University of North Carolina, 1968), pp. 92–8, 106–12, 209–17, Robert E. Burton, 'The New Deal in Oregon', in John A. Braeman, Robert H. Bremner, and David Brody (eds.), *The New Deal*: vol. II *The State and Local Levels* (Ohio State University Press: Columbus, 1975), p. 365, Michael S.

Holmes, *The New Deal in Georgia: An Administrative History* (Greenwood Press: Westport, 1975), pp. 15–59, Jack Irby Hayes Jr, 'South Carolina and the New Deal, 1932–1938' (Ph.D. dissertation, University of South Carolina, 1972), pp. 199–203, James F. Wickens, *Colorado in the Great Depression* (Garland: New York, 1979), pp. 59–62, 70–9, 107–17, Roger D. Tate Jr, 'Easing the Burden: The Era of Depression and New Deal in Mississippi' (Ph.D. dissertation, University of Tennessee, 1978), pp. 63–5, 117–18, 129–32, David J. Maurer, 'Relief Problems and Politics in Ohio', in Braeman *et al.*, *The New Deal*, vol. II, pp. 88–9. For racial discrimination under the FERA, see Harvard Sitkoff, *A New Deal for Blacks: The Emergence of Civil Rights as a National Issue*, vol. I *The Depression Decade* (Oxford University Press: New York, 1978), p. 49, George B. Tindall, *The Emergence of the New South 1913–1945* (Louisiana State University Press: Baton Rouge, 1967), p. 547. For political complaints from Democrats, see Richard C. Keller, *Pennsylvania's Little New Deal* (Garland: New York, 1982), p. 180, and Morgan, 'A Step Towards Altruism', pp. 78–80, 84.

The brief life of the CWA has made it easier for scholars to chart its progress. Forrest A. Walker's competent *The Civil Works Administration: An Experiment in Federal Work Relief, 1933–1934* (Garland: New York, 1979) has been supplanted by Bonnie Fox Schwartz's *The Civil Works Administration, 1933–1934: The Business of Emergency Employment in the New Deal* (Princeton, University Press: Princeton, 1984). Schwartz weaves into her account of national policy-making and administration local case studies of Pennsylvania, Illinois, California, and North Carolina. She argues that professional engineers increasingly took over the running of the CWA from social workers.

The lack of a full-scale history of the FERA is matched by the absence of an overall account of the Works Progress Administration. Searle Charles's biography of Hopkins, *Minister of Relief*, pp. 94–248, and Hopkins's own account, *Spending to Save*, pp. 160–78, again have to serve as basic introductions. Contemporary studies of the WPA also provide a wealth of data, notably Donald S. Howard, *The WPA and Federal Relief Policy* (Da Capo: New York, 1973, reprint of 1943).

Frances Fox Piven and Richard A. Cloward stress the link between disorder and work relief and castigate the Workers'

Alliance for abandoning the tactics of disruption in *Regulating the Poor*, pp. 94–117, and more specifically in *Poor People's Movements: Why They Succeed, How They Fail* (Pantheon Books: New York, 1977), pp. 69–91. The link between welfare cutbacks and disorder is demonstrated by Barbara Blumberg, *The New Deal and the Unemployed: The View From New York City* (Bucknell University Press: Lewisburg, 1977), pp. 39, 52–7, 86–95, 101–3, 107–10, 286–7, and Joseph J. Verdiccio, 'New Deal Work Relief and New York City, 1933–1938' (Ph.D. dissertation, New York University, 1980), pp. 1–10. On the Harlem riot and changes in relief policy, see Mark Naison, *Communists in Harlem during the Depression* (University of Illinois Press: Urbana, 1983), pp. 140–8. Harvey Klehr, *The Heyday of American Communism: The Depression Decade* (Basic Books: New York, 1984), pp. 294–304, argues that the moderate policy of the Workers' Alliance was realistic and inevitable but, less convincingly, that the Alliance was firmly under Communist control.

For the WPA and white-collar projects, see Blumberg, *The New Deal and the Unemployed*, pp. 147–62, and Holmes, *The New Deal and Georgia*, pp. 125–47.; and women, Susan Ware, *Beyond Suffrage: Women in the New Deal* (Harvard University Press: Cambridge, 1981), pp. 108–15, and *Holding Their Own: American Women in the 1930s* (Twayne: Schenectady, 1982), ch. 4; and education, Blumberg, *The New Deal and the Unemployed*, pp. 165–80, Tindall, *The Emergence of the New South*, pp. 493–7, John A. Salmond, *A Southern Rebel: The Life and Times of Aubrey Willis Williams, 1890–1965* (University of North Carolina Press: Chapel Hill, 1983), pp. 121–61; and blacks, Sitkoff, *A New Deal for Blacks*, pp. 49, 69–72, and Blumberg, *The New Deal and the Unemployed*, pp. 78–83, 290–3.

On the problem of localism and the WPA, see Patterson, *The New Deal and the States*, pp. 74–85. For different experiences starting up the WPA locally, see Blumberg, *The New Deal and the Unemployed*, pp. 48–9, Charles H. Trout, *Boston, The Great Depression, and the New Deal* (Oxford University Press: New York, 1977), pp. 164–8, and Bruce M. Stave, *The New Deal and the Last Hurrah: Pittsburgh Machine Politics* (University of Pittsburgh Press: Pittsburgh, 1970), pp. 116–32.

Examples of conservative beneficiaries of political influence in the WPA are provided by Raymond E. Marcello, 'The North

Carolina Works Programme Administration and the Politics of Relief' (Ph.D. dissertation, Duke University, 1969), pp. 59–81, 115–18, 122–6, 136, and Polly Ann Davis, *Alben Barkley: Senate Majority Leader and Vice President* (Garland: New York, 1979), pp. 53–72. But Lyle W. Dorsett uses the political coercion files of the WPA to demonstrate the use of the agency by pro-New Deal city politicians in *Franklin D. Roosevelt and the City Bosses* (National University Publications, Kennikat Press: Port Washington, N.Y., 1977), pp. 31–2, 45–8, 65, 75–7, 88–90, and Bruce Stave demonstrates the role of the WPA in building the Pittsburgh machine in *The New Deal and the Last Hurrah*, pp. 139–61. For a summing-up of the role of the WPA in Louisiana see my 'Huey Long and the New Deal', in Stephen W. Baskerville and Ralph Willett (eds.), *Nothing Else to Fear: New Perspectives on America in the Thirties* (Manchester University Press: Manchester, 1985), pp. 85–7.

John E. Miller, *Governor Philip La Follette, The Wisconsin Progressives and the New Deal* (University of Missouri Press: Columbia, 1982), pp. 61–75, charts the failure of the Wisconsin works plan which aimed to provide for a more comprehensive jobs programme than the WPA could afford. For judicious assessments of the adequacy of the WPA and its attempts to match the legitimacy conferred on workers by private employment, see Blumberg, *The New Deal and the Unemployed*, pp. 281–305, William W. Bremner, 'Along the American Way: The New Deal's Work Relief Program for the Unemployed', *Journal of American History* 42 (1975), 636–52, Lawrence Lashbrook, 'Work Relief in Maine: the administration and progress of the WPA' (Ph.D. dissertation, University of Maine, 1978), pp. 242–6.

The historian strikes gold in the Arts Projects of the WPA. Three of the four programmes are the subjects of excellent monographs: Jane DeHart Mathews, *The Federal Theater, 1935–1939: Plays, Relief and Politics* (Princeton University Press: Princeton, 1967), Richard D. McKinzie, *The New Deal for Artists* (Princeton University Press: Princeton, 1973), Monte N. Penkower, *The Federal Writers' Project: A Study in Government Patronage of the Arts* (University of Illinois Press: Urbana, 1977). A mass of information about the Music Project and the other projects can be dug out of William F. McDonald, *Federal Relief Administration and the Arts: The Origins and Administrative*

History of the Works Project Administration (Ohio State University Press: Columbus, 1969). Jerre Mangione's *The Dream and the
Deal: The Federal Writers' Project, 1935–1943* (Avon Books: New
York, 1972), is more than the vivid memoir of a coordinating
editor on the Writers' Project; it is a scholarly account of the whole
project. The democratic and national cultural goals of Project One
are explored by Jane DeHart Mathews in 'Arts and the People:
the New Deal Quest for a Cultural Democracy', *Journal of
American History* 42 (1973), pp. 316–29. The wider context of the
documentary, popular, radical, and consciously American impulses of cultural expression in the 1930s is provided by Richard
H. Pells, *Radical Visions and American Dreams: Cultural and
Social Thought in the Depression Years* (Harper & Row: New
York, 1973), pp. 194–291, William Stott, *Documentary Expression
and Thirties America* (Oxford University Press: New York, 1973),
pp. 92–118, and Charles C. Alexander, *Here the Country Lies:
Nationalism and the Arts in Twentieth Century America* (Indiana
University Press: Bloomington, 1982).

   For local studies of the Arts Projects, see Blumberg, *The New
Deal and the Unemployed*, pp. 183–217, and Holmes, *The New
Deal in Georgia*, pp. 147–66. On the quality of the work produced
on the Art Project and the trials and tribulations of the Living
Newspaper, see Ralph Willett, ' "Naive, human, eager and alive";
the Federal Art Project and the response from magazines', and
Stuart Cosgrove, 'The Living Newspaper: Strikes, strategies and
solidarity' in Stephen Baskerville and Ralph Willett (eds.),
Nothing Else to Fear, pp. 179–93, 238–57.

   There are three books essential to an understanding of the
policy options in social insurance that had developed in the years
before the Social Security Act: Daniel Nelson, *Unemployment
Insurance: The American Experience, 1915–1935* (University of
Wisconsin Press: Madison, 1969); Roy Lubove, *The Struggle for
Social Security, 1900–1935* (Harvard University Press: Cambridge,
1968); and William Graebner, *A History of Retirement: The
Meaning and Function of an American Institution, 1885–1978*
(Yale University Press: New Haven, 1980). On the rationalising
and preventive imperatives that the Technical Director of the
Committee on Economic Security acquired in his years as a
student, public official, and academic in Wisconsin, see Theron F.
Schlabach, *Edwin E. Witte: Cautious Reformer* (State Historical

Society of Wisconsin: Madison, 1969), pp. 20–97. Schlabach chronicles Witte's role in the deliberations of the Committee on Economic Security and in the passage of the Social Security Act, pp. 98–157. Witte himself wrote an indispensable blow-by-blow account of that process in *The Development of the Social Security Act* (University of Wisconsin Press: Madison, 1963). Witte wrote the account in 1936 but it was not published until after his death. His stress on the practical, constitutional, and congressional restraints on policy formulation is also the thrust of Frances Perkins's own account, *The Roosevelt I Knew* (Viking: New York, 1946), pp. 278–301. Edward Berkowitz and Kim McQuaid, *Creating the Welfare State: The Political Economy of Twentieth-Century Reform* (Praeger: New York, 1980), pp. 96–113, overemphasise the role of 'corporate liberal' businessmen in the development of social security.

On the implementation and early administration of social security, see Charles McKinley and Robert W. Frase, *Launching Social Security: A Capture and Record Account, 1935–37* (University of Wisconsin Press: Madison, 1970). For the wide variations in unemployment compensation and categorical assistance programmes at the local level, see Patterson, *The New Deal and the States*, pp. 85–101; and Tindall, *The Emergence of the New South*, pp. 487–91. In *The Formative Years of Social Security* (University of Wisconsin Press: Madison, 1968), Arthur J. Altmeyer, first a member, then chairman of the Social Security Board, emphasises the successful defence of the programme against conservative challenges but he also demonstrates the steady erosion of early optimism about extending the benefits and scope of the programme. Jerry Cates, *Insuring Inequality: Administrative Leadership in Social Security, 1935–1954* (University of Michigan Press: Ann Arbor, 1982) argues by contrast that Altmeyer and his colleagues used the insurance ideology to fight off liberal as well as conservative challenges. Their success locked the social security programme into a system that benefited the middle class at the expense of the poor.

On housing, the limitations of New Deal policies are thoroughly explained in Kenneth T. Jackson, *Crabgrass Frontier: The Suburbanization of the United States* (Oxford University Press: Oxford and New York, 1985), chs. 10, 11, 12. See also Mark I. Gelfand, *A Nation of Cities: The Federal Government and Urban America,*

1933–1965 (Oxford University Press: New York, 1975), pp. 59–65. One example of an attempt by the FHA to overcome its middle-income, suburban bias is described in Iwan Morgan, 'The Fort Wayne Plan: The FHA and Prefabricated Municipal Housing in the 1930s', *The Historian* 47 (1985), pp. 538–59.

The limitations of the Greenbelt programme are fully explored in Joseph L. Arnold, *The New Deal in the Suburbs: A History of the Greenbelt Programme, 1935–1954* (Ohio State University Press: Columbus, 1971). Paul K. Conkin examines the ideas of colonisation and planning and their implementation in both subsistence homesteads and Greenbelt towns in *Tomorrow a New World: The New Deal Community Program* (Cornell University Press: Ithaca, 1959). The local difficulties of PWA Housing Division projects are covered in Trout, *Boston, The Great Depression, and the New Deal*, pp. 152–4, 286–7, Tindall, *The Emergence of the New South*, pp. 485–6, and Christopher G. Wye, 'The New Deal and the Negro Community: Toward a Broader Conceptualization', *Journal of American History* 41 (1972), pp. 621–39. The campaign for public housing and the passage of the Wagner Housing Act of 1937 is covered in Judith Ann Trolander, *Settlement Houses and the Great Depression* (Wayne State University Press: Detroit, 1975), ch. 8, and Joseph J. Huthmacher, *Senator Robert F. Wagner and the Rise of Urban Liberalism* (Atheneum: New York, 1971), pp. 205–16, 224–30. Richard O. Davies traces the long struggle to extend public-housing legislation in *Housing Reform During the Truman Administration* (University of Missouri Press: Columbia, 1966) and catalogues its disappointing legacy.

The standard work on the New Deal failure to introduce health insurance is Daniel S. Hirshfield, *The Lost Reform: The Campaign for Compulsory Health Insurance in the United States from 1932 to 1943* (Harvard University Press: Cambridge, 1970). Monte M. Poen takes up the story and carries it through to Harry Truman's failed campaigns in *Harry S. Truman vs. the Medical Lobby: The Genesis of Medicare* (University of Missouri Press: Columbia, 1979) which emphasises the difficulty of battling the American Medical Association. In *Health Policies, Health Politics: The British and American Experience, 1911–1965* (Princeton University Press: Princeton, 1986) Daniel M. Fox argues that differences between Britain and America over how individuals should pay for health care obscured a basic similarity in the health care systems. Policy-makers in both countries shared a belief in health care based on 'hierarchical regionalism' in which the results of medical science are dispersed by a regional hierarchy of disseminators. New Deal battles over the payment of medical costs, according to Fox, were sham battles: the real battle was over the organisation of health care provision.

Chapter 6

The best introduction to the politics of the New Deal is John M. Allswang, *The New Deal and American Politics: A Study in Political Change* (Wiley: New York, 1978). Allswang not only provides a shrewd overview; he also makes a bold effort to correlate socio-economic data and voting returns from 3,000 counties.

For the basis of the New Democratic Party, see Arthur M. Schlesinger Jr, *The Politics of Upheaval* (Houghton Mifflin: Boston, 1960), pp. 409–43, 571–600, and Allswang, *The New Deal and American Politics*, pp. 30–7. The 1920s roots of the urban, lower-income voters' shift to the Democratic Party – the 'Al Smith Revolution' – can be traced in David Burner, *The Politics of Provincialism: The Democratic Party in Transition, 1928–1936* (Knopf: New York, 1968), and Samuel Lubell, *The Future of American Politics* (3rd edn., Harper & Row: New York, 1965), pp. 43–55. The consolidation of ethnic and lower-income support for Roosevelt is specified in Lubell, *The Future of American Politics*, pp. 55–68, and Allswang, *The New Deal and American Politics*, pp. 40–6. Kristi Andersen, *The Creation of a Democratic Majority, 1928–1936* (University of Chicago Press: Chicago, 1979), argues that the increase in Democratic support was not the result of the conversion of previously loyal Republican voters but the mobilisation of 'nonimmunized citizens' – non-voters, immigrants, independents, and supporters of minor parties. She supports this contention with a case study of Chicago. For Roosevelt's wooing of Catholic support and the Church's response to New Deal domestic and foreign policy, see George Q. Flynn, *American Catholics and the Roosevelt Presidency, 1932–1936* (University Press of Kentucky: Lexington, 1968).

Lyle W. Dorsett, *Franklin D. Roosevelt and the City Bosses* (National University Publications, Kennikat Press: Port Washington, N.Y., 1977), effectively disposes of any lingering notion that New Deal welfare benefits in themselves undermined city machines. His study of Roosevelt's relations with the major city bosses makes particularly valuable use of the WPA political coercion files, but his analysis is hindered by a curious determination to criticise Roosevelt for failing to act as honourably and loyally as bosses like Pendergast and Crump. The best case study of the New Deal's role in establishing a Democratic city machine is Bruce Stave, *The New Deal and the Last Hurrah: Pittsburgh Machine Politics* (University of Pittsburgh Press: Pittsburgh, 1970). See also Allswang, *The New Deal and American Politics*, pp. 68–87. Mark I. Gelfand traces the policy implications for urban politicians of the new-found potential of federal assistance in *A Nation of Cities: The Federal Government and Urban America, 1933–1965* (Oxford University Press: New York, 1975), pp. 23–70.

The key study of blacks and the New Deal is Harvard Sitkoff, *A New Deal for Blacks: The Emergence of Civil Rights as a National Issue*, vol. 1 *The Depression Decade* (Oxford University Press: New York, 1978). Sitkoff fully acknowledges the New Deal's racial limitations, but argues that it improved over time and that younger New Deal liberals were part of the developing civil rights coalition. His positive view of the 1930s rests in part on his comparison to the previous decade. Nancy Weiss, in *Farewell to the Party of Lincoln: Black Politics in the Age of FDR* (Princeton University Press: Princeton, 1983), views New Deal efforts for blacks less benignly. She provides the fullest data on the shift of black political allegiances and interprets that shift as a realistic response to the economic benefits of the New Deal, not to any substantive achievements by the administration on race. John B. Kirby, *Black Americans in the Roosevelt Era: Liberalism and Race* (University of Tennessee Press: Knoxville, 1980), examines the limitations of racial liberalism amongst New Deal reformers and the ambivalence of black spokesmen about the benefits of federal government intervention.

The discriminatory impact of particular New Deal programmes is best followed in Raymond Wolters' *Negroes and the Great Depression: The Problem of Economic Recovery* (Greenwood:

Westport, 1970) on the NRA and AAA and John A. Salmond's *The Civilian Conservation Corps* (Duke University Press: Durham, 1967), pp. 88–101. The failure of Roosevelt to endorse anti-lynching legislation on a 'must' basis is covered in Robert L. Zangrando, *The NAACP Crusade against Lynching, 1909–1950* (Temple University Press: Philadelphia, 1980), pp. 98–165.

Mark Naison has written an excellent study of black radicalism in the 1930s in a northern ghetto, *Communists in Harlem during the Depression* (University of Illinois Press: Urbana, 1983). He shows how Communist direct action protest during the Depression won the party a following among black intellectuals and led to the development of broad protest coalitions. He also shows that the party's political support was always volatile and vulnerable to the rise of other protest groups in the late 1930s. Historians of the modern civil rights movement are beginning to trace its roots in the strategies of black leadership in the southern communities in the 1930s and 1940s, but so far we lack equivalent studies to Naison's of southern black communities during the Depression, although see Nell Irwin Painter, *The Narrative of Hosea Hudson: His Life as a Negro Communist in the South* (Harvard University Press: Cambridge, Mass., 1979), for a remarkable picture of a black Communist union organiser in Birmingham, Alabama. For the best insights into the political influence blacks could carve out in a hostile environment we have to go back to Ralph J. Bunche's field studies carried out for Gunnar Myrdal's Carnegie-funded study of the American race problem. Bunche's conclusions and the detailed examples of southern black political activity, including voting in AAA crop control referenda, were subsequently published as *The Political Status of the Negro in the Age of FDR* (University of Chicago Press: Chicago, 1973), pp. 24–68, 384–474, 477–515, 547–71. See also George Brown Tindall, *The Emergence of the New South, 1913–1945* (Louisiana State University Press: Baton Rouge, 1967), pp. 540–75, for new directions in southern black experience.

Susan Ware, *Beyond Suffrage: Women in the New Deal* (Harvard University Press: Cambridge, Mass., 1981), describes the impact of the remarkable network of women politicians and administrators in the upper and middle echelons of the New Deal. In *Holding Their Own: American Women in the 1930s* (Twayne: Schenectady, 1982), Ware emphasises the positive gains women made – or at least the protection of what they had already achieved – in the 1930s in government, employment, radical politics, and culture. But along with Lois Scharf, *To Work and to Wed: Female Employment, Feminism, and the Great Depression* (Greenwood: Westport, 1980), and Winifred D. Wandersee, *Women's Work and Family Values, 1920–1940* (Harvard University Press: Cambridge, Mass., 1981), Ware argues that the paramount importance of economic issues, the defence of women's jobs by invoking the contribution their work made to preserving the family, and the persistent commitment of women to traditional notions of family life, all inhibited the development of an explicitly feminist ideology.

The definitive study of Roosevelt's relations with Congress is James T. Patterson, *Congressional Conservatism and the New Deal: The Growth of the Conservative Coalition in Congress, 1933–1939* (University Press of Kentucky: Lexington, 1967). Patterson provides the best account we have of Roosevelt's early success with Congress, the opposition of irreconcilable conservative Democrats, the growing unease of southern Democrats with the non-emergency New Deal, the impact of the Court-packing episode and the recession on active bipartisan conservative cooperation, and Roosevelt's attempt to purge conservative Democrats in 1938.

On Supreme Court reform, Michael E. Parrish provides a useful reminder of how conservative on economic issues the Court was before 1937 in 'The Hughes Court, the Great Depression, and the Historians', *The Historian* 40 (1975), pp. 286–308. Parrish's case is ultimately more convincing than Richard A. Maidment's vigorous defence of the Court's rejection of New Deal legislation in 'The New Deal Court Revisited', in Stepehen W. Baskerville and Ralph Willett (eds.), *Nothing Else to Fear: New Perspectives on America in the Thirties* (Manchester University Press: Manchester, 1985), pp. 38–63. William E. Leuchtenburg has provided the most authoritative accounts of both the origins of the Court reform plan, 'The Origins of Franklin D. Roosevelt's "Court-Packing" Plan', *The Supreme Court Review* (1966), pp. 352–99, and its political impact, 'Franklin D. Roosevelt's Supreme Court "Packing" Plan', in Harold M. Hollingsworth (ed.), *Essays on the New Deal* (University of Texas Press: Austin, 1969), pp. 69–115. It is difficult to imagine that Professor Leuchtenburg's long-awaited full-length study of Court reform can reveal much more than these two formidable essays. The way in which Roosevelt's plan alienated most previously sympathetic progressive Republicans is detailed in Ronald Feinman, *The Twilight of Progressivism: The Western Republican Senators and the New Deal* (Johns Hopkins University Press: Baltimore, 1981), pp. 117–35, and Richard A. Mulder, *The Insurgent Progressives in the United States Senate and the New Deal, 1933–39* (Garland: New York, 1979), pp. 165–213. Richard Polenberg, *Reorganizing Roosevelt's Government: The Controversy over Executive Reorganization* (Harvard University Press: Cambridge, Mass., 1966), explains why, in the aftermath of the Court-packing effort, the president's apparently reasonable proposals to make the government more efficient aroused such fury. David L. Porter, *Congress and the Waning of the New Deal* (National University Publications, Kennikat Press: Port Washington, N.Y., 1980), charts shifting sectional alliances which underlay the New Deal's continuing battle with the conservative coalition in 1939 and 1940 over monetary policy, relief spending, execution reorganisation, transportation regulation, and campaign reform.

The crucial early southern enthusiasm for the New Deal and the later disenchantment with the northern urban orientation of reform is charted in Tindall, *The Emergence of the New South*, pp. 607–49. The distribution of benefits from government spending programmes in the 1930s to southern states can be traced in Don C. Reading, 'A Statistical Analysis of the New Deal's Economic Programs in the Forty-Eight States' (Utah State University: Ph.D. dissertation, 1972), and 'New Deal Activity and the States, 1933 to 1939', *Journal of Economic History* 33 (1973), pp. 792–807.

Lionel Patenaude, *Texans, Politics and the New Deal* (Garland: New York, 1983), examines the influence of Vice-President John Nance Garner in the Senate and Sam Rayburn in the House. He also amply demonstrates the wisdom of the saying 'as thin as the liberalism of a Texas congressman'. A cross-section of southern senators are covered in good biographies: two outright opponents of the New Deal in John Robert Moore, *Senator Josiah William Bailey of North Carolina* (Duke University Press: Durham, 1968), and Monroe Lee Billington, *Thomas P. Gore: The Blind Senator from Oklahoma* (University of Kansas Press: Lawrence, 1967); the influential chairman of the Senate Finance Committee who was increasingly uneasy about Roosevelt's policies in Martha H.

Swain, *Pat Harrison: The New Deal Years* (University of Mississippi Press: Jackson, 1978); the aggressively liberal, former Klans-
man from Alabama in Virginia Vander Veer Hamilton, *Hugo
Black: The Alabama Years* (Louisiana State University Press:
Baton Rouge, 1972).

In *A New Deal for Blacks*, pp. 106–23, Harvard Sitkoff shows
how southern conservatives used the race issue to stir up anti-
Roosevelt sentiment. William Anderson, *The Wild Man from
Sugar Creek: The Political Career of Eugene Talmadge* (Louisiana
State University Press: Baton Rouge, 1975) is a study of one racist
demagogue who was rabidly anti-New Deal from the start.
However, Chester M. Morgan in an important study, *Redneck
Liberal: Theodore G. Bilbo and the New Deal* (Louisiana State
University Press: Baton Rouge, 1985) shows how an equally
notorious racist enthusiastically backed urban liberal New Deal
proposals like public housing, minimum wage legislation, and
relief spending long after most Southerners, notably his Mississippi colleague Pat Harrison, had deserted the New Deal cause.

James MacGregor Burns criticised Roosevelt's half-hearted
commitment to party realignment in *Roosevelt: The Lion and the
Fox* (Harcourt, Brace: New York, 1956), pp. 197–8, 349, 376–9,
and *Deadlock of Democracy: Four-Party Politics in America*
(Prentice-Hall: Englewood Cliffs, N.J., 1963), pp. 151–76. James
T. Patterson emphasised the local obstacles to a full-scale realign-
ment in *The New Deal and the States: Federalism in Transition*
(Princeton University Press: Princeton, 1969), pp. 168–93.

For Roosevelt's willingness to assist progressive non-Democrats
– and the difficulties that ensued – see: Wisconsin, Patrick J.
Maney, *Young Bob La Follette: A Biography of Robert M. La
Follette, Jr, 1895–1953* (University of Missouri Press: Columbia,
1978), pp. 134–46, 190–206, 242–4, 252–301, John E. Miller,
*Governor Philip La Follette, the Wisconsin Progressives and the
New Deal* (University of Missouri Press: Columbia, 1982), pp.
33–99, 127–62, 165–6, 178–80; Minnesota, Millard L. Gieske,
Minnesota Farmer-Laborism: The Third Party Alternative (Uni-
versity of Minnesota Press: Minnesota, 1979), pp. 156–8, 161–72,
222–75; New York City, Dorsett, *Franklin D. Roosevelt and the
City Bosses*, pp. 51–60; Nebraska, Richard W. Lowitt, *George W.
Norris: The Triumph of a Progressive, 1933–1944* (University of
Illinois Press: Urbana, 1978), pp. 138–62, 405–33. For the con-

sequences of *not* backing progressive Republican Bronson Cutting, see William Pickens, 'The New Deal in New Mexico', in John Braeman, Robert Bremner, and David Brody, *The New Deal*, vol. II *The Local and State Levels* (Ohio State University Press: Columbus, 1975), pp. 311–54. Feinman, *The Twilight of Progressivism*, pp. 68–90, 117–56, shows how suspicious of the urban-oriented statist New Deal most of the incurably individualistic progressive Republicans were.

Examples of the New Deal's willingness to intervene within the Democratic Party are provided in Sidney Fine, *Frank Murphy: The New Deal Years* (University of Chicago Press: Chicago, 1979), pp. 225–9, A. Cash Koeniger, 'The New Deal and the States: Roosevelt versus the Byrd Organization', *Journal of American History* 68 (1982), pp. 876–96, Dorsett, *Franklin D. Roosevelt and the City Bosses*, pp. 79–81, 107–11, and Betty M. Field, 'The Politics of the New Deal in Louisiana, 1933–1939' (Tulane University: Ph.D. dissertation, 1973). The best account of Roosevelt's attempt to 'purge' conservative Democrats in the 1938 primaries is Patterson, *Congressional Conservatism and the New Deal*, pp. 250–87. For the local complications in Indiana, see Iwan Morgan, 'Factional Conflict in Indiana Politics During the Later New Deal Years, 1936–1940', *Indiana Magazine of History* 79 (1983), pp. 29–60. For the distinctive context of California politics in the 1930s, see Richard Lowitt, *The New Deal and the West* (Indiana University Press: Bloomington, 1984), pp. 172–88. For the Sinclair campaign, see Jackson K. Putnam, *Old Age Politics in California: From Richardson to Reagan* (Stanford University Press: Stanford, 1970), pp. 32–48. Robert E. Burke provides an excellent analysis of the failure of the liberal Democratic administration of Culbert Olson in *Olson's New Deal for California* (University of California Press: Berkeley, 1953).

James L. Sundquist, *Dynamics of the Party System: Alignment and Realignment of the Political Parties in the United States* (Brookings: Washington, D.C., 1973), pp. 183–244, not only demonstrates the favourable raw electoral material for a liberalised Democratic Party in the northern states but also draws attention to the time-lag before younger issue-oriented liberals emerge. See also John W. Jeffries, *Testing the Roosevelt Coalition: Connecticut Politics in World War II* (University of Tennessee Press: Knoxville, 1979), pp. 3–50.

The transitory attachment of midwestern farmers to the Democrats is described and explained in Allswang, *The New Deal and American Politics*, pp. 48–9, Frances W. Schruben, *Kansas in Turmoil, 1930–1936* (University of Missouri Press: Columbia, 1969), pp. 134, 164, 212, 220, Donald R. McCoy, 'George S. McGill of Kansas and the Agricultural Adjustment Act of 1938', *The Historian* 45 (1983), pp. 186–205, and Lowitt, *George W. Norris: The Triumph of a Progressive*, pp. 305, 454.

For the reluctance of mountain western voters to eschew traditions of individualism and states' rights, despite the unprecedented federal assistance they received, see F. Allan Combs, 'The Impact of the New Deal on Wyoming Politics', Michael P. Malone, 'The Montana New Dealers', and James F. Wickens, 'Depression and the New Deal in Colorado', in Braeman, Bremner, and Brody, *The New Deal*, vol. II *The State and Local Levels*, pp. 222–5, 234, 257, 263. See also James T. Patterson, 'The New Deal and the West', *Pacific Historical Review* 38 (1969).

The liberalising effect on Southerners who came to Washington to work in New Deal agencies is chronicled in Morton Sosna, *In Search of the Silent South: Southern Liberals and the Race Issue* (Columbia University Press: New York, 1977), pp. 60–87, John A. Salmond, *A Southern Rebel: The Life and Times of Aubrey Willis Williams, 1890–1965* (University of North Carolina Press: Chapel Hill, 1983), pp. 43–198, and Hollinger F. Barnard (ed.), *Outside the Magic Circle: The Autobiography of Virginia Foster Durr* (University of Alabama Press: University, 1985), pp. 89–182. Richard B. Henderson, *Maury Maverick: A Politicial Biography* (University of Texas Press: Austin, 1970), celebrates the iconoclastic San Antonio congressman who was the leading light in a group of liberals, Democrats, Progressives, and Farmer-Labor representatives in the House. Antony Dunbar, *Against the Grain: Southern Radicals and Prophets* (University of Virginia Press: Charlottesville, 1981), chronicles the fortunes of a tiny group of southern white radicals – mostly influenced by the Social Gospel – who courageously struggled to organise coal miners, steel workers, and sharecroppers in the 1930s. Numan V. Bartley and Hugh D. Graham discuss the 'time-lag' impact of the New Deal shown in the tentative southern liberal revival of the 1940s in *Southern Politics and the Second Reconstruction* (Johns Hopkins University Press: Baltimore, 1975), pp. 24–50.

The evidence of the fragility of southern liberalism is much greater. For the continued cautious faith in gradualism of those liberals who did not go to Washington, see John T. Kneebone's study of the region's much vaunted liberal newspaper editors, *Southern Liberal Journalists and the Issue of Race, 1920–1944* (University of North Carolina Press: Chapel Hill, 1985), pp. 115–74. Sosna, *In Search of the Silent South*, pp. 88–104, 140–8, and Thomas A. Kreuger, *And Promises to Keep: The Southern Conference for Human Welfare, 1938–1948* (Vanderbilt University Press: Nashville, 1967), demonstrate the failure of the leading pro-New Deal pressure group in the South to attract popular and financial support. The conservative and liberal strategies for tackling the nation's number one economic problem are laid out in Paul E. Mertz, *New Deal Policy and Southern Rural Poverty* (Louisiana State University Press: Baton Rouge, 1978), pp. 223–52. The triumph of conservative business forces in that debate is laid bare by James C. Cobb, *The Selling of the South: The Southern Crusade for Industrial Development, 1936–1980* (Louisiana State University Press: Baton Rouge, 1982), pp. 1–34. The sort of modernisation their triumph would bring is examined by Numan V. Bartley, 'The Era of the New Deal as a Turning Point in Southern History', in James C. Cobb and Michael V. Namaroto, *The New Deal and the South* (University Press of Mississippi: Jackson, 1984), pp. 135–46.

For the uninspiring record of state governments in the 1930s, see Patterson, *The New Deal and the States*, pp. 129–67. Miller, *Governor Philip La Follette*, pp. 25, 101–26, 143–4, and Gieske, *Minnesota Farmer-Laborism*, pp. 142, 153, 189, 191–204, demonstrate the essentially moderate nature of apparently radical governments in Wisconsin and Minnesota. Robert Ingalls, *Herbert H. Lehman and New York's Little New Deal* (New York University Press: New York, 1975), Richard Keller, *Pennsylvania's Little New Deal* (Garland: New York, 1982), and Sidney Fine, *Frank Murphy: The New Deal Years*, pp. 481–528, show what was needed to produce reform in northern states. David Maurer, 'Relief Policies and Politics in Ohio', in Braeman, Bremner, and Brody, *The New Deal*, vol. II *The State and Local Levels*, pp. 91–9 shows that Little New Deals were not inevitable even in the North.

On the right, George Wolfskill and James A. Hudson, *All But the People: Franklin D. Roosevelt and his Critics, 1933–1939*

(Macmillan: New York, 1969), provide the definitive history of the Liberty League. The Republican experience in the 1930s can best be approached through Schlesinger, *The Politics of Upheaval*, pp. 524–47, 601–25, Donald McCoy, *Landon of Kansas* (University of Nebraska Press: Lincoln, 1967), and James T. Patterson, *Mr. Republican: A Biography of Robert A. Taft* (Houghton Mifflin: Boston, 1972). Leo Ribuffo, *The Old Christian Right: The Protestant Far Right from the Great Depression to the Cold War* (Temple University Press: Philadelphia, 1983), shows how the anti-Semitic extremism of William Dudley Pelley, Gerald B. Winrod, and Gerald L. K. Smith interacted with more mainstream conservative assaults on the New Deal.

For the important non-Marxist alternatives to Roosevelt, Donald McCoy provides a straightforward account in *Angry Voices: Left-of-Center Politics in the New Deal Era* (University of Kansas Press: Lawrence, 1958). R. Allan Lawson has written an important intellectual history of those liberals who longed for more thorough-going change in *The Failure of Independent Liberalism, 1930–1941* (Putnam: New York, 1971). He shows that both 'pragmatic radicals' and 'liberal traditionalists' drifted to the centre, disenchanted with collectivism, after Roosevelt's smashing electoral victory in 1936 and the growing menace of fascism at home and overseas. Miller, *Governor Philip La Follette*, pp. 127–62, exposes the weaknesses of the National Progressives of America.

A number of studies helped rescue the Communists from the one-dimensional portrait of the Cold War years. Richard H. Pells examined seriously the Marxist contribution to intellectual and cultural life in the 1930s in *Radical Visions and American Dreams: Culture and Social Thought in the Depression Years* (Harper & Row: New York, 1973). Dan T. Carter, *Scottsboro: A Tragedy of the American South* (Louisiana State University Press: Baton Rouge, 1969), pp. 139–68, and Naison, *Communists in Harlem during the Depression*, interpret Communist efforts as genuine, rather than cynical, attempts to assist blacks. Lowell K. Dyson, *Red Harvest: The Communist Party and American Farmers* (University of Nebraska Press: Lincoln, 1982), examines the dedicated, realistic efforts of Communist organisers in rural areas and their ultimately self-defeating success in Popular Front organisations. The history of rank-and-file militancy in labour and work on the organisation of the unemployed has also highlighted indigenous Communist radicalism. Harvey Klehr, in his overview, *The Heyday of American Communism: The Depression Decade* (Basic Books: New York, 1984), takes full cognizance of this revisionism but is at pains to stress Communist weakness, Moscow manipulation, and liberal gullibility. Theodore Draper both surveys and contributes to the controversy aroused by Klehr in 'American Communism Revisited', *New York Review of Books*, 9 and 23 May 1985.

For the Socialists in the 1930s, see David A. Shannon, *The Socialist Party of America: A History* (Macmillan: New York, 1955), pp. 227–48, Robert S. McElvaine, 'Thunder Without Lightning: Working Class Discontent in the United States, 1929–1937' (State University of New York, Binghamton: Ph.D. dissertation, 1974), ch. 5, and Frank A. Warren, *An Alternative Vision: The Socialist Party in the 1930s* (Indiana University Press: Bloomington, 1976).

There are marvellous vignettes of the dissident demagogues in Schlesinger, *The Politics of Upheaval*, pp. 15–68, but the standard work on them now is Alan Brinkley's calm and sensible overview, *Voices of Protest: Huey Long, Father Coughlin and the Great Depression* (Knopf: New York, 1982). Brinkley accurately assesses the limitations of both their radical ideology and their mass support. His interpretation of Coughlin largely supersedes Charles J. Tull's competent *Father Coughlin and the New Deal* (Syracuse University Press: Syracuse, 1965).

The best account of Dr Townsend is in David H. Bennett, *Demagogues in the Depression: American Radicals and the Union Party, 1932–1936* (Rutgers University Press: New Brunswick, N.J., 1969), pp. 149–80. Bennett also analyses Coughlin, Gerald L. K. Smith, William Lemke, and their alliance in the ill-fated Union Party campaign of 1936. For the Townsend movement, see also Abraham Holtzmann, *The Townsend Movement: A Political Study* (Bookman Associates: New York, 1963), and Jackson K. Putnam, *Old Age Politics in California: From Richardson to Reagan* (Stanford University Press: Stanford, 1970), pp. 49–71. For Gerald L. K. Smith, see also Ribuffo, *The Old Christian Right*, pp. 128–77.

Schlesinger, *The Politics of Upheaval*, pp. 42–69, and Allan P. Sindler, *Huey Long's Louisiana: State Politics, 1920–1952* (Johns

Hopkins University Press: Baltimore, 1956), pp. 45–116 effectively refuted any notion that Huey Long was an incipient fascist
exploiting the status resentments of an irrational mass movement.
They both stressed the very real grievances in Louisiana which
Long exploited. T. Harry Williams, *Huey Long* (Knopf: New
York, 1969), provided a memorable account of the freewheeling
reality of Louisiana's politics as a result of a vast number of
remarkably frank oral history interviews. Williams believed that
Long's sometimes corrupt and ruthless tactics were necessary to
overcome the power of the entrenched conservative oligarchy in
Louisiana and that he offered a genuine challenge to the New
Deal, not from the right but from the left. Brinkley, *The Voices of
Protest*, and Glen Jeansonne, 'Challenge to the New Deal: Huey
P. Long and the Redistribution of National Wealth', *Louisiana
History* 21 (1980), pp. 331–9 are salutary correctives to Williams's
uncritical assessment. I have tried to sum up the arguments about
Long in 'Huey Long and the New Deal', in Stephen W. Basker-
ville and Ralph Willett (eds.), *Nothing Else to Fear: New Perspec-
tives on America in the Thirties* (Manchester University Press:
Manchester, 1985), pp. 65–103.

List of Abbreviations

AAA	Agricultural Adjustment Administration
ACPF	American Commonwealth Political Federation
ADA	Americans for Democratic Action
ADC	Aid to Dependent Children
AFL	American Federation of Labor
AMA	American Medical Association
BAC	Business Advisory Council
BAE	Bureau of Agricultural Economics
CAWIU	Cannery and Agricultural Workers Industrial Union
CCC	Civilian Conservation Corps
CIO	Committee for (later Congress of) Industrial Organization
CWA	Civil Works Administration
ERA	Equal Rights Amendment
FAP	Federal Art Project
FERA	Federal Emergency Relief Administration
FHA	Farmers' Holiday Association
FHA	Federal Housing Administration
FRB	Federal Reserve Board
FSA	Farm Security Administration
GE	General Electric
GM	General Motors
ILGWU	International Ladies' Garment Workers' Union
LIPA	League for Independent Political Action
MWIU	Maritime Workers International Union
NAACP	National Association for the Advancement of Colored People
NAM	National Association of Manufacturers
NLB	National Labor Board
NLRB	National Labor Relations Board

NRA	National Recovery Administration
NWLB	National War Labor Board
NYA	National Youth Administration
POUR	President's Organization for Unemployment Relief
PWA	Public Works Administration
PWAP	Public Works Art Project
RA	Resettlement Administration
REA	Rural Electrification Administration
RFC	Reconstruction Finance Corporation
SCS	Soil Conservation Service
SEC	Securities and Exchange Commission
STFU	Southern Tenant Farmers' Union
SWOC	Steel Workers' Organizing Committee
TERA	Temporary Emergency Relief Administration
TNEC	Temporary National Economic Committee
TVA	Tennessee Valley Authority
UAW	United Automobile Workers
UE	United Electrical, Radio, and Machine Workers
UMW	United Mine Workers
URW	United Rubber Workers
USHA	United States Housing Authority
UTW	United Textile Workers
WIB	War Industries Board
WPA	Works Progress Administration

Index

drafting under the NRA 83–8
implementation 88–94
Cohen, Ben 99, 101
Colorado 15, 56, 194, 209, 284
Collective bargaining
under the NRA 74, 120, 126
in World War II and after 142–4
Collier, John 169, 172, 178–81
Collins, Robert M. 116
Columbia University 61–2
Comintern 133, 289
Commerce Department 42–3, 84
Commissioner of Immigration and
Naturalization 224
Committee on Civic and
Emergency Measures 45
Committee for Economic
Development 116
Committee on Economic Security
227, 231–3, 236–7, 243, 259
Committee for Industrial
Organization (later Congress
of Industrial Organizations)
formation 123–4, 131
success 129
and Communists 133–4
and politics 250
and blacks 255
Committee for the Nation's Health
238
Commodity Credit Corporation
156, 161–2
Commodity Dollar 111
Common Sense 287
Commons, John R. 233
Commonwealth and Southern 175
Communists 3, 8, 297
in coal 19–20, 133, 288
in textiles 20, 133, 288
and farm labourers 27, 133, 183–
4, 189, 288
and tenant farmers 28, 183
and the unemployed 38–40, 133,
201–3, 288
and mass production workers
125, 133–4, 139–40, 143
and the Popular Front 133, 140,
288

and blacks 183, 203, 255, 288
and Roosevelt 288–90
strength of 289
Community Action Programs 308
Community Arts Centers 219, 226
Community Chest 35
Company Unions 120, 126–7, 130
Compensatory fiscal policy 109,
112, 114, 303
Composers Forum Laboratory 220
Compulsory crop control 158,
161–3, 165–6
Concentration and Control 74
Congress
and Depression 48, 52–3, 54–6
and labour 143–4
and farm policy 147, 151, 161,
167–8
hostility to Indian New Deal 179
and politics in relief 209–10
hostility to relief spending 211,
213, 214–15, 243
hostility to Arts programmes
225–6
lack of enthusiasm for Social
Security 234–5
and housing 241, 267, 268, 270
gives power to FDR 245
opposition to New Deal 246,
262–71
support for FDR 260–3, 274–5
pressure for more power to
localities 307
Conkin, Paul 3
Conolly, Colonel 222
Connally Act 97
Connecticut 121
Conservative coalition 2, 113, 143–
4, 246, 298, 309–10
development of 267–71
Conservative Manifesto 113, 267
Consumers
criticism of NRA 89
taxes on 102–3
lack of concern for in farm policy
155, 163–5, 172–4
Consumers Advisory Board 84, 89,
258

Anthony J. Badger is Paul Mellon Professor of American History at Cambridge University. He has also edited *Contesting Democracy* (with Byron E. Shafer) and *F.D.R.: The First Hundred Days* (with Eric Foner).

John Harmon McElroy, *American Beliefs*
Wendy McElroy, ed., *Liberty for Women*
Gerald W. McFarland, *A Scattered People*
Walter Millis, *The Martial Spirit*
Nicolaus Mills, ed., *Culture in an Age of Money*
Nicolaus Mills, *Like a Holy Crusade*
Roderick Nash, *The Nervous Generation*
Keith Newlin, ed., *American Plays of the New Woman*
William L. O'Neill, ed., *Echoes of Revolt: The Masses, 1911–1917*
Gilbert Osofsky, *Harlem: The Making of a Ghetto*
Edward Pessen, *Losing Our Souls*
Glenn Porter and Harold C. Livesay, *Merchants and Manufacturers*
John Prados, *The Hidden History of the Vietnam War*
John Prados, *Presidents' Secret Wars*
Patrick Renshaw, *The Wobblies*
Edward Reynolds, *Stand the Storm*
Louis Rosen, *The South Side*
Richard Schickel, *The Disney Version*
Richard Schickel, *Intimate Strangers*
Richard Schickel, *Matinee Idylls*
Richard Schickel, *The Men Who Made the Movies*
Edward A. Shils, *The Torment of Secrecy*
Robert Shogan, *Bad News*
Geoffrey S. Smith, *To Save a Nation*
John David Smith, *Black Judas*
Robert W. Snyder, *The Voice of the City*
Bernard Sternsher, ed., *Hitting Home: The Great Depression in Town and Country*
Bernard Sternsher, ed., *Hope Restored: How the New Deal Worked in Town and Country*
Bernard Sternsher and Judith Sealander, eds., *Women of Valor*
Athan Theoharis, *From the Secret Files of J. Edgar Hoover*
Nicholas von Hoffman, *We Are the People Our Parents Warned Us Against*
Norman Ware, *The Industrial Worker, 1840–1860*
Robert Weisbrot, *Maximum Danger*
Mark J. White, ed., *The Kennedys and Cuba*
Tom Wicker, *JFK and LBJ: The Influence of Personality upon Politics*
Robert H. Wiebe, *Businessmen and Reform*
T. Harry Williams, *McClellan, Sherman and Grant*
Miles Wolff, *Lunch at the 5 & 10*
Randall B. Woods and Howard Jones, *Dawning of the Cold War*
American Ways Series:
    John A. Andrew III, *Lyndon Johnson and the Great Society*
    Roger Daniels, *Not Like Us*
    J. Matthew Gallman, *The North Fights the Civil War: The Home Front*
    Lewis L. Gould, *1968: The Election That Changed America*
    John Earl Haynes, *Red Scare or Red Menace?*
    Kenneth J. Heineman, *Put Your Bodies Upon the Wheels*
    D. Clayton James and Anne Sharp Wells, *From Pearl Harbor to V-J Day*
    John W. Jeffries, *Wartime America*
    Curtis D. Johnson, *Redeeming America*
    Maury Klein, *The Flowering of the Third America*

Larry M. Logue, *To Appomattox and Beyond*
Jean V. Matthews, *Women's Struggle for Equality*
Iwan W. Morgan, *Deficit Government*
Robert Muccigrosso, *Celebrating the New World*
Daniel Nelson, *Shifting Fortunes*
Thomas R. Pegram, *Battling Demon Rum*
Burton W. Peretti, *Jazz in American Culture*
David Reynolds, *From Munich to Pearl Harbor*
Hal K. Rothman, *Saving the Planet*
John A. Salmond, *"My Mind Set on Freedom"*
William Earl Weeks, *Building the Continental Empire*
Kevin White, *Sexual Liberation or Sexual License?*
Mark J. White, *Missiles in Cuba*

European and World History
Laurie Winn Carlson, *Cattle: An Informal Social History*
John Charmley, *Chamberlain and the Lost Peace*
John K. Dickinson, *German and Jew*
Lee Feigon, *China Rising*
Lee Feigon, *Demystifying Tibet*
Mark Frankland, *The Patriots' Revolution*
Lloyd C. Gardner, *Spheres of Influence*
David Gilmour, *Cities of Spain*
Raul Hilberg, *The Politics of Memory*
Raul Hilberg, et al., eds., *The Warsaw Diary of Adam Czerniakow*
Gertrude Himmelfarb, *Darwin and the Darwinian Revolution*
Gertrude Himmelfarb, *Marriage and Morals Among the Victorians*
Gertrude Himmelfarb, *Victorian Minds*
Thomas A. Idinopulos, *Jerusalem*
Thomas A. Idinopulos, *Weathered by Miracles*
Allan Janik and Stephen Toulmin, *Wittgenstein's Vienna*
Hilton Kramer and Roger Kimball, eds., *The Betrayal of Liberalism*
Ronnie S. Landau, *The Nazi Holocaust*
Filip Müller, *Eyewitness Auschwitz*
Clive Ponting, *1940: Myth and Reality*
David Pryce-Jones, *The Closed Circle*
A.L. Rowse, *The Elizabethan Renaissance: The Life of the Society*
A.L. Rowse, *The Elizabethan Renaissance: The Cultural Achievement*
Scott Shane, *Dismantling Utopia*
Paul Webster, *Petain's Crime*
John Weiss, *Ideology of Death*

Literature, Arts, and Letters
Roger Angell, *Once More Around the Park*
Walter Bagehot, *Physics and Politics*
Sybille Bedford, *Aldous Huxley*
Stephen Vincent Benét, *John Brown's Body*
Isaiah Berlin, *The Hedgehog and the Fox*
F. Bordewijk, *Character*
Robert Brustein, *Cultural Calisthenics*
Robert Brustein, *Dumbocracy in America*

Robert Brustein, *The Siege of the Arts*
Anthony Burgess, *Shakespeare*
Philip Callow, *Chekhov*
Philip Callow, *From Noon to Starry Night*
Philip Callow, *Son and Lover: The Young D. H. Lawrence*
Anton Chekhov, *The Comic Stories*
Bruce Cole, *The Informed Eye*
James Gould Cozzens, *Castaway*
James Gould Cozzens, *Men and Brethren*
Clarence Darrow, *Verdicts Out of Court*
Floyd Dell, *Intellectual Vagabondage*
Theodore Dreiser, *Best Short Stories*
Joseph Epstein, *Ambition*
André Gide, *Madeleine*
Gerald Graff, *Literature Against Itself*
John Gross, *The Rise and Fall of the Man of Letters*
Olivia Gude and Jeff Huebner, *Urban Art Chicago*
Raul Hilberg, *The Politics of Memory*
Irving Howe, *Politics and the Novel*
Irving Howe, *William Faulkner*
Aldous Huxley, *After Many a Summer Dies the Swan*
Aldous Huxley, *Ape and Essence*
Aldous Huxley, *Collected Short Stories*
Roger Kimball, *Experiments Against Reality*
Roger Kimball, *Tenured Radicals*
Hilton Kramer, *The Twilight of the Intellectuals*
Hilton Kramer and Roger Kimball, eds., *Against the Grain*
Hilton Kramer and Roger Kimball, eds., *The Survival of Culture*
F. R. Leavis, *Revaluation*
F. R. Leavis, *The Living Principle*
F. R. Leavis, *The Critic as Anti-Philosopher*
Marie-Anne Lescourret, *Rubens: A Double Life*
Sinclair Lewis, *Selected Short Stories*
Lynne Munson, *Exhibitionism*
William L. O'Neill, ed., *Echoes of Revolt: The Masses, 1911–1917*
Carl Rollyson, *Reading Susan Sontag*
Carl Sandburg, *Poems for the People*
Budd Schulberg, *The Harder They Fall*
Ramón J. Sender, *Seven Red Sundays*
Peter Shaw, *Recovering American Literature*
James B. Simpson, ed., *Veil and Cowl*
Tess Slesinger, *On Being Told That Her Second Husband Has Taken His First Lover, and Other Stories*
Red Smith, *Red Smith on Baseball*
Donald Thomas, *Swinburne*
B. Traven, *The Bridge in the Jungle*
B. Traven, *The Carreta*
B. Traven, *The Cotton-Pickers*
B. Traven, *General from the Jungle*
B. Traven, *Government*
B. Traven, *March to the Montería*

B. Traven, *The Night Visitor and Other Stories*
B. Traven, *The Rebellion of the Hanged*
B. Traven, *Trozas*
Anthony Trollope, *Trollope the Traveller*
Ivan Turgenev, *Literary Reminiscences*
Rex Warner, *The Aerodrome*
Rebecca West, *A Train of Powder*
Thomas Wolfe, *The Hills Beyond*
Wilhelm Worringer, *Abstraction and Empathy*
The Shakespeare Handbooks by Alistair McCallum
    Hamlet
    King Lear
    Macbeth
    Romeo and Juliet

Theatre and Drama

Linda Apperson, *Stage Managing and Theatre Etiquette*
Robert Brustein, *Cultural Calisthenics*
Robert Brustein, *Dumbocracy in America*
Robert Brustein, *Reimagining American Theatre*
Robert Brustein, *The Siege of the Arts*
Robert Brustein, *The Theatre of Revolt*
Stephen Citron, *The Musical from the Inside Out*
Irina and Igor Levin, *Working on the Play and the Role*
Keith Newlin, ed., *American Plays of the New Woman*
Louis Rosen, *The South Side*
Bernard Sahlins, *Days and Nights at The Second City*
David Wood, with Janet Grant, *Theatre for Children*
Plays for Performance:
    Aristophanes, *Lysistrata*
    Pierre Augustin de Beaumarchais, *The Barber of Seville*
    Pierre Augustin de Beaumarchais, *The Marriage of Figaro*
    Georg Büchner, *Woyzeck*
    Anton Chekhov, *The Cherry Orchard*
    Anton Chekhov, *Ivanov*
    Anton Chekhov, *The Seagull*
    Anton Chekhov, *Uncle Vanya*
    Euripides, *The Bacchae*
    Euripides, *Iphigenia in Aulis*
    Euripides, *Iphigenia Among the Taurians*
    Euripides, *Medea*
    Euripides, *The Trojan Women*
    Georges Feydeau, *Paradise Hotel*
    Henrik Ibsen, *A Doll's House*
    Henrik Ibsen, *Ghosts*
    Henrik Ibsen, *Hedda Gabler*
    Henrik Ibsen, *The Master Builder*
    Henrik Ibsen, *When We Dead Awaken*
    Henrik Ibsen, *The Wild Duck*
    Heinrich von Kleist, *The Prince of Homburg*
    Christopher Marlowe, *Doctor Faustus*

Molière, *The Bourgeois Gentleman*
The Mysteries: Creation
The Mysteries: The Passion
Luigi Pirandello, *Enrico IV*
Luigi Pirandello, *Six Characters in Search of an Author*
Budd Schulberg, with Stan Silverman, *On the Waterfront* (the play)
Sophocles, *Antigone*
Sophocles, *Electra*
Sophocles, *Oedipus at Colonus*
Sophocles, *Oedipus the King*
August Strindberg, *The Father*
August Strindberg, *Miss Julie*
The Shakespeare Handbooks by Alistair McCallum
Hamlet
King Lear
Macbeth
Romeo and Juliet

Philosophy
Philosophers in 90 Minutes by Paul Strathern
Thomas Aquinas in 90 Minutes
Aristotle in 90 Minutes
St. Augustine in 90 Minutes
Berkeley in 90 Minutes
Confucius in 90 Minutes
Derrida in 90 Minutes
Descartes in 90 Minutes
Dewey in 90 Minutes
Foucault in 90 Minutes
Hegel in 90 Minutes
Heidegger in 90 Minutes
Hume in 90 Minutes
Kant in 90 Minutes
Kierkegaard in 90 Minutes
Leibniz in 90 Minutes
Locke in 90 Minutes
Machiavelli in 90 Minutes
Marx in 90 Minutes
J. S. Mill in 90 Minutes
Nietzsche in 90 Minutes
Plato in 90 Minutes
Rousseau in 90 Minutes
Bertrand Russell in 90 Minutes
Sartre in 90 Minutes
Schopenhauer in 90 Minutes
Socrates in 90 Minutes
Spinoza in 90 Minutes
Wittgenstein in 90 Minutes